ECCE ROMANI I

A LATIN
READING PROGRAM

FOURTH EDITION

Boston, Massachusetts
Glenview, Illinois
Shoreview, Minnesota
Parsippany, New Jersey
Upper Saddle River, New Jersey

This North American edition of *Ecce Romani* is based on *Ecce Romani: A Latin Reading Course*, originally prepared by The Scottish Classics Group © copyright The Scottish Classics Group 1971, 1982, and published in the United Kingdom by Oliver and Boyd, a division of Longman Group.

Photo Credits appear on page 321, which constitutes an extension of this copyright page.

Cover illustration: Lin Wang
Text art: Lin Wang
Maps: John Burgoyne

13-digit ISBN: 978-0-13-361089-5
10-digit ISBN: 0-13-361089-6

23   18

Series Editor: Gilbert Lawall
Professor Emeritus of Classics
University of Massachusetts, Amherst, Massachusetts

AUTHORS AND CONSULTANTS

Timothy S. Abney
Marquette High School
Chesterfield, Missouri

Jim Bigger
McLean High School
McLean, Virginia

Melissa Schons Bishop
Windermere, Florida

Peter C. Brush
Deerfield Academy
Deerfield, Massachusetts

Penny R. Cipolone
Gateway Regional High School
Woodbury Heights, New Jersey

Gail A. Cooper
Academy of the New Church
Bryn Athyn, Pennsylvania

Sally Davis
Arlington Public Schools
Arlington, Virginia

Pauline P. Demetri
Cambridge Rindge &
Latin School
Cambridge, Massachusetts

Dennis De Young
Montgomery Bell Academy
Nashville, Tennessee

Katy Ganino
Wayland Middle School
Wayland, Massachusetts

Jane Hall
National Latin Exam
Alexandria, Virginia

Sally Hatcher
Winsor School
Boston, Massachusetts

Thalia Pantelidis Hocker
Old Dominion University
Norfolk, Virginia

Anthony L.C. Hollingsworth
Roger Williams University
Bristol, Rhode Island

Dexter Hoyos
Sydney University
Sydney, Australia

Joan C. Jahnige
Kentucky Educational Television
Lexington, Kentucky

Caroline Switzer Kelly
Covenant Day School
Charlotte, North Carolina

Glenn M. Knudsvig
University of Michigan
Ann Arbor, Michigan

Richard A. LaFleur
University of Georgia
Athens, Georgia

Shirley G. Lowe
Wayland Public Schools
Wayland, MA

Maureen O'Donnell
W.T. Woodson High School
Fairfax, Virginia

Ronald B. Palma
Holland Hall School
Tulsa, Oklahoma

David J. Perry
Rye High School
Rye, New York

Kathleen M. Robinson
Harbor Day School
Corona del Mar, CA

Debra Pennell Ross
University of Michigan
Ann Arbor, Michigan

Andrew Schacht
St. Luke's School
New Canaan, Connecticut

Judith Lynn Sebesta
University of South Dakota
Vermillion, South Dakota

**The Scottish Classics
Group**
Edinburgh, Scotland

David M. Tafe
Rye Country Day School
Rye, New York

Rex Wallace
University of Massachusetts
Amherst, Massachusetts

Allen Ward
University of Connecticut
Storrs, Connecticut

Elizabeth Lyding Will
Amherst College
Amherst, Massachusetts

Philip K. Woodruff
Lake Forest High School
Lake Forest, Illinois

CONTENTS

XXIII AT THE PORTA CAPENA

XXIV ALWAYS TOMORROW

REVIEW VI: CHAPTERS 25–27

REFERENCE MATERIALS

MAPS

INTRODUCTION

Ecce Romani

The title of this series of Latin books is *Ecce Romani*, which means "Look! The Romans!" The books in the series will present the Romans to you as you learn the Latin language that they spoke. At first you will meet the members of a Roman family. As you continue reading, you will meet mythological and historical characters that meant much to the Romans and remain part of our cultural heritage today. You will be introduced to a vast and colorful world of ancient Mediterranean and European civilizations that included peoples who spoke many different languages, and you will meet people of many different cultures and social levels, ranging from slaves to emperors. You will read passages from many ancient Roman writers and thus come into direct communication with the ancient Romans themselves.

A Roman Family

Within this vast world, the focus of your attention will be the daily life of a typical upper-class Roman family, consisting of a father named Cornelius, a mother named Aurelia, a son named Marcus, a daughter named Cornelia, and a young boy named Sextus, who is a ward of the family. You will follow the development of Marcus and Cornelia from late childhood to the beginning of their lives as mature Romans.

Baiae

The Latin stories you will be reading about this family take place in A.D. 80, the year following the destruction of Pompeii by the eruption of Mount Vesuvius. The family lives in the great metropolis of Rome, but when you first meet them it is summertime, and they are living at their country home near Baiae in Campania (see map on page xiii).

Baiae, on the Bay of Naples, was a fashionable resort for wealthy Romans, many of whom built splendid country houses or villas there. The shoreline of the Bay of Naples was ringed with villas built on terraces so that their inhabitants could enjoy the beauty of the sparkling waves and the steep cliffs of the islands in the bay. On the terraces the Romans planted gardens and cool arbors of trees under which they could refresh themselves in the heat of the day. Along the shore they built fish ponds, which were flushed daily by the tides.

While the family is at Baiae, you will learn about a number of aspects of Roman culture, such as the family, dress, slavery, names, and life on country estates. When the family returns to Rome, your awareness of Roman culture will expand as you learn about life in the city and life on the frontiers of the Roman empire. You will experience some of the highlights of the cultural life of the city, such as the chariot races and the games in the Colosseum; you will see Cornelius and Aurelia, the parents in our family, fulfill their obligations to society; and you will follow the passage of their children, Marcus and Cornelia, through the rituals of coming of age and marriage. Latin passages adapted from

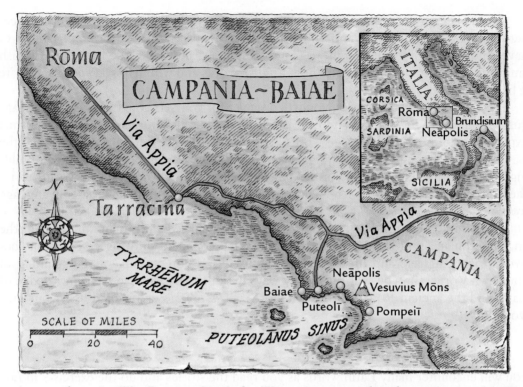

ancient authors in *The Romans Speak for Themselves*, a reader that accompanies *Ecce Romani*, will allow you to hear what the Romans themselves had to say about many of these aspects of their cultural life. All along the way you will have abundant opportunities to compare the cultural life of the Romans with our own today.

The Latin Language

As you read stories about the Roman family in this book, you will be learning Latin, a language that gave birth to a number of languages that are still used today, including Spanish, Portuguese, French, Italian, and Romanian. These modern languages are known as Romance languages, because they come from the language used by the ancient Romans.

In addition, even though the English language developed out of Germanic dialects, as much as sixty percent of English vocabulary comes directly or indirectly from Latin. Many French words of Latin origin were introduced into English by the Normans, a French people who conquered the English in 1066. Many other words of Latin origin came into English during the revival of classical learning in the Renaissance and Enlightenment (1550 and following), and Latin words have come and continue to come into English usage in scientific, medical, and legal terminology. The connections you will make between Latin words and English words will enhance your understanding of English vocabulary, especially of its larger, polysyllabic words. By connecting English words with their Latin roots, you will increase your ability to use English words correctly and effectively.

As you begin to read the Latin stories in this book, you will notice many differences between English and Latin, and you will come to appreciate how different languages have unique ways of expressing ideas. Comparing the structures of the Latin and English languages will help you understand how English works and will help you speak and write it better.

As you read the Latin stories, you will discover for yourself how Latin works as a language and how to understand and translate it. Following the stories you will find formal explanations of how the language works. These explanations will help you visualize the way Latin sentences express meaning, and they will help you learn the elements or building blocks of the language. Be sure to pay close attention as you read the Latin stories themselves and try to discover for yourself as much as you can about how the language works.

In learning the Latin language, in becoming acquainted with the cultural life of the ancient Romans, and in constantly making connections and drawing comparisons between their language and life and yours, you will develop a deeper understanding of your own world, and you will find many ways in which you can use your knowledge of Latin and the ancient Romans to lead a more successful and enjoyable life in your own world.

A Note on Vocabulary

You will encounter many Latin words as you read the stories and do the exercises in *Ecce Romani*. You will not need to learn all of them to the same degree. In the vocabulary lists below the stories and below some of the exercises, some of the Latin words are printed in boldface and some are not. You should acquire an active knowledge of the

The beautiful region of Latium has inspired artists over the centuries. The Roman Campagna with the Claudian Aqueduct, *oil on canvas, 1827, Jean-Baptiste-Camille Corot*

words in boldface. This means that you should be able to give the meaning of the Latin word when you see it in a story or a sentence and that you should also be able to give the Latin word when you see its English equivalent. You will also need to learn other information about these words. These words are for *mastery*. Other words in the vocabulary lists below the stories and below some of the exercises are not in boldface. For these words, you need only recognize the word when you see it and be able to give its meaning. These are words for *recognition*. You must be sure that you learn these words well enough to remember their English meanings when you see them again in stories and sentences. In learning Latin from *Ecce Romani*, you will acquire a rich Latin vocabulary as you read stories about the members of our Roman family in a variety of situations. The distinction we make between words for mastery and words for recognition will make it easier for you to enjoy a wealth of detail and local color in the stories without requiring you to master an excessive number of Latin words.

Go Online

Every chapter of your book contains Web Codes that allow you to Go Online to the *Ecce Romani* Companion Web Site. This Web Site contains activities for additional practice with vocabulary, grammar, and culture and a Self-Test that corresponds to the Review sections in your book. In order to Go Online, go to www.PHSchool.com, type in the Web Code you would like to access, and click on the yellow arrow.

In order to access additional information and links that will be useful to you throughout the year, use the following Web Code:

Go Online
PHSchool.com
Web Code: jfd-0001

Italia

SCALE OF MILES

0   75   150

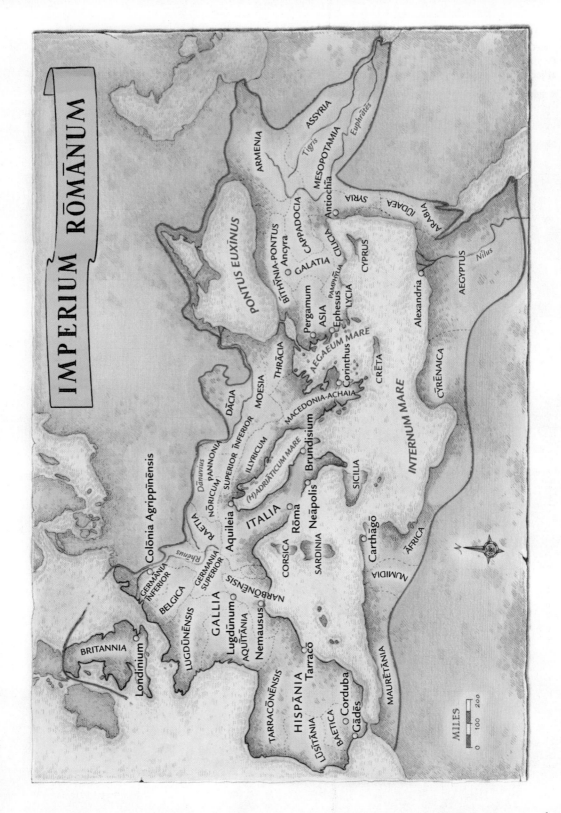

Two Roman Girls

Ecce! In pictūrā est puella, nōmine Cornēlia. Cornēlia est puella Rōmāna quae in Italiā habitat. Etiam in pictūrā est vīlla rūstica ubi Cornēlia aestāte habitat. Cornēlia est laeta quod iam in vīllā habitat. Cornēlia iam sub arbore sedet et legit. Etiam in pictūrā est altera puella, nōmine Flāvia. Flāvia est puella Rōmāna quae in vīllā vīcīnā habitat. Dum Cornēlia legit, Flāvia scrībit. Laeta est Flāvia quod Cornēlia iam in 5 vīllā habitat.

1 **Ecce!** *Look!*
 puella, *(a/the) girl*
 nōmine, *by name, named*
 quae, *who*
2 **habitat,** *(she/he) lives, is living, does live*
 etiam, *also*
 vīlla, *(a/the) country house*
  vīlla rūstica, *(a/the) country house and farm*
 ubi, *where*
 aestāte, *in the summer*
3 **laeta,** *happy*

quod, *because*
iam, *now*
sub arbore, *under the tree*
sedet, *(she/he) sits, is sitting, does sit*
et, *and*
legit, *(she/he) reads, is reading, does read*
4 **altera,** *second, another*
5 **vīcīna,** *neighboring*
 dum, *while*
 scrībit, *(she/he) writes, is writing, does write*

 N.B. Latin does not have articles (*a, an, the*), and so **puella** can mean either *a girl* or *the girl.*

 Latin verbs can be translated several ways, e.g., **habitat** can be translated *(she/he) lives, is living,* or *does live.*

EXERCISE 1a

Respondē Latīnē:

Go Online
PHSchool.com
Web Code: jfd-0001

1. Quis est Cornēlia?
2. Ubi habitat Cornēlia?
3. Cūr est Cornēlia laeta?
4. Quid facit Cornēlia?
5. Ubi habitat Flāvia?
6. Quid facit Flāvia?
7. Cūr est Flāvia laeta?

Quis...? *Who...?*

Cūr...? *Why...?*
Quid facit...? *What is...doing? What does...do?*

BUILDING THE MEANING

Parts of Speech: Nouns, Adjectives, and Verbs

When learning Latin you will be learning how language expresses meaning, and you will need to know certain grammatical terms so that you can talk about how Latin does this. The most important terms are those for the parts of speech, the basic building blocks of meaning in sentences. The most important parts of speech are:

nouns: names of persons, places, things, qualities, or acts;
adjectives: words that describe persons, places, things, qualities, or acts;
verbs: words that denote actions (e.g., *sits*) or existence (e.g., *is*).

In the story on page 3, the words **pictūrā** (1), **Cornēlia** (1), and **Italiā** (2) are nouns; the words **Rōmāna** (1), **rūstica** (2), and **laeta** (3) are adjectives; and the words **est** (1), **habitat** (2), and **sedet** (3) are verbs.

Vergil holds a scroll open to line 8 of the *Aeneid*.
Mosaic, Tunis, early third century A.D.

Portrait, first century A.D.
Encaustic on wood, Egypt

EXERCISE 1b

What part of speech is each of the following (listed in the order in which they occur in the story on page 3):

1. puella
2. vīlla
3. legit
4. altera
5. Flāvia
6. scrībit

EXERCISE 1c

Using story 1 as a guide, give the Latin for:

1. In the picture is a country house and farm.
2. Cornelia is happy.
3. Cornelia is sitting under the tree.
4. Flavia is a Roman girl.
5. Cornelia now lives in the country house.

A Summer Afternoon

Cornēlia est puella Rōmāna. Flāvia quoque est puella Rōmāna. Cornēlia et Flāvia sunt puellae Rōmānae quae in Italiā habitant. Cornēlia et Flāvia sunt amīcae. Hodiē puellae nōn sedent sed in agrīs ambulant. Brevī tempore Cornēlia dēfessa est. Nōn iam ambulat sed sub arbore sedet. Flāvia, quae est puella strēnua, in agrīs currit. Brevī tempore Flāvia quoque est dēfessa. Iam Flāvia et Cornēlia sub arbore sedent quod   5
dēfessae sunt. Dum puellae sub arbore sedent, Cornēlia legit et Flāvia scrībit. Tandem puellae ex agrīs ad vīllam rūsticam lentē ambulant.

1 **quoque,** adv., *also*
2 **sunt,** *(they) are*
  amīcae, *friends*
3 **hodiē,** adv., *today*
  sed, conj., *but*
  in agrīs, *in the fields*
  ambulant, *(they) walk, are walking, do walk*
  brevī tempore, *in a short time, soon*
  dēfessa, *tired*

4 **nōn iam,** adv., *no longer*
  strēnua, *active, energetic*
  currit, *(she/he) runs, is running, does run*
6 **tandem,** adv., *at last*
7 **ex agrīs,** *from/out of the fields*
  ad vīllam rūsticam, *to/toward the country house and farm*
  lentē, adv., *slowly*

EXERCISE 2a

Respondē Latīnē:

1. Ubi habitant Cornēlia et Flāvia?
2. Quid faciunt puellae hodiē?
3. Quid facit Cornēlia quod dēfessa est?
4. Quid faciunt puellae sub arbore?

Quid faciunt…? *What are…doing? What do…do?*

Subjects, Verbs, Linking Verbs, and Complements

Subjects and *verbs* are core elements of sentences. It is important to identify them as you meet them in Latin sentences. You may mark subjects (the person or thing that *is* or *does something*) with the letter S and verbs with the letter V:

     S   V   S   V
  Cornēlia **est** puella Rōmāna.   Puellae in Italiā **habitant.**

The verb **est** is used as a *linking verb* (LV) when it links the subject with a noun or an adjective. This noun or adjective completes the pattern of the sentence and is called a *complement* (C):

     S   LV   C   S   LV   C
  Cornēlia **est** puella.   Flāvia **est** dēfessa.

These sentences may also be written as follows with no change in meaning:

     S   C LV   S   C   LV
  Cornēlia puella **est.**   Flāvia dēfessa **est.**

When **est** and **sunt** appear before the subject and there is no complement, they are normally translated *there is* and *there are*:

  In pictūrā **est** puella. (1:1)   In pictūrā **sunt** puellae.
  There is *a girl in the picture.*   ***There are*** *girls in the picture.*

FORMS

Go Online
PHSchool.com
Web Code: jfd-0002

Verbs: The Endings *-t* and *-nt*

Look at these sentences:

1. Cornēlia es**t** puella Rōmāna.
   Cornelia is a Roman girl.

2. Puella in agrīs curri**t** quod laeta es**t.**
   The girl is running in the fields because she is happy.

3. Cornēlia et Flāvia su**nt** puellae Rōmānae.
   Cornelia and Flavia are Roman girls.

4. Puellae in agrīs curru**nt** quod laetae su**nt.**
   The girls are running in the fields because they are happy.

Girls playing a ball game
Fragment of a Roman relief, second century A.D.

If the subject is singular (e.g., **Cornēlia** and **puella** in the first two sentences), the verb ends in **-t**.

If the subject is plural (e.g., **Cornēlia et Flāvia** and **puellae** in the third and fourth sentences), the verb ends in **-nt**.

You have noticed that vocabulary lists give definitions of verbs as follows: **sedet**, *(she/he) sits, is sitting, does sit.* Verbs may be used with a noun as subject, as in the sentence **Brevī tempore <u>Cornēlia</u> dēfessa est** (line 3 in the story at the beginning of this chapter). If there is no stated subject, as in the sentence **Nōn iam ambulat sed sub arbore sedet**, you must include a pronoun when you translate: thus, *She no longer walks but sits under a tree.* Cornelia continues to be the subject since there is nothing in the sentence to indicate a change of subject.

EXERCISE 2b

Read these fragments of sentences and decide which word at the right best completes each sentence. Then read aloud and translate:

1. Flāvia in vīllā vīcīnā _____.   habitat/habitant
2. Cornēlia et Flāvia sub arbore _____.   sedet/sedent
3. Cornēlia et Flāvia dēfessae _____.   est/sunt
4. Flāvia strēnua _____.   est/sunt
5. Cornēlia et Flāvia sunt _____.   puella Rōmāna/puellae Rōmānae
6. Puellae in agrīs nōn iam _____.   currit/currunt

EXERCISE 2c

Read aloud, mentally noting subjects, verbs, and complements as you read. Note which verbs are linking verbs. Then translate:

Cornēlia est puella Rōmāna quae in vīllā rūsticā aestāte habitat. In vīllā vīcīnā habitat altera puella, nōmine Flāvia, quae est amīca eius. Dum puellae in vīllīs habitant, in agrīs saepe ambulant. Hodiē Cornēlia ad vīllam vīcīnam ambulat ubi in agrīs sub arbore sedet Flāvia. Iam puellae laetae currunt. Brevī tempore, quod dēfessae sunt, nōn iam currunt sed sub arbore sedent.

2 **eius,** *her*   **vīllīs,** *country houses*   3 **saepe,** adv., *often*

In the passage above, how many singular verbs can you find? How many plural verbs?

EXERCISE 2d

Using story 2 as a guide, give the Latin for:

1. Cornelia and Flavia live in Italy.
2. Cornelia and Flavia are walking in the fields.
3. Flavia is running.
4. In a short time the girls are tired and sit under a tree.
5. At last the girls walk slowly to the country house.

Go Online
PHSchool.com
Web Code: jfd-0002

A ROMAN FAMILY

In our family, there is a daughter, Cornelia, who is fourteen, a son, Marcus, sixteen, a father, Gaius Cornelius, and a mother, Aurelia. At the **vīlla,** the education of the children is in the hands of their parents and a Greek slave, Eucleides.

The family of Cornelius traces its lineage far back in Roman history. One of the most distinguished members of the family was Publius Cornelius Scipio Africanus, the Roman general who defeated the Carthaginians in North Africa in the Second Punic War (218–201 B.C.). His daughter, Cornelia, was one of the most famous Roman women of all time and was the mother of the Gracchi brothers, who were great social reformers in the second century B.C. As our Cornelia sits under the tree, she is reading about her namesake in a book given to her by Eucleides, and she is wondering whether she too will become as famous as the Cornelia of old.

Cornelia, mother of the Gracchi, pointing to her sons as her treasures
Cornelia, Mother of the Gracchi, *oil on canvas, 1795, Joseph-Benoît Suvée*

Cornelius is responsible for the estate. As father, he is not only master of his own house, but he legally has power of life and death over his household, although he never exercises it. Aurelia runs the household and teaches her daughter what she will need to know when she gets married and has to run her own household. Aurelia and Cornelia do some wool-spinning and weaving but there are a number of slaves to help with the chores.

The family has living with it a twelve-year-old boy, Sextus, who used to live in Pompeii, where his mother died in the eruption of Mount Vesuvius the year before our story begins. Sextus's father is now on service overseas in Asia Minor, and he has left his son in Italy under the guardianship of his friend Cornelius.

Cornelia's friend Flavia lives in a neighboring country house.

Cornelia with her sons Tiberius and Gaius
Sculpture, Pierre-Jules Cavelier

ADDITIONAL READING:
The Romans Speak for Themselves: Book I: "The Family in Roman Society," pages 1–8.

IN THE GARDEN

In pictūrā est puer Rōmānus, nōmine Mārcus, quī in vīllā rūsticā habitat. Etiam in pictūrā est alter puer, nōmine Sextus, quī in eādem vīllā rūsticā habitat. Mārcus et Sextus sunt amīcī. Hodiē puerī in hortō clāmant et rīdent quod laetī sunt.

Vir quoque est in pictūrā, nōmine Dāvus, quī est servus. In Italiā sunt multī servī quī in agrīs et in vīllīs rūsticīs labōrant. Puerī sunt Rōmānī, sed Dāvus nōn est Rōmānus. Est 5
vir Britannicus quī iam in Italiā labōrat. Sextus et Mārcus, quod sunt puerī Rōmānī, nōn labōrant. Dāvus sōlus labōrat, īrātus quod puerī clāmant et in hortō currunt.

Subitō statua in piscīnam cadit. Sextus rīdet. Mārcus quoque rīdet, sed Dāvus, "Abīte, molestī!" clāmat et ad piscīnam īrātus currit. Puerī ex hortō currunt. Dāvus gemit.

1 **puer,** *(a/the) boy*	5 **in vīllīs rūsticīs,** *in country houses*
quī, *who*	**labōrant,** *(they) work, are working*
2 eādem, *the same*	7 **sōlus,** *alone*
3 **in hortō,** *in the garden*	**īrātus,** *angry*
clāmant, *(they) shout, are shouting*	8 **subitō,** adv., *suddenly*
rīdent, *(they) laugh, are laughing, smile*	**in piscīnam,** *into the fishpond*
4 **vir,** *(a/the) man*	**cadit,** *(he/she/it) falls*
servus, *(a/the) slave*	**Abīte, molestī!** *Go away, pests!*
multī, *many*	9 **gemit,** *(he/she) groans*

Latin words and phrases that are not printed in boldface are for recognition and not for mastery. See Introduction, pages xiv–xv.

EXERCISE 3a

Respondē Latīnē:

1. Quis est Sextus?
2. Suntne Mārcus et Sextus amīcī?
3. Quid faciunt puerī hodiē?
4. Quis est Dāvus?
5. Estne Mārcus servus?
6. Cūr est Dāvus īrātus?
7. Quid in piscīnam cadit?
8. Quid faciunt puerī?

-ne indicates a yes or no question

Minimē! *No!*
Ita vērō! *Yes!*

Go Online
PHSchool.com
Web Code: jfd-0003

Go Online
PHSchool.com
Web Code: jfd-0003

Nouns and Adjectives: Singular and Plural

Note how these nouns change from singular to plural:

Singular	Plural
puell*a*	puell*ae*
serv*us*	serv*ī*
puer	puer*ī*
vir	vir*ī*

Study the following sentences, and note how the nouns and adjectives change from singular to plural:

1. Cornēlia est **puell*a* Rōmān*a***.
   Cornēlia et Flāvia sunt **puell*ae* Rōmān*ae***.

2. Dāvus est **serv*us***.
   Mult*ī* serv*ī* in agrīs labōrant.

3. Mārcus est **puer Rōmān*us***.
   Mārcus et Sextus sunt **puer*ī* Rōmān*ī***.

4. Cornēlius est **vir Rōmān*us***.
   Vir*ī* Rōmān*ī* in Italiā habitant.

Pompeii —

EXERCISE 3b

Change singulars to plurals:

1. amīcus Rōmānus
2. puer sōlus
3. amīca laeta
4. servus dēfessus
5. puella īrāta
6. vir sōlus
7. vīlla rūstica
8. puer dēfessus
9. pictūra Rōmāna
10. vir laetus

Hortus with ***piscīna*** and ***porticus***
Villa of Julia Felix, Pompeii

EXERCISE 3c

Change plurals to singulars:

1. amīcae dēfessae
2. servī īrātī
3. puellae Rōmānae
4. virī dēfessī
5. vīllae vīcīnae
6. amīcī laetī
7. puellae strēnuae
8. virī Rōmānī
9. puellae īrātae
10. puerī sōlī
11. vīllae Rōmānae
12. servī dēfessī

EXERCISE 3d

Based on what you know about singular and plural forms of subjects, verbs, and adjectives, select the correct word or phrase to complete each sentence. Then read aloud and translate:

1. Mārcus et Sextus in eādem vīllā _____.   habitat/habitant
2. Dāvus vir Britannicus _____.   est/sunt
3. In agrīs labōrant _____.   servus/servī
4. Puerī et puellae saepe _____.   gemit/currit/currunt
5. Sunt in agrīs multī _____.   puella/servus/servī
6. In Italiā habitat _____.   Mārcus et Sextus/Mārcus/puellae
7. Mārcus et Sextus sunt puerī _____.   Rōmānus/Rōmānī/Rōmānae
8. Cornēlia et Flāvia sunt puellae _____.   Rōmānus/Rōmānī/Rōmānae
9. Aurēlia est fēmina _____.   Rōmānus/Rōmānī/Rōmāna

fēmina, *(a/the) woman*

EXERCISE 3e

Using stories 2 and 3 as guides, give the Latin for:

1. Today the boy is laughing because he is happy.
2. The tired girls are sitting under a tree.
3. In Italy many slaves work in country houses.
4. In the picture Cornelia is reading and Flavia is writing.
5. While Davus runs to the fishpond, the boys suddenly run out of the garden.

Roman interest in the different cultures of their empire is shown in this bust of a Syrian slave.
Bronze and lead decoration, Rome, second century A.D.

DRESS

When formally dressed, the clothing of a Roman indicated his or her citizenship and status in the multicultural society of the Roman world. The picture opposite shows Cornelius's family and Sextus, the boy who is presently living with the family, all in formal dress. When living at their country villa, they would not always wear such formal attire.

Aurelia wears a simple blue tunic (**tunica**) with sleeves. Over the tunic, she wears a **stola**, a floor-length strapped dress without sleeves. The **stola** indicates that she is both a Roman citizen and the wife of a Roman citizen. She is shown here wearing a dark blue **palla** as well, a single, rectangular piece of material draped over her left shoulder. It could also be put around her body or over her head. She would wear this when out of doors.

Cornelius wears a knee-length tunic. To show that he is a senator, his tunic has broad purple stripes running from near each side of the neck down the front and down the back. On formal occasions in the country and always in the city, he wears a **toga** over his tunic. The toga indicates that he is a Roman citizen. Most Roman men would wear a plain white toga (**toga pūra**), also called a **toga virīlis** (*toga of manhood*), but since Cornelius has held a high magistracy, he wears a toga with a purple border (**toga praetexta**) to signify his rank.

Marcus and Sextus wear tunics with purple stripes that are narrower than those on Cornelius's tunic. Roman boys, before coming of age between fourteen and sixteen, wore the **toga praetexta** with purple border like the toga worn by high government officials. Suspended from their necks, Marcus and Sextus wear a golden **bulla**, a locket containing an amulet or charm to ward off evil and protect them from harm. A boy's father placed a **bulla** around his son's neck at the naming ceremony soon after the boy's birth, and the boy would wear the **bulla** until he came of age. At that time, he would dedicate his **bulla** and the first shavings of his beard to the household gods, the **Larēs** and **Penātēs**, and he would then put on the **toga virīlis**.

Cornelia wears a white tunic like the white ones worn by Marcus and Sextus but without the purple stripes, and she wears the **toga praetexta** to show her status as a Roman citizen. She will dedicate her **toga praetexta** to the goddess of maidenly virtue (**Fortūna Virginālis**) when she marries. Roman girls did not wear a **bulla**.

The footgear shown in the picture is more formal than the simple sandals (**soleae**) that all members of the family would wear when at leisure in the country house and fields.

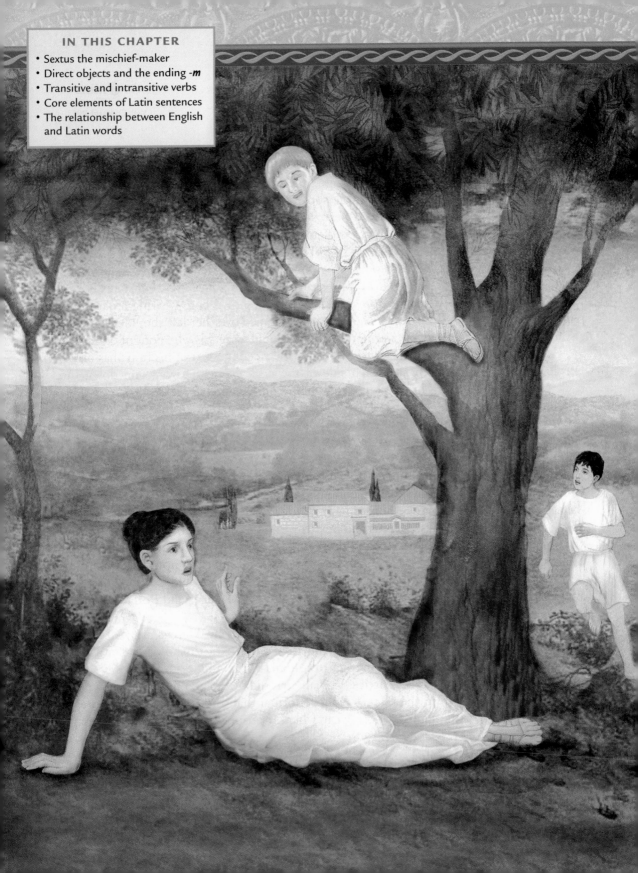

A MISCHIEF-MAKER

Sextus est puer molestus quī semper Cornēliam vexat. Cornēlia igitur Sextum nōn amat. Hodiē sub arbore dormit Cornēlia. Sextus puellam cōnspicit et fūrtim appropinquat. Arborem ascendit et subitō magnā vōce clāmat. Vōcem Cornēlia audit sed Sextum nōn videt. Magna vōx Cornēliam terret. Sollicita est.

Tum Mārcus ad arborem currit. Mārcus puerum molestum cōnspicit et clāmat, 5
"Dēscende, Sexte!"

Sextus clāmat, "Mārce, cūr tū nōn arborem ascendis? Nihil mē terret. Quid tē terret?"

"Cavē, Sexte!" clāmat Mārcus. "Rāmī sunt īnfirmī."

Subitō Mārcus et Cornēlia magnum fragōrem audiunt; Sextus ex arbore cadit. Rīdent Mārcus et Cornēlia, sed nōn rīdet Sextus. 10

1 **molestus,** *troublesome, annoying*	**videt,** *(he/she) sees*
semper, adv., *always*	**vōx,** *(a/the) voice*
vexat, *(he/she) annoys*	**terret,** *(he/she/it) frightens*
igitur, conj., *therefore*	**sollicita,** *anxious, worried*
2 **amat,** *(he/she) likes, loves*	5 **tum,** adv., *at that moment, then*
dormit, *(he/she) sleeps*	6 **Dēscende, Sexte!** *Come down, Sextus!*
cōnspicit, *(he/she) catches sight of*	7 **tū,** *you (subject)*
fūrtim, adv., *stealthily*	**nihil,** *nothing*
3 **appropinquat,** *(he/she) approaches*	**tē,** *you (direct object)*
ascendit, *(he/she) climbs*	8 **Cavē!** *Be careful!*
magnus, *big, great*	**rāmus,** *(a/the) branch*
magnā vōce, *in a loud voice*	**īnfirmus,** *weak, shaky*
4 **audit,** *(he/she) hears, listens to*	9 **fragor,** *(a/the) crash, noise*

In Latin, the form **Sexte** is used when Sextus is addressed by name. (Compare **Mārce**.) No such change is made in English.

EXERCISE 4a

Respondē Latīnē:

1. Quālis puer est Sextus?
2. Quid facit Cornēlia hodiē?
3. Quid facit Sextus?
4. Quid audit Cornēlia?
5. Quō Mārcus currit?
6. Quid clāmat Sextus?
7. Quid audiunt Mārcus et Cornēlia?

Quālis...? *What sort of...?*

Quō...? *Where...to?*

EXERCISE 4b

Review

Select, read aloud, and translate:

1. Mārcus est puer _____.
2. Flāvia et Cornēlia in hortō _____.
3. Mārcus et Sextus sunt _____.
4. Mārcus nōn est _____.
5. Puerī nōn sunt _____.
6. Mārcus arborem nōn _____.
7. _____, cūr tū nōn arborem ascendis?
8. Dāvus est vir _____.
9. Puerī _____ rīdent.
10. Cornēlia et Flāvia sunt _____.
11. _____ servī in Italiā _____.

Rōmānus/Rōmāna
currit/currunt
amīcus/amīcī
servus/servī
servus/servī
ascendit/ascendunt
Mārcus/Mārce
Britannicus/Britannicī
laetus/laetī
dēfessa/dēfessae
Multī/Multae   labōrat/labōrant

BUILDING THE MEANING

Go Online
PHSchool.com
Web Code: jfd-0004

Direct Objects and the Ending -m

Look at these sentences taken from story 4:

        DO
Sextus <u>Cornēlia*m*</u> vexat. (4:1)   *Sextus annoys Cornelia.*

     DO
<u>Vōce*m*</u> Cornēlia audit. (4:3–4)   *Cornelia hears the voice.*

In these sentences, the words that end in *-m*, namely **Cornēlia*m*** and **vōce*m***, are said to be the *direct objects* (DO) of the verbs **vexat** and **audit**. They name the person or thing that receives the action of the verb.

In English, the order of the words in a sentence usually tells us what word is the direct object; the direct object usually follows the verb, e.g., Cornelia hears <u>the voice</u>. In Latin, it is the ending *-m* that indicates the direct object in the sentence **Vōce*m* Cornēlia audit.** The Latin words could be arranged in any order, and they would still convey essentially the same message.

Note that the pronouns **mē** and **tē**, seen in line 7 of the story on page 19, are also direct objects, although they do not have the ending *-m*.

20   CHAPTER 4

Transitive and Intransitive Verbs

Verbs that take direct objects are said to be *transitive verbs* and may be labeled TV. Verbs that do not take direct objects are said to be *intransitive verbs* (IV), e.g., **Cornēlia sub arbore <u>sedet</u>,** *Cornelia sits under the tree* (1:3).

Core Elements of Latin Sentences

A complete sentence usually has at least a subject and a verb. If the verb is a linking verb, a complement will be needed to complete the sentence. If the verb is transitive, a direct object will be needed to complete the sentence.

You have now met three different kinds of Latin sentences, each with a different selection of core elements as follows:

1. Subject and Intransitive Verb:

      S   IV
   Sextus ex arbore **cadit.** (4:9)

2. Subject, Linking Verb, and Complement:

      S LV   C   S   C   LV
   Sextus est puer molestus. (4:1)   Brevī tempore **Cornēlia dēfessa est.** (2:3–4)

3. Subject, Direct Object, and Transitive Verb:

        S   DO   TV   DO   S   TV
   Magna vōx Cornēliam terret. (4:4)   **Vōcem Cornēlia audit.** (4:3–4)

For a fuller discussion of the core elements of Latin sentences and for more examples, see pages 274–275, II.A, B, C, and D.

EXERCISE 4c

Read each sentence aloud, identify core elements, and translate:

1. Sextus Dāvum saepe vexat; Sextum Dāvus nōn amat.
2. Puellae Mārcum et servum cōnspiciunt.
3. Magna vōx puellam terret.
4. Magnam arborem Sextus ascendit.
5. Dāvus, quī fragōrem audit, est īrātus.

EXERCISE 4d

Using story 4 as a guide, give the Latin for:

1. Sextus is always annoying Cornelia.
2. Cornelia is tired and is sleeping under a tree.
3. Marcus runs to the tree and catches sight of the annoying boy.
4. Nothing frightens Sextus.
5. Marcus hears a big noise.

Romans and their style of painting can be remarkably modern looking, as in this artwork from Pompeii.

Word Study I

Latin and English

Over 60 percent of the words in the English language come from Latin. Look again at these words from Chapter 1:

pictūra   **habitat**

It is not difficult to think of English words that come from them:

picture   *inhabit*

The meanings and spellings of these English words show their relationship with Latin. Such words are called *derivatives*, since they are derived from (or come from) another language, in this case, Latin.

Of course, not all of English is derived from Latin. Most of the simple words of everyday English come from Anglo-Saxon, the Germanic ancestor of English. For this reason, many modern German words sound similar to English, such as "Buch" (*book*) and "Nacht" (*night*).

English words derived from Latin are usually the longer or more difficult words. For example, consider the two English words *water* and *aquatic*. The simpler word *water* is derived from the Anglo-Saxon "waeter" and is related to the German "Wasser." The more difficult word *aquatic* comes from the Latin word for water, **aqua**. Even if one did not know the meaning of *aquatic*, Latin would help to answer the following question:

Which of these is an aquatic sport?

(a) horseback riding   (c) swimming
(b) tennis   (d) soccer

Since *aquatic* means "related to water," the correct answer is "swimming." Knowledge of Latin will help with the meanings of over 60 percent of the words in the English language.

EXERCISE 1

Below are some Latin words from Chapters 1–4. Give the meaning of each word. Then, with the meaning in mind, think of at least one English word derived from each Latin word. Use each English word correctly in a sentence.

strēnua	**spectat**
multī	**agrīs**
sōlus	**terret**
nōmine	**dēscende**
servus	**vōx (vōce)**

EXERCISE 2

Match each English word in the column at the left with its meaning in the column at the right. Use the meaning of the Latin word in parentheses as a guide.

1. *legible* (**legit**)
2. *sedentary* (**sedet**)
3. *ridicule* (**rīdet**)
4. *virile* (**vir**)
5. *elaborate* (**labōrat**)
6. *audible* (**audit**)
7. *conspicuous* (**cōnspicit**)
8. *dormant* (**dormit**)
9. *inscribe* (**scrībit**)

a. manly
b. easy to catch sight of
c. to work out carefully
d. to carve letters on stone
e. able to be heard
f. asleep, inactive
g. to make fun of, mock
h. seated, stationary
i. able to be read

The Dictionary

An English dictionary is a useful source not only for finding the meanings of words but also for discovering the languages from which they are derived. Not all dictionaries provide information on derivation, but most larger ones do. In these more complete dictionaries, entries may include:

a. the word
b. a pronunciation guide
c. an abbreviation indicating the part of speech
d. derivation information
e. definition(s)

Locate these items of information in the following dictionary entry:

villain (vil´ ən), n. [O.Fr. *vilain* <L.L. *vīllānus* <L. *vīlla*, a country house]1. a wicked or evil person 2. a scoundrel.

This entry shows that the English word *villain* is a noun that comes from Old French "vilain," which is from the Late Latin **vīllānus**, which derives from Latin **vīlla**, meaning a country house. This derivation is especially interesting since it reveals the negative feelings toward country people that must have been prevalent at the time when the word *villain* came into use in English.

The abbreviations used in notes on derivation will be different from dictionary to dictionary. All abbreviations are explained at the beginning of each dictionary.

EXERCISE 3

Using a dictionary large enough to contain information on derivation, look up the following English words and copy down the complete derivation for each. Be prepared to explain these derivations as in the example above. All these English words are derived from Latin words you have met.

nominal   cadence   virtue   alter   ramify   infirm

MARCUS TO THE RESCUE

Cornēlia et Flāvia in hortō saepe ambulant. Sī diēs est calidus, ex hortō in silvam ambulant quod ibi est rīvus frīgidus. In eādem silvā puerī quoque saepe errant.

Hodiē, quod diēs est calidus, puellae sub arbore prope rīvum sedent. Dum ibi sedent, Flāvia, "Cūr Mārcus arborēs ascendere nōn vult? Estne puer ignāvus?"   5

"Minimē!" respondet Cornēlia. "Cūr tū Mārcum nōn amās? Mārcus neque ignāvus neque temerārius est."

Tum Flāvia, "Sed Mārcus est semper sollicitus. Sextum nihil terret."

Subitō lupum cōnspiciunt quī ad rīvum fūrtim dēscendit. Perterritae sunt puellae. Statim clāmant, "Mārce! Sexte! Ferte auxilium! Ferte auxilium!"   10

Puerī, ubi clāmōrem audiunt, statim ad puellās currunt. Lupus eōs iam cōnspicit. Tum Sextus, quod lupus eum terret, arborem petit et statim ascendit. Sed Mārcus rāmum arripit et lupum repellit. Puellae ē silvā currunt et ad vīllam salvae adveniunt. Brevī

(continued)

1 **sī**, conj., *if*
   diēs, *(a/the) day*
   calidus, *warm*
   in silvam, *into the woods*
2 **ibi**, adv., *there*
   rīvus, *(a/the) stream*
   frīgidus, *cool, cold*
3 **errant**, *(they) wander*
4 **prope**, *near*
5 **vult**, *(he/she) wishes, wants*
   ignāvus, *cowardly, lazy*
6 **respondet**, *(he/she) replies*
   neque...neque..., conj., *neither...nor...*
7 **temerārius**, *rash, reckless, bold*

9 **lupus**, *(a/the) wolf*
   perterritus, *frightened, terrified*
10 **statim**, adv., *immediately*
   Ferte auxilium! *Bring help! Help!*
11 **ubi**, conj., *where, when*
   clāmor, *(a/the) shout, shouting*
   ad puellās, *toward the girls*
   eōs, *them*
12 **eum**, *him*
   petit, *(he/she) looks for, seeks*
13 **arripit**, *(he/she) grabs hold of, snatches*
   repellit, *(he/she) drives off*
   ē silvā, *out of the woods*
   salvae, *safe*
   adveniunt, *(they) reach, arrive (at)*

EXERCISE 5a

Respondē Latīnē:

1. Ubi puellae hodiē sedent?
2. Cūr puellae perterritae sunt?
3. Quid faciunt puerī ubi clāmōrem audiunt?
4. Quem lupus terret?

   Quem...? *Whom...?*
5. Quid facit Mārcus?

Go Online
PHSchool.com
Web Code: jfd-0005

tempore, ubi Mārcus advenit, eum laetae excipiunt. Sextus, puer ignāvus, adhūc sedet in arbore perterritus. Ex arbore dēscendere timet.

14 **excipiunt,** (they) welcome
   adhūc, adv., *still*

15 **timet,** (he/she) fears, is afraid

Respondē Latīnē:

6. Quālis puer est Sextus?

7. Cūr Sextus ex arbore nōn dēscendit?

EXERCISE 5b

Review

Decide whether each sentence is missing a subject or a direct object. Select the correct form of the noun. Then read aloud and translate:

1. Hodiē Sextus _____ ascendit.
   arbor/arborem
2. Sextus _____ cōnspicit.
   Mārcus/Mārcum
3. Nihil _____ terret.
   Sextum/Sextus
4. _____ puellae cōnspiciunt.
   Lupus/Lupum

5. Puerī _____ audiunt.
   clāmōrem/clāmor
6. _____ lupus terret.
   Sextus/Sextum
7. Puellae _____ laetae excipiunt.
   Mārcus/Mārcum
8. Hodiē _____ puerī nōn vexant.
   Dāvus/Dāvum

BUILDING THE MEANING

Go Online
PHSchool.com
Web Code: jfd-0005

The Complementary Infinitive

In the story at the beginning of this chapter, you have seen how the meanings of some verbs may be expanded or completed by forms called *infinitives*. The words **Sextus vult**, *Sextus wants*, do not form a complete thought because we do not know what Sextus wants or wants to do. We can complete the thought as follows:

Sextus arborem **ascendere** vult.   *Sextus wants to climb a/the tree.*

The meaning of the verb **vult** has now been completed with an infinitive **ascendere**, *to climb*, which itself takes the direct object **arborem**.

Here is another example:

Sextus **dēscendere** timet.   *Sextus is afraid to come down.*

The infinitive is a form of a verb that can be recognized by the letters *-re* and is translated *to...*, e.g., **errāre**, *to wander*; **rīdēre**, *to laugh*, **ascendere**, *to climb*, and **dormīre**, *to sleep*.

Infinitives may be used to complete the meaning of verbs such as **vult**, *he/she wishes*, and **timet**, *he/she fears*, as in the sentences above, and of other verbs, some of which you will meet in Exercise 5c (see the list below the exercise).

When the infinitive is used in this way, it is called a *complementary infinitive* because it *completes* the meaning of the verb with which it goes. Note that in Latin a complementary infinitive usually comes *in front of* the verb, the meaning of which it completes, while in English it comes *after* the verb.

EXERCISE 5c

Read aloud, identify infinitives, and translate:

1. Ego ad hortum currō quod Dāvum vexāre volō.
2. Ego arborem nōn ascendō quod in rīvum cadere nōlō.
3. Quod diēs est calidus, tū prope rīvum errāre parās.
4. Lupus ad vīllam fūrtim appropinquat; servus eum repellere nōn potest.
5. Sextus ex arbore dēscendere nōn vult quod lupus eum terret.
6. Ego magnam arborem ascendere timeō.
7. Lupus Sextum in arbore cōnspicere nōn potest.
8. Mārcus lupum cōnspicit, rāmum arripit, lupum repellere parat.
9. Sī diēs est calidus, Mārcus vult ambulāre in silvam ubi prope rīvum frīgidum sedēre potest.
10. In hortum exīre nōlō quod in vīllā labōrāre volō.

    ego, *I*
    volō, *I wish, want*
    nōlō, *I do not wish, want*
    parās, *you prepare, get ready*
    potest, *(he/she) is able, can*
    exīre, *to go out*

EXERCISE 5d

Using story 5 and Exercise 5c as guides, give the Latin for:

1. Cornelia often wishes to wander in the woods.
2. Flavia wishes to climb the large tree.
3. Marcus is able to drive off the wolf.
4. Sextus is afraid to come down out of the tree.
5. Sextus does not want to fall into the stream.

A confrontation between two of the most feared wild animals, a wolf and a bull, is depicted in this mosaic.
Mosaic, Rome

Go Online
PHSchool.com
Web Code: jfd-0005

AENEAS

The members of our Roman family are proud of their heritage, and take particular pride in the deeds accomplished by other Cornelii throughout the history of Rome. As a people, the Romans were also proud of their mythological heritage. They traced their origins to the great Trojan hero, Aeneas, son of the goddess Venus and the mortal Anchises. According to the myth, Aeneas lived over 1200 years before the time we are studying and fought in the Trojan War.

According to legend, the Trojan War began when Paris, the son of King Priam of Troy, abducted Helen, Queen of Sparta, from her home and brought her back to Troy. Helen's outraged husband Menelaus appealed for help to his brother Agamemnon, King of Mycenae, who was then High King of the Greeks. Agamemnon assembled a huge army with contingents drawn from all regions of Greece. Each part of this force was, in turn, led by a king or prince of a region. These were the mighty Homeric heroes, so called because their stories were told by, among others, the Greek poet Homer in his epic poems, the *Iliad* and the *Odyssey*. The Greek army contained the most famous heroes

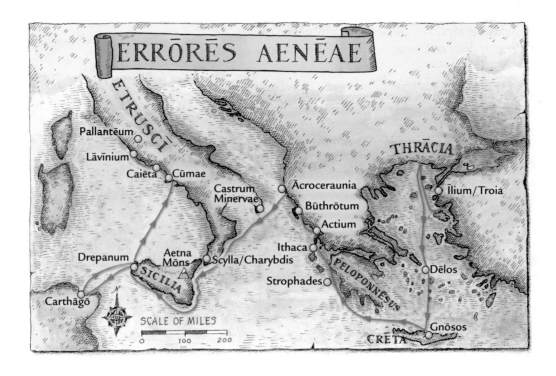

Sinon explains to King Priam why the Greeks left the horse (*top*). The priest Laocoon thrusts his spear into the horse's side to protest accepting the Greek gift (*bottom*).
Episode of The Aeneid: *The Trojan Horse, painted enamel, ca. 1530–1540, Master of* The Aeneid *Series*

of this age, including Ulysses (called Odysseus by the Greeks), the most cunning of the Greeks, and Achilles, the mightiest warrior. With this army Agamemnon set sail for Asia Minor and laid siege to the city of Troy.

The Trojans had their own heroes for defense, primarily the sons of King Priam; the greatest warrior among these was Hector, who commanded the Trojan army. Second to Hector in reputation was Aeneas, a Dardanian from the area north of the city. He had brought his own contingent of Dardanian troops to help in the defense and had moved into Troy with his men and his family early in the war. Powerful though the attacking Greek army was, it was unable to lay an effective siege around such a large city, and the Trojans were able to draw supplies and reinforcements from the surrounding countryside. The resulting stalemate lasted ten years, according to legend.

In the tenth year of the war, after the deaths of many warriors on both sides, including Hector and Achilles, the Greeks finally managed to take the city, owing to a wily deception devised by Ulysses. The Greek army constructed a huge wooden horse, inside of which they hid Greek soldiers. They gave the horse to the Trojans on the pretext that it was a gift to appease the goddess Minerva, whom they had offended, and they pretended to depart the area in force. Actually, though, once the horse was inside the city, the Greek soldiers emerged from its belly and proceeded to lay waste Troy and its inhabitants. That night as the Trojans, caught utterly by surprise, tried desperately to defend their city, the gods themselves spoke to Aeneas. They told him that Troy was destined to fall and that he should not waste his life defending the city. Instead, they revealed that Aeneas's mission was to leave Troy and found a new city where a new nation could be

The arrival of Aeneas at Pallanteum, the future site of Rome
Landscape with the Arrival of Aeneas at Pallanteum, *detail, Claude Lorrain*

established, springing from Trojan stock. Aeneas hurriedly gathered his family and his men and left the city in the confusion of the Greek assault. Although his wife Creusa was tragically lost during the flight, Aeneas and twenty shiploads of companions, together with Anchises his father and Ascanius his son, successfully escaped the ruin of Troy.

Aeneas wandered the lands of the Mediterranean for many years, for although the gods had told him to found a new city, they had not told him where. After abortive attempts to settle in Thrace, on Crete, and at Carthage with Dido, an exiled Phoenician queen, Aeneas finally arrived at Italy where he was destined to found his city. That city was not actually Rome. It was Lavinium, named after Lavinia, the daughter of King Latinus, ruler of Latium, who became the wife of Aeneas. After the marriage of Aeneas and Lavinia, the name of Latins was bestowed upon their combined peoples, the Italians of the kingdom of Latium and the exiled Trojans resettling in the new land.

The story of Aeneas's wanderings from Troy, his many adventures in the waters and lands of the Mediterranean, his struggles and his loves, through to his arrival in Italy and the founding of his city in Latium, was told by the Roman poet Publius Vergilius Maro in his epic poem, the *Aeneid*.

The opening lines of that epic are:

> Of war and a man I sing, who first from Troy's shores, an exile by the decree of fate, came to Italy and Lavinium's shores. Much was he tossed on sea and land by the violence of the gods, because of cruel Juno's unforgetting anger. Much, too, did he endure in war as he sought to found a city and bring his gods to Latium. From him are descended the Latin people, the elders of Alba, and the walls of lofty Rome.

---

1. Why do you suppose the Romans traced their origins back to Aeneas and the Trojan War?
2. In the modern world, there is even a computer virus named after the mythical Trojan Horse. Why does this story have such staying power?

EARLY IN THE DAY

Nōndum lūcet, sed Cornēlia surgit et per vīllam ambulat. Adhūc dormiunt pater et māter et Mārcus. Etiam Sextus dormit neque Cornēliam vexat. Nōn tamen dormiunt servī et ancillae. Omnēs iam surgunt et labōrāre parant quod Cornēlium et Aurēliam timent.

Cornēlia ancillam, nōmine Syram, observat quae vīllam pūrgat et alteram, nōmine Thressam, quae cibum coquere parat. Multī servī mox in agrōs currunt ubi strēnuē labōrant. Aquam ē rīvō in vīllam portant. 5

Iam surgunt Cornēlius et Aurēlia. Cornēlius petit Dāvum quī in hortō est. Īrātus subitō est Cornēlius. Dāvum reprehendit quod sub arbore sedet neque labōrat. Dāvus, ubi Cornēlium audit, statim surgit et labōrāre parat. 10

Aurēlia Cornēliam docet vīllam cūrāre. Ancillae vīllam pūrgant, cibum coquunt, lānam trahunt. Reprehendit Aurēlia ancillās sī ignāvae sunt. Mātrem observat Cornēlia et omnia quae māter facit facere parat. Mātrem adiuvāre vult, sed ipsa neque servum neque ancillam reprehendit. Servī et ancillae nunc strēnuē labōrant. Necesse est neque servum neque ancillam reprehendere. 15

1 **nōndum,** adv., *not yet*	**coquere,** *to cook*
lūcet, *it is light, it is day*	**mox,** adv., *soon, presently*
surgit, *(he/she) gets up, rises*	**strēnuē,** adv., *strenuously, hard*
per vīllam, *through the country house*	7 **aqua,** *water*
pater, *father*	**portant,** *(they) carry*
2 **māter,** *mother*	9 **reprehendit,** *(he/she) blames, scolds*
etiam, adv., *also, even*	11 **docet,** *(he/she) teaches*
neque, conj., *and…not*	**cūrāre,** *to look after, take care of*
tamen, adv., *however*	12 **lānam trahunt,** *(they) spin wool*
3 **ancilla,** *slave-woman*	13 **omnia quae,** *everything that*
omnēs, *all*	**adiuvāre,** *to help*
5 **observat,** *(he/she) watches*	**ipsa,** *she herself*
pūrgat, *(he/she) cleans*	14 **nunc,** adv., *now*
6 **cibus,** *food*	**necesse est,** *it is necessary*

EXERCISE 6a

Respondē Latīnē:

1. Quis surgit?
2. Quī dormiunt?
3. Quid faciunt servī et ancillae?
4. Quid servī ē rīvō in vīllam portant?
   Quī…? *Who…?* (plural)

5. Cūr Cornēlius īrātus est?
6. Quid Aurēlia Cornēliam docet?
7. Quid Cornēlia facere parat?
8. Quid Cornēlia nōn facit?

BUILDING THE MEANING

Infinitive with Impersonal Verbal Phrase

An infinitive usually occurs with the verbal phrase **necesse est**:

> <u>Necesse est</u> neque servum neque ancillam **reprehendere**. (6:14–15)
> *It is necessary* **to scold** *neither slave nor slave-woman.*

The verbal phrase **necesse est** is said to be *impersonal* because we supply the subject "it."

Nouns and Adjectives: Gender

The meaning of basic Latin sentences may be expanded by the addition of modifiers such as adjectives. Compare the following sets of sentences:

Mārcus est <u>puer</u>.   Cornēlia est <u>puella</u>.
Marcus is a <u>boy</u>.   *Cornelia is a <u>girl</u>.*

Mārcus est <u>puer</u> **Rōmānus**. Cornēlia est <u>puella</u> **Rōmāna**.
*Marcus is a **Roman** <u>boy</u>.* *Cornelia is a **Roman** <u>girl</u>.*

The adjectives **Rōmānus** and **Rōmāna** are said to *modify* the nouns that they describe, namely **puer** and **puella**. In order to understand the grammatical relationship between Latin adjectives and the nouns they modify, you need to know more about Latin nouns.

Latin nouns are said to have *gender*. We say that **Mārcus** and **puer** are *masculine* nouns and that **Cornēlia** and **puella** are *feminine* nouns.

Names of men and boys, such as **Cornēlius** and **Mārcus**, and words that designate men and boys, such as **vir** and **puer**, are masculine. Most nouns, such as **hortus**, that end in *-us* are also masculine, even those that do not refer to males.

Names of women and girls, such as **Aurēlia** and **Cornēlia**, and words that designate women and girls, such as **fēmina** and **puella**, are feminine. Most other nouns that end in *-a*, such as **vīlla** and **pictūra**, are also feminine, even those that do not refer to females.

EXERCISE 6b

Tell the gender of each noun below:

1. Aurēlia	4. amīcus	7. rāmus	10. Sextus
2. stola	5. piscīna	8. vir	11. servus
3. Dāvus	6. toga	9. amīca	12. palla

Note that in the following examples the adjective ends in *-us* when it modifies **Mārcus, puer,** and **vir** (masculine nouns) and that it ends in *-a* when it modifies **puella** (feminine):

Mārcus est **Rōmān*us***.   Cornēlius est <u>vir</u> **Rōmān*us***.
Mārcus est <u>puer</u> **Rōmān*us***. Cornēlia est <u>puella</u> **Rōmān*a***.

The endings of both nouns and adjectives change when they become direct objects or become plural:

Masculine	Feminine
Subject or complement singular:	
serv*us* Britannic*us*	puell*a* laet*a*
Object singular:	
serv*um* Britannic*um*	puell*am* laet*am*
Subject or complement plural:	
serv*ī* Britannic*ī*	puell*ae* laet*ae*

The gender of many nouns is not so easy to predict, but you can tell by looking at an adjective used to describe the noun:

Magn*us* <u>clāmor</u> in hortō est.
*There is **great** <u>shouting</u> in the garden.*

<u>Arbor</u> est **magn*a***.
*The <u>tree</u> is **big**.*

<u>Diēs</u> est **calid*us***.
*The <u>day</u> is **hot**.*

The *-us* on **magnus** shows that **clāmor** is masculine, the *-a* on **magna** shows that **arbor** is feminine, and the *-us* on **calidus** shows that **diēs** is masculine.

EXERCISE 6c

Read each sentence aloud. In each sentence identify the adjective and the noun that it modifies or describes. Use the ending on the adjective to determine whether the noun it modifies or describes is masculine or feminine. Then translate the sentence:

1. Cornēlia magnum fragōrem audit.
2. Puerī sunt laetī.
3. Puella sollicita magnam vōcem audit.
4. Magnum clāmōrem nōn amat Dāvus.
5. Sextus est puer strēnuus.
6. Dāvus puerum strēnuum nōn amat.
7. Puerī ad vīllam vīcīnam currunt.
8. Dāvus nōn est Rōmānus.
9. Puellae laetae in agrīs errant.
10. Magnam arborem puerī in agrīs vident.

EXERCISE 6d

Using story 6 as a guide, give the Latin for:

1. Marcus is sleeping because he is tired.
2. The energetic slaves are not sleeping.
3. Cornelius scolds lazy Davus.
4. Many slaves carry cold water.
5. Aurelia scolds a lazy slave-woman.

Romans prized creatively designed glassware, such as this jug.
Second to third century A.D.

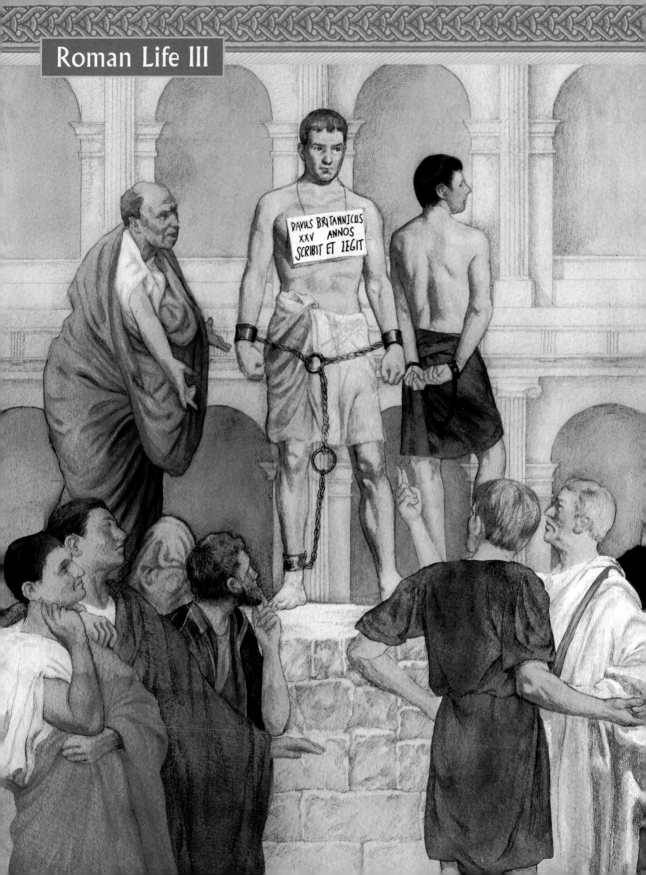

DAVVS BRITANNICVS
XXV ANNOS
SCRIBIT ET LEGIT

THE SLAVE MARKET

Slaves, who were in the early days mainly prisoners of war, were plentiful, and even the poorest Roman household might own one or two. Davus had been captured in Britain and sent to Rome to be sold by auction in the Forum. When his feet were whitened with chalk by the slave-dealer, Davus was mystified, but he soon discovered that this had been done to all new arrivals from abroad. A placard was hung around his neck indicating that he was British and could read and write. He was then put on a revolving stand, and bidding for him began.

He felt pretty uncomfortable standing there like an exhibit at the cattle-market, but he put the best face on it, looking around challengingly at the bidders. Titus Cornelius, father of Gaius Cornelius, was in the Forum that day with the overseer (**vīlicus**) of his farm to purchase some new slaves. He did not pay much attention to the placard—**mangōnēs**, as slave-dealers were called, were notorious swindlers—but when he saw Davus's fine physique, fair hair, and blue eyes he made a bid of 5,000 sesterces, and Davus soon found himself beside the overseer and his new master.

By this time Titus was offering 10,000 sesterces for a Greek from Rhodes. This puzzled Davus because the fellow was a pale, half-starved individual who looked as if a hard day's work would kill him. The overseer, too, looked annoyed at this extravagant bid but said nothing. But when he heard Titus being forced up to 20,000, then 30,000, he could contain himself no longer and muttered angrily, "He's not worth half that, master!" But Titus ignored him and finally paid 35,000 for the Greek Eucleides. The odd qualifications on the placard, "skilled in geometry and rhetoric," must, the overseer thought, have had something to do with the record price!

As Davus, along with the strange Greek, was packed on a cart with some tough-looking Thracians also bought that day, he was filled with fear and doubt as to what might happen to him. But he needn't have worried. Old Titus proved to be the kindest of masters, and now, thirty years later, Davus, himself a grizzled fifty-five, was overseer of the farm. On some of the neighboring estates, he knew, things were not so good.

NEWS FROM ROME

In vīllā sedet vir Rōmānus, nōmine Gāius Cornēlius, quī est pater Mārcī et Cornēliae. Cornēlius est senātor Rōmānus. Sōlus sedet quod multās epistulās scrībere vult. Dum pater occupātus est, Mārcus et Sextus et Cornēlia in agrīs vīcīnīs errant. Ibi multōs servōs labōrantēs spectant.

Subitō nūntium cōnspiciunt quī ad eōs venit. Nūntius, ubi advenit, puerōs salūtat.   5
"Salvē!" respondet Mārcus. "Quem tū petis?"

Nūntius, "Gāium Cornēlium petō," inquit.

Mārcus, "Gāius Cornēlius est pater meus," inquit. "Est in vīllā." Nūntium in vīllam dūcit et patrem petit.

"Pater," inquit Mārcus, "nūntius in vīllā est."   10

Cornēlius statim venit et nūntium salūtat. Epistulam nūntius trādit. Cornēlius, ubi epistulam legit, "Ēheu!" inquit. "Prīnceps senātōrēs Rōmānōs ad urbem revocat. Eōs cōnsulere vult. Necesse est ad urbem redīre."

"Eugepae!" clāmat Sextus, quī Rōmam īre vult. Gemit Cornēlia quod Flāvia ad urbem venīre nōn potest.   15

3 **occupātus,** *busy*
4 labōrantēs, *working*
   spectant, *(they) watch,* look at
5 **nūntius,** *messenger*
   venit, *(he/she) comes*
   salūtat, *(he/she) greets*
6 **Salvē!** *Greetings! Hello!*
7 **inquit,** *(he/she) says*
8 **meus,** *my*
9 **dūcit,** *(he/she) leads,* takes

11 **trādit,** *(he/she) hands over*
12 Ēheu! interj., *Alas! Oh no!*
    prīnceps, *emperor*
    ad urbem, *to the city*
    revocat, *(he/she) recalls*
13 **cōnsulere,** *to consult*
    redīre, *to return*
14 Eugepae! interj., *Hurray!*
    īre, *to go*

EXERCISE 7a

Respondē Latīnē:

1. Cūr Cornēlius sōlus sedet?
2. Ubi Mārcus et Sextus et Cornēlia errant?
3. Quōs spectant in agrīs?   **Quōs…?** *Whom…?* (plural)
4. Quis advenit?
5. Quem nūntius petit?
6. Cūr prīnceps senātōrēs Rōmānōs ad urbem revocat?
7. Quis clāmat "Eugepae!"? Cūr?
8. Cūr gemit Cornēlia?

Go Online
PHSchool.com
Web Code: jfd-0007

Nouns and Adjectives:
The Endings -*ās*, -*ōs*, and -*ēs*

Look at these three sentences:

Mult*ās* epistul*ās* scrībit.	*He writes many letters.*
Mult*ōs* serv*ōs* spectant.	*They watch many slaves.*
Senātor*ēs* Rōmān*ōs* revocat.	*He recalls the Roman senators.*

The words **multās epistulās, multōs servōs,** and **senātōrēs Rōmānōs** introduce you to new endings. You already know that most singular Latin nouns and adjectives end in -*m* when they are used as direct objects (DO) (see page 20). Plural nouns and adjectives used as direct objects usually end in -*s* preceded by a long vowel, e.g., **multās epistulās, multōs servōs,** and **senātōrēs Rōmānōs.**

EXERCISE 7b

Read each sentence aloud. Then locate the direct object in each sentence and say whether it is singular or plural. Also locate any adjectives, identify the nouns that they modify, and give the gender of each of these nouns. Then translate:

1. Cornēlius multās epistulās scrībit.
2. Puerī magnam arborem in agrīs vident.
3. Nūntius quī ad puerōs venit magnōs clāmōrēs audit.
4. Magnās vōcēs audit.
5. Nūntius puerōs dēfessōs salūtat.
6. Prīnceps senātōrēs Rōmānōs ad urbem revocat.
7. Sextus ad magnam urbem īre vult.
8. Cornēlia ad urbem redīre nōn vult quod vīllam rūsticam et amīcam vīcīnam amat.

EXERCISE 7c

Using story 7 as a guide, give the Latin for:

1. Cornelius wants to write many letters.
2. Marcus and Sextus watch many slaves working in the fields.
3. The messenger greets the boys.
4. The messenger is looking for Gaius Cornelius.
5. The messenger hands over a letter.
6. It is necessary to return to the city immediately.
7. Sextus wishes to go to Rome, but Flavia cannot.

Roman writing artifacts

Nouns: Cases and Declensions

Nominative and Accusative Cases

The form of the Latin noun when used as the *subject* of a verb or as a *complement* with **est** or **sunt** is known as the *nominative case*.

The form of the Latin noun when used as the *direct object* of a verb is known as the *accusative case*.

For example:

Nominative	Accusative
Lup*us* eum terret.	Puellae lup*um* vident.
The wolf frightens him.	*The girls see <u>the wolf</u>.*
Lup*ī* puerōs terrent.	Servī lup*ōs* repellunt.
The wolves frighten the boys.	*The slaves drive off <u>the wolves</u>.*
Puell*a* est laet*a*.	Māter puell*am* laet*am* videt.
The girl is <u>happy</u>.	*The mother sees <u>the happy girl</u>.*

Most nouns that you have met belong in the following groups or *declensions*:

Number Case	1st Declension	2nd Declension			3rd Declension	
Singular						
Nominative	puélla	sérvus	púer	áger	páter	vōx
Accusative	puéllam	sérvum	púerum	ágrum	pátrem	vōcem
Plural						
Nominative	puéllae	sérvī	púerī	ágrī	pátrēs	vōcēs
Accusative	puéllās	sérvōs	púerōs	ágrōs	pátrēs	vōcēs

Be sure to learn these forms thoroughly. Note how each word is accented.

NOTES

1. In the 2nd declension, most nouns end in *-us* in the nominative singular (e.g., **servus**), but there are a few like **puer, ager,** and **vir** that end in *-r*. In both types, however, the accusative singular ends in *-um* and the accusative plural in *-ōs*.
2. Although **arbor, pater,** and **māter** end in *-r*, their other endings identify them as 3rd declension nouns.
3. In the 3rd declension, you will note that the nouns you have met end in different ways in the nominative singular (e.g., **arbor, prīnceps, urbs, pater, vōx**). Nevertheless, their accusative singulars all end in *-em*, and both nominative and accusative plurals end in *-ēs*.
4. Most 1st declension nouns are feminine; most 2nd declension nouns are masculine; some 3rd declension nouns are masculine, e.g., **pater**, and some are feminine, e.g., **vōx**.

EXERCISE 7d

In the sentences in Exercise 7b, locate all the nouns and identify their declension, gender, case, and number.

BUILDING THE MEANING

Go Online
PHSchool.com
Web Code: jfd–0007

Reading with Attention to Cases

When you are reading a Latin sentence, identifying the case of each noun *as you meet it* will help you decide what the function of the word will be in the sentence as a whole. As you meet each noun and decide its function, you will form expectations about what is likely to come later to complete the meaning of the sentence.

Consider the following sentences:

1. **Servus currit.**
   The first word we meet is **servus**. We know that it is the subject of the verb because we recognize that it is in the nominative case. The verb (**currit**) then tells us what the slave is "doing."

2. **Servus Dāvum cōnspicit.**
   We go from **servus** (nominative = subject) to **Dāvum** and recognize that **Dāvum** is the direct object of the verb because we recognize it as accusative case. **Dāvum** also tells us that the verb in this sentence is transitive, because **Dāvum** is a direct object and direct objects appear only with transitive verbs. The verb tells us what the slave is "doing" to Davus.

3. **Dāvum puerī vexant.**
   The first word we meet is **Dāvum**. We recognize it as accusative case. The next word is **puerī**. We recognize that it is nominative, and therefore it is *the boys* who are doing something to Davus. The verb **vexant** tells us what they are doing.

4. **Rāmum arripit.**
   We recognize **Rāmum** as accusative case, and we know immediately that someone is doing something to a branch. Since there is no noun in the nominative case, the *ending* of the verb indicates the subject (*he/she*) and the *meaning* of the verb completes the sense.

EXERCISE 7e

Read each sentence aloud. Identify subjects and direct objects, as in the examples above. Then translate:

1. Lupus puellās terret.
2. Puellae silvam amant.
3. Dāvum et servōs puerī vexāre nōn timent.
4. Puerōs et puellās lupī semper terrent.
5. Servī lupōs ex agrīs repellunt.

Mercury, the Roman god of messengers. The wings on the head and feet and the caduceus, or herald's wand, identify this figure as Mercury.
Detail of the ceiling of Palazzo Clerici, Milan, Italy

Nominative or Accusative Plural?
How Do You Decide?

In 3rd declension nouns, the ending of both the nominative and accusative plural is *-ēs*. When you meet a noun with this ending, you cannot tell from the word itself whether it will be a subject or a direct object. To do so in the sentences below, you must first identify the case of the other noun in each sentence. Note the kind of logic modeled below these sentences:

1. Puerī clāmōrēs audiunt.
2. Puerōs clāmōrēs terrent.
3. Prīnceps senātōrēs excipit.
4. Prīncipem senātōrēs excipiunt.
5. Clāmōrēs mātrēs audiunt.
6. Magnōs clāmōrēs patrēs audiunt.
7. Magnī clāmōrēs patrēs terrent.

In sentence 1, since **puerī** is in the nominative case and is therefore the subject of the verb, **clāmōrēs** must be in the accusative case and is therefore the direct object.

In sentence 2, since **puerōs** is accusative, **clāmōrēs** must be nominative.

In sentence 3, since **prīnceps** is nominative, we assume that **senātōrēs** will be accusative. This is confirmed by the singular transitive verb **excipit**.

In sentence 4, since **prīncipem** is accusative, we assume that **senātōrēs** will be nominative. This is confirmed by the fact that the verb **excipiunt** is plural.

In sentence 5, where both nouns end in *-ēs* and the verb is plural, it is the sense that indicates that **clāmōrēs** is accusative and **mātrēs** nominative.

In sentences 6 and 7 the endings on the adjectives tell that **clāmōrēs** is accusative in 6 and nominative in 7.

EXERCISE 7f

Read each sentence aloud. Identify subjects and direct objects, as in the preceding examples. Then translate:

1. Servus senātōrēs videt.
2. Arborēs puerī saepe ascendunt.
3. Clāmōrēs puellās terrent.
4. Patrēs magnōs fragōrēs audiunt.
5. Patrem vōcēs vexant.
6. Vōcēs in hortō audit.
7. Patrēs in viā cōnspiciunt.
8. Patrēs puerōs in viā cōnspiciunt.
9. Patrēs sollicitī clāmōrēs audiunt.
10. Magnās vōcēs patrēs audiunt.

Peristyle of the luxurious *vīlla urbāna* owned by Poppaea Sabina, wife of the emperor Nero, at Oplontis, between Pompeii and Herculaneum
Torre Annunziata, Italy, first century A.D.

ADDITIONAL READING:
The Romans Speak for Themselves: Book I: "Roman Roots in the Country," pages 10–17.

Go Online
PHSchool.com
Web Code: jfd-0007

THE ROMAN VILLA

In cities, the majority of Romans lived in apartment buildings called **īnsulae**, which were several stories high. Cornelius, however, being a wealthy Roman, owned a self-contained house called a **domus**. We shall learn more about these town houses when Cornelius and his family reach Rome.

Like other rich Romans, Cornelius also had a house in the country. Roman country houses often had three distinct areas, each serving a different purpose. One area provided accommodation for the owner and his family when they came to the country from Rome, which they would usually do during the summer months to escape the noisy bustle and heat of the city. This area would include a garden with a fishpond, a dining room, bedrooms, a bakery, a tool room, baths, and a kitchen (see the ground plan on the next page, numbers 1–8). The second area housed the livestock and had quarters for the slaves, who lived on the estate year round and did the agricultural work (ground plan, numbers 9 and 12). The third area contained a room for pressing grapes, olive-pressing rooms, a farmyard with wine vats, a barn for storing grain, and an open space (**ārea**) for threshing grain (ground plan, numbers 10 and 13–16). All three areas taken together could be referred to as a **vīlla rūstica**.

When absent, Cornelius placed the day-to-day running of the **vīlla rūstica** in the capable hands of Davus, his overseer (**vīlicus**), but some landowners had tenant farmers. Roman writers on agriculture stress that the owner should take special care in the selection of his farm staff and in the working relationships between himself and his staff:

> The owner should conduct himself civilly with his tenants, and speak affably, not haughtily, to them; he should be more concerned about their work than their payments of rent, because this offends them less and in the long run is more profitable. For the position of **vīlicus,** a man should be chosen who has borne up under heavy work, one who has been tried by experience. He should be past young manhood and yet not be old, because older men think it beneath them to take orders from a young man, and an old man will break down under heavy labor. Let him be middle-aged, strong, skilled in farming or at least able to learn. As for the other slaves, I myself talk rather familiarly with them for it lightens their toil, and I even make jokes with them and allow them to make jokes. I also now make it my practice to consult them on any new work, as if they were experienced, so that I can come to know their abilities. Moreover, they are more willing to undertake a task on which they think their opinions have been asked and on which I have followed their advice.

Columella, *On Agriculture* I. VII–VIII (extracts)

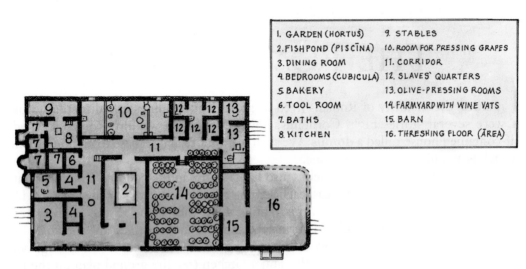

1. GARDEN (HORTUS)
2. FISHPOND (PISCĪNA)
3. DINING ROOM
4. BEDROOMS (CUBICULA)
5. BAKERY
6. TOOL ROOM
7. BATHS
8. KITCHEN
9. STABLES
10. ROOM FOR PRESSING GRAPES
11. CORRIDOR
12. SLAVES' QUARTERS
13. OLIVE-PRESSING ROOMS
14. FARMYARD WITH WINE VATS
15. BARN
16. THRESHING FLOOR (ĀREA)

GROUND PLAN OF *Villa Rūstica* OF THE *Cornēliī*

Reconstructed View of the
Villa Rūstica of the *Cornēliī*

ADDITIONAL READING:
The Romans Speak for Themselves: Book I: "Pliny's Laurentine Villa," pages 18–26, and
"A Pleasant Retreat," pages 27–32.

If Cornelius had been a very wealthy Roman, he might have had a **vīlla urbāna**, literally a "city villa," separate from the accommodations for the farm. Such a **vīlla urbāna** could be very luxurious and could take up almost the whole estate. It could have winter and summer apartments oriented to the seasonal sunlight, baths, and promenades, just like a house in the city. The Roman author Pliny the Younger describes his **vīlla urbāna** near Laurentum in a letter to a friend. Below is a ground plan of his country house. Such country houses by the sea (**mare**) were also called **vīllae maritimae**. These luxury houses offered their owners all the comforts of a city house in the beauty and quiet of the country.

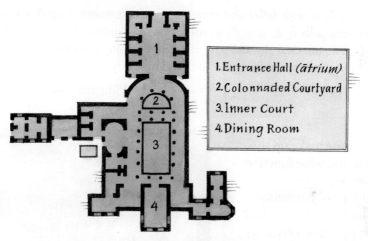

1. Entrance Hall (*ātrium*)
2. Colonnaded Courtyard
3. Inner Court
4. Dining Room

PLAN OF PLINY THE YOUNGER'S
VĪLLA URBĀNA

The Romans loved natural beauty and artistic representations of it. They often had the walls of their houses (in both the city and the country) painted, as Pliny the Younger's uncle, Pliny the Elder, describes them, with pictures "of country houses and landscaped gardens, copses, woods, hills, fish ponds and canals, rivers, coasts, and any other scenery one could desire, and scenes of people strolling along or sailing in a boat, or traveling to the country in carriages, people fishing, fowling and hunting, or gathering grapes" (Pliny the Elder, *Natural History* 35.116).

Pliny the Younger had another **vīlla urbāna** in Etruria with luxurious fountains, pools, and baths, which he describes as follows:

Opposite the dining room at the corner of the colonnade is a large bedroom. From some of its windows you look onto the terrace, from others onto the meadow, while the windows in front overlook an ornamental pool which is a pleasure both to see and hear. For the water, falling from a height, foams white in the marble basin. The bedroom is very warm in winter, being so exposed to the sun, and on a cloudy day the hot air from the nearby furnace takes the place of the sun's heat. From here you pass through a spacious and pleasant changing-room into the "cold bath" room in which there is a large bath out of the full sunlight. But if you want more space to swim in and warmer water, there is a pool in the courtyard and near it a fountain in which you can cool yourself if you've had enough of the heat.

And later in the same letter he tells us why he liked this house so much:

I can relax there with fuller and more carefree enjoyment. I need never wear a toga; nobody calls from next door. All is calm and quiet, which makes the place healthy, as do the clear sky and pure air. There I enjoy health of body and mind, for I keep my mind in training by study and my body by hunting.

Pliny the Younger, *Letters* V.6

1. What three areas make up the **vīlla rūstica**, and what function does each serve?
2. What would Titus Cornelius have been looking for if he had intended to purchase Davus to serve as the **vīlicus** of his estate?
3. Do you find Columella's advice on the treatment of slaves sound? Why or why not?

Wall painting adorning a bedroom of the *vīlla rūstica* of P. Fannius Synistor at Boscoreale near Pompeii. The painting shows an imaginary cityscape. The ground plan and a reconstruction of this villa are shown on page 46. We use this villa at Boscoreale as a model for the villa of the Cornelii at Baiae.
Boscoreale, Pompeii, first century A.D.

Review I: Chapters 1–7

Exercise Ia: The Elements of Sentences pp. 4, 8–9, 20–21, 26–27, 42

In the following sentences from the story in Chapter 7, identify each

subject	transitive verb
intransitive verb	direct object
linking verb	complementary infinitive
complement	

1. In vīllā sedet vir Rōmānus.
2. Cornēlius est senātor Rōmānus.
3. Multās epistulās scrībere vult.
4. Dum pater occupātus est, Mārcus et Sextus et Cornēlia in agrīs errant.
5. Ibi multōs servōs labōrantēs spectant.
6. Flāvia ad urbem venīre nōn potest.

Exercise Ib: Nominative and Accusative pp. 40–43

Identify the declension of each noun. Then change nominatives to accusatives and accusatives to nominatives, keeping the same number (singular or plural):

1. cibus	4. aquae	7. rīvī	10. patrem
2. lānam	5. lupus	8. vōcem	11. rāmī
3. fragōrem	6. virum	9. puerōs	12. clāmōrēs

Exercise Ic: Agreement of Adjectives with Nouns pp. 14, 34–35

Select the appropriate adjective from the pool below to complete each of the following sentences. You may use adjectives more than once. Be sure to use the right ending on the adjective. Translate each sentence:

1. Dāvus _____ est quod puerī clāmant.
2. Sextus arborem ascendit quod _____ est.
3. Flāvia in vīllā _____ habitat.
4. Mārcus _____ rāmum arripit et lupum repellit.
5. Sextus _____ arborem ascendit.
6. Dāvus _____ est quod Sextus in hortō ambulat.
7. Flāvia et Cornēlia puellae _____ sunt et saepe in agrīs currunt.
8. Sextus est puer _____ et puellās terret.
9. Ubi lupus venit, Sextus in arbore sedet, quod puer _____ est.
10. Cornēlius _____ sedet quod epistulās scrībere vult.

sollicitus	vīcīnus	temerārius	strēnuus	ignāvus
sōlus	īrātus	molestus	magnus	

Exercise Id: Reading Comprehension

Read the following passage and answer the questions that follow with full sentences in Latin:

AENEAS LEAVES TROY

Aenēās est vir Troiānus quī urbem Troiam contrā Graecōs dēfendit. Decem annōs Graecī urbem obsident. Decem annōs Troiānī Graecōs repellunt. Tandem per dolum Graecī urbem nocte intrant. Multōs Troiānōs capiunt, multōs necant. Nōn iam urbem dēfendere Aenēās potest. Necesse est igitur ex urbe effugere et urbem novam petere. Multī amīcī quoque ab urbe Troiā effugiunt. 5
Omnēs ad Italiam nāvigāre parant.

Aenēās, dum ex urbe effugit, senem portat. Senex est Anchīsēs, pater Aenēae. Portāre Anchīsēn necesse est quod senex ambulāre nōn potest. Aenēās Anchīsēn portat; portat Anchīsēs Penātēs, deōs familiārēs. Deī Aenēān et Anchīsēn et omnēs amīcōs servant. 10

Aenēās etiam parvum puerum dūcit. Puer est Ascanius, fīlius Aenēae. Dum ex urbe ambulant, Ascanius patrem spectat et manum tenet. Perterritus est Ascanius quod magnōs clāmōrēs, magnōs fragōrēs audit. Valdē Graecōs timet.

Ubi Aenēās et Anchīsēs et Ascanius ex urbe effugiunt, "Ubi est māter?" subitō clāmat Ascanius. Multī amīcī adveniunt, sed nōn advenit Creūsa, māter 15
Ascaniī. Aenēās sollicitus patrem et fīlium et Penātēs relinquit et in urbem redit. Graecī ubīque sunt. Creūsam frūstrā petit.

"Ēheu!" inquit. "Troiam habent Graecī. Fortasse tē quoque habent, Creūsa. Valdē amō Creūsam, valdē Troiam. Sed neque urbem neque Creūsam servāre iam possum. Ad amīcōs igitur redīre necesse est." 20

Tum ad amīcōs redit. Mox ad Italiam nāvigāre parant Aenēās et amīcī.

1 Aenēās: Greek nominative contrā Graecōs, *against the Greeks*	9 deōs familiārēs, *household gods* deī, *the gods* Aenēān: Greek accusative
2 decem annōs, *for ten years* obsident, *(they) besiege*	10 servant, *(they) protect*
3 per dolum, *through a trick* nocte, *at night* intrant, *(they) enter, go into* capiunt, *(they) capture*	11 parvus, *small* fīlius, *son*
	12 manum, *hand* tenet, *(he/she) holds*
4 necant, *(they) kill*	13 valdē, *very much*
5 effugere, *to flee, run away, escape* novus, *new* ab urbe, *from the city*	16 Ascaniī, *of Ascanius* relinquit, *(he/she) leaves*
	17 ubīque, *everywhere* frūstrā, *in vain*
6 nāvigāre, *to sail*	18 habent, *(they) have, hold* fortasse, *perhaps*
7 senem, *old man* Aenēae, *of Aeneas*	19 servāre, *to save*
8 Anchīsēn: Greek accusative	20 possum, *I am able*

1. Who is Aeneas?
2. What do the Greeks do for ten years?
3. How do the Greeks finally enter the city?
4. Why is it necessary for Aeneas to flee?
5. What does Aeneas prepare to do?
6. Whom is Aeneas carrying?
7. What is Anchises carrying?
8. Whom is Aeneas leading?
9. Why is Ascanius frightened?
10. Who is Creusa?
11. Who goes back into the city?
12. Whom does he seek?
13. Is Aeneas able to save Creusa?
14. To where do Aeneas and his friends prepare to sail?

Aeneas carrying his father, Anchises, from the sack of Troy
The Flight of Aeneas from Troy, *1729, Carle van Loo*

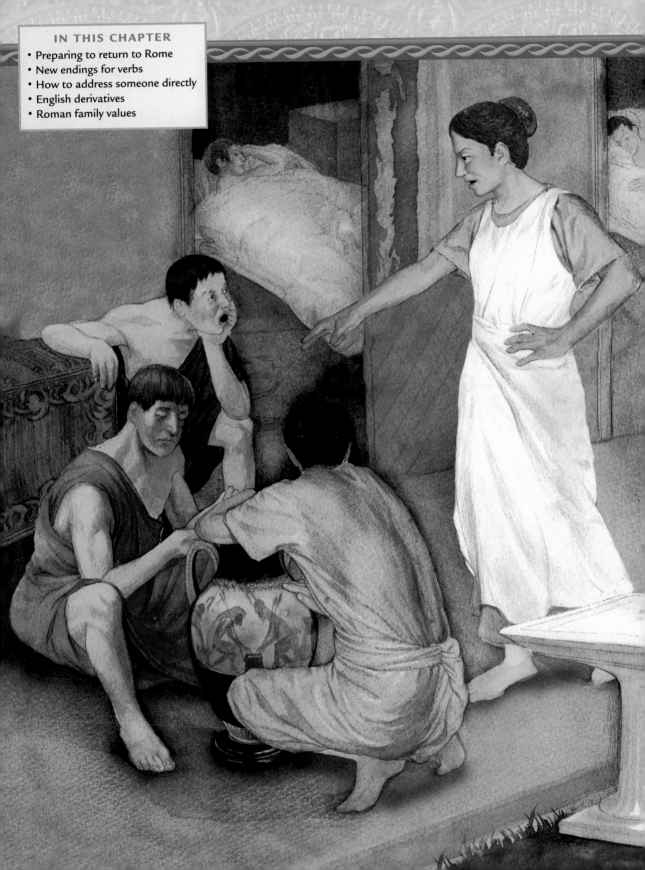

GETTING UP EARLY

Nōndum lūcet, sed Aurēlia, māter Mārcī et Cornēliae, iam in vīllā occupāta est.
Īrāta est quod servōs sedentēs cōnspicit.
    "Agite, molestī servī!" inquit. "Cūr nihil facitis? Cūr vōs ibi sedētis? Cūr nōn
strēnuē labōrātis? Omnia statim parāre necesse est quod nōs hodiē Rōmam redīmus."
Iam strēnuē labōrant servī.   5
    Tum Aurēlia puerōs excitāre parat. Intrat igitur cubiculum Mārcī. Clāmat, "Age,
Mārce! Tempus est surgere. Nōs ad urbem redīre parāmus."
    Mārcus mātrem audit sed nihil respondet. Deinde Aurēlia cubiculum Sextī intrat.
Clāmat, "Age, Sexte! Tempus est surgere." Statim surgit Sextus. Celeriter tunicam et
togam induit et brevī tempore ē cubiculō currit.   10
    Iterum Aurēlia cubiculum Mārcī intrat. Iterum clāmat, "Age, Mārce! Nōs iam
strēnuē labōrāmus. Cūr tū sōlus nōn surgis?"
    Gemit Mārcus. "Ego nōn surgō," inquit, "quod Rōmam redīre nōlō. Cūr mihi
quoque necesse est ad urbem redīre? Patrem meum prīnceps ad urbem revocat. Patrem
cōnsulere vult. Nōn vult cōnsulere Mārcum."   15
    Subitō intrat Gāius, pater Mārcī, et clāmat, "Sed ego volō cōnsulere Mārcum! Cūr,
Mārce, hodiē mē vexās? Cūr nōn surgis? Cūr nōndum tunicam et togam induis, moleste
puer?"
    Nihil respondet Mārcus sed statim surgit quod patrem timet.

1 **iam,** adv., *now, already*
3 **Age!/Agite!** *Come on!*
  vōs, *you* (plural)
4 **nōs,** *we, us*
6 **excitāre,** *to rouse, wake (someone) up*
  intrat, *(he/she) enters*
  cubiculum, *room, bedroom*

7 **tempus,** *time*
8 **deinde,** adv., *then, next*
9 **celeriter,** adv., *quickly*
10 **induit,** *(he/she) puts on*
11 **iterum,** adv., *again, a second time*
13 **mihi,** *for me*

EXERCISE 8a

Respondē Latīnē:

1. Cūr est Aurēlia īrāta?
2. Cūr necesse est omnia statim parāre?
3. Quid Aurēlia in cubiculō Mārcī clāmat?
4. Quid facit Mārcus?

5. Surgitne Sextus?
6. Quid facit Sextus?
7. Cūr Mārcus nōn surgit?
8. Quis subitō intrat?
9. Cūr Mārcus surgit?

Go Online
PHSchool.com
Web Code: jfd-0008

FORMS

Verbs: Persons

Look at these sentences:

Rōmam redīre nōl*ō*.	*I do not want to return to Rome.*
Cūr nōn surgi*s*?	*Why do **you** not get up?*
Aurēlia cubiculum Mārcī intra*t*.	***Aurelia** goes into Marcus's bedroom.*
Iterum clāma*t*.	***She** calls again.*
Ad urbem redīre parā***mus***.	***We** are preparing to return to the city.*
Cūr nōn strēnuē labōrā*tis*?	*Why do **you** not work hard?*
Puerī in agrīs erra***nt***. Servōs	*The **boys** wander in the fields.*
labōrantēs specta***nt***.	***They** watch the slaves working.*

The ending of the verb tells us who is doing something, i.e., whether the subject is 1st, 2nd, or 3rd *person, singular* or *plural* (I, you, he/she/it; we, you, they). In the 3rd person the subject may be a noun (e.g., **Aurēlia** and **puerī**). The 1st person is the speaker or speakers (I, we); the 2nd person is the person or persons spoken to (you, singular or plural); and the 3rd person is the person or thing or persons or things spoken about (he, she, it, they). The personal pronouns **ego, tū, nōs,** and **vōs** are used only for emphasis.

Person	Singular		Plural	
1	-*ō*	*I*	-*mus*	*we*
2	-*s*	*you*	-*tis*	*you*
3	-*t*	*he/she/it*	-*nt*	*they*

These personal endings always have the same meaning wherever they occur.

Person	Singular		Plural	
1	pár*ō*	*I prepare*	parā́***mus***	*we prepare*
2	párā*s*	*you prepare*	parā́*tis*	*you prepare*
3	pára*t*	*he/she prepares*	pára***nt***	*they prepare*

Be sure to learn these forms thoroughly.

Note that the vowel that precedes the personal endings is short before final -*t* and -*nt*. Note how each word is accented.

The following verb is irregular, but it uses the same endings as above (except for -*m* in place of -*ō* in the 1st person singular).

Person	Singular		Plural	
1	su***m***	*I am*	sú***mus***	*we are*
2	e*s*	*you are*	és*tis*	*you are*
3	es*t*	*he/she/it is*	su*nt*	*they are*

Be sure to learn these forms thoroughly.

EXERCISE 8b

Take parts and read these dialogues
aloud several times:

1. NĀRRĀTOR: Sextus est laetus.
   MĀRCUS: Tū es laetus, Sexte. Cūr?
   SEXTUS: Ego sum laetus quod Rōmam
   īre volō.

2. NĀRRĀTOR: Servī sunt dēfessī.
   MĀRCUS: Vōs estis dēfessī, servī. Cūr?
   SERVĪ: Dēfessī sumus quod strēnuē labōrāmus.

3. NĀRRĀTOR: Cornēlius epistulās legit.
   AURĒLIA: Quid legis, Cornēlī?
   CORNĒLIUS: Epistulās legō.

4. NĀRRĀTOR: Mārcus rāmum arripit.
   SEXTUS: Quid arripis, Mārce?
   MĀRCUS: Rāmum arripiō.

5. NĀRRĀTOR: Cornēlia rīdet.
   FLĀVIA: Cūr rīdēs, Cornēlia?
   CORNĒLIA: Rīdeō quod laeta sum.

6. NĀRRĀTOR: Senātōrēs ad urbem redeunt.
   AURĒLIA: Cūr ad urbem redītis, senātōrēs?
   SENĀTŌRĒS: Redīmus quod prīnceps nōs
   cōnsulere vult.

7. NĀRRĀTOR: Puerī lupum nōn timent.
   PUELLAE: Cūr lupum nōn timētis, puerī?
   PUERĪ: Lupum nōn timēmus quod
   temerāriī sumus.

8. NĀRRĀTOR: Puellae clāmant, "Ferte auxilium!"
   PUERĪ: Cūr vōs clāmātis "Ferte auxilium!"?
   PUELLAE: Nōs clāmāmus "Ferte auxilium!"
   quod lupum cōnspicimus.

A woman's well-groomed appearance
reflected her rank and refinement. This
Roman matron is attended by slaves
dressing her hair and holding a mirror.
Relief sculpture, Germany, circa third century A.D.

Nouns and Adjectives: Vocative

You have seen that the forms **Sexte** and **Mārce** are used when Sextus and Marcus are addressed by name. These forms are in the *vocative case*. The vocative case is used when addressing persons or things directly.

The spelling of a noun or adjective in the vocative case is usually the same as the spelling of the word in the nominative. Thus, **Cornēlia, puer,** and **pater** could be either vocative or nominative.

One exception to this rule is that 2nd declension masculine nouns such as **Sextus, Mārcus,** or **servus** and corresponding adjectives such as **magnus** or **strēnuus** change their ending to *-e* when they are used in the vocative singular, e.g., **servus** (nom.) and **serve** (voc.). Thus, among the following vocative forms only **serve** is different from the nominative:

Vocative

	1st Declension	2nd Declension			3rd Declension
Sing.	Cornēlia	serve	puer	ager	pater
Pl.	puellae	servī	puerī	agrī	patrēs

There are three other exceptions. Second declension proper names ending in **-ius,** the noun **fīlius,** *son,* and the adjective **meus,** *my,* have vocatives in *-ī*:

> *Nominative:* Cornēlius   *Vocative:* Cornēlī
> *Nominative:* meus fīlius   *Vocative:* mī fīlī

Identify all words in the vocative in Exercise 8b.

EXERCISE 8c

Read aloud. Identify the person (1st, 2nd, or 3rd) and number (singular or plural) of each verb that is not an infinitive. Then translate:

1. Cūr ē vīllā in silvam saepe ambulātis, puellae?
2. In eādem silvā puerī quoque ambulant.
3. Īrāta sum quod servōs sedentēs cōnspiciō.
4. Arborēs ascendimus quod lupī nōs terrent.
5. "Sexte! Mārce!" clāmat Cornēlia. "Cūr nōn surgitis?"
6. "Ēheu!" inquit Dāvus. "Semper ego labōrō; semper mē vexant puerī; ad Britanniam redīre volō."
7. Omnia parāmus quod Rōmam hodiē redīmus.
8. Servī in vīllā sedent; neque Aurēliam audiunt neque respondent, nam dēfessī sunt.

nam, conj., *for*

EXERCISE 8d

Using story 8 and the charts of forms on pages 54 and 56 as guides, give the Latin for:

1. Slaves: "We are no longer sitting but are working hard."
2. Aurelia: "Marcus, you are still sleeping. Why are you not getting up? Why are you not preparing to return to the city?"
3. Marcus: "Why, Mother, are you waking me up? It is not yet light. I do not want to get up."
4. Aurelia: "We are preparing to return to the city today. Come on, Marcus! It is time to get up."
5. Cornelius: "Troublesome boys, why are you still sleeping? Why aren't you getting up? Why aren't you putting on your tunics and togas?"

Word Study II

Latin Bases into English Verbs

Often the bases of Latin verbs come into English with only minor changes. You can find the base by dropping the letters *-āre, -ēre, -ere,* or *-īre* from the infinitive. Replacing these letters with a silent *-e* will sometimes give you an English verb. For example, **excitāre**, base **excit-**, + silent *-e* becomes *excite* in English. Some Latin bases come into English with no change. For example, **dēscendere** (*to go down*), base **dēscend-**, produces the English *descend*.

Sometimes additional minor spelling changes occur. For example, **exclāmāre** (*to shout out*), becomes *exclaim* in English, adding an *i* in the process.

EXERCISE 1

Give an English verb derived from the base of each of these Latin verbs. Give the meaning of each English verb. In many cases it has the same meaning as the Latin verb:

extendere	salūtāre	revocāre	respondēre	surgere
repellere	vexāre	trādere	errāre	ascendere

Latin Bases into English Nouns and Adjectives

A Latin base may be the source of an English noun or adjective. For example, the base of **errāre** produced the Latin noun **error** and the Latin adjective **errāticus**, from which came the English *error* and *erratic*.

The English words in italics below are derived from the bases of the Latin verbs in parentheses. Determine the meaning of the English word from the meaning of the Latin verb. Is the English word a noun or an adjective?

1. Cornelius was not moved by the runaway slave's *petition*. (**petere**)
2. Sextus's rude behavior was *repellent* to Cornelia and Flavia. (**repellere**)
3. With the *advent* of summer, Cornelius moves his family to their country house at Baiae. (**advenīre**)
4. Cornelius was dictating a letter to his *scribe*. (**scrībere**)
5. "Sextus," scolded Eucleides, "your writing is not *legible*." (**legere**)
6. The *insurgent* senators were severely punished by the emperor. (**surgere**)
7. The Roman army found the *descent* from the mountain more difficult than the *ascent*. (**dēscendere, ascendere**)

One Latin Base into Many English Words

The bases of some Latin words are the source of several English words, representing different parts of speech. For example, **urbs**, *city*, base **urb-**, is the source of:

1. *urban*   adjective, meaning "pertaining to a city"
2. *urbane*   adjective, meaning "elegant and polished in manner" (How does this idea relate to **urbs**?)
3. *urbanity*   noun, meaning "politeness, courtesy, the quality of being urbane"
4. *urbanize*   verb, meaning "to change from country to city"
5. *suburb*   noun, meaning "a residential area at the edge of a city"

The words in each group below are derived from one Latin base. Think of a Latin word that shows this base. With its meaning in mind, determine the meaning of each English word. Finally, give the part of speech of each English word:

1. *magnate, magnificent, magnify*
2. *contemporary, tempo, temporal*
3. *prince, principal, principally*

4. *inscribe, scribble, subscribe*
5. *paternal, paternity, patron*

Go Online
PHSchool.com
Web Code: jfd-0008

PATRIA POTESTAS

M arcus's behavior shows that he respects his father's wishes and fears his displeasure just as strongly. The relationship between Roman parents and children was quite different from that in some modern societies. American children gradually become quite independent of parents by their late teens, even to the extent of choosing their marriage partner themselves. Such independence has developed only quite recently in the history of the family.

The Roman father was the supreme head (**paterfamiliās**) of his family (**familia**), which included his wife, his married and unmarried children, and his slaves. As master (**dominus**), he had the power to sell or kill his slaves. If he married his wife with full legal power (**manus**), he became owner of her property, and she ceased to belong to her own family, becoming legally a member of his. Over his children he exercised a fatherly power (**patria potestās**) that allowed him to determine their lives as he wished.

According to Roman tradition, the concept of **patria potestās** was established by the first king of Rome:

> Romulus gave the Roman father absolute power over his son. This power the father had until he died whether he imprisoned his son, whipped him, threw him into chains and made him labor on the farm, or even killed him. Romulus even let the Roman father sell his son into slavery.

> Dionysius of Halicarnassus, *Roman Antiquities* 2.26–27 (extracts)

The Roman father continued to have complete control even over his adult children, arranging their marriages—and divorces—and managing any property they might own. He exercised his **patria potestās** over *their* children as well.

In most instances, a father's **patria potestās** ended only with his death. A father might, however, "emancipate" his adult son, who then had **patria potestās** over his sons. A daughter who married might remain under her father's **potestās**, but her father could transfer this power into the hands of his son-in-law; such a marriage was called "marriage with **manus**" (literally, "hand").

How strictly and severely a father exercised his **potestās** varied according to personal inclination and situation. Cicero reluctantly accepted one young man as son-in-law due to the urging of his wife and of his daughter, Tullia, and he later ruefully arranged for Tullia's divorce upon her request. Another father slew his adult son in 62 B.C. because he had participated in the Catilinarian conspiracy against the Roman state. There were controls over the exercise of **patria potestās**. The slaying of a child had first to be discussed in a council of adult male relatives. Public opinion also might influence a father. Gradually, too, Roman law imposed some limits, requiring, for instance, that a daughter consent to her marriage.

True love and affection between parent and child were not eliminated by **patria potestās**. However, a father—and mother—were expected primarily to provide a moral education for their children, to prepare sons for service to the state and family through careers as magistrates, and to prepare daughters to educate and rear worthy future members of the family and state. The poet Statius, writing in the last decade of the first century A.D., congratulates his friend, Julius Menecrates, on the upbringing of his sons and daughter:

> From their father may your children learn peaceful ways and from their grandfather may they learn generosity, and from them both eagerness for glorious virtue. Because of their position and birth, the daughter will enter a noble house upon marriage, and the sons as soon as they become men will enter the threshold of Romulus's Senate house.

Statius, to Julius Menecrates (*Silvae* 4.8.57–62, extracts)

The tragic legend of a Roman father who felt compelled to order the execution of his own sons for disloyalty to the state is memorialized in the painting, ***Lictors Bearing the Bodies of His Sons to Brutus.***
Lictors Bearing the Bodies of His Sons to Brutus, *1789, Jacques-Louis David*

The consequences of disregarding a father's instructions were immortalized among the ancients in the legend of Icarus, son of Daedalus the inventor. He perished because he disobediently flew too near the sun on wings of wax his father created. Here is Dürer's engraving of that legend. *Woodcut,* The Fall of Icarus, *1495*

Though the Romans may not have displayed the bond between parent and child as openly and as physically as we do, they considered it sacred: Cicero called parental love **amor ille penitus īnsitus**, "that love implanted deeply within."

A newborn child would be placed at its father's feet, and the father would accept it into the family by lifting it in his arms. Statius expressed his love for his adopted son as follows:

> He was mine, mine. I saw him lying upon the ground, a newborn baby, and I welcomed him with a natal poem as he was washed and anointed. When he demanded air for his new life with trembling cries, I set him in Life's roll.
>
> From your very moment of birth I bound you to me and made you mine. I taught you sounds and words, I comforted you and soothed your hidden hurts. When you crawled on the ground, I lifted you up and kissed you, and rocked you to sleep myself and summoned sweet dreams for you.
>
> Statius, *Silvae* 5.5.69–85 (extracts)

1. Family structure has differed from age to age and society to society. How would you characterize the Roman family in a few sentences?
2. What do the stories of Brutus and his sons and of Daedalus and his son Icarus have in common? How do these stories relate to the concept of **patria potestās**?
3. Parents in many societies use traditional stories to instill personal, familial, and societal values in their children. What traditional stories did your parents tell you to instill such values?

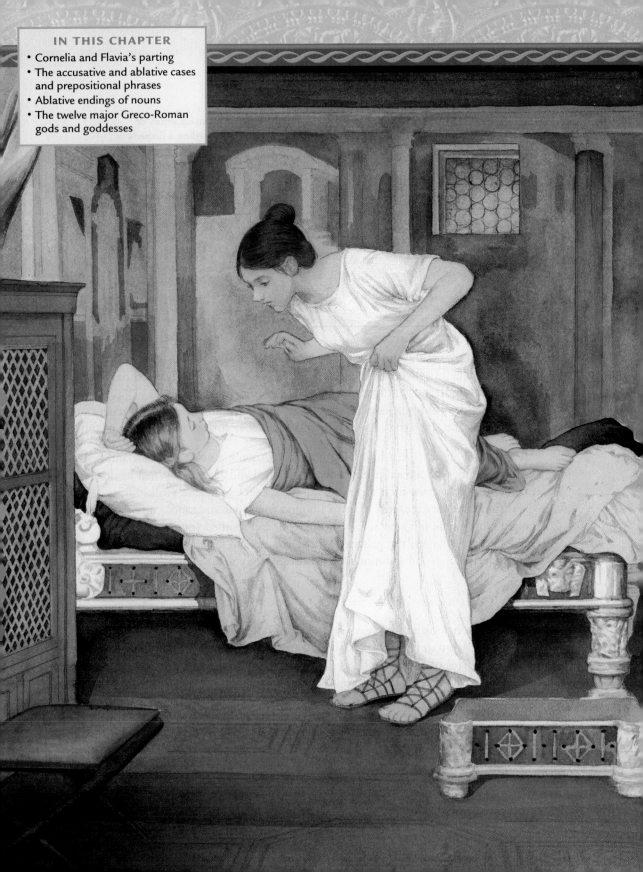

GOODBYE

Cornēlia, ubi surgit, ē vīllā suā fūrtim ambulat et per agrōs ad vīllam amīcae currit. Nōndum lūcet, sed nihil Cornēliam terret. Nēmō eam cōnspicit. Nūllī servī in agrīs labōrant. Etiam iānitor ad iānuam vīllae dormit. Cornēlia, quod tacitē intrat, iānitōrem nōn excitat.

Cornēlia cubiculum Flāviae tacitē intrat et eam excitāre temptat. Adhūc dormit   5
Flāvia. Iterum temptat Cornēlia. Flāvia sēmisomna, "Quis es? Cūr mē vexās?"

Cornēlia respondet, "Sum Cornēlia! Surge!"

Flāvia surgit. Laeta Cornēliam excipit et clāmat, "Quid tū hīc?"

Cornēlia, "Tacē, Flāvia! Nōlī servōs excitāre! Venī tacitē mēcum in agrōs. Ibi nēmō
nōs audīre potest."   10

Cornēlia Flāviam fūrtim ē vīllā in agrōs dūcit. Ubi puellae ad arborēs adveniunt, Cornēlia, "Misera sum," inquit, "quod ego et Mārcus et Sextus et pater et māter Rōmam hodiē redīre parāmus. Prīnceps patrem meum cōnsulere vult. Nōbīs igitur necesse est statim discēdere."

Flāvia clāmat, "Cūr statim, Cornēlia? Cūr nōn pater tuus discēdit sōlus? Cūr   15
vōs omnēs simul discēditis?"

Respondet Cornēlia, "Nesciō, Flāvia. Sed nōbīs secundā hōrā discēdere necesse est."

Flāvia lacrimat, "Ō mē miseram! Vōs omnēs Rōmam redītis. Mihi necesse est hīc manēre. Valē, Cornēlia! Multās epistulās ad mē mitte! Prōmittisne?"

Cornēlia, "Ego prōmittō. Et iam valē!" Cornēlia Flāviam complexū tenet et lacrimāns abit.   20

1 suā, *her own*	**mēcum**, *with me*	Ō mē miseram! *Poor me!*
2 **nēmō**, *no one*	12 **misera**, *unhappy, miserable*	19 **manēre**, *to remain, stay*
nūllī, *no*	13 **nōbīs**, *for us*	**Valē!** *Goodbye!*
3 iānitor, *doorkeeper*	14 **discēdere**, *to go away*	**mitte**, *send*
ad iānuam, *at the door*	15 **tuus**, *your* (sing.)	**prōmittis**, *you promise*
tacitē, adv., *silently*	16 vōs omnēs, *all of you*	20 complexū, *in an embrace*
5 **temptat**, *(he/she) tries*	**simul**, adv., *together*	**tenet**, *(he/she) holds*
6 sēmisomna, *half-asleep*	17 **nesciō**, *I do not know*	lacrimāns, *weeping*
8 **hīc**, adv., *here*	**secundā hōrā**, *at the second hour*	**abit**, *(he/she) goes away*
9 **Tacē!** *Be quiet!*		
Nōlī...excitāre! *Don't wake...up!*	18 **lacrimat**, *(he/she) weeps*	

EXERCISE 9a

Respondē Latīnē:

1. Cūr nēmō Cornēliam cōnspicit?
2. Quō Cornēlia Flāviam dūcit?
3. Cūr est Cornēlia misera?
4. Cūr est Flāvia misera?

Prepositional Phrases: Accusative and Ablative Cases

The meaning of sentences can be expanded by the addition of *prepositional phrases*, which usually modify verbs. Look at the examples in the columns below:

Ad vīllam redit.	*He/She returns to the country house.*
Ad iānuam dormit.	*He/She sleeps at the door.*
Per agrōs currit.	*He/She runs through the fields.*
Puellae prope rīvum sedent.	*The girls sit near the stream.*

The words underlined above form prepositional phrases, in which the prepositions **ad, per,** and **prope** are used with words in the accusative case.

You have seen other prepositions used with words in the ablative case:

Sub arbore dormit.	*He/She sleeps under the tree.*
Ex arbore cadit.	*He/She falls out of the tree.*

Note that **ex** may be written simply as **ē** when the next word begins with a consonant: **ē rāmīs,** *out of the branches.*

Now look at the following examples:

In vīll**am** currit. *He/She runs into the house.*	In vīll**ā** sedet. *He/She sits in the house.*
Statua in piscīn**am** cadit. *The statue falls into the fishpond.*	In rām**ō** sedet. *He/She sits on the branch.*
In urb**em** venit. *He/She comes into the city.*	Prīnceps in urb**e** est. *The emperor is in the city.*

In the left-hand column, the preposition **in** is used with a word in the *accusative case,* and the meaning of the preposition is *into.*

In the right-hand column, the preposition **in** is used with a word in the *ablative case,* and the meaning of the preposition is *in* or *on.*

The preposition **in** can be used with either the accusative or the ablative case, as above, but most other prepositions are used with either one case or the other.

In future vocabulary lists, prepositions will be identified with the abbreviation *prep.* followed by *acc.* or *abl.* to indicate whether the preposition is used with the accusative or the ablative case, e.g., **ad,** prep. + acc., *to, toward, at, near;* **sub,** prep. + abl., *under, beneath.*

Nouns: Cases and Declensions

Ablative Case

Here is a chart showing the groups of nouns and cases you have met so far:

Number Case	1st Declension	2nd Declension			3rd Declension	
Singular						
Nominative	puélla	sérvus	púer	áger	páter	vōx
Accusative	puéllam	sérvum	púerum	ágrum	pátrem	vōcem
Ablative	**puéllā**	**sérvō**	**púerō**	**ágrō**	**pátre**	**vōce**
Vocative	puella	sérve	púer	áger	páter	vōx
Plural						
Nominative	puéllae	sérvī	púerī	ágrī	pátrēs	vōcēs
Accusative	puéllās	sérvōs	púerōs	ágrōs	pátrēs	vōcēs
Ablative	**puéllīs**	**sérvīs**	**púerīs**	**ágrīs**	**pátribus**	**vōcibus**
Vocative	puéllae	sérvī	púerī	ágrī	pátrēs	vōcēs

Be sure to learn these forms thoroughly.

Note that the only difference between the nominative and ablative singular endings of 1st declension nouns is that the ablative has a long vowel: *-ā.*

EXERCISE 9b

Read aloud, identify prepositional phrases, and translate:

1. Mārcus in vīllam currit. Nūntius in vīllā est.
2. Dāvus in hortō labōrat. Mārcus in hortum festīnat.
3. Nūntius in Italiam redīre vult. Cornēlius in Italiā habitat.
4. Puer in arbore sedet. Puella in vīllam intrat.
5. In agrīs puerī ambulāre parant. Puellae in agrōs lentē ambulant.
6. In Italiā sunt multī servī. Aliī in agrīs labōrant, aliī in urbibus.
7. Servī sub arboribus sedēre volunt.
8. Servus ex arbore cadit; ad vīllam currit; in vīllā dormit.
9. Aliī nūntiī ex urbe celeriter veniunt; aliī ad urbem redeunt.
10. Puellae sub rāmīs sedent. Lupus ad puellās currit.
11. Puer ex arbore dēscendere nōn potest.
12. Cornēlia per iānuam in vīllam fūrtim intrat.

festīnat, *(he/she) hurries*
aliī...aliī..., *some...others...*

EXERCISE 9c

Select the correct word to fill each of the gaps, state what case each of these words is, and tell why it is in that case. Then read the sentence aloud and translate it:

1. Mārcus ad _____ sedet.   arborem/arbore
2. Puellae ē _____   silvam/silvā
   ad _____ ambulant.   vīllam/vīllā
3. Multī servī in _____ labōrant.   agrōs/agrīs
4. Cornēlia amīcam ē _____   vīllam/vīllā
   in _____ dūcit.   agrōs/agrīs
5. Servus sub _____ dormit.   rāmōs/rāmīs
6. Puerī per _____ currunt.   agrōs/agrīs
7. Cornēlius ad _____ redīre parat.   urbem/urbe
8. Flāvia prope _____ sedet.   arbore/arborem
9. Sextus ex _____ celeriter exit.   hortō/hortum
10. Servus per _____ festīnat.   agrīs/agrōs

EXERCISE 9d

In story 9, find the Latin for:

1. out of her own country house
2. through the fields
3. to (her) friend's country house
4. in the fields
5. at the door of the country house
6. into the fields
7. out of the country house
8. at the trees
9. to me

Young woman with writing tablet *(tabula)* and pen *(stilus)*. Such tablets, coated with wax, were used by the Romans for writing letters such as Cornelia promises to send to Flavia.

Fresco, Pompeii, mid first century A.D.

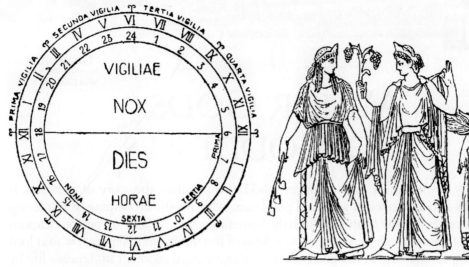

The Romans divided the day into twelve hours, from sunrise to sunset, and the night into four watches (*vigiliae*). Goddesses, called the *Hōrae*, regulated the orderly passage of time, the seasons, and changes of weather.

Hōrae

EXERCISE 9e

Review

Select, read aloud, and translate:

1. Flāvia clāmat, "Ubi _____, Cornēlia?" estis/es
2. Cornēlia iānitōrem nōn _____. excitāre/excitat/excitās
3. Nōs omnēs hodiē Rōmam _____. redīre/redīmus/redītis
4. Cūr patrem _____, Mārce? vexātis/timēs/amātis
5. Necesse est epistulās statim _____. trādit/legere/legimus
6. Prīnceps senātōrēs _____. cōnsulere vult/cōnsulere volunt
7. Cūr vōs omnēs simul _____? discēdere/discēdimus/discēdere parātis
8. Tacē, Flāvia! Nōlī servōs _____. excitāmus/excitāre/surgere
9. Cornēlia amīcam in agrōs _____. adveniunt/dūcit/amat
10. Cūr per agrōs _____, puellae? curritis/excitātis/curris
11. Iānitor Cornēliam nōn _____. audiō/audiunt/audit
12. Ego nōn _____ quod dormīmus/surgere/surgō
    Rōmam redīre _____. nōlō/faciunt/vidētis
13. _____ Cornēlia in agrīs nōn cōnspicit. Servōs/Servī/Servus
14. Nōlī _____ excitāre! puellās/puellae/puella
15. Senātōrēs _____ omnēs in urbe sunt. Rōmānōs/Rōmānī/Rōmānum

Go Online
PHSchool.com
Web Code: jfd-0009

MAJOR GODS AND GODDESSES

The story of Aeneas as told on pages 28–31 is more than the story of a mortal; it involves also a number of gods and goddesses, who are shown helping or hindering Aeneas as he makes his way from Troy to Italy. Sometimes these deities are personifications of the forces of nature, such as Aeolus, who is king of the winds, and Neptune, who is lord of the sea. Jupiter, the king of the gods, intervenes at a critical moment in Aeneas's life by sending the messenger-god Mercury to deliver orders to Aeneas to leave Dido, resume his voyage, and fulfill his destiny by going to Italy. The Greeks and the Romans conceived of their gods as anthropomorphic, having the appearance, the thoughts, and the emotions of men and women, but as being greater and more powerful and above all as being immortal.

The following list gives the names of the twelve major gods and goddesses, who were thought to dwell on Mount Olympus in Greece, with their Greek names in parentheses (Latin spellings of the names are given under the illustrations on the facing page).

Jupiter (*left*) and Juno (*right*, identified by her crown and bird, the peacock) were major state gods of Rome. Both gods were worshiped in Rome and many provincial cities.
Terra cotta sculptures, Tunis, first century A.D.

Iuppiter	Iūnō	Apollō	Mārs	Vesta	Minerva
Mercurius	Diāna	Neptūnus	Venus	Cerēs	Volcānus

JUPITER (ZEUS): king of gods and mortals, wisest of the divinities, and wielder of the thunderbolt.

JUNO (HERA): queen of gods and mortals, sister and wife of Jupiter, and protectress of women and marriage.

APOLLO (PHOEBUS APOLLO): god of archery, music, medicine, and oracles. His priestesses predicted the future at Delphi (in Greece) and Cumae (in Italy).

MARS (ARES): god of war, father of Romulus and Remus.

VESTA (HESTIA): goddess of the hearth, the center of family life, and goddess of the state (a community of families), symbolized by an eternal flame guarded by six maidens ("Vestal Virgins").

MINERVA (ATHENA): goddess of wisdom, strategy in war, spinning, and weaving, creator of the olive tree, and protectress of Athens.

MERCURY (HERMES): god of travelers and thieves and messenger of the gods; he carries the caduceus, a wand twined with two snakes. On his ankles and helmet are wings. He conducts the souls of the dead to the underworld.

DIANA (ARTEMIS): twin sister of Apollo and goddess of the moon and of hunting. She is attended by a chorus of nymphs. The arc of the moon is her bow and its rays are her arrows.

NEPTUNE (POSEIDON): god of the waters and creator of the horse; his symbol is the trident, a three-pronged spear.

VENUS (APHRODITE): goddess of beauty and love, usually attended by her winged son Cupid, whose arrows strike both mortals and immortals. She was the divine mother of Aeneas, the Trojan hero and ancestor of the Romans.

CERES (DEMETER): goddess of the harvest and agriculture, whose daughter Proserpina (Persephone) is queen of the underworld and wife of Pluto (god of the underworld).

VULCAN (HEPHAESTUS): god of fire, blacksmith of the gods, and forger of the thunderbolts of Jupiter and weapons of Aeneas.

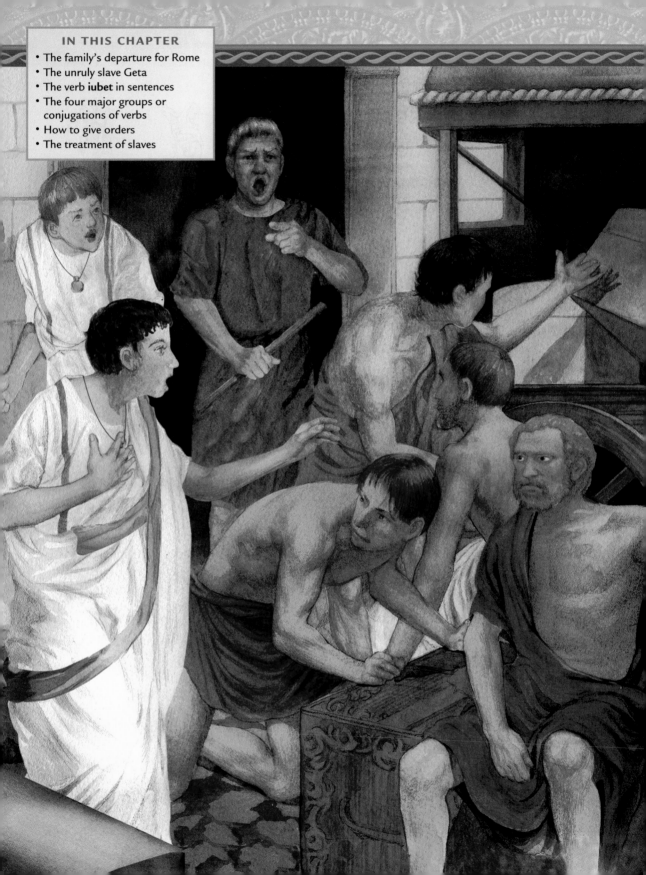

DEPARTURE

Interea in villā Cornēliānā omnēs strēnuē labōrant. Aurēlia tunicam et stolam et pallam gerit. Ancillam iubet aliās tunicās et stolās et pallās in cistam pōnere. Mārcus et Sextus tunicās et togās praetextās gerunt quod in itinere et in urbe togās praetextās līberī gerere solent. Servus aliās tunicās et togās praetextās in cistam pōnit. In cubiculō Gāiī servus togās praetextās in cistam pōnit quod Gāius in urbe togam praetextam gerere solet. Gāius ipse togam praetextam induit. 5

Dāvus, quī ipse omnia cūrat, ad iānuam stat. Servōs iubet cistās ē cubiculīs in viam portāre. Baculum habet et clāmat, "Agite, servī scelestī! Dormītisne? Hodiē, nōn crās, discēdimus."

Mārcus quoque servōs incitat et iubet eōs cistās in raedam pōnere. Servus quīdam, nōmine Geta, cistam Sextī arripit et in raedam iacit. 10

"Cavē, Geta!" exclāmat Sextus sollicitus. "Cūrā cistam meam! Nōlī eam iacere!"

Tandem omnēs cistae in raedā sunt. Ascendunt Mārcus et Sextus. Ascendit Eucleidēs. Ascendit Aurēlia. Gāius ipse ascendere est parātus. Syrus, raedārius, quoque ascendit et equōs incitāre parat. Subitō exclāmat Aurēlia, "Ubi est Cornēlia?"

Eō ipsō tempore in viam currit Cornēlia. Eam Gāius iubet in raedam statim 15 ascendere. Statim raedārius equōs incitat. Discēdunt Cornēliī.

1 **interea**, adv., *meanwhile*
2 **gerit**, *wears*
  iubet, *(he/she) orders*
  alius, *another, other*
  cista, *trunk, chest*
  pōnere, *to put, place*
3 **in itinere**, *on a journey*
4 **līberī**, *children*
  gerere solent, *(they) are accustomed to wear(ing), usually wear*
6 ipse, *himself*
7 **stat**, *(he/she) stands*
  via, *road*

8 **baculum**, *stick*
  habet, *(he/she) has, holds*
  scelestus, *wicked*
  crās, adv., *tomorrow*
9 **incitat**, *(he/she) spurs on, urges on*
  raeda, *carriage*
  servus quīdam, *a certain slave*
10 **iacit**, *(he/she) throws*
13 **parātus**, *ready*
  raedārius, *coachman*
14 **equus**, *horse*
  Ubi...? adv., *Where...?*
15 eō ipsō tempore, *at that very moment*

EXERCISE 10a

Respondē Latīnē:

1. Quid Aurēlia ancillam facere iubet?
2. Cūr Mārcus et Sextus togās praetextās gerunt?
3. Quid Gāius induit?
4. Quid facit Dāvus?
5. Quid clāmat Sextus?
6. Quid raedārius facere parat?
7. Quō currit Cornēlia?
8. Quid Gāius eam facere iubet?
9. Quid tum facit raedārius?
10. Quid faciunt Cornēliī?

Go Online PHSchool.com Web Code: jfd-0010

BUILDING THE MEANING

Accusative and Infinitive

In the preceding reading, you have seen the verb **iubet** used when someone orders someone to do something. The verb is used with an accusative and an infinitive:

Acc.   Infin.

Ancillam <u>iubet</u> aliās tunicās et stolās et pallās in cistam **pōnere**. (10:2)
*She orders **a slave-woman to put** other tunics and stolas and pallas into a chest.*

The infinitive **pōnere** has it own direct objects, **aliās tunicās et stolās et pallās.**

You have also seen this pattern with the verb **docet:**

Aurēlia **Cornēliam** <u>docet</u> vīllam **cūrāre.** (6:11)
*Aurelia <u>teaches</u> **Cornelia** (how) **to take care of** the country house.*

Go Online
PHSchool.com
Web Code: jfd-0010

FORMS

Verbs: Conjugations

Latin verbs, with very few exceptions, fall into four major groups or *conjugations*. You can tell to what conjugation a verb belongs by looking at the spelling of the infinitive: (1) *-āre*, (2) *-ēre*, (3) *-ere*, and (4) *-īre*:

	1st Person Singular		Infinitive	
1st Conjugation	párō	*I prepare*	par**á**re	*to prepare*
2nd Conjugation	hábeō	*I have*	hab**é**re	*to have*
3rd Conjugation	míttō	*I send*	mítt**ere**	*to send*
3rd Conjugation **-iō**	iáciō	*I throw*	iác**ere**	*to throw*
4th Conjugation	aúdiō	*I hear*	aud**í**re	*to hear*

As shown above, some verbs of the 3rd conjugation end in **-iō** in the 1st person singular, just as do verbs of the 4th conjugation. These are called 3rd conjugation **-iō** verbs. Their infinitives show that they belong to the 3rd conjugation.

Hereafter, verbs will be given in the word lists in the 1st person singular form, followed by the infinitive, e.g., **habeō, habēre,** *to have.* The infinitive will tell you to what conjugation the verb belongs. The few exceptions that do not fit neatly into any of the four conjugations will be marked with the notation *irreg.*, e.g., **sum, esse,** irreg., *to be.*

Verbs: The Present Tense

		1st Conjugation	2nd Conjugation	3rd Conjugation		4th Conjugation
Infinitive		par*áre*	hab*ére*	mítt*ere*	iác*ere* (-iō)	aud*íre*
Singular	1	pár*ō*	háb*eō*	míttō	iáciō	aúdiō
	2	pár*ās*	háb*ēs*	míttis	iácis	aúdīs
	3	pára*t*	hábe*t*	míttit	iácit	aúdit
Plural	1	pará*mus*	habé*mus*	mítti*mus*	iáci*mus*	audī*mus*
	2	pará*tis*	habé*tis*	mítti*tis*	iáci*tis*	audī*tis*
	3	pára*nt*	hábe*nt*	míttu*nt*	iáciu*nt*	aúdiu*nt*

Be sure to learn these forms thoroughly. Note that the vowel that precedes the personal endings is short before final *-t* and *-nt*.

In addition to **iaciō, iacere,** you have met the following **-iō** verbs of the 3rd conjugation:

arripiō, arripere　　　　**excipiō, excipere**
cōnspiciō, cōnspicere　　**faciō, facere**

Here are some examples of sentences with verbs in the present tense. Note the English translations:

a. in a simple statement of fact:
　　Cornēliī Rōmam redīre **parant.**
　　The Cornelii **prepare** *to return to Rome.*

b. in a description of an ongoing action:
　　Hodiē Cornēliī Rōmam redīre **parant.**
　　Today the Cornelii **are preparing** *to return to Rome.*

c. in a question:
　　Auditne Dāvus clāmōrem?
　　Does Davus **hear** *the shouting?*

d. in an emphatic statement:
　　Audit clāmōrem.
　　He **does hear** *the shouting.*

e. in a denial:
　　Nōn **audit** clāmōrem.
　　He **does not hear** *the shouting.*

EXERCISE 10b

Read the following verbs aloud. Give the conjugation number and meaning of each:

1. ascendō, ascendere
2. terreō, terrēre
3. arripiō, arripere
4. discēdō, discēdere
5. audiō, audīre
6. repellō, repellere
7. ambulō, ambulāre
8. excitō, excitāre
9. iaciō, iacere
10. currō, currere
11. cūrō, cūrāre
12. excipiō, excipere
13. timeō, timēre
14. nesciō, nescīre
15. rīdeō, rīdēre

EXERCISE 10c

For each of the verbs in Exercise 10b, give the six forms (1st, 2nd, and 3rd persons, singular and plural). Use the chart above as a guide. Translate the 3rd person plural of each.

Verbs: Imperative

The imperative is used in issuing orders:

Positive

Cūrā cistam meam, Geta!
Take care of my trunk, Geta!

Cūrāte cistam meam, servī!
Take care of my trunk, slaves!

Negative

Nōlī eam iacere, Geta!
Don't throw it, Geta! (literally, *refuse, be unwilling to throw it, Geta!*)

Nōlīte eam iacere, servī!
Don't throw it, slaves! (literally, *refuse, be unwilling to throw it, slaves!*)

	1st Conjugation	2nd Conjugation	3rd Conjugation		4th Conjugation
Infinitive	paráre	habére	míttere	iácere (-iō)	audíre
Imperative Singular Plural	párā paráte	hábē habéte	mítte míttite	iáce iácite	aúdī audíte

Be sure to learn these forms thoroughly.
Note the following imperatives, of which some forms are irregular:

dīcō, dīcere, *to say*	dīc! dīcite!
dūcō, dūcere, *to lead, take, bring*	dūc! dūcite!
faciō, facere, *to make, do*	fac! facite!
ferō, ferre, *to bring, carry*	fer! ferte!

EXERCISE 10d

For each of the following verbs, give the imperative forms, singular and plural, positive and negative. Translate each form you give:

1. pōnō, pōnere
2. ferō, ferre
3. sedeō, sedēre
4. dīcō, dīcere
5. arripiō, arripere
6. stō, stāre
7. faciō, facere
8. veniō, venīre
9. dūcō, dūcere

TREATMENT OF SLAVES

Even though in Davus's homeland in Britain his own family had owned a few slaves, it had been difficult for him to adjust to being a slave himself. Adjust he did, however, perhaps by taking advice similar to the following given by an overseer to newly captured slaves:

> If the immortal gods wished you to endure this calamity, you must endure it with calm spirits; if you do so, you will endure the toil more easily. At home, you were free, so I believe; now as slavery has befallen you, it is best to accustom yourselves and to make it easy for your master's commands and for your own minds. Whatever indignities your master commands must be considered proper.

> Plautus, *The Captives* 195–200

Davus enjoys a high position among Cornelius's slaves and takes pride in his responsibilities. Of course he has the good fortune to work for a master who is quite humane by Roman standards. Other slaves had more insensitive masters, who saw their slaves not as human beings but as property. Cato in his treatise on agriculture gave advice to Roman farmers on how to make a profit from their slaves. Notice that he feels no sympathy for his slaves who have grown ill or old in his service; they are "things" just like cattle and tools that a farmer should get rid of when they are no longer of use:

> Let the farmer sell olive oil, if he has a good price, also his wine and his grain.
> Let him sell his surplus too: old oxen, old tools, an old slave, a sick slave.

> Cato, *On Agriculture* II.7 (extracts)

Some masters treated their slaves well and were rewarded by loyalty and good service, but, even when conditions were good, slaves were keenly aware of their inferior position and by way of protest sometimes rebelled or tried to run away. If they were recaptured, the letters FUG (for **fugitīvus**, *runaway*) were branded on their foreheads.

Prison cell with Roman agricultural slaves
Nineteenth-century European engraving, artist unknown

Some owners treated their slaves very badly. Even if the owner were not as bad as the despised Vedius Pollio, who fed his slaves to lampreys, slaves were liable to be severely punished, often at the whim of their master:

> Does Rutilus believe that the body and soul of slaves are made the same as their masters? Not likely! Nothing pleases him more than a noisy flogging. His idea of music is the crack of the whip. To his trembling slaves he's a monster, happiest when some poor wretch is being branded with red-hot irons for stealing a pair of towels. He loves chains, dungeons, branding, and chain-gang labor camps. He's a sadist.
>
> Juvenal, *Satires* XIV.16

Female slaves also were often subjected to ill-treatment by self-centered mistresses. Juvenal tells how a slave-woman was at the mercy of her mistress:

> If the mistress is in a bad mood, the wool-maid is in trouble, the dressers are stripped and beaten, the litter-bearers accused of coming late. The rods are broken over one poor wretch's back, another has bloody weals from the whip, and a third is flogged with the cat-o'-nine-tails. The slave-girl arranging her mistress's hair will have her own hair torn and the tunic ripped from her shoulders, because a curl is out of place.
>
> Juvenal, *Satires* VI.475

Fresco of slaves loading *amphorae*, vessels containing wine or olive oil, onto a wagon
Fresco, Pompeii, mid first century A.D.

On the other hand, Pliny the Younger speaks of owners who treated their slaves fairly and sympathetically. In a letter to a friend he writes:

> I have noticed how kindly you treat your slaves; so I shall openly admit my own easy treatment of my own slaves. I always keep in mind the Roman phrase, "father of the household." But even supposing I were naturally cruel and unsympathetic, my heart would be touched by the illness of my freedman Zosimus. He needs and deserves my sympathy; he is honest, obliging, and well educated. He is a very successful actor with a clear delivery. He plays the lyre well and is an accomplished reader of speeches, history, and poetry. A few years ago he began to spit blood and I sent him to Egypt. He has just come back with his health restored. However, he has developed a slight cough. I think it would be best to send him to your place at Forum Julii where the air is healthy and the milk excellent for illness of this kind.
>
> Pliny the Younger, *Letters* V.19

It was possible for a slave to buy his freedom if he could save enough from the small personal allowance he earned; some masters gave their slaves their freedom in a process called manumission (**manūmissiō**), as a reward for long service. A slave who had been set free was called a **lībertus** and would wear a felt cap called a **pilleus**. Many who were freed and became rich used to hide with "patches" the marks that had been made on their bodies and faces when they were slaves.

> I am very upset by illness among my slaves. Some of them have actually died, including even younger men. In cases like this I find comfort in two thoughts. I am always ready to give my slaves their freedom, so I don't think their deaths so untimely if they die free men. I also permit my slaves to make a "will," which I consider legally binding.
>
> Pliny the Younger, *Letters* VIII.16

Manūmissiō

ADDITIONAL READING:
The Romans Speak for Themselves: Book I: "Slaves and Masters in Ancient Rome," pages 33–39; "Seneca on Slavery and Freedom," pages 40–46.

1. Characterize in a sentence or two the attitudes toward slavery in each of the ancient writers cited in this reading.
2. If you were a Roman slave owner, would you use strict discipline or relative kindness to manage your slaves? Why?

A SLAVE RUNS AWAY

Omnēs Cornēliī iam sunt in raedā. Rōmam per Viam Appiam petunt.
     Intereā in vīllā Dāvus est sollicitus. Dāvus est vīlicus Cornēliī et, sī dominus
abest, vīlicus ipse vīllam dominī cūrat. Dāvus igitur omnēs servōs in āream quae
est prope vīllam venīre iubet. Brevī tempore ārea est plēna servōrum et ancillārum quī
magnum clāmōrem faciunt.   5

Tum venit Dāvus ipse et, "Tacēte, omnēs!" magnā vōce clāmat. "Audīte mē!
Quamquam dominus abest, necesse est nōbīs strēnuē labōrāre."

Tum servī mussant, "Dāvus dominus esse vult. Ecce! Baculum habet. Nōs verberāre
potest. Necesse est igitur facere id quod iubet." Redeunt igitur ad agrōs servī quod
baculum vīlicī timent.   10

Sed nōn redit Geta. Neque vīlicum amat neque īram vīlicī timet. Illā nocte igitur,
quod in agrīs nōn iam labōrāre vult, cibum parat et ē vīllā effugit. Nēmō eum videt,
nēmō eum impedit. Nunc per agrōs, nunc per viam festīnat. Ubi diēs est, in rāmīs arboris
sē cēlat. Ibi dormit.

Intereā, quamquam nōndum lūcet, Dāvus omnēs servōs excitat. In agrōs exīre et ibi   15
labōrāre eōs iubet. Sed Getam nōn videt. Ubi est Geta? Dāvus igitur est īrātus, deinde
sollicitus. Ad portam vīllae stat et viam spectat; sed Getam nōn videt.

1 Via Appia, *The Appian Way*	**verberō, verberāre,** *to beat*
2 **vīlicus,** *overseer, farm manager*	9 id quod, *that which, what*
dominus, *master*	11 **īra,** *anger*
3 **absum, abesse,** irreg., *to be away,*	**illā nocte,** *that night*
be absent	12 **effugiō, effugere,** *to flee, run away,*
ārea, *open space, threshing floor*	escape
4 **plēnus,** *full*	13 **impediō, impedīre,** *to hinder*
7 **quamquam,** conj., *although*	14 **sē cēlāre,** *to hide (himself)*
8 mussō, mussāre, *to mutter*	17 **porta,** *gate*

EXERCISE 11a

Respondē Latīnē:

Go Online
PHSchool.com
Web Code: jfd-0011

1. Quō Dāvus omnēs servōs īre iubet?
2. Quid faciunt servī et ancillae in āreā?
3. Quamquam dominus abest, quid
   facere necesse est?
4. Cūr necesse est facere id quod Dāvus
   iubet?

5. Cūr Geta effugit?
6. Ubi dormit Geta?
7. Cūr est Dāvus īrātus et sollicitus?

BUILDING THE MEANING

The Genitive Case

You have seen how the meanings of sentences can be expanded by the addition of adjectives to modify nouns:

> Dāvus ad **magnam** portam stat.
> *Davus stands near the **large** door.*

A noun can also be modified by the addition of *another noun* in the *genitive case*.

Compare the following sentences:

> Dāvus ad portam stat.
> *Davus stands near the door.*

> Dāvus ad portam **vīllae** stat.
> *Davus stands near the door **of the country house**.*

> Aurēlia est māter.
> *Aurelia is a/the mother.*

> Aurēlia est māter **Mārcī** et **Cornēliae**.
> *Aurelia is the mother **of Marcus** and **Cornelia**.*
> *Aurelia is **Marcus** and **Cornelia's** mother.*

> Servī baculum timent.
> *The slaves fear the stick.*

> Servī baculum **vīlicī** timent.
> *The slaves fear **the overseer's** stick.*

> In rāmīs sē cēlat.
> *He hides in the branches.*

> In rāmīs **arboris** sē cēlat.
> *He hides in the branches **of the tree**.*

In the right-hand column other nouns have been added to the sentences of the left-hand column. These additional nouns are in the genitive case. This case is used to connect one noun with another to make a single phrase. The noun in the genitive case may describe another noun by indicating a family relationship, by showing possession, or by providing some other qualification or description.

Nouns in the genitive case are also used in Latin to fill out the meaning of certain adjectives. This use is parallel to the use of prepositional phrases with "of" in English:

> Ārea est <u>plēna</u> **servōrum** et **ancillārum**. (11:4)
> *The threshing floor is <u>full</u> **of slaves** and **slave-women**.*

Nouns: Cases and Declensions

Genitive and Dative Cases

The following chart includes the genitive forms of 1st, 2nd, and 3rd declension nouns. It also includes the forms of the dative case. You will not study this case formally until Chapter 22. It is the case you use, for example, when you speak of giving something *to someone*. A word or phrase in the dative case can often be translated with the prepositions *to* or *for*:

> Necesse est **servīs** strēnuē labōrāre.
> *It is necessary **for the slaves** to work hard.*

You may wish to learn the forms of the dative case now, even though they are not formally presented until Chapter 22.

Number Case	1st Declension	2nd Declension			3rd Declension	
Singular						
Nominative	puéll*a*	sérv*us*	púer	áger	páter	vōx
Genitive	**puéll*ae***	**sérv*ī***	**púer*ī***	**ágr*ī***	**pátr*is***	**vṓc*is***
Dative	puéll*ae*	sérv*ō*	púer*ō*	ágr*ō*	pátr*ī*	vṓc*ī*
Accusative	puéll*am*	sérv*um*	púer*um*	ágr*um*	pátr*em*	vṓc*em*
Ablative	puéll*ā*	sérv*ō*	púer*ō*	ágr*ō*	pátr*e*	vṓc*e*
Vocative	puéll*a*	sérv*e*	púer	áger	páter	vōx
Plural						
Nominative	puéll*ae*	sérv*ī*	púer*ī*	ágr*ī*	pátr*ēs*	vṓc*ēs*
Genitive	**puell*ā́rum***	**serv*ṓrum***	**puer*ṓrum***	**agr*ṓrum***	**pátr*um***	**vṓc*um***
Dative	puéll*īs*	sérv*īs*	púer*īs*	ágr*īs*	pátr*ibus*	vṓc*ibus*
Accusative	puéll*ās*	sérv*ōs*	púer*ōs*	ágr*ōs*	pátr*ēs*	vṓc*ēs*
Ablative	puéll*īs*	sérv*īs*	púer*īs*	ágr*īs*	pátr*ibus*	vṓc*ibus*
Vocative	puéll*ae*	sérv*ī*	púer*ī*	ágr*ī*	pátr*ēs*	vṓc*ēs*

Be sure to learn the new genitive forms thoroughly.

In future vocabulary lists, nouns will be given as follows: **puella, -ae,** f., *girl;* **servus, -ī,** m., *slave;* **vōx, vōcis,** f., *voice,* i.e.:

> the nominative singular
> the genitive singular ending (**-ae, -ī**) for 1st and 2nd declension nouns
> the entire genitive singular form (**vōcis**) for 3rd declension nouns
> the gender (abbreviated as m. for masculine or f. for feminine)
> the meaning

The genitive singular ending indicates the declension to which a noun belongs: **-ae** = 1st declension, **-ī** = 2nd declension, and **-is** = 3rd declension.

The *base* of a noun is found by dropping the genitive singular ending; the other case endings are then added to this base. Note that in 3rd declension nouns, the base is often slightly different from the nominative (e.g., nominative **vōx,** base **vōc-**).

EXERCISE 11b

Translate the following sentences, completing them where necessary with reference to the family tree:

```
pater————————— māter          parentēs
(Cornēlius)        (Aurēlia)

fīlius               fīlia        līberī
(Mārcus)           (Cornēlia)
```

1. Mārcus est frāter Cornēliae.
2. Cornēlia est soror Mārcī.
3. Cornēlius est vir Aurēliae.
4. Aurēlia est uxor Cornēliī.
5. Mārcus est fīlius Cornēliī et Aurēliae.
6. Cornēlia est _____ Cornēliī et Aurēliae.
7. Cornēlius et Aurēlia sunt _____ Mārcī et Cornēliae.
8. Mārcus et Cornēlia sunt _____ Cornēliī et Aurēliae.
9. Aurēlia est _____ Mārcī et Cornēliae.
10. Cornēlius est _____ Mārcī et Cornēliae.

pater, patris, m., *father*
māter, mātris, f., *mother*
parēns, parentis, m./f., *parent*
frāter, frātris, m., *brother*
soror, sorōris, f., *sister*

fīlius, -ī, m., *son*
fīlia, -ae, f., *daughter*
līberī, līberōrum, m. pl., *children*
vir, virī, m., *man, husband*
uxor, uxōris, f., *wife*

EXERCISE 11c

Supply the genitive ending, read the sentence aloud, and translate:

1. Līberī in raedā senātor_____ sunt.
2. Mārcus est frāter Cornēli_____.
3. Nūntius fīlium Cornēli_____ salūtat.
4. Servī īram vīlic_____ timent.
5. Effugit Geta et in rāmīs arbor_____ sē cēlat.
6. Magna vōx Dāv_____ eum terret.
7. Dāvus, vīlicus Cornēli_____, Getam vidēre nōn potest.
8. Sī Cornēlius abest, Dāvus vīllam domin_____ cūrat.
9. Magnus numerus serv_____ est in āreā.   **numerus, -ī,** m., *number*

EXERCISE 11d

Using story 11 and the information on the genitive case as guides, give the Latin for:

1. Davus is Cornelius's overseer, and Cornelius is Davus's master.
2. The threshing floor is full of many slaves and many slave-women.
3. The slaves fear Davus's stick.
4. Geta fears the anger of the overseer.
5. Geta sleeps in the branches of a tree.

Go Online
PHSchool.com
Web Code: jfd-0011

Genitive Singular or Nominative Plural?
How Do You Decide?

In the 1st and 2nd declensions, the endings of the genitive singular are the same as the endings of the nominative plural. To decide which case is being used, you will need to consider the sentence as a whole.

Look at these sentences:

1. **Celeriter redeunt servī.**

The plural verb **redeunt** raises the expectation of a plural subject, and the noun **servī** meets that expectation. In addition, the genitive usually forms a phrase with another noun. Since **servī** is the only noun in the sentence, it must be nominative plural.

2. **Pater puerī est senātor Rōmānus.**

The word **puerī** could be genitive singular or nominative plural. It must be genitive singular, since **pater** is clearly the subject of the singular verb **est**.

3. **In vīllā puellae sedent.**

The word **puellae** could be genitive singular or nominative plural. The context would help you decide whether the sentence means *The girls sit in the country house* or *They sit in the girl's country house*.

EXERCISE 11e

Look at each sentence. Is it possible to tell whether the nouns in boldface are genitive singular or nominative plural? If so, tell how. Then translate each sentence. Two of the sentences may be correctly translated two different ways:

1. **Puellae** sunt dēfessae.
2. In agrīs **puerī** ambulant.
3. **Puellae** et mātrēs in vīllā sedent.
4. **Puerī** epistulās scrībunt.
5. Pater **Mārcī** in vīllā sedet.
6. Pater vōcem **puellae** audit.
7. **Puerī** vōcem **Mārcī** audiunt.
8. Soror **puellae** per iānuam intrat.

Go Online
PHSchool.com
Web Code: jfd-0011

ROMAN NAMES

The father of the family in our story has three names, **Gāius Cornēlius Calvus**. **Gāius** is his **praenōmen** (first name or personal name), **Cornēlius** is his **nōmen** (the name of his clan), and **Calvus** (*Bald*) is his **cognōmen**, inherited from a distant ancestor. The **cognōmen** was originally a nickname but was often handed on to a man's sons and grandsons so that it came to distinguish a particular family within the larger clan. Roman society was male-oriented, and the name of a Roman boy included the **nōmen** of his father's clan and the **cognōmen** of his father's family. Thus, the name of the son in our story is **Mārcus Cornēlius Calvus**.

Women's names were far simpler. Though in early times a woman, too, might have a **praenōmen**, women came to use only the feminine form of their father's **nōmen**; thus the daughter of **Gāius Cornēlius Calvus** in our story is named simply **Cornēlia**. A second daughter would sometimes be named **Cornēlia secunda** (*the second*) or **Cornēlia minor** (*the younger*), a third daughter, **Cornēlia tertia** (*the third*), and so forth. Cornelia's mother **Aurēlia** would have been the daughter of a man who had **Aurēlius** as his **nōmen**. In the middle of the first century A.D., a little before the time of our story, women began using **cognōmina** that reflected some branch of the family tree.

In very formal naming of girls and women, the father's or husband's full name would be added in the genitive case. Thus, Cornelia would be **Cornēlia Gāiī Cornēliī Calvī (fīlia)** and Aurelia would be **Aurēlia Gāiī Cornēliī Calvī (uxor)**.

In very formal naming of slaves, the master's name would be added in the genitive case, thus, **Dāvus Gāiī Cornēliī Calvī (servus)**. As with formal naming of girls and women, the person in the genitive case represents the person who has authority, whether it be the authority of a master over a slave, of a father over a daughter, or of a husband over a wife.

Below is a transcription of the epitaph of the wife of Gnaeus Cornelius Scipio Hispallus, who served as one of the consuls, the chief magistrates of Rome, in 176 B.C. Note that he had a second **cognōmen**, and note that at this early time his wife had a **praenōmen**.

> ### AVLLA·CORNELIA·CN·F·HISPALLI
> **[P]aulla Cornēlia, Gn(aeī) f(īlia), Hispallī**
> *Paulla Cornelia, daughter of Gnaeus, (wife) of Hispallus*

1. Compare and contrast the Roman naming system with your own name and its cultural tradition.
2. How does Roman naming reflect the Romans' concern with tradition and family?
3. Romans would have been aware of the meanings of their names. Try to learn the meanings of your names.

THE FOUNDING OF ROME

The early history of Rome is a wonderful mixture of myth and fact. The Roman historian Livy admitted that his account of the founding of Rome more than 700 years before his own lifetime was based on a tradition that owed more to poetic tales than to historical fact.

The Romans traced their ancestry to the Trojan hero, Aeneas, who, as we learned in Myth I (pages 28–31), came to Italy after the fall of Troy (traditionally dated 1184 B.C.). Aeneas, after journeying through the underworld with the Sibyl of Cumae and learning of the future greatness of Rome from the ghost of his father Anchises, proceeded to Latium, the district of Italy just south of the Tiber River. There he made an alliance with Latinus, the native king, and married Lavinia, the king's daughter, to ratify the treaty. Aeneas settled the Trojans in a town he named Lavinium in honor of his new wife. Unfortunately, Turnus, king of the neighboring Rutulians and Lavinia's husband-to-be prior to Aeneas's arrival, could not accept the arrangements that Latinus made with Aeneas, and he stirred the native peoples to make war against Aeneas. Both Latinus and Turnus were killed in this war, and Aeneas then united his Trojans with the native peoples and named this Italo-Trojan nation the Latins.

Faustulus and his wife with Romulus and Remus and the she-wolf
Romulus and Remus, *oil on canvas, 1700, Charles de Lafosse*

Romulus, Remus, and the she-wolf
Sculpture, Rome, fifth century B.C.

Aeneas had come from Troy with a son, Ascanius, also known as Iulus, whom Julius Caesar's family later claimed as their ancestor. After his father's death, Ascanius left Lavinium, now a strong and rich city, and established a new city that he named Alba Longa because the colony stretched out along the ridge of Mount Albanus. Ascanius's son, Silvius ("born in the woods"), succeeded his father to the throne and began the Silvian dynasty, which ruled Alba Longa for perhaps 300 years.

In the 8th century B.C. Amulius, an Alban prince, seized the throne from his older brother, Numitor; he then murdered his nephews and appointed his niece, Rhea Silvia, a priestess of Vesta (goddess of the hearth) so that she could bear no future rival heirs to the throne. When Romulus and Remus, twin sons of Rhea Silvia and the god Mars, were born, Amulius was furious. He ordered the priestess mother of the twins put into prison and gave instructions that the infants be set adrift in the Tiber. By luck, the river was in flood, and those assigned to expose Romulus and Remus happened to set the basket containing the twins in a shallow spot, expecting that it would be carried out into the mainstream and that the twins would be drowned. Attracted by the infants' crying, a she-wolf came and nursed the babies. Faustulus, the king's shepherd, discovered the wolf licking the twins and took them home to his wife. They raised Romulus and Remus as their own sons.

When Romulus and Remus grew up, they discovered their true heritage, and they then helped Numitor, their grandfather, to assassinate Amulius and regain the throne of Alba Longa.

They next decided to found a new city on the Tiber in the place where they had been exposed and raised. Since they were twins, they turned to augury and asked the gods who should give his name to this city and rule over it. On the Aventine Hill Remus saw the first omen, six vultures. No sooner had that sign been reported than a flock of twelve vultures flew over the Palatine Hill, where Romulus was standing. The followers of each twin argued whether the right to rule belonged to the one who first sighted birds or the one who sighted twice the number, and Remus died in the ensuing riot. Livy supplies an alternative version of the story: when Remus as a joke jumped over the rising city walls, Romulus was enraged and killed his brother on the spot, shouting, "This is what will happen to anyone else who jumps over my walls!" By either account, on April 21, 753 B.C. Romulus founded on the Palatine Hill that city we still call Rome.

---

1. Imagine you are a Roman with a traditional belief in family. What elements in the story of Romulus and Remus would trouble you and why?
2. As you continue your study of Latin, you will learn much more about mythology and religion. If this story were all you knew about the Romans' beliefs, what conclusions would you draw about Roman religion?

Archaeologists have found on the Palatine Hill the postholes for a simple hut such as this. The very first inhabitants of Rome lived in this kind of hut.

CAPTURE

Dāvus est sollicitus, nam necesse est Getam invenīre. Ubi servī effugiunt, dominī saepe vīlicōs reprehendunt. Saepe etiam eōs verberant. Cornēlius est dominus bonus, sed ubi Cornēlius īrātus est—

Servōs igitur Dāvus in āream statim convocat et rogat, "Ubi est Geta?" Nēmō respondēre potest. Dāvus igitur aliōs servōs in hortum, aliōs in agrōs, aliōs in vīneās 5 mittit. In hortō et agrīs et vīneīs Getam petunt. Neque in hortō neque in fossīs agrōrum neque in arboribus vīneārum Getam inveniunt.

Dāvus igitur servōs iubet canēs in āream dūcere. Aliī servī tunicam Getae in āream ferunt. Canēs veniunt et tunicam olfaciunt. Mox Dāvus servōs in agrōs cum canibus dūcit. Lātrant canēs. Per agrōs Cornēliī, deinde per agrōs vīcīnārum vīllārum currunt. 10 Neque rīvī neque fossae canēs impediunt. Vēstīgia Getae inveniunt, sed Getam invenīre nōn possunt. Tandem Dāvus eōs in silvam incitat.

Geta in arbore adhūc manet et ibi dormit. Canēs lātrantēs eum excitant. Nunc tamen Geta effugere nōn potest et in rāmīs sedet, immōbilis et perterritus. Canēs, ubi ad arborem appropinquant, Getam ipsum nōn cōnspiciunt, sed olfaciunt. Lātrant canēs; 15 appropinquant servī. Miserum servum vident quī in rāmīs arboris sē cēlat.

"Dēscende, Geta!" clāmat Dāvus. Geta dēscendit. Dāvus eum tunicā arripit et baculō verberat. Deinde servōs iubet Getam ad vīllam trahere et in fronte litterās FUG inūrere.

1	**inveniō, invenīre,** *to find*		
2	**bonus,** *good*	10	**lātrō, lātrāre,** *to bark*
4	**convocō, convocāre,** *to call together*	11	**vēstīgia,** *tracks, footprints, traces*
	rogō, rogāre, *to ask*	14	**immōbilis,** *motionless*
5	vīnea, -ae, f., *vineyard*	17	**tunicā,** *by the tunic*
6	**fossa, -ae,** f., *ditch*	18	**trahō, trahere,** *to drag*
8	**canis, canis,** m./f., *dog*		in fronte litterās inūrere, *to brand*
9	**ferō, ferre,** irreg., *to bring, carry*		*the letters on his forehead*
	olfaciō, olfacere, *to catch the scent*		
	of, smell		

cum, prep. + abl., *with*

EXERCISE 12a

Respondē Latīnē:

1. Cūr est Dāvus sollicitus?
2. Quō Dāvus servōs mittit?
3. Inveniuntne Getam?

4. Quid canēs faciunt?
5. Cūr Geta effugere nōn potest?
6. Ubi servī litterās FUG inūrunt?

The Ablative Case

You have learned how the meaning of sentences can be expanded by the addition of prepositional phrases, which usually modify verbs (page 64).

Prepositions used with the ablative case may modify the verbs in their sentences by answering the questions:

Ubi...?	*Where...?*
Unde...?	*From where...?*
Quōcum...? or **Quibuscum...?**	*With whom...?*

For example, questions introduced by the words at the left could be answered by statements that might include the prepositional phrases with the ablative case at the right:

Ubi...?	*Where...?*	**in vīllā**	*in the farmhouse*
Ubi...?	*Where...?*	**sub arboribus**	*under the trees*
Unde...?	*From where...?*	**ē rīvō**	*out of the stream*
Quōcum...?	*With whom...?*	**cum patre**	*with his/her father*
Quibuscum...?	*With whom...?*	**cum amīcīs**	*with his/her friends*

You will also find nouns and phrases in the ablative case without prepositions, often with predictable meanings. These also answer certain questions, as follows:

1. They may answer the question *When...?* (**Quandō...?**), in expressions referring to time:

septimā hōrā	*at the seventh hour*
nocte	*at night*
aestāte	*in the summer*
tribus diēbus	*in three days*
brevī tempore	*in a short time, soon*

This is called the *ablative of time when* or *within which*.

2. They may answer the question *How...?* (**Quō īnstrūmentō...?** or **Quōmodo...?**) and can often be translated with the words *with* or *by* and sometimes with *in*:

a. Answering the quesion **Quō īnstrūmentō...?** *With what instrument...? By what means...? How...?*

Servum **baculō** verberat.   *with a stick*
Dāvus Getam **tunicā** arripit.   *by the tunic*
Cornēlia Flāviam **complexū** tenet.   *in an embrace*

This is called the *ablative of instrument* or *means.*

b. Answering the question **Quōmodo...?** *In what manner...? How...?*

Mārcus **magnā vōce** clāmat.   *with a loud voice*
                                                 (= *loudly*)

This is called the *ablative of manner* and sometimes uses a preposition, e.g., **magnā cum vōce.**

From the very beginning of the course, you have seen another use of the ablative case:

In pictūrā est puella, **nōmine** Cornēlia. (1:1)
*There is a girl in the picture, Cornelia **with respect to her name/by name.***
*There is a girl in the picture, **named** Cornelia.*

This use of the ablative without a preposition is called the *ablative of respect.*

EXERCISE 12b

Read each sentence aloud, locating the words in the ablative case and prepositional phrases with the ablative. Then translate and give in Latin the question or questions that each sentence answers:

1. Cornēlia Flāviam ē vīllā dūcit.
2. Servus molestus dominum togā arripit.
3. Secundā hōrā discēdere necesse est.
4. Dāvus magnā vōce servōs tacēre iubet: "Tacēte, omnēs!"
5. Brevī tempore ārea est plēna servōrum et ancillārum.
6. Dāvus cum servīs et canibus Getam in hortō et agrīs et vīneīs petit.
7. Vīlicus Getam baculō verberāre vult.

EXERCISE 12c

Using story 12 as a guide, answer in Latin:

1. Ubi servī Getam petunt?
2. Quibuscum servī Getam petunt?
3. Unde dēscendit Geta?
4. Quō īnstrūmentō Dāvus Getam arripit?
5. Quō īnstrūmentō Dāvus Getam verberat?

Review

Select the word or phrase in the correct case, read aloud, and translate:

1. Geta in _____ sē cēlat.   arborem/arbore/arboris
2. Prope _____ vīllae servī stant.   portae/portam/porta
3. Aliī in _____, aliī in   cubiculum/cubiculō
   _____ sedent.   āreā/āreae/āream
4. Servī in fossīs _____ Getam nōn   agrīs/agrī/agrōs
   vident.
5. Dāvus servōs in agrōs cum _____   canēs/canem/canibus
   dūcit.
6. Est magnus numerus _____ et   puerī/puerōs/puerōrum
   _____ in vīllā vīcīnā.   puellārum/puella/puellam
7. Dāvus est vīlicus _____ _____.   dominus bonus/dominō bonō/dominī bonī
8. Dāvus Getam _____ verberat.   baculum/baculī/baculō
9. Dāvus servōs iubet canēs ex _____   agrī/agrīs/agrum
   in āream dūcere.

ADDITIONAL READING:
The Romans Speak for Themselves: Book I: "The Responsibilities of a Farm Manager," pages 47–52.

"Cavē canem!"
Watchdogs were commonly chained to the wall within the entrance to a *domus*, but more often, visitors found a substitute "watchdog" depicted in the mosaic floor of the entryway.
Mosaic, second to third century A.D.

Review II: Chapters 8–12

Go Online
PHSchool.com
Web Code: jfd-0012

Exercise IIa: Nouns; Singular and Plural p. 81

Change singulars to plurals and plurals to singulars, keeping the same case:

1. vīlicō (*abl.*)
2. cistae (*gen.*)
3. noctem
4. dominī (*nom.*)
5. ancillā
6. canēs (*nom.*)
7. equōs
8. āream

9. vōx
10. fossae (*nom.*)
11. cibī (*gen.*)
12. patribus (*abl.*)
13. puerum
14. raedīs (*abl.*)
15. frontem
16. fīlius

17. portārum
18. virōrum
19. fragōrēs (*acc.*)
20. serve
21. raedāriīs (*abl.*)
22. canis (*gen.*)
23. equum
24. arbore

Exercise IIb: Verbs; Conjugations and pp. 72–74
Personal Endings

Supply the appropriate form of each of the verbs below to complete each sentence. Read the complete sentence aloud and translate it:

| portō, portāre | pōnō, pōnere | inveniō, invenīre |
| habeō, habēre | iaciō, iacere | |

Singular

1. Ego cistam _____.
2. Tū cistam _____.
3. Puer cistam _____.

Plural

4. Nōs cistam _____.
5. Vōs cistam _____.
6. Puerī cistam _____.

Imperatives

7. _____ cistam, puer!
8. _____ cistam, puerī!

Exercise IIc: Verbs; Identification of Forms pp. 72–74

Give the 1st person singular, infinitive, and conjugation number of each of the following verbs. Then translate the form that is given:

For example: **surgimus**   Answer: **surgō, surgere,** 3; *we rise*

1. intrātis
2. iubēs
3. habent
4. impedīte
5. reprehendimus

6. convocā
7. rogat
8. manē
9. mussātis
10. cūrō

11. prōmittis
12. festīnāte
13. verberāmus
14. olfaciunt

Exercise IId: Prepositional Phrases with Accusative  pp. 64, 90–91
and with Ablative Cases; Ablative Case without
a Preposition

Complete the following sentences to match the English. Translate each sentence:

1. Cornēlia et Mārcus et Sextus _____ in vīllā habitant. (in summer)
2. Mārcus et Sextus _____ sedent. (under the tree)
3. Nūntius sollicitus _____ currit. (to the country house)
4. Puer temerārius _____ cadit. (out of the tree)
5. Cornēlia _____ ad vīllam vīcīnam fūrtim ambulat. (that night)
6. Servus _____ dormit. (at the door)
7. Cornēlius sōlus _____ epistulam scrībit. (in the country house)
8. Servī per agrōs _____ currunt. (with the dogs)
9. Statua _____ cadit. (into the fishpond)
10. Dāvus _____ Getam verberat. (with a stick)
11. Puella amīcam _____ tenet. (in an embrace)

Exercise IIe: Reading Comprehension

Read the following passage and answer the questions with complete sentences
in Latin:

ON THE BANKS OF THE TIBER
IN THE EIGHTH CENTURY B.C.

In Italiā prope fluvium Tiberim habitat pastor quīdam, nōmine Faustulus.
Hodiē ad casam redit et uxōrem, nōmine Accam Lārentiam, magnā vōce vocat,
"Uxor! Venī celeriter ad mē!"

Lārentia venit et virum rogat, "Quid est, coniūnx? Cūr mē vocās?"

"Venī mēcum ad rīpam fluviī," respondet Faustulus. "Rem mīram tibi 5
ostendere volō. Necesse est nōbīs festīnāre."

Pastor et uxor ē casā currunt et ad Tiberim festīnant. Lārentia virum multa
rogat. Vir tamen nihil respondet sed uxōrem ad rīpam fluviī dūcit. Ubi adveniunt,
Lārentia rīpam spectat. Ibi videt lupam, quae puerōs geminōs alit. Lupa puerōs
dīligenter cūrat et linguā lambit. 10

"Age, Faustule," clāmat Lārentia. "Rāmum arboris arripe et lupam repelle!"

"Cūr mē lupam repellere iubēs?" rogat vir. "Lupa puerōs neque vexat neque
terret. Ecce! Puerōs cūrat quod eōs amat."

"Ita vērō," respondet uxor, "sed ego puerōs ad casam nostram portāre volō.
Ego et tū puerōs velut līberōs nostrōs cūrāre dēbēmus." 15

Faustulus ad lupam appropinquat. Eam rāmō repellere parat. Lupa tamen
neque lātrat neque pastōrem petit sed puerōs lambit et in silvam effugit. Tum
pastor et uxor puerōs ad casam portant. "Sine dubiō," exclāmat Faustulus, "sunt
puerī mīrābilēs."

1 fluvius, -ī, m., *river*
  Tiberis, Tiberis, m., *the Tiber River*
  pastor, pastōris, m., *shepherd*
2 casa, -ae, f., *hut, cottage*
  vocō, vocāre, *to call*
4 coniūnx, coniugis, m./f., *spouse,*
    husband or *wife*
5 rīpa, -ae, f., *bank*
  rem mīram, *a wonderful thing*
  tibi, *to you*
6 ostendō, ostendere, *to show*
7 multa, *many things*

9 geminus, *twin*
  alō, alere, *to feed, nourish*
10 dīligenter, *carefully*
  lingua, -ae, f., *tongue*
  lambō, lambere, *to lick*
14 noster, *our*
15 velut, adv., *just as*
  dēbēmus, *we ought*
17 petō, petere, *to look for, seek, attack*
18 sine dubiō, *without a doubt*
19 mīrābilis, *extraordinary, wonderful*

1. Who is Faustulus?
2. Whom does he call with a loud voice?
3. To what place is it necessary to hurry?
4. What does Larentia see when she gets there?
5. What is the she-wolf doing?
6. What does Larentia want to do with the boys?
7. What are the last two things that the she-wolf does?
8. What, in Faustulus's judgment, are the boys?

Exercise IIf: Identification of Forms

In the passage on page 94, identify the following:

1. One 1st person singular verb.
2. Two 2nd person singular verbs.
3. One 1st person plural verb.
4. Three imperatives.
5. Three words in the genitive case and the noun that each modifies.
6. Three prepositional phrases with the accusative case.
7. Three prepositional phrases with the ablative case.
8. Four uses of the ablative case without a preposition.

DISASTER

Intereā Cornēliī per Viam Appiam iter faciēbant. Cornēlius, quod ad urbem tribus diēbus advenīre volēbat, Syrum identidem iubēbat equōs incitāre. Syrus igitur equōs virgā verberābat. Dum per viam ībant, Aurēlia et Cornēlia spectābant rūsticōs quī in agrīs labōrābant. Mārcus et Sextus spectābant omnēs raedās quae per Viam Appiam ībant.   5

Septima hōra erat. Diēs erat calidus. In agrīs rūsticī nōn iam labōrābant sed sub arboribus quiēscēbant. In raedā Cornēlius et Aurēlia iam dormiēbant. Mārcus pede vexābat Cornēliam quae dormīre volēbat. Sextus cum raedāriō Syrō sedēbat; viam et vehicula spectābat.

Subitō, "Ecce, Mārce!" exclāmat Sextus. "Est aurīga!"   10

Mārcus magnō rīsū respondet, "Nōn est aurīga, fatue! Est tabellārius quī epistulās cīvium praeclārōrum ab urbe fert. Tabellāriī semper celeriter iter faciunt quod epistulās ab urbe ad omnēs partēs Italiae ferunt."

"Quam celeriter iter facit!" clāmat Sextus. "Equōs ferōciter virgā incitat. Cavē tabellārium, Syre! Tenē equōs! Cavē fossam! Cavē fossam!"   15

Syrus equōs tenet et tabellārium vītat, sed raeda in fossam magnō fragōre dēscendit.

1	**iter,** *journey*	9	**vehicula,** *vehicles*
	iter faciēbant, *(they) were traveling*	10	**aurīga, -ae,** m., *charioteer*
2	tribus diēbus, *in three days*	11	**magnō rīsū,** *with a loud laugh*
	volēbat, *(he/she) wanted*		fatuus, *stupid*
	identidem, adv., *again and again*		**tabellārius, -ī,** m., *courier*
	iubēbat, *(he) ordered, kept ordering*	12	**cīvis, cīvis,** gen. pl., **cīvium,** m./f., *citizen*
3	**virga, -ae,** f., *stick, switch*		**praeclārus,** *distinguished*
	verberābat, *(he) kept beating, whipping*		**ab** or **ā,** prep. + abl., *from*
	ībant, *(they) were going*	13	**pars, partis,** gen. pl., **partium** f., *part*
	rūsticus, -ī, m., *peasant*	14	**Quam...!** adv., *How...!*
6	septimus, *seventh*		**ferōciter,** adv., *fiercely*
	erat, *(it) was*		**Cavē...!** *Watch out (for)...!*
7	**quiēscēbant,** *(they) were resting*	16	**vītō, vītāre,** *to avoid*
	pēs, pedis, m., *foot*		

EXERCISE 13a

Respondē Latīnē:

1. Quid Cornēliī faciēbant?
2. Cūr Cornēlius Syrum identidem iubēbat equōs incitāre?
3. Cūr rūsticī nōn iam labōrābant?
4. Quis celeriter appropinquat?
5. Vītatne Syrus tabellārium?
6. Quō dēscendit raeda?

3rd Declension i-stem Nouns

Some 3rd declension nouns such as **cīvis** and **pars** end in *-ium* instead of *-um* in the genitive plural. These are called *i-stem nouns*, and they will be identified in vocabulary lists by inclusion of the genitive plural form.

Verbs: The Imperfect Tense I

Up to the beginning of this chapter all of the verbs in the Latin stories described actions that were going on in the present with respect to the time of the story. All of these verbs are said to be in the present tense. (The word tense came into English from Old French *tens*, "tense," "time," which came from the Latin **tempus**, *time*.) Tense refers to the time when an action is conceived as taking place.

Look at the following sentences from the story at the beginning of this chapter:

Per Viam Appiam iter **faciēbant**. (13:1)	*They **were traveling** along the Appian Way.*
Ad urbem tribus diēbus advenīre **volēbat**. (13:1–2)	*He **wanted** to reach the city in three days.*
Syrus equōs **verberābat**. (13:2–3)	*Syrus **kept whipping** the horses.*

The Latin verbs in bold type are examples of the *imperfect tense*. This tense is easily recognized by the tense sign *-ba-* that appears before the personal endings. The verbs in the imperfect tense in these sentences describe actions that took place in past time and that were continuous or repeated.

N.B. The imperfect forms of **sum, esse**, *to be*, and **possum, posse**, *to be able*, are irregular. They may be recognized by the letters **era-**:

| <u>era</u>t, *(he/she/it) was* | pot<u>era</u>t, *(he/she/it) was able* |
| <u>era</u>nt, *(they) were* | pot<u>era</u>nt, *(they) were able* |

EXERCISE 13b

Read aloud, say whether the verb is present or imperfect, and translate:

1. Cornēlia sub arbore sedet.
2. Flāvia in agrīs ambulābat.
3. Rōmānī in Italiā habitant.
4. Servī Getam invenīre nōn poterant.
5. Lātrant canēs; appropinquant servī.
6. Mārcus et Sextus raedās spectābant.
7. Erant rūsticī prope Viam Appiam.
8. Puerī saepe currunt in agrīs.
9. Geta labōrāre nōlēbat.
10. Tabellāriī epistulās ab urbe in omnēs partēs Italiae ferēbant.

EXERCISE 13c

Using story 13 and the information on the imperfect tense as guides, give the Latin for:

1. Again and again Cornelius kept ordering Syrus to spur on the horses.
2. The day was warm, and it was the seventh hour.
3. The peasants were resting under the trees, and Cornelius and Aurelia were asleep in the carriage.
4. Marcus was sitting in the carriage and annoying Cornelia with his foot.
5. Sextus was looking at a courier who was going along the road.

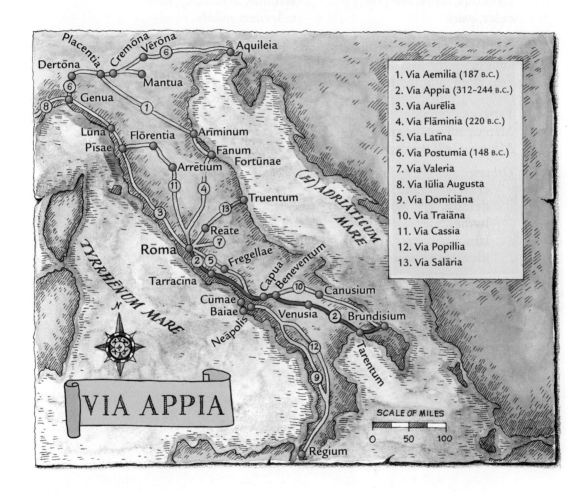

1. Via Aemilia (187 B.C.)
2. Via Appia (312–244 B.C.)
3. Via Aurēlia
4. Via Flāminia (220 B.C.)
5. Via Latīna
6. Via Postumia (148 B.C.)
7. Via Valeria
8. Via Iūlia Augusta
9. Via Domitiāna
10. Via Traiāna
11. Via Cassia
12. Via Popillia
13. Via Salāria

VIA APPIA

SCALE OF MILES

0   50   100

BUILDING THE MEANING

Adverbs

You have seen a number of ways in which the meaning of simple Latin sentences can be expanded by the addition of modifiers. One commonly used modifier is the *adverb*. Adverbs can modify verbs ("She ran *quickly*"), adjectives ("She is *very* beautiful"), or other adverbs ("She ran *very* quickly").

Latin adverbs are sometimes formed from adjectives by using the ending *-ē* or *-iter*:

Adjective	Adverb
strēnuus, *active, energetic*	**strēnuē,** *strenuously, hard*
celer, *quick*	**celeriter,** *quickly*

But you have met many adverbs that are not formed from adjectives and do not have these endings. See the lists below.

Adverbs often indicate the *time, place,* or *manner* of the action of the verb:

Time:
Mārcus **adhūc** dormit.
*Marcus is **still** sleeping.*

Others:
crās, *tomorrow*
deinde, *then, next*
hodiē, *today*
iam, *now, already*
identidem, *again and again, repeatedly*
intereā, *meanwhile*
iterum, *again, a second time*
mox, *soon, presently*
nōn iam, *no longer*

nōndum, *not yet*
nunc, *now*
saepe, *often*
semper, *always*
simul, *together, at the same time*
statim, *immediately*
subitō, *suddenly*
tandem, *at last, at length*
tum, *at that moment, then*

Place:
"Quid tū **hīc**?" (9:8)
*"What (are) you (doing) **here**?"*

Other:
ibi, *there*

Manner:

Sextus **celeriter** tunicam et togam induit. (8:9–10)
*Sextus **quickly** puts on his tunic and toga.*

Others:

> **ferōciter,** *fiercely*
> **fūrtim,** *stealthily*
> **lentē,** *slowly*
> **strēnuē,** *strenuously, hard*
> **tacitē,** *silently*

Other Adverbs:

> **etiam,** *also, even*
> **Ita vērō!** *Yes! Indeed!*
> **Minimē!** *No! Not at all!*
> **nōn,** *not*
> **Quam...!** *How....!*
> **quoque,** *also*
> **tamen,** *however, nevertheless*

Note that some of the adverbs on the previous page and above end with letters that are used in case endings of nouns and adjectives: **-ās, -e, -am, -em, -ā, -um,** and **-ō.** Be sure that you know that the words on these pages are adverbs and not nouns or adjectives.

Rome

Some sections of the ancient Appian Way have survived over time. The wheel ruts shown in the picture are the result of the heavy traffic over the road throughout the centuries.
Via Appia Antica, Rome

Word Study III

Latin Suffix -or

The suffix *-or*, when added to the base of a Latin verb, creates a 3rd declension noun that means "the act of" or "the result of" that particular verb. The base of a verb is found by dropping the *-āre, -ēre, -ere,* or *-īre* ending from its infinitive. For example, **clāmāre** (base: **clām-**) becomes **clāmor, clāmōris** m., *shouting*. The Latin noun formed in this way often comes into English unchanged. The derivative *clamor* means "a loud outcry."

EXERCISE 1

Create a 3rd declension noun from each verb below. Give the nominative and genitive singular of the noun. Give an English derivative, if there is one.

terrēre	**tenēre**	**stupēre** (*to be amazed*)
errāre	**timēre**	**valēre** (*to be strong*)

English Suffix -(i)fy

The Latin verb **facere,** *to make, do,* is the source of the English verb suffix *-(i)fy,* meaning "to make." The English word *beautify* means "to make beautiful." Often the base to which the suffix is added is also of Latin origin. The Latin word **magnus** provides the base for the English word *magnify,* "to make large."

EXERCISE 2

Give the English verbs made by adding the suffix *-(i)fy* to the bases of these Latin words.

terrēre	**satis** (*enough*)
quālis	**ūnus** (*one*)
nūllus	**signum** (*sign*)

EXERCISE 3

Match each English word in the column at the left with its meaning in the column at the right. Use the meaning of the Latin word in parentheses as a guide.

1. *fraternity* (**frāter**)
2. *novelty* (**novus**)
3. *pedestrian* (**pēs, pedis**)
4. *procrastinate* (**crās**)
5. *ancillary* (**ancilla**)
6. *tacit* (**tacitē**)
7. *simultaneous* (**simul**)
8. *dominate* (**dominus**)

a. unspoken
b. put off until tomorrow
c. brotherhood
d. be master over
e. traveler on foot
f. something new
g. at the same time
h. serving as helper

Latin Mottoes

Although Latin is an ancient language, its words and phrases are still part of our life today. Look at the inscriptions on a penny, nickel, dime, or quarter. Find the Latin words E PLURIBUS UNUM. This is the motto of the United States, meaning "out of many, one." It refers to the many colonies that were united to make one nation.

Many states, universities, and other organizations have Latin mottoes, which serve as symbols of their purpose, for example:

SEMPER FIDELIS *always faithful* (U.S. Marine Corps)

VOX CLAMANTIS IN DESERTO *the voice of one crying in the wilderness* (Dartmouth College)

VERITAS VOS LIBERABIT *the truth will set you free* (Johns Hopkins University)

NIL SINE MAGNO LABORE *nothing without great effort* (Brooklyn College)

MIHI CURA FUTURI *I care for the future* (Hunter College)

VOLENS ET POTENS *willing and able* (4th Army Engineers)

IN ARDUIS FIDELIS *faithful in adversity* (Medical Corps)

AD ASTRA PER ASPERA *to the stars through difficulties* (Kansas)

DUM SPIRO, SPERO *while I breathe, I hope* (South Carolina)

CAVEAT EMPTOR *let the buyer beware* (proverb)

CARPE DIEM *seize the day* (Horace)

COGITO ERGO SUM *I think, therefore I am* (Descartes)

ERRARE HUMANUM EST *to err is human* (Seneca)

ARS LONGA, VITA BREVIS *art is long, but life is brief* (Horace)

FESTINA LENTE *make haste slowly* (Augustus)

O TEMPORA! O MORES! *O the times, O the values!* (Cicero)

A MARI USQUE AD MARE *from sea to sea* (national motto of Canada)

GRANDESCUNT AUCTA LABORE *by work, all things increase and grow* (McGill University)

EXERCISE 4

Find further examples of mottoes in English, Latin, or other languages used by any of the following:

a. your home state or city
b. military units, such as the army, navy, or air force
c. local colleges, universities, or academies
d. local organizations: community service groups, political groups, unions, or clubs

Make up a motto for your family, best friend, pet, favorite movie star, or sports hero.

WHO IS TO BLAME?

Ubi dēscendit raeda in fossam, concidunt omnēs. Nēmō tamen ē raedā cadit. Mox cūnctī in viam ē raedā dēscendunt, sollicitī sed incolumēs. Cornēlius, quamquam gaudet quod omnēs sunt incolumēs, raedārium miserum reprehendit.

"Age, Syre! Nōlī cessāre! Extrahe statim raedam ē fossā!"

Syrus igitur equōs incitat. Equī raedam strēnuē trahunt, sed frūstrā. Raeda in fossā 5
haeret immōbilis. Syrus eam movēre nōn potest.

"Ō sceleste!" inquit Cornēlius. "Tuā culpā raeda est in fossā. Quid tū faciēbās ubi cisium appropinquābat? Dormiēbāsne?"

Interpellat Sextus, "Syrus nōn dormiēbat, sed per viam placidē ībat dum appropinquābat cisium. Ego et Mārcus spectābāmus cisium, quod celerrimē appropinquābat. 10
Deinde tabellārius equōs ad raedam nostram dēvertēbat. Perīculum erat magnum. Syrus cisium vītāre poterat et iam nōs omnēs sumus incolumēs quod Syrus raedam magnā arte agēbat."

Tum Cornēlius rogat, "Tūne cisium spectābās, Mārce, ubi appropinquābat?"

"Ita vērō, pater!" respondet Mārcus. "Omnia observābam. Erat culpa tabellāriī, nōn 15
Syrī. Syrus raedam magnā arte agēbat."

Sed Cornēlius, magnā īrā commōtus, virgam arripit et raedārium miserum verberat.

1 **concidō, concidere,** *to fall down*
2 **cūnctī,** *all*
   incolumis, *unhurt, safe and sound*
   gaudeō, gaudēre, *to be glad*
3 **quod,** conj., with verbs of feeling, *that*
4 **cessō, cessāre,** *to be idle, do nothing*
   extrahō, extrahere, *to drag out*
5 **frūstrā,** adv., *in vain*
6 **haereō, haerēre,** *to stick*
   moveō, movēre, *to move*
7 **culpa, -ae,** f., *fault, blame*
      tuā culpā, *because of your fault, it's your fault that*

8 **cisium,** *light two-wheeled carriage*
9 interpellō, interpellāre, *to interrupt*
   placidē, adv., *gently, peacefully*
10 **quod,** *which*
   celerrimē, adv., *very fast*
11 **noster,** *our*
   dēvertēbat, *he began to turn aside*
   perīculum, *danger*
12 **ars, artis,** gen. pl., **artium,** f., *skill*
13 **agō, agere,** *to do, drive*
14 Tūne…spectābās, *Were you watching?*
17 **commōtus,** *moved*

EXERCISE 14a

Respondē Latīnē:

1. Quid accidit ubi raeda in fossam dēscendit?
2. Cūr Cornēlius gaudet?
   accidit, *happens*

3. Dormiēbatne Syrus ubi cisium appropinquābat?
4. Quōmodo commōtus est Cornēlius?

Go Online
PHSchool.com
Web Code: jfd-0014

Go Online
PHSchool.com
Web Code: jfd-0014

Verbs: The Imperfect Tense II

You have now met all the endings of the imperfect tense:

Singular			Plural		
	1	-bam		1	-bāmus
	2	-bās		2	-bātis
	3	-bat		3	-bant

Note that the vowel is short before final *-m, -t,* and *-nt.*

These are the endings of the imperfect tense of *all* Latin verbs (except **esse** and its compounds, of which **posse** is one; see page 98).

Compare the following chart showing verbs in the imperfect tense with the chart showing present tense forms on page 73.

		1st Conjugation	2nd Conjugation	3rd Conjugation		4th Conjugation
Infinitive		par*āre*	hab*ēre*	mít*tere*	iá*cere* (-*iō*)	aud*īre*
Singular	1	par*ábam*	hab*ébam*	mitt*ébam*	iaci*ébam*	audi*ébam*
	2	par*ábās*	hab*ébās*	mitt*ébās*	iaci*ébās*	audi*ébās*
	3	par*ábat*	hab*ébat*	mitt*ébat*	iaci*ébat*	audi*ébat*
Plural	1	par*ābámus*	hab*ēbámus*	mitt*ēbámus*	iaci*ēbámus*	audi*ēbámus*
	2	par*ābátis*	hab*ēbátis*	mitt*ēbátis*	iaci*ēbátis*	audi*ēbátis*
	3	par*ábant*	hab*ébant*	mitt*ébant*	iaci*ébant*	audi*ébant*

Be sure to learn these forms thoroughly.

Note that the personal endings are the same as those given for the present tense on page 54, except that in this tense the 1st person singular ends in *-m* (compare **sum**).

The imperfect tense shows action *in the past* that was

    a.   going on for a time:

           Ego et Mārcus **spectābāmus** cisium. (14:10)
           *Marcus and I **were watching** the carriage.*

           Cornēlia dormīre **volēbat.** (13:8)
           *Cornelia **wanted** to sleep.*

    b.   repeated:

           Mārcus **vexābat** Cornēliam. (13:7–8)
           *Marcus **kept annoying** Cornelia.*

    c.   habitual or customary:

           Dāvus in Britanniā **habitābat.**
           *Davus **used to live** in Britain.*

d. beginning to happen:

> Equōs ad raedam nostram **dēvertēbat**. (14:11)
> He **began to turn** the horses **aside** in the direction of our carriage.

Let the context guide you to an appropriate translation.

Exercise 14b

Read aloud, paying special attention to the tenses of verbs. Then translate:

1. Tabellārium līberī spectābant.
2. Cornēlius, ubi epistulās scrībēbat, uxōrem et līberōs vidēre nōlēbat.
3. Gaudēbat Cornēlius quod omnēs incolumēs erant.
4. Cīvēs tabellāriōs ex urbe saepe mittunt.
5. Syrus tabellārium vītāre poterat quod equōs tenēbat.
6. Dormiēbāsne, Syre? Minimē vērō, domine! Ego placidē per viam ībam.
7. Quid vōs faciēbātis, puerī? Nōs omnēs raedās spectābāmus, pater.
8. Appropinquābatne cisium placidē? Minimē! Celerrimē per viam ībat.
9. Cūr mē semper vexās, Mārce? Dormīre volō.

Exercise 14c

Select, read aloud, and translate:

1. Tabellārius equōs ferōciter _____.   incitābam/incitābat/incitābant
2. Pater et māter ē raedā _____.   dēscendēbās/dēscendēbat/dēscendēbant
3. Cūr tū celeriter iter _____?   faciēbās/faciēbant/faciēbāmus
4. Nōs omnēs in raedā _____.   dormiēbam/dormiēbātis/dormiēbāmus
5. Ego et Mārcus saepe in agrīs _____.   currēbāmus/currēbant/currēbat

Exercise 14d

Supply the appropriate imperfect tense endings, read aloud, and translate:

1. Tabellārius multās epistulās ab urbe portā_____.
2. Cornēlia, quae dēfessa era_____, in cubiculō dormiē_____.
3. Nōs raedās magnā arte agē_____.
4. Sub arboribus vīneārum et in olīvētīs vōs Getam petē_____.
5. Latrā_____ canēs; per agrōs currē_____; Getam invenīre nōn potera_____.
6. "Servumne, Dāve, baculō verberā_____?"
7. Aliī servī in vīllā, aliī in vīneīs labōrā_____.
8. Sextus identidem clāmā_____, "Ecce! Aurīga!"

   olīvētum, *olive grove*

Verbs: Irregular Verbs I

The infinitives of a few Latin verbs show that they do not belong to one of the four regular conjugations. They are therefore called *irregular verbs*. Two of these are the verbs **sum, esse,** *to be*, and **possum, posse,** *to be able*; *I can*, a verb consisting of **pos-** or **pot-** + the forms of **sum**:

		Present	Imperfect	Present	Imperfect
Infinitive		ésse		pósse	
Singular	1	sum	éram	póssum	póteram
	2	es	érās	pótes	póterās
	3	est	érat	pótest	póterat
Plural	1	súmus	erámus	póssumus	poterámus
	2	éstis	erátis	potéstis	poterátis
	3	sunt	érant	póssunt	póterant

Be sure to learn these forms thoroughly.

EXERCISE 14e

From the chart above, select the verb form that will complete the Latin sentence to match the English cue. Then read aloud and translate the entire sentence:

1. Dāvus sollicitus est, nam Getam invenīre nōn _____. (*is able/can*)
2. Tū _____ raedārius scelestus, Syre! (*are*)
3. Flāvia misera erat quod Cornēlia in vīllā manēre nōn _____. (*was able/could*)
4. Vōs incolumēs _____ quod Syrus equōs magnā arte agēbat. (*are*)
5. Getam, Dāve, in agrīs invenīre nōs nōn _____. (*were able/could*)
6. Canēs, quī Getam olfacere _____, lātrant. (*are able/can*)
7. Quamquam Cornēlius _____, servī strēnuē labōrābant. (*was away*)
8. Ō mē miserum! Quō īnstrūmentō ego raedam ē fossā extrahere _____? (*am able/can*)
9. Equī cisium sed nōn fossam vītāre _____. (*were able/could*)
10. Dāvus vōs verberāre vult, nam Getam invenīre vōs nōn _____. (*were able/could*)

EXERCISE 14f

Using story 14 and the material on verbs in this chapter as guides, give the Latin for:

1. Although all were unhurt, Cornelius was scolding the coachman.
2. Cornelius: "Why were you not able to drag the coach out of the ditch, Syrus?"
3. Syrus and Sextus: "We were not sleeping when the light carriage was approaching."
4. Cornelius: "Were you watching the light carriage that was approaching very fast, Syrus and Sextus?"
5. Syrus and Sextus: "We were able to avoid the light carriage, and although we are in the ditch we are all unhurt."

THE KINGS OF ROME

According to legend, seven kings ruled Rome over a span of 243 years. Myth, legend, and history are intertwined in the accounts of their rule.

Romulus, as the founding king, devised a set of laws for his Romans, a group of fellow shepherds and a motley crew of rough men who had come together to start new lives in a new place for a variety of reasons. They could not very well found a society, however, without women and the prospect of children.

When ambassadors who had been sent to arrange marriage treaties with neighboring states returned empty-handed, rebuffed, and ridiculed, Romulus adopted a bold plan. He invited these neighbors to a grand festival in honor of Neptune. Largely out of curiosity and a desire to see the new city, many came to Rome, including Sabines who brought along their whole families. Impressed by the grand tour, the guests sat attentively, watching the spectacle. At a signal from Romulus, suddenly the young Roman men rushed in and carried off the young unmarried Sabine girls. Most grabbed the first potential bride they encountered. A few senators had their followers grab some of the especially pretty ones they had picked out ahead of time.

Romulus and the other Romans persuaded the Sabine women, with assurances of deep love and lasting marriages, to accept their new roles as Roman wives (**mātrōnae**). Their families, who had fled from the fracas, attacked Rome to reclaim their daughters. As the Sabine and Roman armies opened battle on the future site of the Roman Forum, however, the Sabine women intervened and begged them to stop fighting, saying they did not wish to become both widows and orphans on the same day. In response, the Sabines and Romans united to form one state with Rome as the capital city.

After the second king of Rome, Numa Pompilius, had devoted much attention to legal and religious institutions, the third king, Tullus Hostilius, renewed the state's emphasis on its military posture. Tullus declared war on the Albans because of cattle-raiding. Both sides agreed to settle the conflict by having the Horatii, a set of Roman triplets, battle a set of Alban triplets, the Curiatii. As their armies watched, the two sets of triplets clashed. Two of the Romans died; all three Albans were wounded. Outnumbered three to one, but unscathed, the surviving Roman, Horatius, took flight, counting on the strategic assumption that the three Curiatii would pursue him and thus be separated. One by one he was able to turn back and face each of his foes until he had dispatched all three Albans and Rome claimed victory.

When the Albans later proved disloyal and tried to desert the Romans in a battle against the cities of Fidenae and Veii, Tullus destroyed Alba Longa and moved her citizens to Rome. But as Tullus prepared further campaigns, he fell ill and turned to religion for deliverance from a plague. Legend has it that he performed a sacrifice to Jupiter incorrectly and consequently was struck by a bolt of lightning, perishing in flames with his palace.

Ancus Marcius, grandson of Numa, who was elected the fourth king of Rome, turned his attention to major construction projects: new city walls, a prison, a bridge across the Tiber (the **Pōns Sublicius** or bridge built on piles), and the seaport of Rome at Ostia, located at the mouth of the Tiber River.

The fifth king of Rome, Lucius Tarquinius Priscus, from Etruria to the north of Rome, gained the throne by fraud and was subsequently murdered at the instigation of the sons of Ancus Marcius. Priscus's wife, Tanaquil, then engineered the ascent to the throne of her daughter's husband, Servius Tullius.

Servius was a much respected king. After he solidified his status with a victory in war against Veii, he went to work on the organization of Roman society. He held the first census and established the practice of assigning all Roman citizens to classes based on wealth. He further enlarged the physical boundaries of Rome to accommodate the increased population, bringing the city to its total of seven hills.

Palace intrigues, however, continued. Tullia, Servius's daughter, engineered the murder of her sister and her own husband and then goaded her new husband, Lucius Tarquinius, into proclaiming himself King Tarquinius and confronting her father before the Roman senate. Tarquinius threw Servius out of the Senate House bodily, and his agents murdered the king in the street. Tullia arrived to be the first to hail her husband the seventh king of Rome. Heading home, she ordered her horrified carriage driver to run over the body of her father lying in the road—an act immortalized by the street's name, **Vīcus Scelerātus** (Street of Crime).

That seventh and final king of Rome soon earned his name Tarquinius Superbus, Tarquin the Proud, by executing many senators and refusing to seek the counsel of that body. He did achieve military successes and oversaw construction of the great temple of Jupiter on the Capitoline hill and the **cloāca maxima**, the main sewer of Rome. But the penchant for crime continued to run in the veins of

To settle the dispute between Rome and Alba Longa, the three Horatii brothers swear, in the presence of their father, mother, and sisters to fight the three Curiatii brothers.
The Oath of the Horatii, *oil on canvas, 1784, Jacques-Louis David*

Sextus demands that Lucretia yield to him (*left*). Lucretia's husband and friends find her overcome with shame (*right*). Lucretia's body is shown to the Romans, and Brutus demands that they avenge her (*center*).
The Tragedy of Lucretia, *oil on wood, ca. 1500–1501, Sandro Botticelli*

the Tarquin family. The youngest son, Sextus Tarquinius, developed a passion for Lucretia, the wife of his cousin, Tarquinius Collatinus, and raped her. Lucretia, after telling her husband, father, and Lucius Junius Brutus what had happened, stabbed herself and died. That was cause enough to inspire Brutus, Collatinus, and other worthy Romans to persuade the citizens to oust Tarquinius Superbus and everyone in his family and to replace the kingship with a new form of government, the Republic. This was accomplished in 509 B.C.

Fact and fiction are intertwined in these legends from the age of the kings. Historical record indicates that after Romulus a king chosen by the assembly of the people and the Senate (made up of the heads of the most important families) was granted a form of power (**imperium**) that amounted to despotism. The arrival of the Tarquin family may reflect an Etruscan takeover, which was interrupted by the reign of Servius and then thrown off when the last of the kings, Tarquinius Superbus, was banished. That the area of the Forum was drained and paved over and that the first buildings appeared on the Capitoline Hill in the period that corresponds roughly with the arrival of the Tarquins are facts that the archaeologists confirm.

---

1. Summarize the reign of each king in a sentence or two. What overall trends do you find in this period of three centuries?
2. Romans always seemed ambiguous about their kings. What would they find positive and negative about the period of the monarchy?
3. If you had to live in Rome during the monarchy, under which king would you choose to live and why?

VEHICLE SPOTTING

Dum raeda in fossā manēbat, Mārcus et Sextus vehicula exspectābant. Longum erat silentium.

Diū nūllum vehiculum appāret. Tandem Mārcus murmur rotārum audit et procul nūbem pulveris cōnspicit.

Sextus, "Quid est, Mārce? Estne plaustrum?"   5

Mārcus, "Minimē, fatue! Plaustra onera magna ferunt. Tarda igitur sunt. Sed illud vehiculum celeriter appropinquat."

Sextus, "Ita vērō! Praetereā equī illud vehiculum trahunt. Bovēs plaustra trahunt. Fortasse est raeda."

"Nōn est raeda," inquit Mārcus, "nam quattuor rotās habet raeda. Illud vehiculum   10 duās tantum rotās habet."

"Est cisium!" clāmat Sextus. "Ecce, Mārce! Quam celeriter appropinquat! Fortasse est vir praeclārus quī ab urbe Neāpolim iter facit."

"Minimē, Sexte!" respondet Mārcus. "Nōn est vir praeclārus, nam tunicam, nōn togam, gerit. Fortasse est alius tabellārius."   15

Praeterit cisium. Tum nūbem pulveris tantum vident et murmur rotārum audiunt. Tandem silentium.

1 **exspectō, exspectāre,** *to look out for*
  longus, *long*
3 **diū,** adv., *for a long time*
  appāreō, appārēre, *to appear*
  rota, -ae, f., *wheel*
4 **procul,** adv., *in the distance, far off*
  nūbēs, nūbis, gen. pl., **nūbium,** f.,
    cloud
  pulvis, pulveris, m., *dust*
5 **plaustrum, -ī,** n., *wagon, cart*
6 **onus, oneris,** n., *load, burden*

  tardus, *slow*
  illud, *that*
8 **praetereā,** adv., *besides*
  bōs, bovis, m./f., *ox*
9 **fortasse,** adv., *perhaps*
10 **quattuor,** *four*
11 **duae,** *two*
   tantum, adv., *only*
13 Neāpolim, *to Naples*
16 **praetereō, praeterīre,** irreg., *to go past*

EXERCISE 15a

Respondē Latīnē:

1. Quid puerī faciēbant ubi raeda in fossā manēbat?
2. Erantne multa vehicula in viā?
3. Quid Mārcus audit et cōnspicit?
4. Cūr vehiculum plaustrum esse nōn potest?
5. Cūr vehiculum raeda esse nōn potest?
6. Quid est?
7. Estne vir praeclārus in cisiō?

Go Online
PHSchool.com
Web Code: jfd-0015

Go Online
PHSchool.com
Web Code: jfd–0015

Nouns: Neuter

Some Latin nouns end with the same letters in the nominative and accusative singular and with the letter *-a* in the nominative and accusative plural. Second declension nouns of this type end with the letters *-um* in the nominative and accusative singular. These are *neuter* nouns. **Neuter** is the Latin word for "neither"; neuter nouns are neither masculine nor feminine (for the concept of gender, see page 34).

Look at the following sentences in which nouns ending with the letters *-um* in the singular and *-a* in the plural are used first as subject and then as direct object:

Baculum Dāvī in vīllā est.	S	*Davus's **stick** is in the farmhouse.*
Dāvus **baculum** habet. (11:8)	DO	*Davus has a **stick**.*
Vēstīgia Getae in silvā sunt.	S	*Geta's **footprints** are in the woods.*
Vēstīgia Getae inveniunt. (12:11)	DO	*They find Geta's **footprints**.*

The words **baculum** and **vēstīgia** are neuter nouns of the 2nd declension. Both the 2nd and the 3rd declensions have neuter nouns:

Number Case	2nd Declension	3rd Declension
Singular		
Nominative	bácul**um**	nṓmen
Genitive	bácul**ī**	nṓmin**is**
Dative	bácul**ō**	nṓmin**ī**
Accusative	bácul**um**	nṓmen
Ablative	bácul**ō**	nṓmin**e**
Vocative	bácul**um**	nṓmen
Plural		
Nominative	bácul**a**	nṓmin**a**
Genitive	bacul**ṓrum**	nṓmin**um**
Dative	bácul**īs**	nōmín**ibus**
Accusative	bácul**a**	nṓmin**a**
Ablative	bácul**īs**	nōmín**ibus**
Vocative	bácul**a**	nṓmin**a**

Most neuter nouns of the 2nd declension end in *-um* in the nominative and the accusative singular.

The nominative and accusative singular forms of neuter nouns of the 3rd declension, such as **nōmen** and **murmur**, are not predictable, but the other cases are formed by adding the usual 3rd declension endings to the base, which is found by dropping the ending from the genitive singular form.

Remember that the accusative singular of neuter nouns is always the same as the nominative singular and that the nominative and accusative plurals always end in *-a*.

Most 1st declension nouns are feminine. Most 2nd declension nouns are either masculine or neuter. The 3rd declension contains many nouns that are masculine, many that are feminine, and a number of neuter nouns. See the chart on page 267 at the end of this book for examples of nouns of the different genders in each declension.

Examples of neuter nouns are:

2nd Declension
auxilium, -ī, n., *help*
baculum, -ī, n., *stick*
cisium, -ī, n., *light two-wheeled carriage*
cubiculum, -ī, n., *room, bedroom*
olīvētum, -ī, n., *olive grove*
perīculum, -ī, n., *danger*
plaustrum, -ī, n., *wagon, cart*
silentium, -ī, n., *silence*
vehiculum, -ī, n., *vehicle*
vēstīgium, -ī, n., *track, footprint, trace*

3rd Declension
iter, itineris, n., *journey*
murmur, murmuris, n., *murmur, rumble*
nōmen, nōminis, n., *name*
onus, oneris, n., *load*
tempus, temporis, n., *time*

BUILDING THE MEANING

Go Online
PHSchool.com
Web Code: jfd-0015

Nominative, Accusative, or Genitive Plural? How Do You Decide?

At the top of page 114 you saw the words **baculum** and **vēstīgia** used in sentences, first as subjects and then as direct objects. To decide which case is being used, you need to consider the sentence as a whole, just as you have learned to do when other nouns are present that have endings that could be more than one case.

Up to now, the case ending *-a* has indicated a 1st declension nominative singular, e.g., **puella**, but now you can see that if the noun is neuter the ending *-a* could indicate either nominative or accusative plural, e.g., **bacula** or **onera**.

Up to now, the ending *-um* has indicated either a 2nd declension accusative singular of a masculine noun, e.g., **puerum**, or a 3rd declension genitive plural, e.g., **mātrum**, but now you can see that if a noun is 2nd declension and neuter the ending *-um* could indicate either a nominative or accusative singular, e.g., **baculum**.

Note also that the nominative and accusative singular forms of some 3rd declension neuter nouns end with the letters *-us*, e.g., **onus**. You need to know that this is a 3rd declension neuter noun rather than a 2nd declension masculine noun such as **servus**. The word **servus** could only be nominative, while **onus** could be either nominative or accusative.

Now that neuter nouns have been introduced, it is particularly important to note the gender and declension of a noun when you learn vocabulary.

EXERCISE 15b

Read each sentence aloud. Identify each neuter noun and its declension. How can you tell the case of each noun ending in *-a* or *-um*? Translate each sentence:

1. Nūllum vehiculum cōnspicere poterant puerī.
2. Prīnceps magnās vōcēs senātōrum audīre nōlēbat.
3. Nox erat; raeda in fossā immōbilis manēbat; nēmō auxilium ferēbat.
4. Canis lātrābat quod murmur rotārum audiēbat.
5. Sorōrem clāmōrēs frātrum vexābant.
6. Magna onera ferēbant plaustra.
7. Erant multa vehicula in viā; cisium tarda vehicula praeterībat.
8. Magnum onus fert plaustrum.
9. Necesse erat iter Rōmam facere.
10. Servī vēstīgia canum in agrīs inveniunt.
11. Ubi cisium praeterit, est magnum perīculum.
12. Magnum onus nōn fert raeda.

Roman Numerals and Latin Numbers

I	**ūnus, -a, -um,** *one*	VIII **octō,** *eight*
II	**duo, -ae, -o,** *two*	IX **novem,** *nine*
III	**trēs, trēs, tria,** *three*	X **decem,** *ten*
IV	**quattuor,** *four*	L **quīnquāgintā,** *fifty*
V	**quīnque,** *five*	C **centum,** *a hundred*
VI	**sex,** *six*	D **quīngentī, -ae, -a,** *five hundred*
VII	**septem,** *seven*	M **mīlle,** *a thousand*

The words above are adjectives. The masculine, feminine, and neuter endings or forms are given for the numbers one, two, three, and five hundred. The others never change their form. Here are forms for **ūnus, duo,** and **trēs:**

Case	Masc.	Fem.	Neut.	Masc.	Fem.	Neut.	Masc.	Fem.	Neut.
Nom.	ūnus	ūna	ūnum	dúo	dúae	dúo	trēs	trēs	tría
Gen.	ūníus	ūníus	ūníus	duórum	duárum	duórum	tríum	tríum	tríum
Dat.	ūnī	ūnī	ūnī	duóbus	duábus	duóbus	tríbus	tríbus	tríbus
Acc.	ūnum	ūnam	ūnum	dúōs	dúās	dúo	trēs	trēs	tría
Abl.	ūnō	ūnā	ūnō	duóbus	duábus	duóbus	tríbus	tríbus	tríbus

In the stories, you have met the following other adjectives that have *-īus* in the genitive singular and *-ī* in the dative singular: **alius, -a, -ud,** *another, other* (10); **alter, altera, alterum,** *second, one (of two), the other (of two), another;* (1); **nūllus, -a, -um,** *no, not any* (9); and **sōlus, -a, -um,** *alone* (3).

All roads to Rome radiated from the center of the city, a point marked by the Emperor Augustus with the *mīliārium aureum*, a gilded, inscribed bronze milestone. Shown here are peoples of the world who came to Rome, circling the *mīliārium aureum*.
Seventeenth-century European engraving, artist unknown

EXERCISE 15c

Answer the questions by supplying the Latin words for the appropriate numbers, read aloud, and translate:

1. Quot rotās raeda habet? _____ rotās raeda habet.
2. Quot rotās plaustrum habet? _____ rotās plaustrum habet.
3. Quot rotās cisium habet? _____ rotās cisium habet.
4. Quot equī raedam trahunt? _____ equī raedam trahunt.
5. Quot bovēs plaustrum trahunt? _____ bovēs plaustrum trahunt.
6. Quot līberōs in raedā vidēs? In raedā _____ puellam et _____ puerōs videō.
7. Quot parentēs in raedā vidēs? _____ parentēs in raedā videō.
8. Quot līberī cum quot parentibus Rōmam raedā iter faciēbant?
   _____ puella et _____ puerī cum _____ parentibus Rōmam raedā iter faciēbant.

   Quot...? *How many...?*

EXERCISE 15d

Respondē Latīnē:

1. Sī duo puerī et octō puellae iter faciunt, quot līberī iter faciunt?
2. Sī duae puellae et trēs puerī iter faciunt, quot līberī iter faciunt?
3. Sī sex parentēs et trēs puellae iter faciunt, quot hominēs iter faciunt?
4. Sī quīnque parentēs et trēs puerī iter faciunt, quot hominēs iter faciunt?
5. Sī quattuor puerī et sex puellae iter faciunt, quot līberī iter faciunt?
6. Sī quattuor puellae et quīnque puerī iter faciunt, quot līberī iter faciunt?
7. Sī quattuor puellae et trēs puerī iter faciunt, quot līberī iter faciunt?

   hominēs, hominum, m. pl., *people*

WHY IS SEXTUS A PEST?

Iam nōna hōra erat. Adhūc immōbilis in fossā haerēbat raeda. Sed nihil facere
Sextum taedēbat, nam puer strēnuus erat. Subitō igitur ad raedam currit et cistam
aperit. Tum ē cistā pilam extrahit.

"Vīsne pilā lūdere, Mārce?" clāmat. Pilam ad Mārcum statim iacit. Mārcus eam
excipit et ad Sextum mittit. Identidem puerī pilam iaciēbant, alter ad alterum. Tum   5
Sextus, quī semper Cornēliam vexāre vult, per iocum pilam iacit et Cornēliam ferit.

Statim īrāta Cornēlia ad mātrem sē vertit et, "Cūr mē semper vexat Sextus, māter?"
clāmat. "Cūr pilam in mē iacit? Quam molestus puer est Sextus!"

"Venī ad mē, cārissima," respondet māter et fīliam complexū tenet. "Sextus tē ferīre
in animō nōn habēbat. Est puer strēnuus, est puer temerārius, nōn tamen est puer   10
scelestus."

"Sed cūr Sextus apud nōs habitat?" rogat Cornēlia, quae adhūc īrāta est. "Cūr pater
Sextī eum ad nōs mittit?"

(continued)

1 nōnus, *ninth*	**alter…alterum,** *the one…the other*
2 Sextum taedēbat, *it bored Sextus*	6 **iocus, -ī,** m., *joke, prank*
3 **aperiō, aperīre,** *to open*	per iocum, *as a prank*
pila, -ae, f., *ball*	**feriō, ferīre,** *to hit, strike*
4 Vīsne…? *Do you want…?*	7 **vertō, vertere,** *to turn*
lūdō, lūdere, *to play*	9 cārissima, *dearest*
pilā lūdere, *to play ball*	10 **animus, -ī,** m., *mind*
eam, *her, it*	**in animō habēre,** *to intend*
5 **excipiō, excipere,** *to welcome, receive,*	12 **apud,** prep. + acc., *at the house of, with*
catch	

EXERCISE 16a

Respondē Latīnē:

1. Cūr nihil facere Sextum
   taedēbat?
2. Quid facit Sextus?
3. Quid faciēbant puerī?

4. Cūr est Cornēlia īrāta?
5. Habēbatne Sextus in animō
   Cornēliam ferīre?
6. Quālis puer est Sextus?

Go Online
PHSchool.com
Web Code: jfd-0016

"Pater Sextī ad Asiam iter facit. Quod pater abest, necesse erat Sextum in Italiā relinquere. Itaque, quod pater Sextī hospes patris tuī est, Sextus apud nōs manet." 15

"Quid tamen dē mātre Sextī?" rogat fīlia. "Cūr illa fīlium nōn cūrat?"

"Ēheu!" respondet Aurēlia. "Māter Sextī, ut scīs, iam mortua est. Mātrem nōn habet Sextus." Tacēbat Cornēlia, nōn iam īrā commōta.

Eō ipsō tempore tamen Sextus, "Vīsne nōbīscum lūdere, Cornēlia?" exclāmat. "Quamquam tū es puella, pilam iacere fortasse potes." Dum clāmābat, iam rīdēbat et 20 effugiēbat. Iterum īrāta Cornēlia, "Abī, moleste puer!" clāmat. "Pilā lūdere nōlō."

15 **relinquō, relinquere,** *to leave behind*
   itaque, adv., *and so, therefore*
   hospes, hospitis, m./f., *host, guest, friend*
16 **dē,** prep. + abl., *down from, concerning, about*

   illa, *she*
17 **ut,** conj., *as*
   sciō, scīre, *to know*
   mortuus, -a, -um, *dead*
19 nōbīscum = cum nōbīs, *with us*

Respondē Latīnē:

7. Cūr Sextus cum Cornēliīs habitat?
8. Cūr māter Sextī fīlium nōn cūrat?
9. Vultne Cornēlia pilā lūdere?

BUILDING THE MEANING

Nouns and Adjectives: Agreement I

In Chapter 6, you learned the general principle that an adjective always agrees with the noun it describes or modifies. Adjective agreement must be considered from three points of view:

1. The adjective must be the same *gender* as the noun it modifies:

   magn**us** canis   (masculine)
   magn**a** vōx   (feminine)
   magn**um** iter   (neuter)

2. The adjective must be the same *case* as the noun it modifies:

   magn**us** canis   (nominative)
   magn**ī** canis   (genitive)
   magn**um** canem   (accusative)
   magn**ō** cane   (ablative)

3. The adjective must be the same *number* (singular or plural) as the noun it modifies:

magn**us** canis	(singular)	magn**ī** canēs	(plural)
magn**a** vōx	(singular)	magn**ae** vōcēs	(plural)
magn**um** iter	(singular)	magn**a** itinera	(plural)

The fact that adjectives must agree with their nouns does *not* mean that the adjective and noun will always have identical endings, as the examples above show. Most of the adjectives you have met use the same endings as the 2nd declension masculine noun **servus** when they modify masculine nouns; they use the same endings as the 1st declension noun **puella** when they modify feminine nouns; and they use the same endings as the 2nd declension neuter noun **baculum** when they modify neuter nouns. For this reason they are referred to as *1st and 2nd declension adjectives*. Here is a complete chart of the 1st and 2nd declension adjective **magnus, magna, magnum.** Note the order of the columns in the chart: masculine (2nd), feminine (1st), neuter (2nd):

Number Case	1st and 2nd Declensions		
	Masc.	**Fem.**	**Neut.**
Singular			
Nominative	mágn**us**	mágn**a**	mágn**um**
Genitive	mágn**ī**	mágn**ae**	mágn**ī**
Dative	mágn**ō**	mágn**ae**	mágn**ō**
Accusative	mágn**um**	mágn**am**	mágn**um**
Ablative	mágn**ō**	mágn**ā**	mágn**ō**
Vocative	mágn**e**	mágn**a**	mágn**um**
Plural			
Nominative	mágn**ī**	mágn**ae**	mágn**a**
Genitive	magn**órum**	magn**árum**	magn**órum**
Dative	mágn**īs**	mágn**īs**	mágn**īs**
Accusative	mágn**ōs**	mágn**ās**	mágn**a**
Ablative	mágn**īs**	mágn**īs**	mágn**īs**
Vocative	mágn**ī**	mágn**ae**	mágn**a**

Look at the following example:

Cum senātōr**e** Rōmān**ō** iter facit.

In this sentence **Rōmānō** is masculine ablative singular in agreement with **senātōre.** The endings are different since the noun belongs to the 3rd declension, while the adjective uses 1st and 2nd declension endings (2nd declension for masculine, as here). Sometimes, of course, the endings may be the same, when the adjective and noun belong to the same declension:

Cum vir**ō** Rōmān**ō** iter facit. Cum fēmin**ā** Rōmān**ā** iter facit.

SUMMARY: Adjectives agree with the nouns they describe in *gender, case,* and *number.* The adjective and the noun it modifies may belong to different declensions and end with different letters.

In future vocabulary lists, 1st and 2nd declension adjectives will be given as follows: **magnus, -a, -um**, *big, great, large, loud (voice, laugh)*, showing the masculine nominative singular form and the endings of the feminine and neuter nominative singular forms.

EXERCISE 16b

For each noun below, first identify the declension of the noun, then tell what gender, case, and number it is, and finally give the proper form of the adjective **bonus, -a, -um** to modify the noun:

1. cubiculī
2. fīliārum
3. clāmōrem
4. vōcum
5. itinere
6. servīs
7. auxilium (3 possibilities)
8. puellam
9. nōminis
10. artem
11. patrēs (3 possibilities)
12. cīvis (6 possibilities)

EXERCISE 16c

Read each sentence aloud. Identify all noun-adjective pairs. Check your identification by noting the gender, case, and number of both items in each pair. Then translate:

1. Aliī servī equōs dominī in viam dūcēbant, aliī ē vīllā currēbant et magnās cistās in raedam pōnēbant.
2. Ubi Cornēlius multās epistulās scrībit, nēmō eum impedit.
3. Sī līberōrum magnae vōcēs patrem vexant, Aurēlia puerōs strēnuōs in hortum mittit.
4. Puellārum nōmina vocat ancilla nova; sed strēnuae puellae magnam vōcem ancillae nōn audiunt.
5. Plaustrum duās habet rotās; in plaustra onera magna rūsticī pōnunt; plaustra bovēs tardī per viās in magnam urbem nocte trahunt.
6. Magnum numerum servōrum Cornēlius in vīneā vīcīnā spectābat.
7. Cūnctī servī spectābant Getam, quī in rāmīs arboris dormiēbat.

   vocō, vocāre, *to call*   **novus, -a, -um,** *new*

EXERCISE 16d

Make the adjectives in parentheses agree with the nouns (if necessary, use the Latin to English vocabulary list at the end of the book to find the gender of the nouns):

1. aestātem (calidus)
2. nocte (frīgidus)
3. sorōribus (bonus)
4. urbis (magnus)
5. ars (novus)
6. nōminum (alius)
7. onera (magnus)
8. viātōrēs (tardus) (2 possibilities)
9. bovēs (tardus) (4 possibilities)
10. fragōris (magnus)

Word Study IV

Numbers

The Latin words for numbers provide English with a great many words. For example, the English word *unite* (to bring together as *one*) comes from the Latin number **ūnus**. The English word *duet* (music for *two* performers) is derived from **duo** in Latin, and *triple* (*three* fold) traces its ancestry to the Latin **trēs**.

EXERCISE 1

Match these English words with their meanings:

1. sextet
2. unique
3. decimate
4. quadrant
5. duplex
6. septuagenarians
7. octagon
8. triad
9. quintuplets
10. century

a. five babies born together
b. an eight-sided figure
c. one-of-a-kind, without equal
d. people in their seventies
e. to destroy one tenth of
f. a set of three
g. one fourth of a circle
h. a period of 100 years
i. a group of six
j. a two-family house or an apartment on two levels

The Roman Number System

The origin of Roman numerals from one to ten is in the human hand. The Roman numeral I is one finger held up; the numeral II is two fingers, and so on. The numeral V comes from the v-shape between the thumb and the other four fingers pressed together, and it therefore represents five. When two V's are placed with their points touching, the numeral X is formed, representing ten. A limited number of letters were used by the Romans to express numerals: I = 1, V = 5, X = 10, L = 50, C = 100, D = 500, and M = 1000. All Roman numerals are based on these.

The number system of the Romans may seem awkward compared with the Arabic system we use today. As Roman numerals grew larger, they became increasingly hard to read. Although no longer used in mathematics, Roman numerals are still part of our everyday experience: on the face of a clock, in the chapter headings of our books, and in writing the year of an important date.

Here are some rules to remember about Roman numerals:

1. A numeral followed by a smaller numeral represents addition: VI = 5 + 1 = 6.
2. A numeral followed by a larger numeral represents subtraction: IV = 5 - 1 = 4.
3. A smaller numeral between two larger numerals is subtracted from the second of the larger numerals: MCM = 1000 + (1000 - 100) = 1900.

Roman milestone of A.D. **217/218**
Trentino, Alto Adige

EXERCISE 2

Give the following in Arabic numerals:

1. XXI
2. DC
3. XL
4. LVII
5. XIX
6. XXXIV
7. LXXXVIII
8. MDLXXIII
9. MCMXLVI
10. MDCCCLXIV

EXERCISE 3

Give the following in Roman numerals:

1. your age
2. the year of our story, A.D. 80
3. the current year
4. the year Rome was founded, 753 B.C.
5. your age in 25 years time

EXERCISE 4

Find five examples of Roman numerals in use in your environment.

EXERCISE 5

In Chapter 19 you will read the Roman poet Horace's account of his journey from Rome to Brundisium. On page 125 is a map showing the route of his journey, along with his itinerary indicating the distances in Roman numerals. Convert each Roman numeral into its corresponding Arabic numeral, and give the Roman numeral for the total miles that Horace traveled.

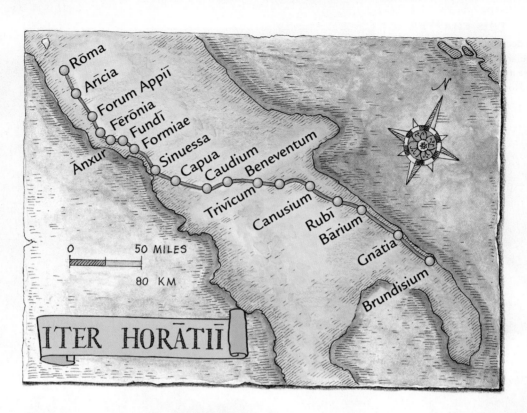

ITER HORĀTIĪ

	Stage of Journey	Distance
Day 1:	Rome to Aricia	XV miles
Day 2:	Aricia to Forum Appii	XXIII miles
Day 3:	Canal boat to Feronia	XV miles
	Feronia to Anxur	IV miles
	Anxur to Fundi	XIII miles
	Fundi to Formiae	XV miles
Day 4:	Formiae to Sinuessa	XXIV miles
Day 5:	Sinuessa to Capua	XXXV miles
	Capua to Caudium	XX miles
Day 6:	Caudium to Beneventum	XV miles
Day 7:	Beneventum to Trivicum	XXIII miles
Day 8:	By coach to unnamed town	XXVIII miles
Day 9:	To Canusium	XXX miles
	Canusium to Rubi	XXV miles
Day 10:	Rubi to Barium	XXIII miles
Day 11:	Barium to Gnatia	XXX miles
Day 12:	Gnatia to Brundisium	XXXVIII miles

DO WE STAY AT AN INN?

Erat ūndecima hōra. Raeda adhūc in fossā manēbat quod raedārius eam movēre nōn poterat. Aurēlia sollicita erat; Cornēlia lacrimābat; etiam puerī perīcula iam timēbant; Cornēlius in viā stābat sollicitus et caelum spectābat quod iam advesperāscēbat.

Tandem Eucleidēs, "Vidēsne illud aedificium, domine?" inquit.

"Videō," Cornēlius respondet. "Quid est?" 5

"Caupōna est. Vīsne igitur ibi pernoctāre, domine?"

Clāmat Aurēlia, "Ō mē miseram! Caupōnās nōn amō. Saepe ibi perīcula sunt magna. Fortasse caupō aliōs equōs habet. Fortasse equī caupōnis raedam ē fossā extrahere possunt. In caupōnā pernoctāre timeō."

"Cūr timēs, mea domina?" Eucleidēs rogat. "Nūllum est perīculum. Nōn omnēs 10 caupōnae sunt perīculōsae. Nōn omnēs caupōnēs sunt scelestī. Ille caupō est amīcus meus. Graecus est et vir bonus."

Tum Aurēlia, "Cornēlius est senātor Rōmānus. Senātōrēs Rōmānī in caupōnīs nōn pernoctant."

Cornēlius tamen, "Quid facere possumus?" inquit. "Hīc in Viā Appiā pernoctāre nōn 15 possumus. Nūlla vehicula iam appārent quod advesperāscit. Est nūllum auxilium. Illa caupōna nōn procul abest. Necesse est igitur ad caupōnam īre. Agite, puerī!"

Itaque, dum Eucleidēs Cornēliōs ad caupōnam dūcēbat, raedārius sōlus in viā manēbat; raedam et equōs custōdiēbat.

1 ūndecimus, -a, -um, *eleventh*	**pernoctō, pernoctāre,** *to spend the*
3 **caelum, -ī,** n., *sky*	*night*
advesperāscit, advesperāscere, *it*	8 **caupō, caupōnis,** m., *innkeeper*
gets dark	11 **perīculōsus, -a, -um,** *dangerous*
4 **aedificium, -ī,** n., *building*	12 Graecus, -a, -um, *Greek*
6 **caupōna, -ae,** f., *inn*	19 **custōdiō, custōdīre,** *to guard*

EXERCISE 17a

Respondē Latīnē:

1. Cūr raeda in fossā manēbat?
2. Cūr Cornēlius sollicitus erat?
3. Quid videt Eucleidēs?
4. Ubi pernoctāre possunt?
5. Cūr Aurēlia in caupōnā pernoctāre nōn vult?
6. Ubi Cornēliī pernoctāre nōn possunt?
7. Quis raedam et equōs custōdiēbat?

Go Online
PHSchool.com
Web Code: jfd-0017

Verbs: Regular Verbs (Review)

Most Latin verbs are regular and belong to one of four conjugations. Review the present and imperfect forms of such verbs, as given on page 271 of the Forms section at the end of this book. Practice by giving the present and imperfect and imperatives of the following verbs: **amō, amāre; iubeō, iubēre; currō, currere; faciō, facere;** and **dormiō, dormīre.**

Verbs: Irregular Verbs II

Some verbs are irregular, like **sum, esse** and its compounds (see page 108). Four other common irregular verbs, like **sum** and its compounds, do not belong to any one of the four conjugations: **volō, velle,** *to wish, want, be willing;* **nōlō** (= **nōn volō**), **nōlle,** *not to wish, not to want, to be unwilling;* **ferō, ferre,** *to bring, carry;* and **eō, īre,** *to go.* You will notice that these irregular verbs have the same personal endings as the regular verbs:

The Present Tense				
Infinitive	vélle	nōlle	férre	īre
Imperative	—	nōlī	fer	ī
	—	nōlīte	férte	īte
Singular 1	vólō	nōlō	férō	éō
2	vīs	nōn vīs	fers	īs
3	vult	nōn vult	fert	it
Plural 1	vólumus	nōlumus	férimus	īmus
2	vúltis	nōn vúltis	fértis	ītis
3	vólunt	nōlunt	férunt	éunt

The Imperfect Tense				
Singular 1	volébam	nōlébam	ferébam	ībam
2	volébās	nōlébās	ferébās	ībās
3	volébat	nōlébat	ferébat	ībat
Plural 1	volēbámus	nōlēbámus	ferēbámus	ībámus
2	volēbátis	nōlēbátis	ferēbátis	ībátis
3	volébant	nōlébant	ferébant	ībant

Be sure to learn these forms thoroughly.

EXERCISE 17b

Read aloud and translate:

1. In fossam dēscendere nōlō.
2. Plaustrum onus fert.
3. Cornēliī et Eucleidēs ad caupōnam eunt.
4. Syrus raedam ē fossā extrahere vult.
5. Cistās ad raedam ferimus.
6. Cum amīcīs Rōmam eō.

7. Aurēlia in caupōnā pernoctāre nōn vult.
8. Ī, fatue!
9. Servī cistās ferunt.
10. Ubi pernoctāre vīs, domine?
11. Nōlī in caupōnam īre, Cornēlia!
12. Fer aquam, serve!

EXERCISE 17c

Read each question aloud. Then give an answer in a complete sentence in Latin:

1. Ubi Sextus manēbat?
2. Unde Cornēliī veniunt?
3. Cūr Rōmam īre nōn poterant?
4. Quid fers, Dāve?
5. Quid faciēbātis, servī?
6. Erātisne diū in fossā?
7. Quō Cornēliī īre volunt?
8. Quid puellae in agrīs faciēbant?
9. Quid Dāvus servōs et ancillās facere iubēbat?
10. Poterāsne clāmāre?
11. Quō ītis, Cornēliī?
12. Quid ferēbās, Dāve?
13. Quid facitis, servī?
14. Quid in viā vidēs, Sexte?
15. Ubi haeret raeda?
16. Cūr in viā pernoctāre nōn vultis?
17. Quō ībant Cornēliī?
18. Cūr ad urbem īre Cornēlia nōn vult?
19. Unde veniēbās, Cornēlia?
20. Scelestusne sum?
21. Quō Syrus equōs dūcit?
22. Cūr equī īre nōn possunt?
23. Quid nōn procul aberat?
24. Cūr in caupōnā pernoctāre nōlēbātis?

EXERCISE 17d

Give the Latin for the following (use irregular verbs):

1. Carry the chests to the inn, slaves!
2. Marcus, why are you carrying Sextus's chest?
3. We do not wish to spend the night in an inn.
4. We were going to Rome.
5. Sextus wants to see the great Roman buildings.
6. Do you wish to see the buildings, Marcus?
7. We are going to Rome today.
8. The slow wagon is carrying a large load.
9. All the Roman senators are going to the city.
10. I am going to my country house.

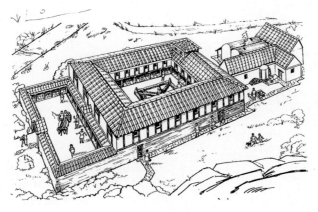

A Roman country inn

Bedroom (*cubiculum*) in the *villa rūstica* of P. Fannius Synistor at Boscoreale near Pompeii.
We use this villa at Boscoreale as a model for the villa of the Cornelii at Baiae.
Fresco, second style ca. 40–30 B.C.

Review III: Chapters 13–17

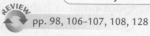
Web Code: jfd-0017

Exercise IIIa: Present and Imperfect of Regular and Irregular Verbs

pp. 98, 106–107, 108, 128

In each sentence below supply the appropriate form of each of the following verbs or verbal phrases, first in the present and then in the imperfect tense. Read aloud and translate each sentence you make:

cūrō	cōnspiciō	portāre volō
moveō	custōdiō	portāre nōlō
extrahō	portāre possum	ferō

1. Ego cistam _____.
2. Tū cistam _____.
3. Servus cistam _____.
4. Nōs cistam _____.
5. Vōs cistam _____.
6. Servī cistam _____.

In each sentence below, supply the appropriate form of the verb **eō** first in the present and then in the imperfect tense. Translate each sentence you make:

1. Ego Rōmam _____.
2. Tū Rōmam _____.
3. Cornēlius Rōmam _____.
4. Nōs Rōmam _____.
5. Vōs Rōmam _____.
6. Cornēliī Rōmam _____.

Exercise IIIb: Neuter Nouns

pp. 114–115

Change the nouns and adjectives in italics to plural, make any other necessary changes, read aloud, and translate:

1. Puerī in *cubiculō* dormiēbant.
2. Servus *onus magnum* portat.
3. Sextus *murmur* rōtārum in viā audiēbat.
4. Cornēliī nōn in *cisiō* iter faciēbant.
5. *Magnum perīculum* in viīs est.
6. Cornēlius servōs *baculō* verberābat.
7. Senātor ad urbem *iter* facit.
8. *Raeda* est *vehiculum Rōmānum*.
9. *Rūsticus* in *plaustrō* dormit.
10. *Rōta cisiī īnfirma* erat.

Exercise IIIc: Numbers

pp. 116, 123

Read the following sentences aloud, filling in the blanks as you go with Latin words for the appropriate numbers:

1. Quot fīliōs habet Cornēlius? Cornēlius _____ fīlium habet.
2. Quot fīliās habet Cornēlius? Cornēlius _____ fīliam habet.
3. Numerus līberōrum Cornēliī est _____.
4. Quot pedēs habet lupus? Lupus _____ pedēs habet.
5. Quot līberī ad urbem iter faciunt? _____ līberī ad urbem iter faciunt.

(continued)

6. Quot rotās habent raeda et cisium? Raeda et cisium _____ rotās habent.
7. Quot pedēs habent duo lupī? Duo lupī habent _____ pedēs.
8. Quot nōmina habet Cornēlius? Cornēlius _____ nōmina habet.
9. Quot nōmina habet Cornēlia? Cornēlia _____ nōmen habet.
10. Quot pedēs habent trēs puerī? Trēs puerī _____ pedēs habent.

Exercise IIId: Nouns and Cases p. 81

Select the correct word, read the sentence aloud, and translate it:

1. In agrīs errābant _____.   puerōs/puerī/puerōrum
2. Cornēlius multōs _____ habēbat.   canēs/servum/ancillās/amīcī
3. Quid facit _____?   Aurēliam/Aurēlia/Aurēliae
4. Rūsticī _____ baculīs excitant.   canis/bovēs/equus
5. Quam molesta est _____!   Sextus/puellae/Flāvia/Cornēliam
6. Sub arborum rāmīs dormit _____.   cīvēs/servus/rūsticōs
7. Canēs lātrantēs _____ timēbant.   puer/puerī/puella
8. In agrīs _____ sunt multae arborēs.   Cornēliī/vīllā/vīneam
9. Ancillae līberōrum _____ cūrābant.   tunica/tunicae/canis/cistās
10. _____ novās _____ induere   puella/puellae/tunica/tunicās
    volunt.

Exercise IIIe: Agreement of Adjectives and Nouns pp. 120–121

For each adjective below, select the noun or nouns that are in the correct gender, case, and number for the adjective to modify them. Explain your choices:

1. magna   nox, onera, fragore, rotā
2. magnīs   nocte, oneribus, servīs, fēminās, rotīs
3. magnae   dominī, rotae, onerī, vōcis
4. magnōs   vōcēs, fragōrēs, fīliōs, pedēs
5. magnum   onus, vōcum, baculum, cistam

Exercise IIIf: Adverbs pp. 100–101

Often nouns and adverbs have the same endings. Identify the adverbs in the following sets of words. Give the meaning of each adverb:

1. fortasse
   frātre
   saepe
   sorōre

2. fossā
   frūstrā
   intereā
   pictūrā
   praetereā

3. etiam
   iam
   iānuam

4. iānitōrem
   identidem
   tandem

5. iter
   iterum

6. deinde
   mātre
   nōmine

7. nōndum
   numerum

8. rāmō
   rārō
   silentiō
   subitō

Exercise IIIg: Adverbs from 1st and 2nd Declension Adjectives

pp. 100–101

Make adverbs from the following adjectives. Give the meanings of the adverbs:

1. temerārius, -a, -um
2. scelestus, -a, -um
3. praeclārus, -a, -um
4. perīculōsus, -a, -um
5. novus, -a, -um
6. strēnuus, -a, -um
7. miser, misera, miserum
8. tacitus, -a, -um
9. lentus, -a, -um
10. īrātus, -a, -um

Exercise IIIh: Reading Comprehension

Read the following passage and answer the questions with full sentences in Latin:

ONE HERO WINS A WAR

Ubi Tullus Hostilius, rēx tertius, Rōmānōs regēbat, pugnābant Rōmānī cum cīvibus Albae Longae, urbis quae nōn procul aberat. Pugnāre tamen volēbant neque Rōmānī neque Albānī, nam multī Rōmānī aut amīcōs aut propinquōs in urbe Albā Longā habēbant. Itaque Rōmānī cōnsilium capiunt et nūntiōs ad Albānōs mittunt.   5

Nūntiī, "Nōn necesse est," inquiunt, "cūnctīs Rōmānīs cum cūnctīs Albānīs pugnāre. Nōs inter mīlitēs nostrōs frātrēs habēmus trigeminōs, nōmine Horātiōs. Vōs quoque inter mīlitēs vestrōs frātrēs habētis trigeminōs, nōmine Cūriātiōs. Sī vultis, hī frātrēs cum illīs pugnābunt, et proeliī victōrēs victōriam bellī prō patriā suā reportābunt."   10

Hoc cōnsilium Albānōs dēlectat. Frātrēs in proelium festīnant. Ferōciter pugnant Horātiī Cūriātiīque. Ūnus ē Cūriātiīs vulnus accipit, tum alter, deinde tertius. Cūriātiī tamen duōs ē Horātiīs necant. Ūnus Horātius contrā trēs Cūriātiōs vulnerātōs stat, sōlus sed incolumis. Horātius tamen nōn timet sed cōnsilium capit.   15

Ex illō locō iam currit Horātius et ā Cūriātiīs effugit. Cūriātiī Horātium petunt sed, quod vulnerātī sunt, magnīs intervallīs currunt. Itaque, ubi ūnus Cūriātius frātrēs praeterit, Horātius sē vertit et eum necat. Iterum effugit Horātius; iterum sē vertit et ūnum ē Cūriātiīs necat. Hōc modō omnēs trēs Cūriātiōs necat Horātius ūnus. Victor est Horātius et victōriam bellī habent Rōmānī.   20

1 rēx, rēgis, m., *king*	victor, victōris, m., *conqueror, victor*
tertius, -a, -um, *third*	bellum, -ī, n., *war*
regō, regere, *to rule*	prō, prep. + abl., *for, on behalf of*
pugnō, pugnāre, *to fight*	patria, -ae, f., *nation, native land*
3 aut…aut, conj., *either…or*	10 reportābunt, *(they) will bring back*
propinquus, -ī, m., *relative*	11 dēlectō, dēlectāre, *to please*
4 cōnsilium, -ī, n., *plan*	12 -que, enclitic conj., *and*
cōnsilium capere, *to form a plan*	ē Cūriātiīs, *of the Curiatii*
6 cūnctīs Rōmānīs, *for all the Romans*	vulnus, vulneris, n., *wound*
7 inter, prep. + acc., *between, among*	accipiō, accipere, *to accept, receive*
mīles, mīlitis, m., *soldier*	13 necō, necāre, *to kill*
trigeminus, -a, -um, *triplet*	contrā, prep. + acc., *against*
8 vester, vestra, vestrum, *your*	14 vulnerātus, -a, -um, *wounded*
9 hī…illīs, *these…those*	17 magnīs intervallīs, *with big gaps*
pugnābunt, *(they) will fight*	*between them*
proelium, -ī, n., *fight, battle*	19 hōc modō, *in this way*

1. With whom were the Romans fighting?
2. Were the Romans and Albans eager to fight?
3. Why or why not?
4. What do the Romans do before joining battle?
5. Whom do the Romans have among their soldiers?
6. Whom do the Albans have?
7. How do the Horatii and Curiatii fight?
8. Who receive wounds?
9. Who kills whom?
10. What does the surviving Horatius do when he forms a plan?
11. Why do the Curiatii seek Horatius with big gaps between them?
12. What does Horatius do when one of the Curiatii runs ahead of another?
13. How many Curiatii does Horatius kill?
14. Who is the winner?

Exercise IIIi: Identification of Forms

In the passage on page 134, identify the following:

1. Five imperfect verb forms.
2. Four neuter nouns.
3. Four adverbs.
4. All examples of the Latin words for "one," "two," and "three."
5. Two prepositional phrases using the accusative case and two using the ablative case.

Tradition identifies this tomb as that of the legendary Horatii and Curiatii brothers.
Albano Laziale, Italy, first half of first century B.C.

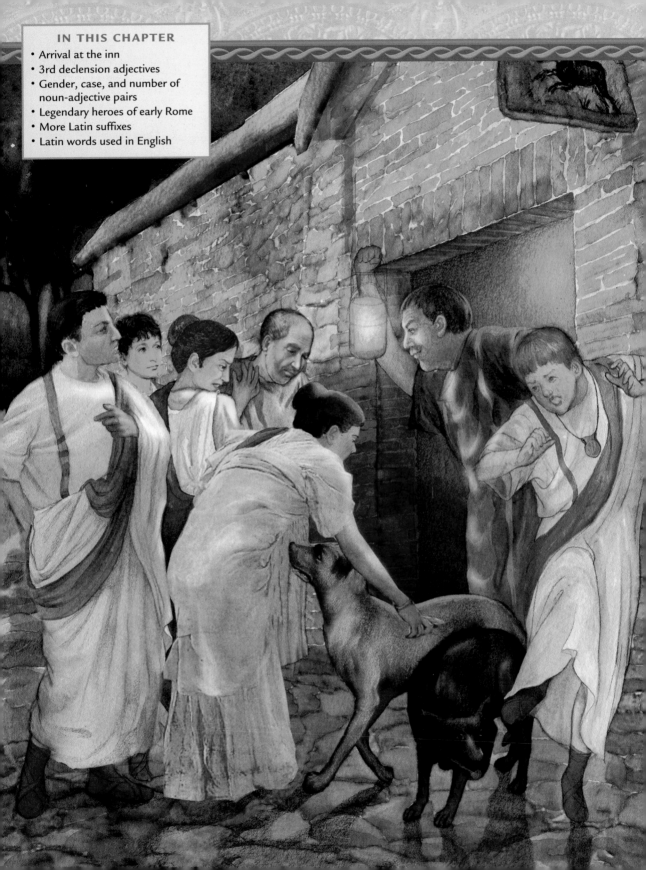

ARRIVAL AT THE INN

Raeda in fossā haerēbat. Cornēliī per viam ībant ad caupōnam, quae nōn procul aberat. Cornēlia, quae nōn iam lacrimābat, cum Eucleide ambulābat. Puerōs, quod praecurrēbant, identidem revocābat Cornēlius. Aurēlia, quamquam in caupōnā pernoctāre adhūc nōlēbat, lentē cum Cornēliō ībat.

Mox ad caupōnam appropinquābant. Nēminem vidēbant; vōcēs tamen hominum audiēbant. 5

Subitō duo canēs ē iānuā caupōnae sē praecipitant et ferōciter lātrantēs Cornēliōs petunt. Statim fugit Sextus. Stat immōbilis Mārcus. Aurēlia perterrita exclāmat. Cornēlius ipse nihil facit. Cornēlia tamen nōn fugit sed ad canēs manum extendit.

"Ecce, Mārce!" inquit. "Hī canēs lātrant modo. Nūllum est perīculum. Ecce, Sexte! 10 Caudās movent."

Eō ipsō tempore ad iānuam caupōnae appāruit homō obēsus, quī canēs revocāvit.

"Salvēte, hospitēs!" inquit. "In caupōnā meā pernoctāre vultis? Hīc multī cīvēs praeclārī pernoctāvērunt. Ōlim hīc pernoctāvit etiam lēgātus prīncipis."

"Salvē, mī Apollodōre!" interpellāvit Eucleidēs. "Quid agis?" 15

"Mehercule!" respondit caupō. "Nisi errō, meum amīcum Eucleidem agnōscō."

"Nōn errās," inquit Eucleidēs. "Laetus tē videō. Quod raeda dominī meī in fossā haeret immōbilis, necesse est hīc in caupōnā pernoctāre."

"Doleō," inquit caupō, "quod raeda est in fossā, sed gaudeō quod ad meam caupōnam nunc venītis. Intrāte, intrāte, omnēs!" 20

3 praecurrō, praecurrere, *to run ahead*
5 **homō, hominis,** m., *man*
7 sē praecipitant, (*they*) *hurl themselves, rush*
8 **fugiō, fugere,** *to flee*
9 **manum,** *hand*
10 hī canēs, *these dogs*
   modo, adv., *only*
11 cauda, -ae, f., *tail*
12 **appāruit,** (*he*) *appeared*
   obēsus, -a, -um, *fat*

revocāvit, (*he*) *called back*
14 **pernoctāvērunt,** (*they*) *have spent the night*
   ōlim, adv., *once (upon a time)*
   lēgātus, -ī, m., *envoy*
15 **Quid agis?** *How are you?*
16 Mehercule! interj., *By Hercules! Goodness me!*
   nisi errō, *unless I am mistaken*
   agnōscō, agnōscere, *to recognize*
19 doleō, dolēre, *to be sad*

Go Online
PHSchool.com
Web Code: jfd-0018

EXERCISE 18a Respondē Latīnē:

1. Quō ībant Cornēliī?
2. Volēbatne Aurēlia in caupōnā pernoctāre?
3. Quid canēs faciunt?
4. Quālis homō ad iānuam caupōnae appāruit?
5. Quālēs cīvēs in caupōnā pernoctāvērunt?
6. Cūr necesse est in caupōnā pernoctāre?

Adjectives: 1st/2nd Declension and 3rd Declension

You learned in Chapter 16 that some adjectives have endings like those of 1st and 2nd declension nouns. There are also other adjectives, which have 3rd declension endings, as shown in the right-hand column in the following chart:

Number Case	1st and 2nd Declensions			3rd Declension		
	Masc.	Fem.	Neut.	Masc.	Fem.	Neut.
Singular						
Nominative	mágn**us**	mágn**a**	mágn**um**	ómn**is**	ómn**is**	ómn**e**
Genitive	mágn**ī**	mágn**ae**	mágn**ī**	ómn**is**	ómn**is**	ómn**is**
Dative	mágn**ō**	mágn**ae**	mágn**ō**	ómn**ī**	ómn**ī**	ómn**ī**
Accusative	mágn**um**	mágn**am**	mágn**um**	ómn**em**	ómn**em**	ómn**e**
Ablative	mágn**ō**	mágn**ā**	mágn**ō**	ómn**ī**	ómn**ī**	ómn**ī**
Vocative	mágn**e**	mágn**a**	mágn**um**	ómn**is**	ómn**is**	ómn**e**
Plural						
Nominative	mágn**ī**	mágn**ae**	mágn**a**	ómn**ēs**	ómn**ēs**	ómn**ia**
Genitive	magn**órum**	magn**árum**	magn**órum**	ómn**ium**	ómn**ium**	ómn**ium**
Dative	mágn**īs**	mágn**īs**	mágn**īs**	ómn**ibus**	ómn**ibus**	ómn**ibus**
Accusative	mágn**ōs**	mágn**ās**	mágn**a**	ómn**ēs**	ómn**ēs**	ómn**ia**
Ablative	mágn**īs**	mágn**īs**	mágn**īs**	ómn**ibus**	ómn**ibus**	ómn**ibus**
Vocative	mágn**ī**	mágn**ae**	mágn**a**	ómn**ēs**	ómn**ēs**	ómn**ia**

Be sure to learn these forms thoroughly.

NOTES

1. Some 1st and 2nd declension adjectives end in *-er* in the masculine nominative singular, e.g., **miser**, and keep the **-e-** before the **-r** in all other forms. The feminine and neuter of this adjective are **misera** and **miserum**. Compare the 2nd declension noun **puer**, gen., **puerī**, which also keeps the **-e-** in all its forms.

   Some 1st and 2nd declension adjectives that end in *-er* in the masculine nominative singular drop the **-e-** in all other forms, e.g., **noster, nostra, nostrum**; gen., **nostrī, nostrae, nostrī**. Compare the 2nd declension noun **ager**, gen., **agrī**.

2. Most 3rd declension adjectives have identical forms in the masculine and feminine, as does **omnis** above.

3. The ablative singular of 3rd declension adjectives ends in *-ī* (not *-e*), and the genitive plural ends in *-ium*. The neuter nominative and accusative plurals end in *-ia*. Compare these endings with those of 3rd declension nouns that you learned in Chapters 11, 13, and 15.

4. You have met the following 3rd declension adjectives:

   brevis, -is, -e, *short*
   immōbilis, -is, -e, *motionless*
   incolumis, -is, -e, *unhurt, safe and sound*

   omnis, -is, -e, *all, the whole, every, each*
   Quālis, -is, -e…? *What sort of…?*

In future vocabulary lists, most 3rd declension adjectives will be given in this way, with the masculine nominative singular form spelled out in full and only the endings given for the feminine and neuter nominative singular forms.

BUILDING THE MEANING

Nouns and Adjectives: Agreement II

You learned in Chapter 16 that adjectives agree with the nouns they modify in gender, case, and number. Consider the following sentence:

> Multās vīllās, multōs agrōs, multās arborēs vident.

Since **vīllās** is a feminine noun in the accusative plural, **multās** has a feminine accusative plural ending. Similarly, **multōs** is masculine accusative plural agreeing with **agrōs**, and **multās** is feminine accusative plural agreeing with **arborēs**. An adjective will agree with the noun it describes in gender, case, and number.

You already know that 1st and 2nd declension adjectives may be used to modify nouns of any declension (see the example above). Third declension adjectives may also be used to describe nouns of any declension:

> Omnēs vīllās, omnēs agrōs, omnēs arborēs vident.

Note that the adjective **omnēs** has the same endings all three times in this sentence while two different forms, **multās** and **multōs**, are used in the sentence above. Why is this?

What Noun Does an Adjective Modify?
How Do You Decide?

Gender, Case, and Number

Identifying the gender, case, and number of an adjective will help you decide what noun it modifies.

EXERCISE 18b

Read each sentence aloud. What noun does each adjective modify?
Explain your decisions. Then translate:

1. Canis magnus ossa habet.   os, ossis, n., *bone*
2. Meus canis magna ossa habet.
3. Ossa multī canēs habent.
4. Canis magnum os habet.
5. Ossa magnus canis habet.
6. Dominus bonum canem habet.
7. Dominus obēsus canem habet.
8. Canem magnum dominus habet.

Position

In English, adjectives usually come immediately before the nouns they modify, e.g., "the good boy," "the good girls." The opposite is true in Latin; the more significant word comes first, and usually this is the noun and not the adjective:

Ad iānuam caupōnae appāruit **homō** <u>obēsus</u>. (18:12)

Numbers, adjectives meaning *this* and *that*, and adjectives expressing quantity, however, normally precede the nouns they modify:

duo canēs   hī canēs   multī cīvēs   omnēs cīvēs

The adjective **bonus, -a, -um** also often precedes the noun it modifies: **Māter bonās puellās laudat,** *The mother praises the good girls.* In Latin, an adjective may be placed before a noun for emphasis; observe how the adjective **meus, -a, -um** is placed sometimes before (for emphasis) and sometimes after the noun it modifies in the story at the beginning of this chapter (lines 13, 15, 16, 17, and 19). Examples of these rules for the placement of adjectives may be found in the sentences in Exercise 18b. Note that **magnus, -a, -um** may be placed before or after the noun it modifies.

An adjective may be separated from the noun it modifies. This often occurs in prepositional phrases, e.g., **magnīs in aedificiīs,** *in big buildings,* and **magnā cum cūrā,** *with great care.*

Sense

In the following sentence, both position and sense suggest that the adjective goes with the preceding rather than the following noun:

Puellam <u>ignāvam</u> epistulam scrībere iubēmus.
*We order the **lazy girl** to write a letter.*

EXERCISE 18c

Read each sentence aloud. Identify all 3rd declension adjectives. Tell what noun each modifies and what gender, case, and number each is. Then translate:

1. Omnēs viātōrēs ad caupōnās vesperī adveniēbant.
2. Apollodōrus est dominus omnium servōrum quī sunt in caupōnā.
3. In omnī urbe sunt magna aedificia.
4. Aurēlia nōn est fēmina fortis, nam in caupōnīs perīculōsīs pernoctāre nōn vult.
5. Omnēs līberī erant laetī quod Syrus, raedārius bonus, raedam celerrimē agēbat.
6. Cornēlia laudat Mārcum, puerum fortem, quī omnēs lupōs magnā in silvā repellit.
7. Puer fortis canēs nōn timet.
8. Canēs manum puellae fortis olfaciunt.
9. Sextus omnēs arborēs ascendere vult.
10. Brevia itinera laetī saepe facimus.

omnis, -is, -e, *all, every*
viātor, viātōris, m., *traveler*
vesperī, *in the evening*

fortis, -is, -e, *brave, strong*
laudō, -āre, *to praise*

LEGENDARY HEROES
OF EARLY ROME

Once Tarquinius Superbus had been expelled for tyranny in 509 B.C., the monarchy was replaced by a republican form of government, in which two consuls, elected annually, held equal power and ruled with the advice of the Senate. For the next 250 years, Rome's history was one of constant struggle and conflict, as she vied with other city-states for supremacy in Italy. The story of Rome's conquests is studded with patriots, whose actions reflect the character of early Rome and emphasize the virtue of **pietās**, firm loyalty and devotion to one's country, gods, and family. The stories of these patriots were told by the Roman historian Livy (1st century B.C.–1st century A.D.), on whom the following accounts are based.

Horatius at the Bridge

The king of Clusium in Etruria, Lars Porsenna, was goaded by Tarquinius Superbus into leading an army to attack Rome and restore the monarchy. As the Etruscans advanced to cross the Pons Sublicius, the access route into the city across the Tiber, they were thwarted by one man, Horatius Cocles. He instructed his fellow citizens to demolish the bridge behind him, promising to hold back the attack of the enemy as well as one man could. The sight of a single armed man standing at the entrance to the bridge astounded the Etruscan army. Two comrades helped Horatius stave off the first attack and then retired into the city over what still remained of the bridge. Horatius taunted the Etruscans and

The goddess Victory crowns Horatius Cocles as he defends the bridge. Father Tiber, with water jar, watches (*below*). Horatius Cocles Defending the Bridge, *oil on canvas, 1643, Charles LeBrun*

with his shield blocked the many spears they threw at him as they advanced. As the last of the bridge fell, the loud crash behind him and the cheers of the Romans inside the city stopped the advancing enemy in their tracks. "Father Tiber," prayed Horatius, "receive these weapons and this soldier in your kind waters!" and he jumped into the river and swam through a shower of spears to safety with his fellow citizens in the city.

Mucius Scaevola

Porsenna then decided to besiege the Romans into submission. Gaius Mucius, a young Roman noble, got permission from the senators to infiltrate the Etruscan camp and kill the king. Mucius happened to arrive at the camp on the soldiers' payday. As he mingled with the crowd, he noticed that two similarly dressed important people were talking with the troops from a raised platform. Since Mucius realized he could not ask someone in the crowd, "Which one is King Porsenna?" he made a guess, pulled his sword, and slew the king's scribe. Seized by the royal bodyguards and dragged before the king, he said, "I am a Roman citizen. They call me Mucius. As an enemy I wanted to kill my enemy, nor do I have less courage for death than for killing." When the furious king threatened to have Mucius burned alive, "Watch this," he said, "so you may know how cheap the body is to men who have their eye on great glory." With that, Mucius plunged his right hand into the fire on an altar and held it there. The king, astounded because Mucius showed no feeling of pain, jumped up and ordered his guards to pull him from the fire. "Go back," said Porsenna, "since you do more harm to yourself than to me." After informing the king that he was but one of a number of young Romans who had sworn to assassinate the king, Mucius returned to Rome, where he received rewards of honor and the cognomen Scaevola, "Lefty."

Cloelia

Frightened by the news that others like Mucius Scaevola would attempt to kill him, Porsenna offered to withdraw his troops in exchange for Roman hostages. Cloelia was one of the girls included among the hostages. Inspired by Mucius's act of heroism, when she realized that the Etruscan camp was near the Tiber, Cloelia led a group of girls to elude their guards, swim across the river through a shower of spears, and reach safety on the Roman side. Incensed, Porsenna demanded Cloelia's return, only to honor her by sending her home with other hostages of her choosing and calling her deed greater than those of Cocles and Mucius. After friendship had thus been restored and the treaty renewed, the Romans honored Cloelia by setting up in the Forum a statue of a girl seated on a horse.

Cincinnatus

Lucius Quinctius Cincinnatus was a model Roman citizen-farmer, a statesman idolized in legend for virtues other than being a fine patriot and military leader. In 458 B.C., the Aequi, a neighboring people with whom the Romans had been fighting for half a century,

History and myths of antiquity are full of legendary women, some of whom are pictured here.
Great Women of Antiquity, *pencil and watercolor, 1902, Frederick D. Wallenn*

had surrounded a Roman army and its commander, a consul, near Mt. Algidus in the Alban Hills southeast of Rome. Deeming the other consul not up to the challenge of rescuing the besieged army, the Senate decreed that Cincinnatus should be named dictator, a special office that in times of crisis permitted them to put the best qualified citizen in charge of the state for up to six months. The Senate's representatives found Cincinnatus at his four-acre farm across the Tiber, intent on his work of digging ditches and plowing. After an exchange of greetings, they asked him to put on his toga and hear the Senate's instructions. The startled Cincinnatus ordered his wife to run to their hut and fetch his toga. Once he had wiped off the dust and sweat and put on his toga, the senators hailed him as dictator, asked him to come to the city, and explained the dangerous circumstances of the army. The next day Cincinnatus ordered every citizen of military age to muster on the Campus Martius, armed, provided with five days' supply of food, and each carrying twelve poles to be used for building a palisade. With this army Cincinnatus marched from Rome and arrived at Mt. Algidus at midnight. In the darkness he deployed his troops in a circle, surrounding the enemy. On command, his army started shouting as they dug a trench and built a palisade that fenced the Aequi in between the two Roman armies. The enemy quickly surrendered. Within days Cincinnatus resigned his dictatorship and returned to his farm. Here, indeed, was a Roman driven by **pietās** rather than by hunger for wealth or power.

The Romans passed along legendary anecdotes such as these about their heroes from generation to generation as an inspiration to their children.

1. Explain how each of these heroes embodied **pietās**.
2. All Roman children learned these stories as part of their education. How do *you* react to heroes such as Horatius Cocles and Cloelia?
3. George Washington was referred to as a modern Cincinnatus. In what ways do you find this comparison appropriate or inappropriate?

Word Study V

Latin Suffixes -*(i)tūdō* and -*(i)tās*

Some Latin adjectives may form nouns by adding the suffix -*(i)tūdō* or the suffix -*(i)tās* to their bases. The base of a Latin adjective may be found by dropping the ending from the genitive singular, e.g., the base of **magnus** (genitive, **magnī**) is **magn-**. Nouns formed in this way are in the 3rd declension, they are feminine, and they convey the meaning of the adjective in noun form:

	Adjective			Base	Noun
Nom.	*Gen.*				
magnus	**magnī**	*big, great*		**magn-**	**magnitūdō, magnitūdinis,** f., *size, greatness*
obēsus	**obēsī**	*fat*		**obēs-**	**obēsitās, obēsitātis,** f., *fatness*

In English words derived from these nouns, -*(i)tūdō* becomes -*(i)tude* and -*(i)tās* becomes -*(i)ty*. The meaning of the English derivative is usually the same as that of the Latin noun, e.g., *magnitude* (size), *obesity* (fatness).

EXERCISE 1

Give the Latin nouns that may be formed from the bases of the adjectives below. In numbers 1–4, use the suffix -*(i)tūdō*, and in numbers 5–10, use the suffix -*(i)tās*. Give the English word derived from each noun formed, and give the meaning of the English word:

1. **sōlus, -a, -um**
2. **multus, -a, -um**
3. **longus, -a, -um**
4. **sollicitus, -a, -um**
5. **ūnus, -a, -um**
6. **brevis, -is, -e**
7. **īnfirmus, -a, -um**
8. **timidus, -a, -um**
9. **vīcīnus, -a, -um**
10. **hūmānus, -a, -um**

Manus manum lavat. *One hand washes the other.* (Petronius, *Satyricon* 45)
Errāre est hūmānum. *To err is human.* (Seneca)
Nōn omnia possumus omnēs. *We cannot all do everything.* (Vergil, *Eclogues* VIII.63)

Latin Suffixes *-īlis, -ālis, -ārius*

The suffixes *-īlis, -ālis,* and *-ārius* may be added to the bases of many Latin nouns to form adjectives. The base of a Latin noun may be found by dropping the ending from the genitive singular, e.g., the base of **vōx** (genitive, **vōcis**) is **vōc-.** Adjectives formed in this way mean *pertaining to* the meaning of the noun from which they are formed:

	Noun		Base	Adjective
Nom.	*Gen.*			
vir	**virī**	*man*	**vir-**	**virīlis, -is, -e,** *pertaining to a man or men, manly*
vōx	**vōcis**	*voice*	**vōc-**	**vōcālis, -is, -e,** *pertaining to the voice, vocal*
statua	**statuae**	*statue*	**statu-**	**statuārius, -a, -um,** *pertaining to statues*

Some adjectives ending in *-ārius* are used as nouns, e.g., **statuārius, -ī,** m., *sculptor.* Can you think of similar words made from the nouns **raeda, -ae,** f., *coach,* and **tabella, -ae,** f., *tablet, document*?

English words derived from these adjectives make the following changes in the suffixes:

> *-īlis* becomes *-il* or *-ile,* e.g., **virīlis,** *virile*
> *-ālis* becomes *-al,* e.g., **vōcālis,** *vocal*
> *-ārius* becomes *-ary,* e.g., **statuārius,** *statuary*

The meaning of the English derivative is similar to or the same as that of the Latin adjective, e.g., **virīlis** in Latin and *virile* in English both mean "manly." Sometimes the English word ending in *-ary* may be used as a noun, e.g., *statuary,* "a group or collection of statues," "sculptor," or "the art of sculpting."

EXERCISE 2

For each English word below, give the following:
  a. the Latin adjective from which it is derived
  b. the Latin noun from which the adjective is formed
  c. the meaning of the English word

You may need to consult a Latin and an English dictionary for this exercise.

auxiliary	principal
civil	puerile
literary	servile
nominal	temporal

Combining Suffixes

Some English words end with a combination of suffixes derived from Latin. For example, the English word *principality* (domain of a prince) is derived from the Latin **prīnceps, prīncipis**, m., base **prīncip-** > English *princip-* plus the suffixes *-al* (from Latin *-ālis*) and *-ity* (from Latin *-itās*).

EXERCISE 3

For each word below, give the related English noun ending in the suffix *-ity*. Give the meaning of the English word thus formed and give the Latin word from which it is derived:

civil	immobile
dual	partial
facile	servile
hospital	virile

English Replaced by Latin Derivatives

In the following exercise, the italicized English words are not derived from Latin. Note that these words are usually simpler and more familiar than the Latin derivatives that replace them. Latin can help with the meanings of many of these more difficult English words.

EXERCISE 4

Replace the italicized words with words of equivalent meaning chosen from the pool on the next page. Use the Latin words in parentheses to determine the meanings of the English words in the pool:

1. Staying at an inn was much too *risky* for Aurelia.
2. While he was away, Cornelius left the children in the *guardianship* of Eucleides.
3. Although the driver *handled* the reins skillfully, he was unable to avoid disaster.
4. It was *easy to see* that Eucleides was a friend of the innkeeper.
5. The *runaway* slave was captured and returned to the farm.
6. The innkeeper offered his *friendly welcome* to the Cornelii.
7. The heat made the slaves' work more *burdensome*.
8. The Via Appia is full of *traveling* merchants, who sell their wares from town to town.
9. Cornelia cast a *sorrowful* glance as she waved goodbye to Flavia.
10. This *country* inn was host to all the local farmers.

custody (**custōs**)	hospitality (**hospes**)
itinerant (**iter**)	fugitive (**fugere**)
apparent (**appārēre**)	perilous (**perīculum**)
doleful (**dolēre**)	onerous (**onus**)
manipulated (**manus**)	rustic (**rūsticus**)

Latin Words in English

Some Latin words are used in English in their Latin form. Many of these words have become so familiar in English that they are pluralized using English rules:

senator	plural: *senators*
area	plural: *areas*

Others retain their Latin plurals:

alumnus	plural: *alumni*
alumna	plural: *alumnae*
medium	plural: *media*

Sometimes both an English and a Latin plural are used:

index	plurals: *indexes, indices*
memorandum	plurals: *memorandums, memoranda*

Occasionally the use of two plurals reflects more than one meaning of the word. For example, the word *indexes* usually refers to reference listings in a book, whereas *indices* are signs or indicators, e.g., "the indices of economic recovery."

EXERCISE 5

Look up these nouns in both an English and a Latin dictionary. For each noun, report to the class on similarities or differences between the current meaning in English and the original meaning in Latin. Be sure to note carefully the English plurals and their pronunciation (one word does not have an English plural):

antenna	consensus	formula
appendix	crux	stadium
campus	focus	stimulus

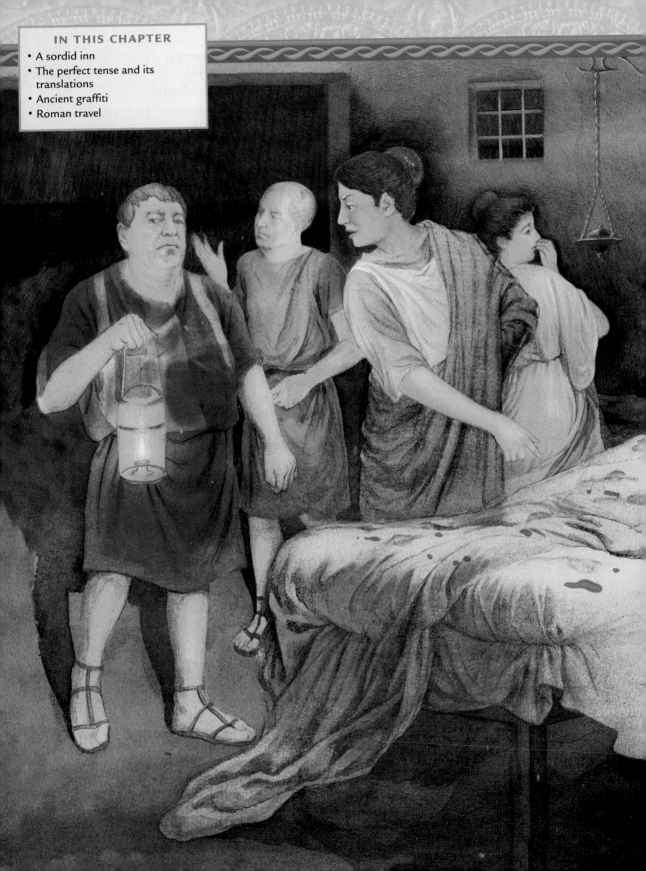

SETTLING IN

Cūnctī in caupōnam intrāvērunt.

    "Nōnne cēnāre vultis?" inquit caupō. "Servī meī bonam cēnam vōbīs statim parāre possunt."

    "Ego et Cornēlia hīc cēnāre nōn possumus," inquit Aurēlia. "Dūc nōs statim ad cubiculum nostrum." 5

    Servōs caupō statim iussit cēnam Cornēliō et Mārcō et Sextō parāre. Ipse Aurēliam et Cornēliam ad cubiculum dūxit. Aurēlia, ubi alterum duōrum lectōrum vīdit, gemuit.

    "Hic lectus est sordidus," inquit. "Neque ego neque Cornēlia mea in sordidō lectō dormīre potest. Necesse est alium lectum in cubiculum movēre."

    Caupō respondit, "Cūr mē reprehendis? Multī viātōrēs ad meam caupōnam venīre 10 solent. Nēmō meam caupōnam reprehendit."

    Iam advēnit Eucleidēs. Ubi Aurēlia rem explicāvit, Eucleidēs quoque caupōnem reprehendit.

    Caupō mussāvit, "Prope Viam Appiam caupōnam meliōrem invenīre nōn potestis. In caupōnā meā nūllī lectī sunt sordidī." 15

    Sed servōs iussit alium lectum petere. Brevī tempore servī alium lectum in cubiculum portāvērunt. Caupō iam cum rīsū clāmāvit, "Ecce, domina! Servī meī alium lectum tibi parāvērunt. Nōnne nunc cēnāre vultis?"

    "Ego nōn iam ēsuriō," inquit Cornēlia. "Volō tantum cubitum īre."

    "Ego quoque," inquit Aurēlia, "sum valdē dēfessa." 20

    Nōn cēnāvērunt Aurēlia et Cornēlia, sed cubitum statim iērunt. Aurēlia mox dormiēbat sed Cornēlia vigilābat.

1 **intrāvērunt,** *(they) entered*	**sordidus, -a, -um,** *dirty*
2 **cēnō, cēnāre,** *to dine, eat dinner*	12 **rem explicāre,** *to explain the situation*
cēna, -ae, f., *dinner*	14 **melior,** *better*
vōbīs, *for you* (pl.)	17 **tibi,** *for you* (sing.)
6 **iussit,** *(he) ordered*	19 **ēsuriō, ēsurīre,** *to be hungry*
Cornēliō, *for Cornelius*	**cubitum īre,** *to go to bed*
7 **dūxit,** *(he) led*	20 **valdē,** adv., *very, very much, exceedingly*
lectus, -ī, m., *bed*	21 **iērunt,** *they went*
8 **hic lectus,** *this bed*	22 **vigilō, vigilāre,** *to stay awake*

Web Code: jfd-0019

EXERCISE 19a Respondē Latīnē:

1. Quid servī caupōnis parāre possunt?
2. Vultne Aurēlia statim cēnāre?
3. Quid fēcit Aurēlia ubi lectum vīdit?
   Quid fēcit…? *What did…do?*
4. Quid servī in cubiculum portāvērunt?
5. Cūr Cornēlia cēnāre nōn vult?
6. Quid faciēbant Aurēlia et Cornēlia?

Verbs: Perfect Tense I

Compare the following pairs of sentences:

Caupō **mussat**.	*The innkeeper **mutters**.*
Caupō **mussāvit**.	*The innkeeper **muttered**.*

Dāvus servōs **iubet** canēs dūcere.	*Davus **orders** the slaves to lead the dogs.*
Caupō servōs **iussit** cēnam parāre.	*The innkeeper **ordered** the slaves to prepare dinner.*

Mārcus **gemit**.	*Marcus **groans**.*
Aurēlia **gemuit**.	*Aurelia **groaned**.*

Mārcus nūntium in vīllam **dūcit**.	*Marcus **leads** the messenger into the house.*
Cornēliam ad cubiculum **dūxit**.	*He **led** Cornelia to the bedroom.*

In each of the pairs of examples listed above, the verb in the first example is in the present tense, and the verb in the second example is in the *perfect tense*.

Meanings and translations of the perfect tense:

1. The perfect tense ("perfect" comes from Latin **perfectus**, *completed*) refers not to an action that *is happening* (present tense) or that *was happening* (imperfect tense; "imperfect" = "not completed"), but to an action that *happened* or to something that someone *did* in past time:

    Present:
    Caupō **mussat**.   *The innkeeper **mutters**.*

    Imperfect:
    Caupō **mussābat**.   *The innkeeper **was muttering/used to mutter**.*
    (imperfect = continuous or repeated action in past time)

    Perfect:
    Caupō **mussāvit**.   *The innkeeper **muttered**.*
    (perfect = a single action, completed in the past)

Note that in questions, emphatic statements, or denials we may use the helping verb "did" in translating a verb in the perfect tense:

Cēnāvitne Aurēlia?	*Did Aurelia **eat** dinner?*
Cēnāvit Aurēlia.	*Aurelia **did eat** dinner.*
Aurēlia nōn **cēnāvit.**	*Aurelia **did** not **eat** dinner.*

2. The perfect tense may also refer to an action that someone *has completed* as of present time:

| Servus meus alium lectum tibi **parāvit.** | *My slave **has prepared** another bed for you.* |
| Hīc multī cīvēs praeclārī **pernoctāvērunt.** | *Many famous citizens **have spent the night** here.* |

In the perfect tense, the ending of the 3rd person singular is *-it*; the ending of the 3rd person plural is *-ērunt.*

In many verbs, the stem for the perfect tense ends in **-v-** or **-s-** or **-u-** or **-x-**:

| mussāv- | iuss- | gemu- | dūx- |

The perfect endings are then added to the perfect stem:

| mussāv*it* | iuss*it* | gemu*it* | dūx*it* |
| mussāv*ērunt* | iuss*ērunt* | gemu*ērunt* | dūx*ērunt* |

The perfect stems of some verbs are recognized not by letters such as those given above but by a lengthened vowel:

| Iam Eucleidēs **advenit.** (present) | *Now Eucleides **arrives**.* |
| Iam Eucleidēs **advēnit.** (perfect) | *Now Eucleides **arrived**.* |

Note how **currō** forms its perfect stem; its perfect tense is **cucurrit**, and its perfect stem is **cucurr-**. This is called a *reduplicated stem.*

Sometimes there are no letters such as **-v-**, **-s-**, **-u-**, or **-x-** or any other marker for the perfect stem, and the perfect stem is the same as the present. Third conjugation verbs of this sort are spelled the same in the 3rd person singular in the present and the perfect tenses, and only the context can tell you the tense of the verb (find an example in lines 12–13 of the story).

EXERCISE 19b

Give the missing forms and meanings to complete the following table:

| Perfect Tense | | Perfect Stem Marker | Infinitive | Meaning |
Singular	Plural			
intrāvit	intrāvērunt	-v-	intrāre	to enter
_____	custōdīvērunt	_____	_____	_____
timuit	_____	_____	_____	_____
_____	cēnāvērunt	_____	_____	_____
	trāxērunt	_____	_____	_____
mīsit	_____	_____	_____	_____
spectāvit	_____	_____	_____	_____
doluit	_____	_____	_____	_____
_____	mānsērunt	_____	_____	_____
	voluērunt	_____	_____	_____
haesit	_____	_____	_____	_____

EXERCISE 19c

Read aloud, paying special attention to tenses of verbs. Then translate:

Cornēliī per viam ad caupōnam lentē ambulābant.

Sextus, "Nōnne ille tabellārius equōs vehementer incitāvit, Mārce?"

Cui respondit Mārcus, "Ita vērō! Eōs ferōciter verberāvit. Equī cisium celeriter trāxērunt. Raedārius noster, 'Cavē, sceleste!' magnā vōce exclāmāvit. Tum raedam dēvertēbat, sed frūstrā. Tabellārius tamen neque cisium dēvertit 5 neque raedam vītāvit. Itaque equī raedam in fossam trāxērunt. Gemuit raedārius; gemuērunt pater et māter; lacrimāvit Cornēlia."

"Pater tuus certē īrātus erat," interpellāvit Sextus. "Statim virgam arripuit et miserum raedārium verberābat. Cornēlia, ubi hoc vīdit, iterum lacrimāvit. 'Pater! Pater!' inquit. 'Nōlī miserum hominem verberāre!'" 10

"Tum pater," inquit Mārcus, "Cornēliam tacēre iussit. Omnēs sollicitī caelum spectāvērunt quod iam advesperāscēbat. Pater igitur Eucleidem nōs ad caupōnam dūcere iussit."

2 **vehementer**, adv., *very much,
    violently, hard*
3 cui, *to whom, to him, to her*

8 **certē**, adv., *certainly*
    arripuit, *he seized*
9 **hoc**, *this*

EXERCISE 19d

Locate all verbs in the perfect tense in the story above. Copy them onto a sheet of paper in six columns, each headed with one of the markers of the perfect stem ("-v-," "-s-," "-u-," "-x-," "lengthened vowel," and "no stem marker").

ADDITIONAL READING:
The Romans Speak for Themselves: Book I: "Stopping at an Inn," pages 53–58.

Go Online
PHSchool.com
Web Code: jfd–0019

GRAFFITI FROM ANCIENT INNS

Numerous graffiti were scratched or painted on the walls of inns and taverns in Pompeii, and many of them have been recovered by archaeologists while excavating this city that was destroyed by the eruption of Mount Vesuvius in A.D. 79. Some of the graffiti were written by the proprietors, others by the guests. They concern food, drink, conditions at the inn, and experiences of the guests. Sometimes they are prose, sometimes verse, and sometimes they are in dialogue form. Here is a sample:

I
Viātor, audī. Sī libet, intus venī:
tabula est aēna quae tē cūncta perdocet.
Traveler, listen. Come inside if you like:
there's a bronze tablet that gives you all the information.

II
Assibus hīc bibitur; dīpundium sī dederis, meliōra bibēs;
    quattus sī dederis, vīna Falerna bibēs.
A drink is had here for one as; *if you pay two, you'll drink better (wines);*
    if you pay four, you'll drink Falernian.

III
Tālia tē fallant utinam mendācia, caupō:
    tū vēndis aquam et bibis ipse merum.
I hope these deceptions get you into trouble, innkeeper:
    you sell water and drink the pure wine yourself.

IV
Mīximus in lectō. Fateor, peccāvimus, hospes.
    Sī dīcēs, "Quārē?" Nūlla matella fuit.
I wet the bed. I have sinned, I confess it, O host.
    If you ask why: there was no chamber-pot.

Write a graffito that one of our characters might write after a night at the inn.

Scene from an inn at Pompeii. Sausages and meat hang from the rack.

Go Online
PHSchool.com
Web Code: jfd-0019

ROMAN TRAVEL

Gaius Cornelius and his family traveled by land from Baiae to Rome along a section of the Via Appia, which ran south from Rome to Brundisium—a distance of 358 miles or 576 kilometers. It was part of a network of major highways that radiated from the Golden Milestone (**mīliārium aureum**) in the Forum at Rome to all parts of the Empire. These roads, originally built by the legions to make easy movement of troops possible, were laid on carefully made foundations with drainage channels at both sides and were usually paved with slabs of basalt. Although land travel was safer and easier than at any time before the "Railway Age," it was nevertheless extremely slow by modern standards. The **raeda** seldom averaged more than five miles or eight kilometers per hour; a man walking might manage twenty-five miles or forty kilometers a day; an imperial courier on urgent business might, with frequent changes of horse, manage to cover over 150 miles or 240 kilometers in twenty-four hours. Since carriage wheels had iron rims and vehicles lacked springs, a journey by road was bound to be uncomfortable. Some **raedae** were open or covered only with a canopy and would subject travelers to clouds of dust and attacks of insects. Others were enclosed with leather, cloth, or wood but could be uncomfortable in hot weather.

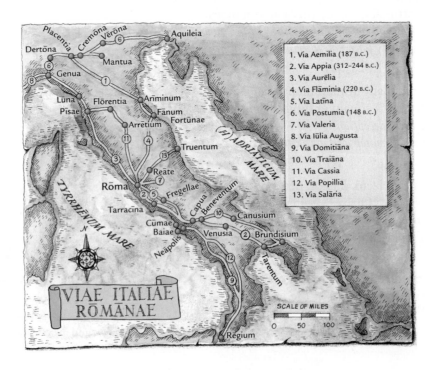

Map legend:

1. Via Aemilia (187 B.C.)
2. Via Appia (312–244 B.C.)
3. Via Aurēlia
4. Via Flāminia (220 B.C.)
5. Via Latīna
6. Via Postumia (148 B.C.)
7. Via Valeria
8. Via Iūlia Augusta
9. Via Domitiāna
10. Via Traiāna
11. Via Cassia
12. Via Popillia
13. Via Salāria

VIAE ITALIAE ROMANAE

SCALE OF MILES
0   50   100

Whether a journey was over land or water, the trip was filled with hazards and discomforts. The following passage illustrates some of these discomforts:

> When I had to make my way back from Baiae to Naples, to avoid the experience of sailing a second time, I easily convinced myself that a storm was raging. The whole road was so deep in mud that I might as well have gone by sea. That day I had to endure what athletes put up with as a matter of course: after being anointed with mud, we were dusted with sand in the Naples tunnel. Nothing could be longer than that prison-like corridor, nothing dimmer than those torches that do not dispel the darkness but merely make us more aware of it. But even if there were light there, it would be blacked out by the dust, which, however troublesome and disagreeable it may be in the open, is, as you can imagine, a thousand times worse in an enclosed space where there is no ventilation and the dust rises in one's face. These were the two entirely different discomforts that we suffered. On the same day and on the same road we struggled through both mud and dust.

Seneca, Moral Epistles LVII

Roman mosaic showing travel by boat on the Nile
Mosaic, Landscape crossed by the Nile, Palestrina, second to third century B.C.

Horace's Journey

The Roman poet Horace describes a journey that he took on the Appian Way from Rome to Brundisium in 38 or 37 B.C. He describes some of the hazards with which travelers might be faced:

After I had left great Rome, I put up in Aricia in a humble inn. My companion was Heliodorus, a teacher of rhetoric. From there we went to Forum Appii, a town packed with boatmen and grasping innkeepers. We were idle enough to take this part of the journey in two stages; for the more energetic it is only one; the Appian Way is less tiring for leisurely travelers. Here, because of the water, which is very bad, I suffered an upset stomach; and it was in a bad temper that I waited for my companions to finish their evening meal. As we were about to go on board, the boatmen began to argue. A whole hour went past while the fares were being collected and the mule harnessed. The vicious mosquitoes and marsh-frogs made sleep impossible, while the boatman, who had drunk too much cheap wine, sang of his absent girlfriend, and a passenger joined in the singing.

At last the weary passengers fell asleep, and the idle boatman turned the mule out to graze, fastened its halter to a stone, and lay on his back snoring.

At dawn we realized we weren't moving. A hot-tempered passenger leapt up and beat the boatman and the mule with a stick. When at last we disembarked, it was almost ten o'clock. With due reverence and ceremony we washed our hands and faces in the fountain of Feronia.

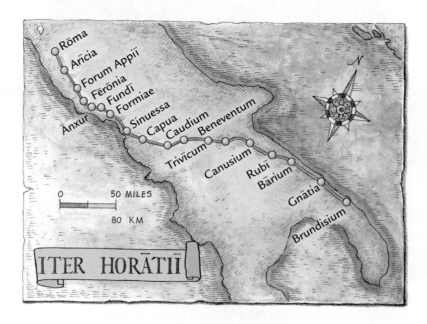

After lunch we "crawled" the three miles to Anxur, which is perched on rocks that shine white in the distance. There our very good friend Maecenas was due to meet us. As my eyes were giving me trouble, I smeared black ointment on them. Meanwhile, Maecenas arrived with that perfect gentleman, Fonteius Capito. We were glad to leave Fundi behind, with its self-appointed "praetor" Aufidius Luscus. How we laughed at the official get-up of the ambition-crazy clerk, his toga praetexta and the tunic with the broad stripe. At last, tired out, we stayed in the city of Formiae, where Murena provided accommodation and Capito a meal.

The next day we reached Sinuessa and were met by Varius, Plotius, and Vergil—friends to whom I was most attached. Then a small villa next to the Campanian bridge gave us shelter, and the official purveyors, as they were obliged to do, provided us with wood and salt. After we left here, our pack-mules were unsaddled early at Capua. Maecenas went to play ball, Vergil and I to sleep; for ball games are bad for a man with sore eyes and an upset stomach. After Capua, Cocceius received us in a house with ample provisions built above the inns of Caudium.

From here we made our way right on to Beneventum, where the overworked innkeeper nearly burned the place down while roasting lean thrushes on a spit. Soon after leaving Beneventum, I saw again the familiar mountains of my native Apulia. We would never have struggled over those mountains if we had not found lodgings at Trivicum. There the smoke made our eyes water, for they put green branches on the fire, leaves and all. There also I waited until midnight for a deceitful girl who never showed up. What a fool I was!

From here we sped on twenty-four miles in carriages, intending to lodge in a small town, the name of which I cannot fit into the rhythm of my verse. Here they charge for the cheapest of all commodities—water. The bread, however, is very good indeed, so that the experienced traveler usually takes some away in his bag; for the bread at Canusium is as hard as a stone, and the water supply is no better.

From here we arrived at Rubi, tired out—as was to be expected—for the stage was long and the road conditions difficult because of heavy rain. After this the weather was better, but the road worse as far as Barium, a fishing town. Then Gnatia provided us with laughter and amusement: the people tried to convince us that in the temple there frankincense melts without a flame. I don't believe it!

Brundisium is the end of my long account and of my long journey.

Horace, *Satires* I.5 (abridged)

1. Explain the origin of the saying "All roads lead to Rome" in light of the reading and the map on page 154. To what degree is the saying accurate?
2. What do you think Horace enjoyed the most on his journey? What the least?

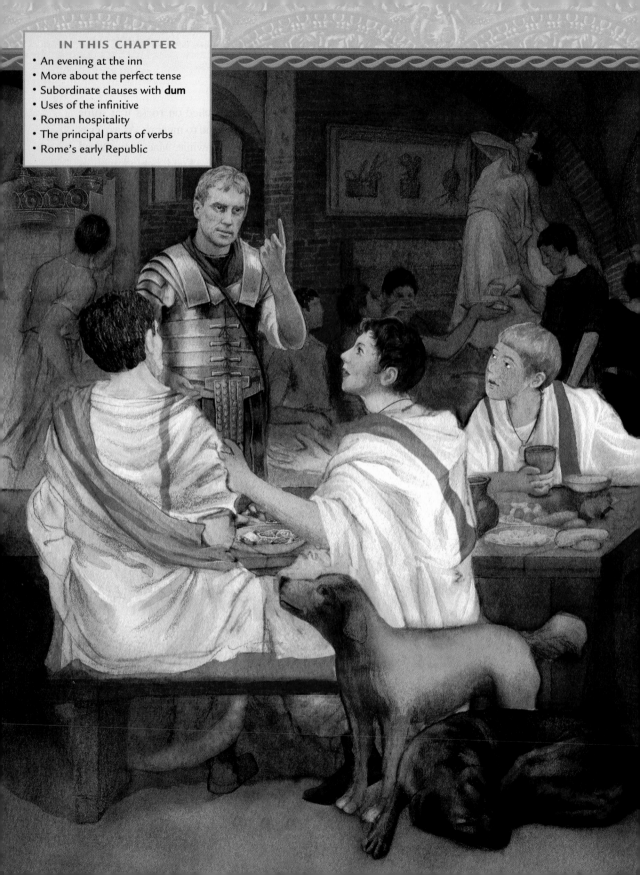

CHANCE ENCOUNTER

Ubi Cornēlia et māter cubitum iērunt, Mārcus et Sextus cum Cornēliō mānsērunt. Cum Cornēliō cēnāre et post cēnam ad mediam noctem vigilāre in animō habuērunt, nam omnia vidēre et omnia audīre voluērunt.

Mārcus, "Ēsuriō, pater," inquit. "Ēsurīsne tū quoque, Sexte?"

"Ita vērō!" respondit Sextus.   5

"Semper ēsurītis, tū et Mārcus!" exclāmāvit Cornēlius.

"Licetne nōbīs," inquit Mārcus, "hīc cēnāre?"

Paulisper tacēbat pater, sed tandem, "Estō!" inquit. "Tibi et Sextō licet hīc cēnāre. Post cēnam tamen necesse est statim cubitum īre."

Rīsērunt puerī quod laetī erant. "Gaudēmus, pater," inquit Mārcus, "quod nōs in   10 cubiculum nōn statim mīsistī. Voluimus enim hīc manēre et aliōs viātōrēs spectāre."

Tum Cornēlius caupōnem iussit cibum parāre. Brevī tempore servus cibum ad eōs portāvit. Dum puerī cibum dēvorant, subitō intrāvit mīles quīdam. Cornēlium attentē spectāvit. "Salvē, vir optime!" inquit. "Salvēte, puerī! Cūr vōs in hanc caupōnam intrā- vistis? Cūr nōn ad vīllam hospitis istis? Nōnne tū es senātor Rōmānus?"   15

(continued)

1 **mānsērunt,** *(they) stayed*	**enim,** conj., *for*
2 **post,** prep. + acc., *after*	13 Dum…dēvorant, *While…were*
medius, -a, -um, *mid-, middle of*	*devouring*
media nox, *midnight*	**mīles, mīlitis** m., *soldier*
7 **Licetne nōbīs…?** *Is it allowed for*	14 vir optime, *sir*
us…? May we…?	**optimus, -a, -um,** *best, very good*
8 **paulisper,** adv., *for a short time*	**in hanc caupōnam,** *into this inn*
Estō! *All right!*	15 Cūr nōn…istis? *Why didn't you go?*
11 **mīsistī,** *you have sent*	
voluimus, *we wanted*	

EXERCISE 20a

Respondē Latīnē:

1. Quid Mārcus et Sextus facere voluērunt?
2. Ēsuriuntne puerī?
3. Licetne Mārcō et Sextō in caupōnā cēnāre?
4. Cūr puerī laetī sunt?
5. Quis intrāvit dum puerī cibum dēvorant?

"Senātor Rōmānus sum," respondit Cornēlius. "Nōs in hanc caupōnam intrāvimus quod raeda nostra in fossā haeret immōbilis. In agrīs nocte manēre nōlēbāmus, sed numquam anteā in caupōnā pernoctāvimus. Certē in agrīs pernoctāre est perīculōsum."

Tum mīles, "Etiam in caupōnā pernoctāre saepe est perīculōsum."

"Cūr hoc nōbīs dīcis?" rogāvit Cornēlius. "Estne hic caupō homō scelestus? Dē   20
Apollodōrō quid audīvistī?"

"Dē Apollodōrō nihil audīvī, sed semper est perīculōsum in caupōnā pernoctāre. Vōsne audīvistis illam fābulam dē caupōne nārrātam? Ille caupō hospitem necāvit."

"Minimē!" inquit Cornēlius. "Illam fābulam nōn audīvī. Cūr igitur nōbīs illam nōn nārrās dum cēnāmus?"   25

18	**numquam**, adv., *never*		**nārrātus, -a, -um**, *told*
	anteā, adv., *before*		**necō, necāre**, *to kill*
20	**dīcō, dīcere**, *to say, tell*	25	**nārrō, nārrāre**, *to tell (a story)*
23	**fābula, -ae**, f., *story*		

Respondē Latīnē:

6. Cūr Cornēlius in agrīs pernoctāre nōlēbat?
7. Quid mīles dē Apollodōrō audīvit?
8. Quid fēcit caupō in fābulā?

FORMS

Go Online
PHSchool.com
Web Code: jfd-0020

Verbs: Perfect Tense II

You have now met all the endings of the perfect tense:

Singular	1	*-ī*	Plural	1	*-imus*
	2	*-istī*		2	*-istis*
	3	*-it*		3	*-ērunt*

These are the endings of the perfect tense of *all* Latin verbs, e.g.:

Singular	1	mī́s**ī**	Plural	1	mī́s**imus**
	2	mīs**ístī**		2	mīs**ístis**
	3	mī́s**it**		3	mīs**ḗrunt**

EXERCISE 20b

Read each incomplete sentence to yourself. Identify all subjects and use the chart above to supply the correct perfect tense endings for the verbs. Then read aloud and translate:

1. Ego līberōs in hortō petīv_____; tū eōs in silvā invēn_____.
2. Ubi tunica Sextī in rāmīs haerēbat, nōs omnēs rīs_____.

3. Quō iit Cornēlia? Ego et Mārcus patrem hoc rogāv_____, sed ille nihil respond_____.
4. Quamquam Sextus fuit molestus, servī eum nōn verberāv_____.
5. Ubi heri fu_____, Mārce et Cornēlia? Pater et māter nōs iuss_____ hīc manēre.
6. Postquam vōs cēnāv_____, cubitum īre volu_____.
7. Heri nōs in urbe erāmus, sed mātrem ibi nōn vīd_____.
8. "Unde vēn_____, amīcī?" rogāv_____ caupō. "Quō nunc ītis?"
9. Tūne Cornēlium vīd_____, ubi tū Rōmam advēn_____? Ego certē eum nōn vīd_____.
10. Ille, postquam haec audīv_____, ē caupōnā sē praecipitāv_____.

ille, *he*
fuit, *(he/she/it) was*
heri, adv., *yesterday*

postquam, conj., *after*
haec, *these things, this*

BUILDING THE MEANING

Go Online
PHSchool.com
Web Code: jfd-0020

Subordinate Clauses with the Conjunction *dum*

Look at the following sentences, in which subordinate clauses are introduced by the conjunction **dum**:

> **Dum** Cornēliī **cēnant**, mīles fābulam **nārrat.**
> *While/As long as the Cornelii eat dinner*, the soldier *tells* a story.

> **Dum** Cornēliī **cēnābant**, mīles fābulam **nārrābat.**
> *While/As long as the Cornelii were eating dinner*, the soldier *was telling* a story.

In the first sentence, the verb in each clause is in the present tense, and the sentence describes two actions that are taking place at the same time.

In the second sentence, the verb in each clause is in the imperfect tense, and the sentence describes two actions that were taking place over the same period of time in the past.

Now look at the following sentence:

> **Dum** puerī cibum **dēvorant**, subitō **intrāvit** mīles quīdam. (20:13)
> *While the boys were devouring their food*, a certain soldier suddenly *entered*.

Here the verb in the subordinate clause is in the present tense (**dēvorant**), and the verb of the main clause is in the perfect tense (**intrāvit**). The subordinate clause, introduced by **dum**, describes an action that was continuing over a period of time in the past when suddenly a single, simple action occurred, namely a soldier entered. Contrary to expectation, Latin uses the present tense and not the imperfect in subordinate clauses introduced by **dum** when the verb of the main clause is in the perfect tense. Translate as above: *While the boys were devouring their food. . . .*

Uses of the Infinitive (Consolidation)

You have met the following uses of the infinitive in your reading:

a. Complementary infinitive:

> Mārcus arborēs **ascendere** nōn vult.
> *Marcus does not want* **to climb** *trees.*

> Multī viātōrēs ad meam caupōnam **venīre** solent.
> *Many travelers are accustomed* **to come** *to my inn.*
> *Many travelers are in the habit of coming to my inn.*

In addition to **nōlle** and **solēre**, the verbs **parāre**, **posse**, **timēre**, and **velle** and the phrase **in animō habēre** are commonly accompanied by complementary infinitives.

b. Infinitive with impersonals:

> Nōbīs necesse est statim **discēdere**. (9:13–14)
> *It is necessary for us* **to leave** *immediately.*
> *We must leave immediately.*

> Vōbīs licet hīc **cēnāre**.
> *It is allowed for you* **to dine** *here.*
> *You may dine here.*

The verbal phrase **necesse est** and the verb **licet** are said to be *impersonal*, because we may supply a subject, *it*, and translate them with the impersonal phrases *it is necessary* and *it is allowed*. The infinitives, however, are actually the grammatical subjects, and we may translate very literally and rather awkwardly as follows:

> **To leave** *immediately is necessary for us.*
> **To dine** *here is allowed for you.*

c. Infinitive as subject of the verb **est**:

> Certē in agrīs **pernoctāre** est perīculōsum. (20:18)
> **To spend the night** *in the fields is certainly dangerous.*
> *It is certainly dangerous* **to spend the night** *in the fields.*

The infinitive is here being used as a *verbal noun*, and as such it is neuter in gender, hence the neuter complement **perīculōsum**.

d. Accusative and infinitive with verbs such as **docēre** and **iubēre**:

> Aurēlia **Cornēliam** docet vīllam **cūrāre**. (6:11)
> *Aurelia teaches* **Cornelia** *(how)* **to take care of** *the country house.*

> **Ancillam** iubet aliās tunicās et stolās et pallās in cistam **pōnere**. (10:2)
> *She orders* **a slave-woman to put** *other tunics and stolas and pallas into a chest.*

EXERCISE 20c

In the story at the beginning of this chapter, locate all infinitives and explain their uses.

EXERCISE 20d

Read aloud and translate. Explain uses of **dum** and of infinitives:

1. Cūr, Mārce et Sexte, ad mediam noctem vigilāre in animō habētis?
2. Omnia vidēre et audīre volumus quod numquam anteā in caupōnā pernoctāvimus.
3. Dum puerī in caupōnā erant, dormīre nōlēbant.
4. Cūr voluistī hīc pernoctāre, Mārce?
5. Cūr in caupōnā pernoctāvistis, puerī? Licetne fīliō senātōris in caupōnam intrāre?
6. Cornēlius servum in cubiculum īre iussit.
7. In viā pernoctāre perīculōsum est.
8. Dum Cornēlius et puerī cēnant, intrāvit mīles quīdam.
9. Vōbīs in caupōnā cēnāre licet.
10. Ego et tū cubitum īre nōluimus.

EXERCISE 20e

Using story 20 and the charts of forms showing perfect tense endings as guides, give the Latin for:

1. Cornelia: "I wanted to go to bed."
2. Boys: "We stayed with Cornelius."
3. Boys: "We intended to stay awake until midnight."
4. Cornelius: "Why did you laugh, boys?"
5. Soldier: "Why, sir, did you enter this inn?"
6. Cornelius: "I entered this inn because my carriage is stuck in a ditch."

Wine and other liquids, such as olive oil, were transported in large clay jars called *amphorae*, each capable of holding several gallons of liquid.

Go Online
PHSchool.com
Web Code: jfd-0020

ROMAN HOSPITALITY

Because inns were dirty and often dangerous, well-to-do Romans tried to avoid staying in them. Instead, they tried to plan their journeys so that they could stay at the **vīlla** of a **hospes**. This word means "host" or "guest," but it is also translated as "friend," although in this special sense it has no exact equivalent in English. It describes a relationship of friendship and trust between two men that could be continued by their descendants. As a result of such a relationship, a traveler could go to the house of his **hospes**—whom in some cases he personally might never have met—and claim **hospitium** for the night, producing, if need be, some token such as a coin that had been halved as proof of the link between the two men. The relationship could extend to other situations. For instance, if a Roman had business interests in one of the provinces, someone residing there might look after them for him. In return, he might have some service done for him in Rome. Cornelius, you may remember, is taking care of Sextus while his father is in Asia.

This open-air dining area of the so-called House of Neptune at Herculaneum is adorned with mosaic-covered niches for statues.
Open-air trīclīnium *of House of Neptune at Herculaneum, first century A.D.*

FORMS

Verbs: Principal Parts

A dictionary entry for a Latin verb normally gives the four principal parts, from which all forms of that verb may be derived. Since Chapter 10 you have been seeing the first two principal parts of verbs in vocabulary lists. All four principal parts of the verb **parō** are:

parō:	1st person singular, present tense = *I prepare, I am preparing, I do prepare*
parāre:	present infinitive = *to prepare, to be preparing*
parāvī:	1st person singular, perfect tense = *I prepared, I did prepare, I have prepared*
parātus, -a, -um:	perfect passive participle (verbal adjective) = *having been prepared, prepared, ready*

	Present	Infinitive	Perfect	Perfect Passive Participle	Meaning of the Verb
1st Conj.	párō	paráre	parávī	parátus	*to prepare*
2nd Conj.	hábeō	habére	hábuī	hábitus	*to have*
3rd Conj.	míttō	míttere	mísī	míssus	*to send*
-iō	iáciō	iácere	iḗcī	iáctus	*to throw*
4th Conj.	aúdiō	audíre	audívī	audítus	*to hear*

NOTES

1. The perfect stem is found by dropping the **-ī** from the end of the third principal part of the verb. The perfect endings are then added directly to this stem.

2. The fourth principal part of a Latin verb will usually be the *perfect passive participle*, which has the forms of a 1st and 2nd declension adjective. Sometimes perfect passive participles function as simple adjectives as in the following sentence from Chapter 10:

   Gāius ipse ascendere est **parātus**. (10:13)
   *Gaius himself is **ready** to climb [into the carriage].*

   Other examples are: **perterritus, -a, -um,** *frightened, terrified* (5:9); **commōtus, -a, -um,** *moved* (14:17); and **nārrātus, -a, -um,** *told* (20:23). You will study the perfect passive participle more fully later in the course.

3. Intransitive verbs do not have perfect passive participles, and the *future active participle* will be given as the fourth principal part instead:

   veniō, venīre, vēnī, ventūrus, *to come*

The future active participle **ventūrus** may be translated *being about to come* or simply *about to come*. You will study this form later.

4. The principal parts of most verbs of the 1st, 2nd, and 4th conjugations are predictable and follow the patterns on the previous page.

5. In future vocabulary lists, the principal parts of verbs of the 1st, 2nd, and 4th conjugations that follow the set patterns will appear as follows:

   parō, -āre, -āvī, -ātus, *to prepare*
   habeō, -ēre, -uī, -itus, *to have, hold*
   audiō, -īre, -īvī, -ītus, *to hear*

6. When verbs of the 1st, 2nd, and 4th conjugations do not follow the set patterns, their principal parts will be given in full, so that you can see how the stems change and note any irregularities:

   lavō, lavāre, lāvī, lautus, *to wash*

7. There is no set pattern for 3rd conjugation verbs. Their principal parts will be given in vocabulary lists in full:

   dūcō, dūcere, dūxī, ductus, *to lead*

8. The principal parts of irregular verbs will be given in full with the notation *irreg.*:

   sum, esse, fuī, futūrus, irreg., *to be*
   eō, īre, iī or **īvī, itūrus,** irreg., *to go*

9. The perfect tense of irregular verbs is formed by adding the perfect endings to the perfect stem in the same way as for all other verbs, e.g., **fuī, fuistī, fuit,** etc. Note, however, that in the perfect tense forms of the verb **īre**, formed from the stem **i-**, the double **i**'s become **ī** before **s**:

	Sing.	Pl.
1	íī	íimus
2	ístī	ístis
3	íit	iérunt

This verb also has forms from the stem **īv-**: īvī, īvistī, īvit, īvimus, īvistis, īvērunt.

10. It is very important that you learn the principal parts of Latin verbs.

To help you do this, the principal parts of new verbs that do not follow the set patterns or are irregular will be given in separate verb lists following the stories in which they first appear from this point on.

The principal parts of verbs that you have already met that do not follow the set patterns or are irregular will also be given in these separate verb lists following the stories in which they first reappear from this point on.

New verbs that follow the set patterns in the 1st, 2nd, and 4th conjugations will be given with their principal parts abbreviated in the regular vocabulary lists.

EXERCISE 20f

Read aloud and translate each verb form given at the left below. Then deduce and give the first three principal parts for each verb. Note that there are no 3rd conjugation **-iō** verbs in this list.

	1st Sing. Present	Present Infinitive	1st Sing. Perfect
necāmus, necāvimus intrant, intrāvērunt errās, errāvistī tenēs, tenuistī mittunt, mīsērunt manēmus, mānsimus iubet, iussit discēdimus, discessimus haeret, haesit dormiunt, dormīvērunt petunt, petīvērunt custōdīmus, custōdīvimus gemitis, gemuistis	necō	necāre	necāvī

Can you give the first three principal parts for the following?

estis, fuistis			

THE EARLY REPUBLIC

The Roman Republic grew steadily from 509 B.C., when the election of Lucius Junius Brutus and Lucius Tarquinius Collatinus as its first consuls signaled its birth, until 264 B.C., the start of the First Punic War. Rome expanded physically, until through military conquests she gained control of all of Italy south of the Rubicon River. Political growth came about through the adaptation of the constitution to meet the changing needs of society and circumstances. This constitution was not a formal, written document but a set of practices and policies. A major cause of change was the long, yet successful, struggle of the common people, the plebs, to acquire legal and political equality with the upper-class patricians.

The Consuls and the Magistrates

The two consuls, essentially co-presidents, were both heads of the civil government and generals of the Roman army. The election of two leaders to a one-year term of office was a consciously dramatic change from the installation of a single king for life, and it assured that no one person could have unlimited power.

As time went on, to assist the consuls in managing the affairs of state, other officers were named: praetors, who directed the judicial system; aediles, who supervised commerce and public works; tribunes, who championed the lower classes; and quaestors, who handled financial matters. These magistrates, like the consuls, were elected annually. To maintain the balance of power, two or more individuals generally bore the same title and either shared the same duties or performed matching roles in the government. As Rome grew and the Roman government had greater responsibilities to fulfill, the number of quaestors, aediles, and praetors was increased. Censors, moreover, were chosen every five years to revise the list of members of the Senate and carry out the census that assigned citizens to specific classes. In times of crisis, a dictator could be appointed to take over the government for a period of no more than six months, as did Cincinnatus. An ambitious Roman's political career might carry him up the steps of a series of offices, the **cursus honōrum**: election as quaestor, followed by appointment to the Senate, then terms as praetor, consul, and censor. After being quaestor, one might become an aedile before becoming a praetor.

The Centuriate assembly (**comitia centuriāta**) had its origin in the army, which was originally divided into centuries or groups of a hundred men. It passed laws, ratified treaties, issued declarations of war, and elected consuls, praetors, aediles, the censors, and the priests of the state religion. A citizen was assigned to his century or voting block in the Centuriate assembly according to his wealth, originally equalling the amount of military equipment he could afford. The cavalry or horsemen, **equitēs**, made up the eighteen richest of the 193 centuries. The next richest class made up eighty centuries of infantry or foot soldiers. At the bottom of the ranking were the citizens who owned no property, the proletariat, all heaped into one century. Each century cast a single vote, determined by the majority of the entire group, like the American electoral college. Since the ninety-eight votes of the two wealthiest classes could constitute the majority when the entire assembly voted, and since clients in the lower ranks usually voted according to the wishes of their richer patrons, it is easy to guess how the voting went.

The Tribal assembly (**comitia tribūta**), an outgrowth of the Council of Plebeians, issued plebiscites, which eventually were as binding as laws passed by the Centuriate assembly. It also elected aediles and the tribunes, who, with their power of veto, could intercede in the passage of laws and in practices that were unjust to the plebeians.

The Senate, an advisory council whose members were former magistrates, controlled finances and foreign policy. In practice, they were the major influence in the government, for the magistrates followed the senators' advice and matters were brought before the assemblies only after the Senate had voiced its approval.

A Roman triumphal procession
A Roman Triumph, *oil on canvas, ca. 1630, Peter Paul Rubens*

The Citizen Army

For Rome to survive its continual battles with her neighboring states, especially those in the hills, a larger citizen army was needed. The plebeian class provided that human resource, and once they had assumed the burden of military duty, they began to demand full equality as citizens. Military successes brought spoils of war and property grants and made the lower class more prosperous and ambitious. The wealthier plebeians especially were eager to attain equality with the patricians. By organizing a mass strike and refusing to perform their military service, the plebeians could force changes. Their leadership came from the tribunes, originally military officers, who gained acceptance as plebeian representatives before the Senate. As a first step, existing legal practices were codified and written down on bronze tablets. This first collection of Roman law, the Laws of the Twelve Tables, guaranteed every Roman citizen the right to justice. The Tribal assembly became an official body, with formal powers to pass plebiscites and elect aediles and tribunes. Then the right to hold office, including the consulship, allowed the plebeians to become senators. And once the plebiscites of the Tribal assembly came to be equal to laws passed by the Centuriate assembly, Rome achieved a fairly representative form of government, in which a senatorial aristocracy of patricians and wealthy plebeians formed the new ruling class of citizens.

The Conquest of Italy

The progress of the Roman military conquest of Italy is not a simple story, since the conquered did not always stay conquered. A new generation was likely to bring a new war with an old foe. The first victories came in the struggle to survive against the threats of neighbors: the Sabines, Aequi, and Volsci from the mountains inland; the Etruscans, pushing across the Tiber from the north; the Latins to the south. When the Gauls invaded Italy from the north in 390 B.C., going so far as to occupy all of Rome except the Capitoline Hill, the Romans, under the command of the legendary Camillus, led a unified Italian force that chased out the invaders, who were interested more in plunder than conquest. The Romans then revamped their military operations. A standing army was formed. The legions, now armed with spears and short swords, arranged in units or maniples that could maneuver quickly and attack in three waves, proved more effective than the old phalanx formation. The practice of establishing a camp with a fixed plan, even when the army was on the move over the growing network of Roman roads, provided a safety-measure of defense.

Following the military conquest of their neighbors and the Gallic invaders, the Romans faced new opponents. They confronted the Samnites and the Greek cities in southern Italy. When Pyrrhus, king of the Greek nation of Epirus, was invited to assist his fellow Greeks in repelling the Romans, he brought such novelties as elephants to Italy, but could win battles only at the expense of great losses to his manpower. After one of his famous Pyrrhic victories such as those at Heraclea in 280 B.C. and at Ausculum in 279 B.C., the king reckoned the human cost and made his legendary remark, "One more victory like this, and we shall be truly ruined." After Pyrrhus went home to Greece, Rome was left master of Italy. From the time of the Gallic invasion, moreover, Rome ceased to be simply a vengeful conqueror and adopted the policy of forming an alliance with each city she won. These allies gave Rome military allegiance and control of foreign policy, but they retained home rule in the governing of their own states. To many neighbors, too, Rome offered Roman citizenship. Elsewhere throughout Italy, she planted colonies that provided a Roman presence. Thus Rome became not simply a strong city-state, but the head of a confederacy of cities in Italy.

---

1. What groups of people have been totally omitted from this discussion, and why?
2. In what ways did the plebs gain greater power during this period?
3. What were the main offices of the **cursus honōrum**, and what do you learn about them in the reading?

MURDER

Mīles hanc fābulam nārrāvit:
"Duo amīcī, Aulus et Septimus, dum iter in Graeciā faciunt, ad urbem
Megaram vēnērunt. Aulus in caupōnā pernoctāvit, in vīllā hospitis Septimus.
Mediā nocte, dum Septimus dormit, Aulus in somnō eī appāruit et clāmāvit. 'Age,
Septime! Fer mihi auxilium! Caupō mē necāre parat.'   5

"Septimus, somniō perterritus, statim surrēxit et, postquam animum recuperāvit,
'Nihil malī,' inquit. 'Somnium modo fuit.'

"Deinde iterum obdormīvit. Iterum tamen in somnō Aulus suō amīcō appāruit;
iterum Septimō clāmāvit, 'Ubi ego auxilium petīvī, tū nōn vēnistī. Nēmō mē adiuvāre
nunc potest. Caupō enim mē necāvit. Postquam hoc fēcit, corpus meum in plaustrō   10
posuit et stercus suprā coniēcit. In animō habet plaustrum ex urbe crās movēre. Necesse
est igitur crās māne plaustrum petere et caupōnem pūnīre.'   (continued)

4 **somnus, -ī,** m., *sleep*
  eī, *to him*
	8 obdormiō, -īre, -īvī, -ītūrus, *to go to
	  sleep*

6 **somnium, -ī,** n., *dream*
  animum recuperāre, *to regain one's
  senses, wake up*
	10 **corpus, corporis,** n., *body*

7 nihil malī, *nothing of a bad thing, there
  is nothing wrong*
  malus, -a, -um, *bad*
	11 stercus, stercoris, n., *dung, manure*
	  suprā, adv., *above, on top*

	12 **māne,** adv., *early in the day, in the
	  morning*
	  pūniō, -īre, -īvī, -ītus, *to punish*

6 **surgō, surgere, surrēxī, surrēctūrus,** *to get up*, rise
7 **sum, esse, fuī, futūrus,** irreg., *to be*
9 **adiuvō, adiuvāre, adiūvī, adiūtus,** *to help*
11 **pōnō, pōnere, posuī, positus,** *to place, put*
   coniciō, conicere, coniēcī, coniectus, *to throw*

EXERCISE 21a

Respondē Latīnē:

1. Ubi est Megara?
2. Ubi pernoctāvit Aulus? Ubi erat amīcus Aulī?
3. Quandō Aulus Septimō appāruit?   **Quandō...?** *When...?*
4. Quid fēcit Septimus postquam animum recuperāvit?
5. Ubi caupō corpus Aulī posuit? Quid in animō habuit?

Go Online
PHSchool.com
Web Code: jfd-0021

"Iterum surrēxit Septimus. Prīmā lūce ad caupōnam iit et plaustrum petīvit. Ubi plaustrum invēnit, stercus remōvit et corpus extrāxit. Septimus, ubi amīcum mortuum vīdit, lacrimāvit. Caupō scelestus quoque lacrimāvit, nam innocentiam simulābat. 15 Septimus tamen caupōnem statim accūsāvit. Mox cīvēs eum pūnīvērunt."

Postquam mīles fābulam fīnīvit, silentium fuit. Subitō Cornēlius exclāmāvit, "Agite, puerī! Nōnne vōs iussī post cēnam cubitum īre? Cūr ad cubiculum nōn īstis?"

Sed Sextus, "Nōs quoque fābulam mīlitis audīre voluimus. Nōn dēfessī sumus. Nōn 20 sērō est."

Hoc tamen dīxit Sextus quod cubitum īre timēbat. Dum enim fābulam mīlitis audiēbat, caupōnem spectābat. Cōgitābat, "Quam scelestus ille caupō vidētur! Certē in animō habet mediā nocte mē necāre. Necesse est vigilāre."

Etiam Mārcus timēbat. Cōgitābat tamen, "Sī hic caupō est scelestus, gaudeō quod mīles in caupōnā pernoctat. Eucleidēs certē nōs adiuvāre nōn potest." 25

Invītī tandem puerī cubitum iērunt, vigilāre parātī. Mox tamen sēmisomnī fuērunt. Brevī tempore obdormīvit Mārcus.

13 **prīmus, -a, -um,** *first*	17	**fīniō, -īre, -īvī, -ītus,** *to finish*
lūx, lūcis, f., *light*	20	**sērō** adv., *late*
prīmā lūce, *at dawn*	22	**cōgitō, -āre, -āvī, -ātus,** *to think*
14 **mortuus, -a, -um,** *dead*		**vidētur,** *(he) seems*
15 **simulō, -āre, -āvī, -ātus,** *to pretend*	26	**invītus, -a, -um,** *unwilling*

13 **eō, īre, iī** or **īvī, itūrus,** irreg., *to go*
   petō, petere, petīvī, petītus, *to look for, seek, head for, aim at, attack*
14 **inveniō, invenīre, invēnī, inventus,** *to come upon, find*
   removeō, removēre, remōvī, remōtus, *to remove, move aside*
   extrahō, extrahere, extrāxī, extractus, *to drag out, take out*
15 **videō, vidēre, vīdī, vīsus,** *to see*
18 **iubeō, iubēre, iussī, iussus,** *to order, bid*
19 **volō, velle, voluī,** irreg., *to wish, want, be willing*
21 **dīcō, dīcere, dīxī, dictus,** *to say, tell*
25 **possum, posse, potuī,** irreg., *to be able; I can*

Respondē Latīnē:

6. Quid Septimus prīmā lūce fēcit?
7. Quandō lacrimāvit Septimus?
8. Cūr lacrimāvit caupō?
9. Quid cīvēs fēcērunt?
10. Quid Sextus facere timēbat?
11. Cūr Mārcus gaudet?
12. Quōmodo puerī cubitum iērunt?
13. Quid Mārcus et Sextus facere in animō habuērunt?

EXERCISE 21b

The following sentences contain errors of fact in the light of the last story you read. Explain these errors and give new Latin sentences that correct them:

1. Duo amīcī, Aulus et Septimus, urbem Rōmam intrāvērunt.
2. Aulus et Septimus frātrēs Mārcī erant.
3. Septimus mediā nocte surrēxit quod ēsuriēbat.
4. Aulus auxilium petīvit quod lectus sordidus erat.
5. Cīvēs, postquam Septimum necāvērunt, corpus sub stercore cēlāvērunt.
6. Caupō Septimum accūsāvit postquam cīvem mortuum invēnit.
7. Septimus cīvēs pūnīre in animō habuit quod scelestī erant.
8. Cīvēs corpus in caupōnā sub lectō invēnērunt.
9. Mārcus cubitum īre timēbat quod silentium erat.
10. Cornēlius caupōnem pūnīvit quod Mārcus eum accūsāvit.

Vēnī, vīdī, vīcī. *I came, I saw, I conquered.* (Julius Caesar, after the battle of Zela, 47 B.C.; reported in Suetonius, *Julius Caesar* XXXVII)

Nihil sub sōle novum. *There's nothing new under the sun.* (Vulgate, *Ecclesiastes* I.10)

Mēns sāna in corpore sānō. *A sound mind in a sound body.* (Juvenal X.356)

EXERCISE 21c

Using the lists of principal parts given in the vocabularies on pages 173 and 174, give the Latin for:

1. What did you want, boys?
2. They got up suddenly.
3. The boys went to bed at last.
4. Septimus looked for the wagon.
5. What have you seen, girls?
6. We went to the inn.
7. What did you say, Marcus?
8. We ordered Cornelia to go to sleep.
9. What have they found?
10. He placed the body in the wagon.

EXERCISE 21d

Read aloud and translate. Identify the tense of each verb:

1. Mārcus sub arbore sedēbat sed subitō surrēxit.
2. Iam advesperāscēbat et viātōrēs aedificia urbis cōnspexērunt.
3. Dāvus in hortō saepe labōrābat.
4. Servī cēnam parāvērunt et nunc cēnāre possumus.
5. Aurēlia in caupōnā pernoctāre nōluit.
6. "Ego," Cornēlius inquit, "in caupōnā numquam pernoctāvī."
7. Cornēlia manum ad canem identidem extendēbat.
8. Sextus ā cane fūgit.
9. Quamquam Mārcus dormiēbat, Sextus obdormīre nōn potuit.

    nōlō, nōlle, nōluī, irreg., *not to wish, not to want, to be unwilling*

EXERCISE 21e

Read aloud, paying special attention to tenses of verbs. Then translate:

SEXTUS CAN'T SLEEP

Sextus tamen nōn obdormīvit, nam dē mīlitis fābulā cōgitābat. Itaque diū vigilābat et dē Aulō mortuō cōgitābat. Tandem, "Mārce!" inquit. "Tūne timēbās ubi illam fābulam audīvistī?"

Sed Mārcus nihil respondit. Iterum, "Mārce!" inquit. "Tūne caupōnem spectābās?" Iterum silentium! Deinde Sextus, iam timidus, "Mārce! Mārce!" 5 inquit. "Cūr tū obdormīvistī? Cūr tū nōn vigilāvistī?"

Subitō sonitum in cubiculō audīvit Sextus. "Ō mē miserum! Audīvitne sonitum Aulus ille miser ubi caupō eum necāre parābat? Quālis sonitus fuit?"

Sonitum Sextus iterum audīvit. "Ō Eucleidēs!" inquit. "Cūr ad cubiculum nōndum vēnistī? Ō pater! Cūr mē in Italiā relīquistī? Voluistīne ita mē ad mortem 10 mittere? In Asiam ad tē īre volō. Ibi enim nūllum est perīculum, sed perīculōsum est hīc in Italiā habitāre."

Multa sē rogābat Sextus, nam, quamquam puer temerārius esse solēbat, nunc mediā nocte in cubiculō tremēbat.

Itaque Sextus, per tōtam noctem vigilāre parātus, diū ibi sedēbat. "Quōmodo 15
iam ē manibus caupōnis scelestī effugere possum? Suntne omnēs caupōnēs
scelestī? Fortasse caupō mē, fīlium cīvis praeclārī, necāre in animō habet.
Quamquam Aulus aurum habuit, ego nihil habeō, neque aurum neque pecūniam."
     Ita cōgitābat Sextus. Iterum sonitum audīvit. Timēbat sed tandem surrēxit
invītus, nam omnēs cubiculī partēs īnspicere volēbat. Mox tamen rīsit. Ecce! Sub 20
lectō erat fēlēs, obēsa et sēmisomna. Prope fēlem Sextus mūrem mortuum vīdit.
Mussāvit Sextus, "Nōn necesse est hoc corpus sub stercore cēlāre!"

7	**sonitum**, *sound*	15	**tōtus, -a, -um**, *all, the whole*
10	**ita**, adv., *thus, so, in this way*	18	**aurum, -ī**, n., *gold*
	ad mortem, *to my death*		**pecūnia, -ae**, f., *money*
	mors, mortis, gen. pl.,	21	**fēlēs, fēlis**, gen. pl., **fēlium**, f., *cat*
	mortium, f., *death*		**mūs, mūris**, m., *mouse*

 4 **respondeō, respondēre, respondī, respōnsūrus**, *to reply*
10 **relinquō, relinquere, relīquī, relictus**, *to leave behind*
14 **tremō, tremere, tremuī**, *to tremble*
15 **sedeō, sedēre, sēdī, sessūrus**, *to sit*
16 **effugiō, effugere, effūgī**, *to run away, escape*
20 **īnspiciō, īnspicere, īnspexī, īnspectus**, *to examine*
    rīdeō, rīdēre, rīsī, rīsus, *to laugh (at), smile*

EXERCISE 21f

In the first twelve lines of the passage on page 176, locate the following in
sequence:

1. All verbs in the present tense.
2. All verbs in the imperfect tense.
3. All verbs in the perfect tense.

ADDITIONAL READING:
The Romans Speak for Themselves: Book I: "Ghosts," pages 59–64.

Go Online
PHSchool.com
Web Code: jfd-0021

EAVESDROPPING

It was quite dark. Cornelia was still wide awake. All kinds of exciting sounds were floating up from the inn downstairs, inviting her to go down and have a look. She slipped out of bed, put a shawl around her shoulders, and tiptoed into the corridor where Eucleides was on guard.

"Take me downstairs, Eucleides," she wheedled. "I've never seen the inside of an inn before." This was quite true, because an upper-class Roman away from home preferred to stay in a friend's villa and avoided inns if possible.

Eucleides took a lot of persuading, but Cornelia could always get around him; he soon found himself downstairs, looking into the main room, with Cornelia peering from behind his arm.

It was pretty dark inside, despite the lamps. The atmosphere was thick with smoke and reeked of garlic. On the far side Cornelia could see her father; and nearer were other customers seated on stools at rough tables, and an evil-looking group they were.

"Stay away from them, Cornelia," whispered Eucleides. "Those rogues would murder their own mothers for a silver **dēnārius**."

But Eucleides needn't have worried because they were all absorbed in what was going on at the far end of the low room, where a girl was dancing. Above the hum of conversation her singing could be heard to the accompaniment of a rhythmic clacking noise she seemed to be making with her fingers. "Makes that noise with castanets," whispered Eucleides. "Dancing girl from Spain, probably Gades."

But one person was not paying much attention to the entertainment—the **tabellārius**, whose reckless driving had forced their **raeda** into the ditch. He had not come out of the incident unscathed. One of his horses had gone lame, and he was making the most of the enforced delay, drinking the innkeeper's best Falernian wine.

As Cornelia and Eucleides entered, the innkeeper was bringing forward a young man to introduce him to the courier. "This is Decimus Junius Juvenalis, sir, a soldier like yourself." The **tabellārius**, unbending slightly as a rather haggard young man came forward wearing the insignia of a junior officer, dismissed the innkeeper with a look and said pleasantly enough, "Greetings, young man! Where are you from?"

"I'm on my way back from service in Britain, sir. What a place! They don't have any climate there, just bad weather! Mist, rain, hail, snow—the lot! Hardly a blink of sunshine!"

"Let me see!" said the **tabellārius**. "Who's governor of Britain these days? A chap called Agricola, I hear."

"That's right!" replied Juvenalis. "A madman, if you ask me. He's not content with conquering the bit of Britain that's near Gaul, where you can get something profitable, like silver or wool or hides or those huge hunting dogs. Before I left, he had gone to the

From silver mined in places like Britain and Spain, the Romans fashioned beautiful pieces such as this cavalry officer's mask.

very edge of the world where the Caledonii live. They say that there, in the middle of winter, the sun doesn't shine at all! But I can't vouch for that myself!"

"I've been to Britain too," said the **tabellārius**, much interested. "I'm not an ordinary **tabellārius**, you know. I personally carry dispatches only if they are confidential messages from—"

And here he whispered something in Juvenalis's ear, which Cornelia could not catch.

The innkeeper sidled up again with some more wine.

"We get lots of interesting people stopping here on the Via Appia," he confided. "Not only military gentlemen like yourselves, or that scum of humanity there"—jerking his thumb toward the dancer's audience—"but special envoys to the Emperor himself. When Nero was Emperor, we had one of this new Jewish religious sect who lodged here on a journey all the way from Judaea, to be tried by the Emperor himself no less! He was called Paul or something—"

Suddenly Cornelia felt her ear seized between finger and thumb and looked around into the eyes of a very angry Aurelia. She found herself upstairs and back in bed before she knew what had happened.

Take parts, read aloud, and translate:

EARLY THE NEXT MORNING

Nōndum lūcēbat, sed Cornēlia, ut solēbat, iam surgēbat. Tunicam induit et tacitē ē cubiculō exiit, quod mātrem excitāre nōlēbat. Ē cubiculīs caupōnae nihil nisi silentium. Omnēs adhūc dormiēbant, sed Cornēlia audīre poterat vōcem ancillae quae iam in culīnā labōrābat. Cornēlia igitur ad culīnam appropinquāvit et fēminam cōnspexit. Dum Cornēlia spectat, fēmina cibum coquit et cantat. 5
Cornēlia intrat.
CORNĒLIA: Nōnne tū es fēmina quae saltat? Quid tibi nōmen est?
ANCILLA: Ita vērō! Saltātrīx sum. Mē appellant Ēlissam. Quis es tū?
CORNĒLIA: Ego sum Cornēlia. Quis tē saltāre docuit?
ANCILLA: (*cum rīsū*) Ubi in urbe Gādibus habitābam cum parentibus, māter mē 10
   cum crotalīs saltāre, cantāre, multa alia facere docuit.
CORNĒLIA: Sī tū saltātrīx es, cūr cibum coquis?
ANCILLA: Quamquam sum saltātrīx, ancilla tamen sum.
CORNĒLIA: Tū ancilla es? Quōmodo ad Italiam vēnistī?
ANCILLA: Pīrātae mē in Hispāniā cēpērunt et ad Italiam tulērunt. Apollōdorus 15
   mē in urbe Rōmā ēmit.
CORNĒLIA: Cūr nōn effugis et ad Hispāniam redīs?
ANCILLA: Quōmodo effugere possum? Nūllōs amīcōs in Italiā habeō et ad
   Hispāniam sōla redīre nōn possum. Praetereā Apollodōrus dominus bonus
   est quod ipse servus fuit. Mē numquam verberat et omnia dat quae volō. 20
CORNĒLIA: Praeter lībertātem.
ANCILLA: Ita vērō! Praeter lībertātem.

4 **culīna, -ae,** f., *kitchen*
5 cantō, -āre, -āvī, -ātus, *to sing*
7 saltō, -āre, -āvī, -ātūrus, *to dance*
8 saltātrīx, saltātrīcis, f., *dancer*
   appellō, -āre, -āvī, -ātus, *to call, name*
10 Gādēs, Gādium, f. pl., *Gades (Cadiz, a town in Spain)*
11 crotalum, -ī, n., *castanet*
15 pīrāta, -ae, m., *pirate*
21 **praeter,** prep. + acc., *except*
   lībertās, lībertātis, f., *freedom*

   5 **cōnspiciō, cōnspicere, cōnspexī, cōnspectus,**
      to catch sight of
  11 **doceō, docēre, docuī, doctus,** *to teach*
  15 **capiō, capere, cēpī, captus,** *to take, capture*
      ferō, ferre, tulī, lātus, irreg., *to bring, carry*
  16 **emō, emere, ēmī, ēmptus,** *to buy*
  20 **dō, dare, dedī, datus,** *to give*

The seven-stringed cithara is one of the forerunners of today's guitar.
Second style fresco, Villa of P. Fannius Synistor, Boscoreale, ca. 40–30 B.C.

Exercise IVa: Agreement of Adjectives and Nouns pp. 138–140

Complete the following sentences with 3rd declension adjectives to match the English cues. Make the adjective agree with the underlined noun. Read aloud and translate:

1. <u>Cornēliī</u> ē raedā dēscendērunt _____. (unhurt)
2. Pater <u>fīliam</u> _____ laudāvit. (brave)
3. <u>Puer</u> _____ lupum repellit. (brave)
4. In _____ <u>caupōnā</u> lectī sunt sordidī. (every)
5. Nōn _____ <u>caupōnēs</u> sunt scelestī. (all)
6. <u>Puella</u> _____ stat et manum ad canem extendit. (motionless)
7. Prīnceps _____ <u>senātōrēs</u> Rōmam redīre iussit. (all)
8. _____ <u>Cornēliī</u> Rōmam redeībant. (all)
9. Servī per agrōs cum <u>canibus</u> _____ currunt. (brave)
10. Cornēlia et Flāvia sunt <u>puellae</u> strēnuae et _____. (brave)

Review the present, imperfect, and perfect tenses of regular verbs and of the irregular verbs **esse, velle, nōlle,** and **īre** in the charts on pages 271–273 before doing exercises IVb–IVd.

Exercise IVb: Identification of Verb Forms;  pp. 150–151, 160, 165–167
Principal Parts

Identify the tense, person, and number of each of the following verb forms. Then give the principal parts of each verb:

	Tense	Person	Number
1. veniēbātis	___	___	___
	___	___	___
2. cōgitāvistis	___	___	___
	___	___	___
3. coniciēbam	___	___	___
	___	___	___
4. iussērunt	___	___	___
	___	___	___
5. surrēxī	___	___	___
	___	___	___
6. removēbās	___	___	___
	___	___	___
7. clāmāvistī	___	___	___
	___	___	___
8. obdormiēbāmus	___	___	___
	___	___	___

Exercise IVc: Imperfect, Present, and Perfect Tenses

pp. 106–107, 108, 150–151, 160, 166

Change the following irregular verbs to the present tense and then to the perfect tense. Keep the same person and number:

	Present	Perfect
1. volēbam	_____	_____
2. erāmus	_____	_____
3. volēbās	_____	_____
4. ībant	_____	_____
5. erās	_____	_____
6. ībās	_____	_____
7. nōlēbat	_____	_____
8. ībātis	_____	_____
9. erant	_____	_____
10. nōlēbātis	_____	_____

Exercise IVd: Uses of *Dum* and of Infinitives

pp. 161, 162

Read aloud and translate. Explain the tenses used with **dum,** and explain uses of infinitives:

1. Dum Cornēliī ad caupōnam appropinquant, subitō canis appāruit.
2. Cornēliī in caupōnā pernoctāre in animō habuērunt.
3. Perīculōsum nōn est in hāc caupōnā pernoctāre.
4. Cornēliōs caupō intrāre iussit.
5. Aurēlia et Cornēlia in caupōnā cēnāre nōluērunt.
6. Puerīs licet vigilāre et mīlitis fābulam audīre.
7. Dum mīles fābulam nārrābat, puerī vigilābant et audiēbant.
8. "Hic lectus est sordidus," inquit Aurēlia. "Necesse est alium lectum petere."
9. Aurēlia et Cornēlia in cubiculō manent, dum servī alium lectum petunt.
10. Aurēlia in lectō sordidō dormīre nōluit.
11. Dum Aurēlia et Cornēlia in cubiculō manent, servī alium lectum in cubiculum portāvērunt.

Exercise IVe: Reading Comprehension

Read aloud and translate:

MUCIUS GIVES A LESSON IN ROMAN VIRTUE

Porsenna, rēx Clūsīnōrum, urbem Rōmam iam diū obsidēbat. Rōmānī igitur, quod cibum in urbem ferre nōn poterant, famē perībant. Tum mīles quīdam Rōmānus, Gāius Mūcius nōmine, quī cīvēs patriamque servāre volēbat, Porsennam necāre cōnstituit.

Itaque Mūcius ad senātōrēs Rōmānōs iit et, "Tiberim trānsīre," inquit, "et 5
castra hostium intrāre in animō habeō. Ibi rēgem Porsennam necāre volō."

Respondērunt senātōrēs, "Sī hoc temptāre vīs, tibi licet." Laetus domum rediit Mūcius. Gladium arripuit et sub tunicā cēlāvit. Trāns Tiberim festīnāvit et castra hostium fūrtim intrāvit. Ibi magnam multitūdinem mīlitum vīdit. Ad mēnsam ante mīlitēs sedēbant duo hominēs. Alter pecūniam mīlitibus dabat, alter eōs spectābat. Cōgitābat Mūcius, "Uter est rēx? Nōnne ille est, quī omnia facit? Necesse est illum necāre!"

Mūcius ad mēnsam appropinquāvit et virum gladiō necāvit. Stupuērunt omnēs mīlitēs. Ē castrīs effugiēbat Mūcius, sed mīlitēs eum cēpērunt.

"Ō sceleste!" inquiunt. "Cūr scrībam rēgis necāvistī?"

"Rēgem, nōn scrībam, necāre volēbam," respondit Mūcius.

Rēx, ubi haec audīvit, īrātus erat et mīlitēs iussit Mūcium pūnīre. Superbē respondit Mūcius: "Cīvis Rōmānus sum. Mē Gāium Mūcium vocant. Castra intrāvī quod urbem Rōmam servāre in animō habēbam. Mē cēpistī sed poenās nōn timeō."

Eō ipsō tempore stābat Mūcius prope āram et ignem. Subitō dextram manum in ignem iniēcit. Rēx statim surrēxit et mīlitēs iussit virum ab igne trahere. "Quamquam," inquit, "hostis es, tē ad cīvēs tuōs iam remittō quod vir fortissimus es."

Postquam Mūcius Rōmam rediit, rem tōtam nārrāvit. Cīvēs Mūcium nōn modo laudābant sed, quod iam sinistram modo manum habēbat, eum appellāvērunt Scaevolam.

1	rēx, rēgis, m., *king*	11	Uter…? *Which (of the two)…?*
	Clūsīnī, -ōrum, m. pl., *the people of Clusium*		ille, *that one*
		13	stupeō, -ēre, -uī, *to be amazed*
2	famē perīre, *to die of hunger*	15	scrība, -ae, m., *scribe*
3	patria, -ae, f., *native land*	17	superbē, adv., *proudly*
	-que, enclitic conj., *and*	19	poenae, -ārum, f. pl., *punishment*
	servō, -āre, -āvī, -ātus, *to save*		
5	Tiberis, Tiberis, m., *the Tiber River*	21	āra, -ae, f., *altar*
6	castra, -ōrum, n. pl., *camp*		ignis, ignis, gen. pl., ignium, m., *fire*
	hostēs, hostium, m. pl., *the enemy*		dexter, dextra, dextrum, *right*
8	gladius, -ī, m., *sword*	23	fortissimus, -a, -um, *very brave*
	trāns, prep. + acc., *across*	26	sinister, sinistra, sinistrum, *left*
9	multitūdō, multitūdinis, f., *crowd*	27	Scaevola, -ae, m., *Scaevola (nickname derived from the adjective scaevus, -a, -um, left)*
10	mēnsa, -ae, f., *table*		
	ante, prep. + acc., *in front of*		
	mīlitibus, *to the soldiers*		

1 obsideō, obsidēre, obsēdī, obsessus, *to besiege*
4 cōnstituō, cōnstituere, cōnstituī, cōnstitūtus, *to decide*
5 trānseō, trānsīre, trānsiī or trānsīvī, trānsitus, irreg., *to cross*
22 iniciō, inicere, iniēcī, iniectus, *to throw into*, *thrust into*
23 remittō, remittere, remīsī, remissus, *to send back*

FROM THE INN TO ROME

Iam diēs erat. Prīmā lūce raedārius auxiliō servōrum caupōnis raedam ē fossā extrāxit et ad caupōnam admōvit. Tum servī cistās Cornēliōrum raedāriō trādidērunt. Intereā in caupōnā, dum omnēs sē parābant, Sextus, iam immemor terrōris nocturnī, mīlitis fābulam Cornēliae nārrābat; Eucleidēs mandāta servīs dabat. Cornēlius ipse Aurēliae et līberīs clāmābat, "Agite, omnēs! Nōlīte cessāre! Tempus est discēdere." 5

Tandem cūnctī ē caupōnā vēnērunt et in raedam ascendērunt.

"Valē!" clāmāvērunt puerī.

"Valēte!" respondit caupō, quī in viā stābat. "Nōlīte in fossam iterum cadere! Nōn in omnibus caupōnīs bene dormīre potestis."

Tum raedārius habēnās sūmpsit et equōs verberāvit. Tandem Rōmam iterum petēbant. 10

In itinere Sextus omnia dē mūre mortuō Mārcō explicāvit; Cornēlius mīlitis fābulam uxōrī nārrāvit. Iam urbī appropinquābant, cum subitō puerī ingēns aedificium cōnspexērunt.

(continued)

1 **auxiliō**, *with the help*	4 **Cornēliae**, *to Cornelia*
2 **raedāriō**, *to the coachman*	**mandātum, -ī**, n., *order, instruction*
3 **sē parāre**, *to prepare oneself, get ready*	9 **bene**, adv., *well*
immemor, immemoris + gen.,	10 **habēnae, -ārum**, f. pl., *reins*
forgetful	12 **uxōrī**, *to his wife*
nocturnus, -a, -um, *happening during*	**cum**, conj., *when*
the night	**ingēns, ingentis**, *huge*

2 admoveō, admovēre, admōvī, admōtus, *to move toward*
  trādō, trādere, trādidī, trāditus, *to hand over*
5 **discēdō, discēdere, discessī, discessūrus**, *to go away, depart*
6 **ascendō, ascendere, ascendī, ascēnsus**, *to climb, climb into (a carriage)*
8 **stō, stāre, stetī, statūrus**, *to stand*
  cadō, cadere, cecidī, cāsūrus, *to fall*
10 **sūmō, sūmere, sūmpsī, sūmptus**, *to take, take up*

EXERCISE 22a

Respondē Latīnē:

Go Online
PHSchool.com
Web Code: jfd-0022

1. Cui Sextus mīlitis fābulam nārrābat?
2. Quid Eucleidēs faciēbat?
3. Quid dīxit caupō ubi Cornēliī discēdēbant?
4. Quid fēcit raedārius?
5. Quid Sextus Mārcō explicāvit?
6. Quid puerī cōnspexērunt?

Mārcus patrem, "Quid est illud?" rogāvit.

Atque Sextus, "Quis in illō aedificiō habitat?"   15

Cui Cornēlius, "Nēmō ibi habitat," cum rīsū respondit. "Est sepulcrum Messallae Corvīnī, quī erat ōrātor praeclārus. Hīc sunt sepulcra multōrum et praeclārōrum cīvium quod Rōmānīs nōn licet intrā urbem sepulcra habēre."

Mox alterum aedificium magnum vīdērunt.

"Estne id quoque sepulcrum, pater?" rogāvit Mārcus.   20

"Ita vērō!" Cornēlius respondit. "Est sepulcrum Caeciliae Metellae. Nōnne dē Caeciliā Metellā audīvistī?"

Sed Mārcus patrī nihil respondit. Iam enim urbem ipsam vidēre poterat. "Ecce Rōma!" clāmāvit.

"Ecce Rōma! Ecce Rōma!" clāmāvērunt Sextus et Cornēlia.   25

Tum Cornēlius, "Brevī tempore ad Portam Capēnam adveniēmus et Titum, patruum vestrum, ibi vidēbimus. Epistulam enim per servum mīsī et omnia eī explicāvī. Titus mox nōs prope Portam excipiet."

14 illud, *that*	**patruus, -ī,** m., *uncle*
15 **atque,** conj., *and, and also*	27 **vester, vestra, vestrum,** *your* (pl.)
16 **sepulcrum, -ī,** n., *tomb*	**vidēbimus,** *we will see*
18 **intrā,** prep. + acc., *inside*	28 **excipiet,** *he will welcome*
26 **adveniēmus,** *we will come*	

28 **excipiō, excipere, excēpī, exceptus,** *to welcome, receive*

Respondē Latīnē:

7. Cūr sepulcra nōn sunt intrā urbem?
8. Cuius est alterum sepulcrum?   **Cuius**…? Whose…?
9. Audīvitne Mārcus dē Caeciliā Metellā?
10. Quis Cornēliōs ad Portam Capēnam excipiet?

Amīcus omnibus amīcus nēminī. *A friend to everyone is a friend to no one.*

FORMS

Nouns: Cases and Declensions: Dative Case

Look at the following sentences:

1. Mandāta **servīs** dabat. (22:4)
   *He was giving orders **to the slaves**.*

2. Omnia **Mārcō** explicāvit. (22:11)
   *He explained everything **to Marcus**.*

3. Cornēlius fābulam **uxōrī** nārrāvit. (22:11–12)
*Cornelius told the story **to his wife**.*

4. Servī meī bonam cēnam **vōbīs** parāre possunt. (19:2–3)
*My slaves are able to prepare a good dinner **for you**.*

The Latin words in bold type are all in the *dative case* and may be translated using *to...* or *for....*

Here is a chart showing the groups of nouns and cases, including the dative:

Number Case	1st Declension Fem.	2nd Declension Masc.	Masc.	Masc.	Neut.	3rd Declension Masc.	Fem.	Neut.
Singular								
Nom.	puélla	sérvus	púer	áger	báculum	páter	vōx	nómen
Gen.	puéllae	sérvī	púerī	ágrī	báculī	pátris	vōcis	nóminis
Dat.	**puéllae**	**sérvō**	**púerō**	**ágrō**	**báculō**	**pátrī**	**vōcī**	**nóminī**
Acc.	puéllam	sérvum	púerum	ágrum	báculum	pátrem	vōcem	nómen
Abl.	puéllā	sérvō	púerō	ágrō	báculō	pátre	vōce	nómine
Voc.	puélla	sérve	púer	áger	báculum	páter	vōx	nómen
Plural								
Nom.	puéllae	sérvī	púerī	ágrī	bácula	pátrēs	vōcēs	nómina
Gen.	puellárum	servōrum	puerōrum	agrōrum	baculōrum	pátrum	vōcum	nóminum
Dat.	**puéllīs**	**sérvīs**	**púerīs**	**ágrīs**	**báculīs**	**pátribus**	**vōcibus**	**nōmínibus**
Acc.	puéllās	sérvōs	púerōs	ágrōs	bácula	pátrēs	vōcēs	nómina
Abl.	puéllīs	sérvīs	púerīs	ágrīs	báculīs	pátribus	vōcibus	nōmínibus
Voc.	puéllae	sérvī	púerī	ágrī	bácula	pátrēs	vōcēs	nómina

Be sure to learn the new dative forms thoroughly.

NOTES

1. In each declension dative and ablative plurals have the same endings.
2. The datives of the pronouns are as follows:

Singular		Plural	
Nominative	*Dative*	*Nominative*	*Dative*
ego	**mihi**	**nōs**	**nōbīs**
tū	**tibi**	**vōs**	**vōbīs**
is, ea, id	**eī**	**eī, eae, ea**	**eīs**
Quis...?	**Cui...?**	**Quī...?**	**Quibus...?**

Here is a chart showing the adjectives, including the dative case:

Number	1st and 2nd Declensions			3rd Declension		
Case	Masc.	Fem.	Neut.	Masc.	Fem.	Neut.
Singular						
Nom.	mágn**us**	mágn**a**	mágn**um**	ómn**is**	ómn**is**	ómn**e**
Gen.	mágn**ī**	mágn**ae**	mágn**ī**	ómn**is**	ómn**is**	ómn**is**
Dat.	**mágnō**	**mágnae**	**mágnō**	**ómnī**	**ómnī**	**ómnī**
Acc.	mágn**um**	mágn**am**	mágn**um**	ómn**em**	ómn**em**	ómn**e**
Abl.	mágn**ō**	mágn**ā**	mágn**ō**	ómn**ī**	ómn**ī**	ómn**ī**
Voc.	mágn**e**	mágn**a**	mágn**um**	ómn**is**	ómn**is**	ómn**e**
Plural						
Nom.	mágn**ī**	mágn**ae**	mágn**a**	ómn**ēs**	ómn**ēs**	ómn**ia**
Gen.	magn**órum**	magn**árum**	magn**órum**	ómn**ium**	ómn**ium**	ómn**ium**
Dat.	mágn**īs**	mágn**īs**	mágn**īs**	ómn**ibus**	ómn**ibus**	ómn**ibus**
Acc.	mágn**ōs**	mágn**ās**	mágn**a**	ómn**ēs**	ómn**ēs**	ómn**ia**
Abl.	mágn**īs**	mágn**īs**	mágn**īs**	ómn**ibus**	ómn**ibus**	ómn**ibus**
Voc.	mágn**ī**	mágn**ae**	mágn**a**	ómn**ēs**	ómn**ēs**	ómn**ia**

You should now have thoroughly learned all of the forms above and on the previous page.

3rd Declension Adjectives of One Termination

Most 3rd declension adjectives have two different endings in the nominative singular, one that is used when the adjective modifies masculine or feminine nouns (e.g., **omn***is* **ager, omn***is* **vīlla**) and a second ending that is used when the adjective modifies neuter nouns (e.g., **omn***e* **sepulcrum**).

Some 3rd declension adjectives use the same form in the nominative when the adjective modifies masculine, feminine, *or* neuter nouns, as **immemor**, *forgetful*, and **ingēns**, *huge*. Thus, we can say **ingēns ager** (masculine), **ingēns vīlla** (feminine), and **ingēns sepulcrum** (neuter). Adjectives of this sort are called *adjectives of one termination*. The nominative and genitive are given in vocabulary entries for this type of adjective: **immemor, immemoris**, and **ingēns, ingentis**. The base is found by dropping the *-is* ending from the genitive singular, and to this base are added the same endings as for **omnis**. As always, the neuter nominative, accusative, and vocative are the same in the singular and in the plural.

EXERCISE 22b
Write out a full set of the forms of **immemor**.

BUILDING THE MEANING

The Dative Case

1. The sentence below illustrates a basic pattern with which you have been familiar since Chapter 4:

   >   S   DO   TV
   > Cornēlius fābulam nārrāvit.
   > *Cornelius told the story.*

   You will often find sentences of this type with a subject (S), direct object (DO), and a transitive verb (TV) expanded with a word or phrase in the *dative case* that will modify the verb. In the sentence below the word in the dative case tells *to whom* the story was told:

   >   S   DO   IO   TV
   > Cornēlius fābulam **uxōrī** nārrāvit. (22:11–12)

   The word in the dative case, **uxōrī**, is called the *indirect object* (IO). Words or phrases in the dative case functioning as indirect objects will often be found with verbs of *giving* (e.g., **dare**, **trādere**), *showing* (e.g., **mōnstrāre**), and *telling* (e.g., **dīcere**, **nārrāre**). They answer the question "to whom…?"

   Note that sentences with indirect objects can often be translated two ways in English. For example, the sentence above can be translated:

   > *Cornelius told the story* **to his wife**. or *Cornelius told* **his wife** *the story.*

2. Note also that sometimes a word or phrase in the dative case can best be translated *for…* instead of *to…*:

   > Servī meī bonam cēnam **vōbīs** parāre possunt. (19:2–3)
   > *My slaves are able to prepare a good dinner* **for you**.

3. The dative case may also be found in sentences in which the verb is intransitive and does not have a direct object:

   > Aulus **Septimō** clāmāvit. (21:8–9)   Aulus in somnō **eī** appāruit. (21:4)
   > *Aulus shouted* **to Septimus**.   *Aulus appeared* **to him** *in (his) sleep.*

4. The intransitive verb **appropinquāre**, *to approach*, is sometimes used with the preposition **ad** + acc.:

   > Mox **ad caupōnam** appropinquābant.
   > *Soon they were coming near* **to the inn**/*approaching* **the inn**.

   It may also be used with a word or phrase in the dative case:

   > Iam **urbī** appropinquābant. (22:12)
   > *Already they were coming near* **to the city**/*approaching* **the city**.

5. You have also seen the dative case used with the impersonal verbal phrase **necesse est**, *it is necessary*, and the impersonal verb **licet**, *it is allowed*, with infinitives as their subjects:

> Cūr **mihi** quoque necesse est ad urbem redīre? (8:13–14)
> *Why is to return to the city necessary **for me** too?*
> *Why is it necessary **for me** too to return to the city?*

> "Licetne **nōbīs**," inquit Mārcus, "hīc cēnāre?" (20:7)
> *"Is to eat dinner here allowed **for us**?" said Marcus.*
> *"Is it allowed **for us**," said Marcus, "to eat dinner here?"*
> *"May **we** eat dinner here?" said Marcus.*

EXERCISE 22c

Reword the sentence **Cornēlius fābulam <u>uxōrī</u> nārrāvit** to say that Cornelius told the story to each of the following in turn: **Septimus, Flāvia, puellae, mīles, puerī, raedārius, senātōrēs, caupō, viātōrēs.**

EXERCISE 22d

In each sentence identify the word or phrase in the dative case and the reason for its use. Then read the sentence aloud and translate it:

1. Patruus pecūniam puerīs dat.
2. Ancilla invīta caupōnī scelestō cibum trādit.
3. Omnia patrī meō semper dīcō.
4. Nihil lēgātō prīncipis dīxit.
5. Cornēlius epistulam ad Titum mīsit et omnia eī explicāvit.
6. Mārcus, "Tacē, Sexte!" inquit. "Nōbīs nōn licet hīc clāmāre."
7. In somnīs Aulus amīcō Septimō appāruit.
8. Dum Cornēliī urbī appropinquābant, Titus omnia eīs parābat.
9. Apollodōrus Cornēliīs cubicula mōnstrat.   **mōnstrō, -āre, -āvī, -ātus,** *to show*
10. Servī alium lectum Aurēliae parāvērunt.

EXERCISE 22e

Give the Latin for:

1. Suddenly a soldier appeared to them.
2. "May I stay awake and hear the soldier's story?" asked Marcus.
3. It was necessary for Aurelia and Cornelia to go to bed, for they were tired.
4. Sextus told the soldier's story to Cornelia.
5. They were approaching the tomb of Caecilia Metella.

Nouns: Dative or Ablative? How Do You Decide?

You will have noticed that the dative and ablative cases often have identical endings, e.g., **servō, puellīs, mīlitibus**. How are you to tell which case is used in a particular sentence? Ask yourself these two questions:

a. Is the noun preceded by a preposition? If it is, the noun will be in the ablative case because no preposition governs the dative case.

b. If there is no preposition, does the noun refer to a *person*? If it does, it will normally be in the dative because nouns referring to persons are usually governed by a preposition if they are in the ablative. If the noun refers to a *thing*, it is more likely to be ablative than dative (exception: a word in the dative case with the verb **appropinquāre** often refers to a thing).

Consider the following sentences, noting each word and each group of words as you meet it:

1. **Canem nostrum puerō dedit.**
   The words **canem nostrum** are obviously accusative. When we reach **puerō**, knowing that **puer** refers to a person, we can say that it must be in the dative case because it would be governed by a preposition if it were in the ablative case. A Roman reading as far as **puerō** would have known before he reached the verb that the sentence deals with giving or showing "our dog" in some way or other "to the boy."

2. **Puerō canem nostrum dedimus.**
   The fact that **puerō** comes first in the sentence does not alter the reasoning. Since it refers to a person and is not governed by a preposition, it must be in the dative case.

3. **Mārcus lupum baculō repellit.**
   When we come to **baculō**, knowing that **baculum** refers to a thing, we can be sure because of the sense that it is in the ablative case. A Roman would have understood as soon as he reached **baculō** that Marcus is "doing" something to the wolf *with* a stick.

4. **Baculō lupum repellit.**
   Again, the fact that **baculō** appears as the first word makes no difference. We again know that **baculō** must be in the ablative case because it refers to a thing, and when we come to **lupum** we know that someone is "doing" something to the wolf *with* a stick.

Remember that some 3rd declension nouns end in **-ō** in the nominative singular, e.g., **caupō, caupōnis**. In addition, do not mistake the 3rd declension dative singular ending **-ī**, e.g., **caupōnī**, for a 2nd declension genitive singular or nominative plural ending.

EXERCISE 22f

Use the reasoning given in the preceding discussion to help you with the words in boldface that could be dative or ablative in form. Identify each as dative or ablative and then translate the entire sentence:

1. Septimus omnia dē Aulō mortuō **cīvibus** explicāvit.
2. Mihi necesse est **equīs meīs** cibum dare.
3. Mārcus **rāmō** lupum repellit.
4. Sextus **raedāriō** clāmāvit, "Tenē equōs! Cavē fossam!"
5. Raedārius **habēnīs** equōs dēvertēbat.
6. Cūr tū **ancillīs** lībertātem nōn dedistī?
7. Raedārius habēnās **manibus** sūmpsit.
8. Nōs bonam cēnam **hospitibus** parāvimus, domine.
9. **Puerīs** quoque cibum date!
10. Ego in animō habeō corpus et stercus **plaustrō** ē caupōnā removēre.
11. Mediā nocte Aulus in somnō **amīcō suō** appāruit.
12. **Rūsticīs** necesse erat bovēs tardōs **clāmōribus** et **baculīs** incitāre.
13. Mercātōrēs togās et tunicās **cīvibus** mōnstrant.

mercātor, mercātōris, m., *merchant*

EXERCISE 22g

Here is the inscription from the tomb of Caecilia Metella on the Appian Way. Which words in the inscription are in the dative case, and which are in the genitive?

The tomb of Caecilia Metella is situated on the Appian Way. The crenelations on the top of the rotunda are a medieval addition. *Via Appia, Rome, 60 B.C.*

CAECILIAE
Q·CRETICI·F
METELLAE·CRASSI

Caeciliae
Q(uīntī) Crēticī f(īliae)
Metellae Crassī

(the tomb dedicated) to Caecilia Metella, daughter of Quintus (Caecilius Metellus) Creticus, (wife) of Crassus

Go Online
PHSchool.com
Web Code: jfd-0022

ROME AND NORTHERN EUROPE

When we think of the Roman conquest of parts of northwestern Europe and the subsequent spread of Roman civilization to these areas, we most often visualize the Roman general Julius Caesar and his army subjugating what is now France, called **Gallia** by the Romans, from 58 to 51 B.C. and invading Britain in 55 and 54 B.C. Or we think of Agricola, legate of the Twentieth Legion in Britain (A.D. 71–73), who, when governor of Britain (A.D. 78–83), led Roman troops as far as the Scottish Highlands, where the Caledonii lived (Agricola was mentioned in "Eavesdropping" on pages 178–179).

These images of the northward expansion of Roman power and control are quite correct, but there were men, other than these commanders, who brought about the Romanization of the native peoples in these areas. Perhaps these men had greater influence

Germany
France

Vercingetorix surrendering to Caesar, who is seated on the red dais in the distance, 52 B.C.
Vercingetorix before Caesar, *oil-acrylic, 1886, Henri-Paul Motte*

than their commanders because they had closer contact with the ordinary people. These men were the **mīlitēs legiōnāriī**, the ordinary foot soldiers of the legions. What follows is an imaginary account of how a common soldier might have helped to bring about the Romanization process somewhere in **Gallia** or **Germānia** shortly after the Roman conquest of those areas.

Our soldier, whom we will call Lucius, is a man in the Twentieth Legion (**Legiō XX Valeria**). This legion was transferred from Illyricum to the site of the modern Cologne (called **Āra Ubiōrum**, "Altar of the Ubii," by the Romans) on the Rhine River (**Rhēnus**), a site inhabited by a German tribe known as the Ubii and protected since 38 B.C. by a permanent Roman camp (**castra**). The legion was transferred there to help defend the Roman frontier shortly after the destruction of three Roman legions by the Germans in the Teutoburg Forest in A.D. 9 during the reign of the first emperor, Augustus (emperor 27 B.C.– A.D. 14). Lucius falls in love with Helge, an Ubian girl. A number of years before,

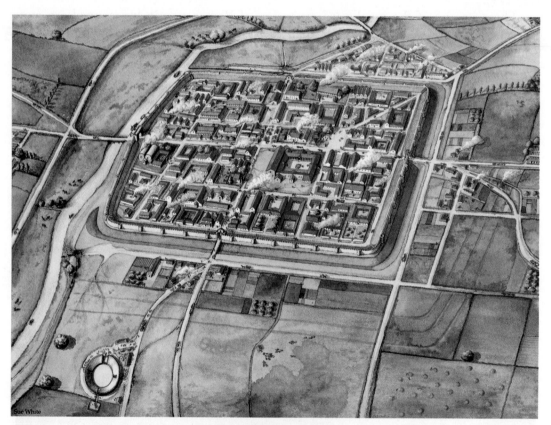

Reconstruction of the Roman town of *Venta Icenōrum*, Britain
Sue White, artist

Helge's family had been given land by Marcus Vipsanius Agrippa, when he moved the Ubii at their request from the eastern to the western bank of the Rhine in 38 B.C.

When Lucius learns that Helge is carrying his child, he arranges to marry her, although Roman law stipulated that any marriage contracted by a Roman soldier below the rank of centurion was invalid. However, many of the legionaries held marriage ceremonies with local women who lived in the area near the **castra** or legionary camp. Thus, before his bunkmates (**contubernālēs**), Lucius placed a small gold ring on the third finger of Helge's left hand, and she, prompted by Lucius, recited the traditional marriage vow, **Ubi tū Gāius, ego Gāia**, "Where you are Gaius, I am Gaia." Although the girl knew only a few words of Latin, she understood that this stocky and swarthy man was now her "husband."

Before the marriage ceremony, Lucius and his comrades had built a small hut for Helge. However, instead of building the hut in any open space that suited them, as the Germans did in their villages, the men carefully selected a location in accordance with the plan of streets established by surveyors (**agrimēnsōrēs**) when the Roman settlement of Ara Ubiorum began to be transformed into an outpost town about 12 B.C. There were two main streets, the north-south axis or **cardō**, and the **decumānus**, the east-west axis, oriented to the sunrise on September 23, the birthday of Augustus Caesar. This plan provided locations for a **forum**, which included a marketplace with shops, a **tabulārium** for the keeping of records, a theater, temples with altars not only to the Roman gods but also to Helge's gods such as the Three Mothers, and houses for the town's inhabitants. This foresight and planning were very different from the haphazard way Helge's people built their settlements, and the girl felt new respect and admiration for her husband's people, the Romans.

---

1. If Roman law did not allow foot soldiers to marry, why would officers and officials have overlooked "marriages" such as that of Lucius to Helge?
2. Judging from this story, what facilitated Romanization on the frontier with Germany?

English Words from the Fourth Principal Part of Latin Verbs

The stem of the fourth principal part of a Latin verb may be the source of other Latin words and of English derivatives. This stem is found by dropping the *-us* or the *-ūrus* from the end of the fourth principal part, e.g., the stem of **vīsus** is **vīs-**. Here are some common types of words formed from the stem of the fourth principal part:

1. No suffix.

   The stem may form an English word with no change:

   invent (**invent-**)   fact (**fact-**)

2. Silent *-e*.

   An English word may be formed by adding silent *-e* to the stem:

   narrate (**nārrāt-**)   finite (**finīt-**)

3. Suffix *-or*.

   When added to the stem of the fourth principal part, the Latin suffix *-or* creates a 3rd declension, masculine noun, which means *one who does* the action of the verb. These nouns are often borrowed into English with no change in spelling, although there is sometimes a change in meaning:

	Latin Noun & Meaning	English Word
nārrātus (nārrāre)	**nārrātor, nārrātōris,** m., *storyteller*	narrator
spectātus (spectāre)	**spectātor, spectātōris,** m., *onlooker, observer*	spectator
āctus (agere)	**āctor, āctōris,** m., *driver, doer, actor*	actor

4. Suffix *-iō*.

   The Latin suffix *-iō*, when added to the stem of the fourth principal part, forms a 3rd declension, feminine noun, which means the *act of, state of,* or *result of* the action of the verb. The genitive singular of these nouns ends in *-iōnis*, and the base has *-iōn-*, which is the source of English words ending in *-sion* and *-tion*. The meaning of the English word is similar or identical to that of the Latin noun, which takes its meaning from the Latin verb:

	Latin Noun & Meaning	English Word
vīsus (vidēre)	**vīsiō, vīsiōnis,** f., *act of seeing, vision*	vision
nārrātus (nārrāre)	**nārrātiō, nārrātiōnis,** f., *act of telling (a story), narrative, narration*	narration

   Note that whether the English word ends in *-sion* or *-tion* depends on whether the word from which it is derived ends in *-sus* or *-tus*.

EXERCISE 1

Using the preceding information, create a 3rd declension Latin noun and an English derivative from each of the following. Check in a Latin dictionary to verify the existence of each noun and compare its meaning with that of its English derivative:

1. audītus (audīre)
2. cautus (cavēre)
3. exclāmātus (exclāmāre)
4. factus (facere)
5. mānsūrus (manēre)
6. missus (mittere)
7. petītus (petere)
8. positus (pōnere)

EXERCISE 2

Give the meaning of each English word below. Then give the fourth principal part, the infinitive, and the meaning of the Latin verb from which the English word is derived. You may have to find some of the fourth principal parts in the Vocabulary at the back of this book:

1. apparition
2. cogitate
3. diction
4. habitation
5. inventor
6. motor
7. session
8. state
9. tacit

Latin Expressions in English

Latin phrases and expressions are often used in English. Some are very familiar, such as et cetera (etc.), *and the rest*. Others are more specialized, such as ipso facto, *by the fact itself*, a legal expression used to describe an assumption that has obvious truth, e.g., "A slave, ipso facto, had no right to vote."

While Latin expressions may sometimes be used in English as mere affectations, there are occasions when they are very effective in summarizing an idea succinctly. For example, the term *de facto segregation* refers to a long history of racial segregation that occurred *in fact*, even though no legal measures were taken to achieve it. De jure segregation, on the other hand, was achieved *by law*. These two Latin phrases capsulize these notions in a minimum of words, thereby making communication more efficient.

EXERCISE 3

Look up the following Latin expressions in an English dictionary. Use each expression in a sentence that illustrates its special use in English:

1. ad hoc
2. ad infinitum
3. modus operandi
4. non sequitur
5. per capita
6. per se
7. quid pro quo
8. sine qua non
9. status quo

AT THE PORTA CAPENA

Intereā Titus, patruus Mārcī et Cornēliae, eōs prope Portam Capēnam exspectābat.
Cīvēs, mercātōrēs, servī per portam ībant atque hūc illūc currēbant. Titus tamen in
lectīcā sedēbat. Ubi Cornēliōs cōnspexit, ē lectīcā dēscendit. Ē raedā dēscendērunt
Cornēliī. Interdiū enim raedās intrā urbem agere Rōmānīs nōn licēbat.

Stupuit Sextus ubi multitūdinem cīvium, servōrum turbam vīdit. Undique erat   5
strepitus plaustrōrum, undique clāmor mercātōrum, viātōrum, raedāriōrum.

Titus Cornēlium et Aurēliam et līberōs maximō cum gaudiō salūtāvit. "Quam laetus,"
inquit, "vōs omnēs excipiō! Nōnne estis itinere dēfessī?"

"Valdē dēfessī," respondit Cornēlius. "Mihi necesse est celeriter ad Cūriam īre, sed
prīmum Aurēliam et Cornēliam domum dūcam."   10

"Ita vērō!" inquit Titus. "Ecce! Lectīcāriī, quōs vōbīs condūxī, vōs domum ferent.
Ego puerōs cūrābō. Multa et mīra vidēbunt puerī, atque ego omnia eīs explicābō."

(continued)

2 **hūc illūc,** adv., *this way and that*	10 **prīmum,** adv., *first*
3 **lectīca, -ae,** f., *litter*	**domum,** *homeward, home*
4 interdiū, adv., *during the day*	**dūcam,** *I will take*
5 **stupeō, -ēre, -uī,** *to be amazed, gape*	11 **ferent,** *(they) will carry*
turba, -ae, f., *crowd, mob*	12 **cūrābō,** *I will take care of*
undique, adv., *on all sides*	multa et mīra, *many wonderful things*
6 strepitus, *noise, clattering*	**mīrus, -a, -um,** *wonderful, marvelous*
7 **maximus, -a, -um,** *greatest, very great*	
gaudium, -ī, n., *joy*	**vidēbunt,** *(they) will see*
9 Cūria, -ae, f., *Senate House*	

2 **currō, currere, cucurrī, cursūrus,** *to run*
3 **dēscendō, dēscendere, dēscendī, dēscēnsūrus,** *to come/go down, climb down*
4 **agō, agere, ēgī, āctus,** *to do, drive*
11 condūcō, condūcere, condūxī, conductus, *to hire*

EXERCISE 23a

Respondē Latīnē:

1. Quis Cornēliōs exspectābat?
2. Quī hūc illūc currēbant per portam?
3. Ubi sedēbat Titus?
4. Cūr Cornēliī ē raedā dēscendērunt?
5. Quid Sextus prope portam vīdit?

6. Quid Sextus prope portam audīvit?
7. Quōmodo Titus Cornēliōs salūtāvit?
8. Quō necesse est Cornēliō īre?
9. Quis lectīcāriōs condūxit?
10. Quis puerīs multa et mīra explicābit?

Go Online
PHSchool.com
Web Code: jfd-0023

Itaque per viās urbis lectīcāriī patrem, mātrem, fīliam celeriter domum tulērunt. Postquam eō advēnērunt, Aurēlia et Cornēlia, itinere dēfessae, sē quiētī dedērunt. Cornēlius tamen sē lāvit, aliam togam praetextam induit, iterum in lectīcā cōnsēdit. 15
"Ad Cūriam celeriter!" inquit.

14 **eō** adv., *there, to that place*
sē quiētī dare, *to rest*
    quiēs, quiētis, f., *rest*

    14 **adveniō, advenīre, advēnī, adventūrus,** *to reach, arrive (at)*
    15 **induō, induere, induī, indūtus,** *to put on*
        cōnsīdō, cōnsīdere, cōnsēdī, *to sit down*

Respondē Latīnē:

11. Quō lectīcāriī Cornēlium et Aurēliam et Cornēliam tulērunt?
12. Quid Aurēlia et Cornēlia ibi fēcērunt?
13. Quid fēcit Cornēlius postquam domum advēnit?

BUILDING THE MEANING

Go Online
PHSchool.com
Web Code: jfd-0023

Adjectives as Substantives

In the sentence in line 12 of the story, **Multa et mīra vidēbunt puerī, atque ego omnia eīs explicābō,** the words **multa, mīra,** and **omnia** are adjectives, but they are here used with no nouns for them to modify. The adjectives themselves are used as *substantives,* i.e., as words that function as nouns.

The neuter gender and plural number of these particular substantives (**multa, mīra,** and **omnia**) imply the idea of *things,* and you may therefore translate *many and wonderful things* and *all things.* Note that Latin uses a conjunction between **multa** and **mīra,** while we would say merely "many wonderful things." Note also that we normally say "everything" instead of "all things," the literal translation of **omnia.**

You have also seen adjectives in the masculine or feminine used as substantives, e.g., **Cūnctī in caupōnam intrāvērunt** (19:1). Masculine adjectives so used, as here, refer to people in general, and **cūnctī** may be translated *everybody.* You have seen **omnēs** used in this way a number of times. A feminine adjective would refer to women, e.g., **bonae,** *good women.* We often use adjectives as substantives in English as well, e.g., "the good," "the brave," "the wise."

FORMS

Go Online
PHSchool.com
Web Code: jfd–0023

Verbs: Future Tense I

Look at these sentences:

Ego omnia eīs **explicābō.**	*I will explain* everything to them.
Multa et mīra **vidēbunt** puerī.	*The boys* ***will see*** *many wonderful things.*
Ego Cornēliam domum **dūcam.**	*I will take* Cornelia home.
Brevī tempore ad Portam Capēnam **adveniēmus.**	*In a short time* ***we will arrive*** *at the Porta Capena.*

The words in boldface are examples of the *future tense*. The endings of the future tense are shown in the chart below:

		1st and 2nd Conjugations	3rd and 4th Conjugations
Singular	1	*-bō*	*-am*
	2	*-bis*	*-ēs*
	3	*-bit*	*-et*
Plural	1	*-bimus*	*-ēmus*
	2	*-bitis*	*-ētis*
	3	*-bunt*	*-ent*

Note that in the future tense the endings of verbs in the 3rd and 4th conjugations are quite different from the endings of verbs in the 1st and 2nd conjugations.

Note also that the *-e-* of the ending in the 3rd and 4th conjugations is short before final *-t* and *-nt*.

Note in the chart below that the letter *i* precedes the endings *-am, -ēs, -et,* etc., in 3rd conjugation **-iō** verbs (**iaciam, iaciēs, iaciet,** etc.) and in 4th conjugation verbs (**audiam, audiēs, audiet,** etc.).

		1st Conjugation	2nd Conjugation	3rd Conjugation		4th Conjugation
Infinitive		par*ā́re*	hab*ḗre*	mít*tere*	iác*ere* (-iō)	aud*ī́re*
Singular	1	par*ā́bō*	hab*ḗbō*	mítt*am*	iáci*am*	aúdi*am*
	2	par*ā́bis*	hab*ḗbis*	mítt*ēs*	iáci*ēs*	aúdi*ēs*
	3	par*ā́bit*	hab*ḗbit*	mítt*et*	iáci*et*	aúdi*et*
Plural	1	par*ā́bimus*	hab*ḗbimus*	mitt*ḗmus*	iaci*ḗmus*	audi*ḗmus*
	2	par*ā́bitis*	hab*ḗbitis*	mitt*ḗtis*	iaci*ḗtis*	audi*ḗtis*
	3	par*ā́bunt*	hab*ḗbunt*	mítt*ent*	iáci*ent*	aúdi*ent*

Be sure to learn these forms thoroughly.

EXERCISE 23b

Read aloud, identify all verbs in the future tense, and translate:

1. Titus nōs prope Portam Capēnam exspectābit; omnēs maximō cum gaudiō salūtābit.
2. Hodiē magna sepulcra Rōmānōrum praeclārōrum vīdimus; crās Cūriam et alia aedificia Rōmāna vidēbimus.
3. Fortasse patruus noster nōs ad Cūriam dūcet.
4. Cornēliī omnēs sē parant; brevī tempore ad urbem iter facient.
5. Multa et mīra vident puerī; lectīcāriī eōs mox domum portābunt.
6. Cornēlius ē raedā dēscendet, nam raedam intrā urbem agere nōn licet.
7. Quam diū in urbe manēbis, pater?
8. Bene dormiētis, puerī. Longum enim iter hodiē fēcistis.
9. Cornēlia, itinere longō dēfessa, sē quiētī dabit.
10. Puerī multa rogābunt dē aedificiīs quae in urbis viīs vidēbunt.

faciō, facere, fēcī, factus, *to make, do*   **maneō, manēre, mānsī, mānsus,** *to remain, stay, wait (for)*

EXERCISE 23c

Using story 23, its verb list, and the charts of the future tense as guides, give the Latin for:

1. Will you run home, boys?
2. We will sit near the Porta Capena.
3. When will the Cornelii climb down out of the carriage?
4. Cornelius, will you drive your carriage inside the city during the day?
5. Who will hire the litter-bearers?
6. Litter-bearers, will you carry us home?
7. Where will Cornelius wash himself?
8. What will you put on, Cornelius?
9. We will all sit down in two litters.

Detail of a reconstructed view of the *Forum Rōmānum*, early third century A.D. Clockwise from the upper left-hand corner: Temple of Concord, Arch of Septimius Severus, Curia Julia, Basilica Aemilia, Temple of Antoninus and Faustina, Regia (Temple of the Divine Julius in front of it), Temple of Castor (roof only), and Basilica Julia.

Watercolor, Peter Connolly

Present or Future Tense? How Do You Decide?

Look at these sentences:

Cornēlius multōs servōs hab**et**.	Cornelius **has** many slaves.
Scelestōs servōs ad vīllam rūsticam mitt**et**.	He **will send** the wicked slaves to the country house and farm.
Hodiē in caupōnā man**ēmus**.	Today we **remain** in the inn.
Crās Rōmam adveni**ēmus**.	Tomorrow we **will reach** Rome.

It is important to know to which conjugation a verb belongs in order to determine its tense.

The endings *-ēs, -et, -ēmus, -ētis, -ent* can denote the present tense of verbs of the 2nd conjugation or the future tense of verbs of the 3rd and 4th conjugations. If there is an *i* before the *e*, the verb will be the future tense of a 3rd conjugation **-iō** verb or the future tense of a 4th conjugation verb.

EXERCISE 23d

Following the examples, identify and translate the remainder of the verb forms below:

Verb	Conjugation	Tense	Meaning
habent	2	present	they have
mittent	3	future	they will send
vident			
iubent			
ascendent			
admovent			
timent			
dūcent			
rīdent			
facient			

EXERCISE 23e

Look carefully at the verbs in the following sentences. Decide the conjugation number first (this will help you get the tense right). Then read aloud and translate:

1. Puerī Eucleidem nōn vident sed vōcem eius audient.
2. Vidēsne senātōrēs in viīs? Quandō Cornēlius veniet?
3. Servī celeriter current, nam Cornēlium timent.
4. Sextus māne surget; in animō habet exīre.
5. Ego et Cornēlia tacēmus; patrem timēmus.

Read the dialogue below to yourself, mentally noting all verbs in the imperfect, perfect, and future tenses. Then take parts and read the dialogue aloud:

Intereā Eucleidēs et puerī cum Titō extrā Portam Capēnam stābant.

TITUS: Salvēte, puerī! Quid in itinere vīdistis? Vīdistisne rūsticōs in agrīs? Agrōsne colēbant?

SEXTUS: Rūsticōs vīdimus. Agrōs nōn colēbant, sed sub arboribus quiēscēbant. At caupōnam vīdimus; nostra raeda in fossā haerēbat et nōbīs necesse erat in 5 caupōnā pernoctāre.

MĀRCUS: Ita vērō! Gaudēbam quod pater meus in illā caupōnā pernoctāre cōnstituit. Caupō erat vir Graecus, amīcus Eucleidis.

SEXTUS: Ego quoque gaudēbam, nam mīles bonam fābulam nōbīs nārrāvit. In illā fābulā caupō quīdam hospitem necāvit. Tālēs fābulās amō. Sed quid nunc 10 faciēmus? Ego volō Circum Maximum vīsitāre. Ecce! Nōnne Circum Maximum suprā mūrōs urbis exstantem vidēre possum?

MĀRCUS: Ita vērō! Est Circus Maximus. Nōn procul abest.

TITUS: Nōn possumus omnia hodiē vidēre. Crās satis temporis habēbimus.

SEXTUS: Sed quid est illud aedificium? Nōnne pontem ingentem suprā portam videō? 15

MĀRCUS: Nōn pontem hīc vidēs, ō stulte! Est aquaeductus, Aqua Mārcia. Per illum aquaeductum Rōmānī aquam in urbem ferunt. Cavē imbrem, Sexte!

SEXTUS: Sed nōn pluit.

TITUS: Semper hīc pluit, Sexte. Rīmōsa enim est Aqua Mārcia.

1	**extrā**, prep. + acc., *outside*	15 **pōns, pontis**, gen. pl., **pontium**, m., *bridge*
4	**at**, conj., *but*	
10	**tālis, -is, -e**, *such*	16 **stultus, -a, -um**, *stupid, foolish*
11	Circus Maximus, *the Circus Maximus (a stadium in Rome)*	17 Cavē imbrem! *Watch out for the rain!* **imber, imbris**, gen. pl., **imbrium**, m., *rain*
12	**suprā**, prep. + acc., *above* **mūrus, -ī**, m., *wall* exstantem, *standing out, towering*	19 rīmōsus, -a, -um, *full of cracks, leaky*
14	satis temporis, *enough of time, enough time*	

3 **colō, colere, coluī, cultus**, *to cultivate*
4 **quiēscō, quiēscere, quiēvī, quiētūrus**, *to rest, keep quiet*
7 **cōnstituō, cōnstituere, cōnstituī, cōnstitūtus**, *to decide*
18 **pluit, pluere, pluit**, usually found only in 3rd person singular, *it rains, is raining*

Go Online
PHSchool.com
Web Code: jfd-0023

Verbs: Future Tense II

The following are the future tenses of the irregular verbs you have met:

Infinitive		ésse	pósse	vélle	nṓlle	férre	íre
Singular	1	érō	pótero	vólam	nṓlam	féram	íbō
	2	éris	póteris	vólēs	nṓlēs	férēs	íbis
	3	érit	póterit	vólet	nṓlet	féret	íbit
Plural	1	érimus	potérimus	volḗmus	nōlḗmus	ferḗmus	íbimus
	2	éritis	potéritis	volḗtis	nōlḗtis	ferḗtis	íbitis
	3	érunt	póterunt	vólent	nṓlent	férent	íbunt

Note that **velle, nōlle, ferre,** and **īre** have future tense endings like those of regular verbs. Note also where long vowels occur in the endings of these verbs. The tenses of the compounds of irregular verbs are formed in the same way as those of the uncompounded verbs, e.g., the future tense of **exeō** is **exībō**.

| **Cistern** | **Water wheel** | **Spring-fed watering channel** |

EXERCISE 23g

Read aloud, identify all verbs in the future tense, and translate:

1. Ībisne ad Cūriam, pater? Ita vērō! Ad Cūriam celeriter ībō.
2. Quandō domum redībis, pater? Nesciō.
3. Fortasse Cornēlius domum redīre brevī tempore poterit.
4. Eucleidēs et puerī in urbem māne exiērunt.
5. Necesse erat diū in urbe manēre.
6. Nocte vehicula magna onera in urbem ferent.

    redeō, redīre, rediī or **redīvī, reditūrus,** irreg., *to return, go back*
    exeō, exīre, exiī or **exīvī, exitūrus,** irreg., *to go out*

(continued)

7. Puerī Circum Maximum crās vidēre volent.
8. Ubi līberī māne erunt? Tū līberōs nōn vidēbis, nam ē domō nostrō mox exībunt.
9. Sī equī strēnuē labōrābunt, raedam ē fossā extrahere poterunt.
10. Sī pluet, ad silvam ambulāre nōlam.
11. Ferēsne cistam meam in caupōnam? Minimē! Tū ipse eam fer!
12. Redībitisne ad vīllam rūsticam? Fortasse redīre poterimus.
13. Volētisne crās ad Circum Maximum īre? Ita vērō! Crās illūc īre volēmus.
14. "Ego īre nōlam," inquit Aurēlia.
15. Post cēnam puerī cubitum īre nōlēbant.

ē domō nostrō, *out of our house*　　　**illūc**, adv., *there, to that place*

Note that in sentences 9 and 10 the verbs in both clauses are in the future tense because the actions in both clauses are conceived of as taking place at the same time in the future. English, however, normally uses the present tense in the *if* clause in this type of conditional sentence.

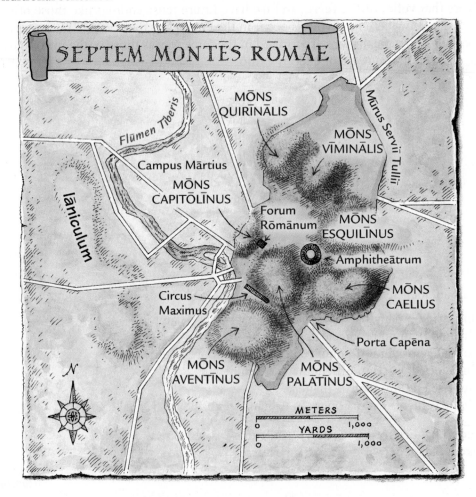

Go Online
PHSchool.com
Web Code: jfd-0023

AQUEDUCTS

One feature of the city that the Cornelii would notice as they approached Rome was the evidence of the Romans' passion for water. Abundant water for baths and fountains and pools was a vital necessity to the Romans, and water was brought in by aqueducts, whose arches strode into Rome from all directions. By A.D. 80, nine aqueducts were in use, carrying water across the plains to Rome from sources up to fifty-six miles or ninety kilometers distant.

The drawing on page 209 shows the arches supporting the water channel and a cross-section of the channel itself. To maintain the downhill flow, experts recommended a fall of six inches or fifteen centimeters in every ninety-eight feet or thirty meters. Tunnels, with inspection shafts built into them, were driven through those hills that were impossible to bypass. Sometimes, by using the principle that water rises to its own level, a U-shaped arrangement of the tunnel allowed an uphill flow.

The first aqueduct, named the Aqua Appia after its builder Appius Claudius, was built in 312 B.C. and ran underground for much of its route in order to speed its construction

France

A Roman aqueduct in southern France, called the Pont du Gard

This 8.5 mile long Roman aqueduct brought water to the city of Segovia into the twentieth century.

Roman aqueduct, Segovia, Spain

and to hide its presence from Rome's enemies. Its waters supported the growth in Rome's population during the fourth century B.C. Appius's pride in its construction was commemorated in his epitaph, which lists this accomplishment on a par with his victories in war.

Later aqueducts had to supply water to the more hilly and elevated districts of Rome. Since the Romans used a gravity system to propel the flow of water, sources higher in the Sabine and Alban Hills had to be found.

The Romans then hit on the idea of using arches to support the water channel. The arches turned out to be beautiful structures in themselves, but the Romans had adopted them for quite different reasons. The arches required less brick and stone than a solid wall and allowed people and animals to pass through easily. An arched structure could be easily repaired, as workmen could take the building materials from one side to the other.

Admiring comments about the aqueducts abound from native and foreigner alike. "Just as impressive," says one writer, "as the pyramids, but how much more useful!" Not only so, but we also have an astonishing book, *De aquis urbis Romae*, by Frontinus, Superintendent of Aqueducts, written about A.D. 97, describing the system in detail and the difficulties of organizing and maintaining it. He reports that, through bribery of watermen, supplies were sometimes diverted into private estates and never reached Rome at all. Householders in Rome itself often succeeded in bribing inspectors (who were, after all, slaves) to replace a narrow pipe by one of wider bore, while they continued to pay at the old rate!

The emperor appointed the Superintendent of Aqueducts, who, with his staff, had responsibility for maintaining and cleaning the whole vast system. Concern for the health of the immense population of Rome made the emperors keenly aware of the importance of maintaining a supply of clean water. In his official statement of his accomplishments, Augustus took justifiable pride in his improvement of the water supply of Rome:

> In many places I rebuilt the channels of the aqueducts that had collapsed due to old age, and the aqueduct which is called the Marcia I doubled in quantity, by means of a new source flowing into its channel.

Augustus, Res gestae 20

According to the latest available figures, the daily consumption of water in a large city today is about 120 gallons or 455 liters per person. According to Frontinus, in his day the Roman aqueducts could deliver over 264 million gallons or one billion liters in twenty-four hours, providing a daily allowance of about 240 gallons or 900 liters per person! The aqueducts leaked dreadfully, as the Cornelii found at the Porta Capena, and what with water thieves and corrupt inspectors, all this water did not actually reach Rome. For all that, the Roman citizen still had a lot of water at his disposal. Did he use it all? The answer is "Yes," because as one Roman writer put it, "The waters, having provided the city with the life-giving element, passed on into the sewers." The Roman, you see, hardly ever turned the tap off. For him, running water was quite literally running water!

Sketch of the Pont du Gard showing the water channel

1. Appius Claudius was responsible for both the first aqueduct and the first great Roman road, the Via Appia used by our characters. Both these projects took place in 312 B.C. What does this construction boom tell us about the Roman world of that year?
2. From the eassays that have appeared so far in this book, how would you characterize the Romans? What does this essay on aqueducts add to your characterization of the Romans?

ADDITIONAL READING:
The Romans Speak for Themselves: Book I: "The Aqueducts of Ancient Rome," pages 65–74.

ALWAYS TOMORROW

Simulac Titus et puerī et Eucleidēs urbem per Portam Capēnam intrāvērunt, clāmāvit Sextus, "Quid nōs prīmum faciēmus? Quō ībimus? Vīsitābimusne— ?"

"Quō tū nōs dūcēs, patrue?" interpellāvit Mārcus. "Vidēbimusne Cūriam et Forum? Sextus multa dē Rōmā lēgit et audīvit et nunc, patrue, omnia vidēre vult."

Titus, "Tacēte! Tacēte!" inquit. "Forum crās vīsitābimus. Crās, Eucleidēs, tibi licēbit 5
puerōs eō dūcere. Tum erit satis temporis. Hodiē tamen, puerī, vōs domum per urbem
dūcam et omnia in itinere vōbīs dēmōnstrābō."

Iam advēnerant ad Circum Maximum, quī nōn procul aberat. Stupuit Sextus ubi
mōlem Circī Maximī vīdit. Mārcus quoque stupuit, quamquam Circum anteā vīderat.
Stupuit Titus, attonitus nōn mōle, sed silentiō Circī. 10

"Ēheu! Ēheu!" inquit Titus. "Hodiē Circus est clausus. Tribus diēbus tamen prīnceps
ipse, Titus Flāvius Vespasiānus, lūdōs magnificōs faciet."

"Nōnne tū nōs eō dūcēs?" rogāvit Mārcus.

"Ēheu! Ego nōn poterō vōs dūcere," inquit Titus. "Fortasse Eucleidēs vōs dūcet."

(continued)

1 **simulac**, conj., *as soon as*
8 **advēnerant**, *they had arrived*
9 mōlēs, mōlis, gen. pl., mōlium, f.,
    mass, huge bulk
  vīderat, *he had seen*

10 **attonitus, -a, -um**, *astonished,
    astounded*
11 **clausus, -a, -um**, *shut, closed*
12 **lūdī, -ōrum**, m. pl., *games*

4 **legō, legere, lēgī, lēctus**, *to read*
5 **licet, licēre, licuit** + dat., usually found only in 3rd person singular
    and infinitive, *it is allowed*

EXERCISE 24a

Respondē Latīnē:

Go Online
PHSchool.com
Web Code: jfd-0024

1. Quis puerōs crās ad Forum dūcet?
2. Vīderatne Sextus anteā Circum Maximum?
3. Eratne Titus attonitus mōle Circī?
4. Cūr Circum hodiē puerī nōn intrant?
5. Quid faciet prīnceps tribus diēbus?
6. Dūcetne Titus puerōs ad lūdōs?

"Minimē!" respondit Sextus. "Librōs, nōn lūdōs amat Eucleidēs."

"Agite, puerī!" interpellāvit Titus. "Nunc circumībimus Montem Palātīnum et Forum intrābimus ad arcum Tiberiī. Ibi fortasse patrī tuō occurrēmus, Mārce. Mox senātōrēs ē Cūriā exībunt."

Itaque Circum relīquērunt et Palātīnum circumiērunt. Titus in itinere mōnstrāvit puerīs mīra aedificia quae prīncipēs in Palātīnō aedificāverant. Tandem ad arcum Tiberiī 20 advēnērunt, iam labōre et aestū dēfessī.

"Hic est arcus," inquit Titus, "quem— "

"Omnia vidēre poteritis crās," interpellāvit Cornēlius, quī eō ipsō tempore ad arcum ē Cūriā advēnerat. "Cum ad Forum crās redieritis, Eucleidēs omnia vōbīs explicābit. Iam sērō est. Agite! Iam domum ībimus." 25

15 **liber, librī,** m., *book*	21 aestū, *from the heat*
16 Mōns Palātīnus, Montis Palātīnī,	22 quem, acc., *which*
m., *the Palatine Hill*	24 **redieritis,** *you* (pl.) *will have returned,*
17 **arcus,** *arch*	*you return*
20 **aedificō, -āre, -āvī, -ātus,** *to build*	

16 **circumeō, circumīre, circumiī** or **circumīvī, circumitus,**
     irreg., *to go around*

17 **occurrō, occurrere, occurrī, occursūrus** + dat., *to meet, encounter*

Respondē Latīnē:

7. Quid amat Eucleidēs?
8. Quī mīra aedificia in Palātīnō aedificāverant?

9. Quis puerīs prope arcum Tiberiī occurrit?
10. Quō Cornēlius puerōs hodiē dūcet?

Go Online
PHSchool.com
Web Code: jfd-0024

BUILDING THE MEANING

Dative with Intransitive Compound Verbs

Look at the following sentence:

Ibi fortasse **patrī tuō** occurrēmus. (24:17) *Perhaps we will meet **your father** there.*

The verb **occurrere** is a compound verb, that is, it consists of the intransitive verb **currere** plus the prefix **ob-** *against,* which becomes **oc-** by assimilation to the initial consonant of the verb. The compound verb is still intransitive, and its meaning (*to run against, to meet*) is completed not by a direct object in the accusative case but by a word or phrase in the *dative case,* here **patrī tuō.**

You have also seen the intransitive compound verb **appropinquāre** (= the prefix **ad-** + **propinquāre**) used with the dative:

Iam **urbī** appropinquābant. (22:12)
*Already they were coming near **to the city**/approaching **the city.***

Sentences with compound verbs and the dative such as these give us another basic pattern of Latin sentences (see pages 8 and 21).

Ablative of Cause

You have met words or phrases in the ablative case assigning blame for something that has happened or stating the cause of someone's being in a certain state:

> **Tuā culpā** raeda est in fossā. (14:7)
> *Because of your fault* the carriage is in the ditch.
> *It's your fault* that the carriage is in the ditch.

> **magnā īrā** commōtus (14:17)   *moved **because of/by great anger***

> **itinere** dēfessī (23:8)   *tired **because of/from the journey***

> attonitus nōn **mōle**… (24:10)   *astonished not **because of/by the mass**…*

This is called the *ablative of cause*; note that no preposition is used in Latin.

Go Online
PHSchool.com
Web Code: jfd-0024

FORMS

Verbs: Pluperfect Tense

Look at this sentence:

> Mārcus quoque stupuit, quamquam Circum anteā **vīderat.** (24:9)
> *Marcus too was amazed, although **he had seen** the Circus before.*

The verb in the subordinate clause in this sentence is in the *pluperfect tense*. A verb in the pluperfect tense describes an action that was completed *before* some other action in the past took place. Thus, Marcus had seen the Circus *before* the occasion when he saw it in our story.

Verbs in the pluperfect tense can nearly always be translated with *had…* in English.

The endings of the pluperfect tense are the same for *all* Latin verbs. They look like the imperfect tense of **esse**:

Singular			Plural		
	1	-eram		1	-erāmus
	2	-erās		2	-erātis
	3	-erat		3	-erant

These endings are added to the perfect stem, which is found by dropping the *-ī* from the end of the third principal part, e.g., **relinquō, relinquere, relīquī,** perfect stem **relīqu-.**

Singular			Plural		
	1	relīqueram		1	relīquerāmus
	2	relīquerās		2	relīquerātis
	3	relīquerat		3	relīquerant

EXERCISE 24b

Read each sentence aloud. Identify each pluperfect verb and explain how the action it describes was completed before the action of the other verb took place. Then translate:

1. Eucleidēs puerōs ad urbem māne dūxerat et omnia eīs dēmōnstrābat.
2. Aurēlia laeta erat quod servī cēnam bonam iam parāverant.
3. Hodiē librum diū legēbam quem mihi herī dederās.
4. Dēfessus eram quod multās epistulās iam scrīpseram.
5. Vix domum advēnerant puerī, cum Eucleidēs in hortum intrāvit.

scrībō, scrībere, scrīpsī, scrīptus, *to write*   **vix**, adv., *scarcely*

EXERCISE 24c

Substitute the corresponding pluperfect form for each verb in parentheses (all present tense), read the sentence aloud, and translate:

1. Tantum sonitum numquam anteā (audīmus) _____.
2. Mārcus laetus erat quod patrī prope Cūriam (occurrit) _____.
3. Via erat plēna hominum quī ad urbem (veniunt) _____.
4. Lectīcāriī, quī Cornēlium per urbis viās (ferunt) _____, extrā Cūriam eum exspectābant.
5. Titus, quod Circum (invenit) _____ clausum, puerōs domum dūcēbat.
6. Sextus, ubi ad urbem advēnit, laetus erat quod numquam anteā in urbe Rōmā (est) _____.
7. Arcus, quem Tiberius (aedificat) _____, erat ingēns.
8. Senātōrēs iam ē Cūriā (exeunt) _____, cum puerī ad Forum advēnērunt.
9. Mārcus multa aedificia quae iam (videt) _____ iterum vīsitābat.
10. Sextus, quod multa dē Rōmā (audit) _____ et (legit) _____, omnia vidēre volēbat.

tantus, -a, -um, *so great, such a big*

NORTH AFRICA

Numidia

Mummy portraits such as these reflect the multicultural, multiethnic society of Roman Africa.
Funerary portraits from Roman Egypt, first to third centuries A.D.

Cornelius has been recalled to Rome due to urgent messages the emperor and consuls have received from the governor of the province of Africa (who is appointed by the Senate) and the prefect (administrator) of Numidia (see map, page 244). One of the fierce nomadic tribes of Africa, the Nasamones, has made several attacks on two of the colonies lately established in the province of Africa. The agricultural territory given to these colonies was seized from the Nasamones, who were consequently restricted to pasturing their flocks on poorer ground. Because these colonies contributed to the large supply of grain sent from Africa to Rome for free distribution to its inhabitants, the emperor asked the consuls to summon an extraordinary session of the Senate to consider what should be done to end the raids.

Cornelius's opinions and advice will be of particular interest to the emperor and Senate in their deliberations. At age seventeen Cornelius began his political career by serving as military tribune in the army stationed in Numidia and came to know some young men who are now leaders of the Nasamones. His subsequent experience in government offices has given him a good understanding of the potential danger posed by these raids. His first post after the army was on the Board of Twenty (**Vīgintīvirī**), where he and two others were placed in charge of the state mint. At age twenty-seven, elected as one of forty quaestors, he was in charge of the grain supply from Africa at Rome's port city, Ostia. As an ex-quaestor, Cornelius automatically became a member of the Senate and has attended its meetings regularly. At age thirty-two, he was elected curule aedile and was in charge of regulating the grain supply at Rome. Two years ago as the officer in charge of lawsuits involving foreigners (**praetor peregrīnus**) he adjudicated lawsuits of non-Roman citizens; because of his prior stay in Africa, he specialized in suits of non-Roman citizens of Africa. His friends in the Senate think he will be elected consul in a few years and that the Senate will probably appoint him governor of Africa after his year in that office.

264–241 B.C. AND
218–201 B.C.

Go Online
PHSchool.com
Web Code: jfd-0024

THE FIRST AND
SECOND PUNIC WARS

A s we learned in the essay on North Africa on page 215, Cornelius was recalled to Rome to take part in senatorial deliberations over attacks by native tribesmen on recently founded Roman colonies in Africa. Rome's involvement with North Africa already spanned hundreds of years—going back as far, in fact, as the Punic Wars of the third and second centuries B.C.

Rome, the great land power of Italy, engaged Carthage, the great sea power of North Africa, in a long struggle for control of Sicily and the western Mediterranean Sea that lasted through three wars and spanned more than a century (264–146 B.C.) A strong navy protected the flourishing commercial center of Carthage, colonized as an outpost centuries earlier by the Phoenicians, whom the Romans called **Pūnicī**. In the First Punic War (264–241 B.C.), the Romans were quick to realize that if they wanted to win they too must take to the sea. Roman marines shocked the Carthaginians when they dropped gangways with sharp metal points on one end, called "crows" (**corvī**), onto their decks; these held the enemy ships fast while the Romans boarded them with their superior soldiers. The birth of the Roman fleet ultimately led to a Roman victory.

Just as significant was the hatred between the two nations that the war produced. Roman legend confidently reports that Hannibal Barca, when he was a boy of nine years old, stood before an altar with his father, Hamilcar, and swore his undying hatred of the Romans. When Hannibal was twenty-six, troops loyal to Hamilcar, who had been slain in battle in Spain,

Hamilcar invites his son Hannibal to swear eternal enmity to Rome. Hamilcar points his sword at the she-wolf nursing Romulus and Remus, and Roman legionary standards lie on the ground.
Hannibal Swearing Eternal Enmity to Rome, *oil on canvas,* *Jacopo Amigoni*

were quick to pledge allegiance to Hannibal. Determined to fulfill his father's dreams of revenge on the Roman conquerors and of a new Carthaginian empire, Hannibal set out for Italy to ignite the Second Punic War (218–201 B.C.).

With an army of Carthaginians and mercenaries, Hannibal left Spain, crossed the Pyrenees, proceeded up the coast of France, and arrived at the great barrier into northern Italy, the Alps. Thirty-seven elephants, including Hannibal's pet, Syrus, were the most memorable members of the forces that Hannibal led up the Alps.

Fending off the attacks of mountain tribesmen, battling against snow and cold and slippery paths, the fiercely loyal troops reached a promontory high in the Alps where Hannibal, pointing to the vista of Italy far below his troops, proclaimed: "Now you are crossing not only the walls of Italy, but those of Rome." When a rockslide blocked their way down, Hannibal ordered his men to build fires that heated the rocks; according to the Roman historian Livy, the rocks split apart when sour wine was poured on them, clearing a path that the Carthaginian army descended, elephants and all.

Employing clever tactics, Hannibal dealt the Romans crushing defeats as he swept southward through Italy. The worst occurred at Lake Trasimene, where mist rising off the water prevented the Romans from realizing that they were heading into an ambush until the trap had already been sprung. At Cannae, a year later, Hannibal led the center of his line in a planned retreat, luring the Romans into a trap again. Hannibal's cavalry closed in from the flanks and dealt a crippling blow to the Roman army.

Hannibal did not have a large enough force at his command to march on the city of Rome, however. He waited, expecting that Rome's Italian allies would revolt and come

BELLUM PŪNICUM
SECUNDUM
218 – 201 B.C.

Saguntum
Carthāgō Nova
Rhodanus
Ticīnus
Padus
Trebia
Trasumennus
Lacus
(H)ADRIATICUM MARE
Roma
Capua
Cannae
TYRRHĒNUM MARE
Tarentum
Messāna
Syrācūsae
Rēgium
Carthāgō
Zama
IŌNIUM MARE

☐ Carthaginian Territory
☐ Roman Territory
⟶ Hannibal's Route

SCALE OF MILES
0   250   500

over to his side. They did not. For years Hannibal and the wary Romans played cat and mouse. In 207 B.C., Hasdrubal, Hannibal's brother, crossed the Alps with a relief force but was intercepted by the Romans—a disaster Hannibal learned about when a Roman cavalryman tossed Hasdrubal's head into his camp.

Publius Cornelius Scipio, the Roman commander, after victories over Carthaginian forces in Spain, returned to Italy and convinced the Roman Senate to send him to Africa with a Roman army. Scipio achieved so much success there that Hannibal, after fifteen years of fighting in Italy, was summoned to return home and defend Carthage. On the plain of Zama, Scipio, employing Hannibalic tactics against his foe, claimed the decisive victory of the war. Scipio received the title (**cognōmen**) **Africānus.** Hannibal, Rome's most memorable enemy, was forced into exile.

1. Summarize the three famous military encounters of the Second Punic War: Trasimene, Cannae, and Zama.
2. In Vergil's *Aeneid*, Dido, Queen of Carthage, when abandoned by Aeneas, curses the Trojans. With her dying breath, she calls upon **aliquis ultor** (*some avenger*) to arise from her bones. How would Vergil's Roman audience have interpreted this curse?
3. What are some ways in which the course of Western history might have been different if Hannibal and his Carthaginians had defeated Rome?

FORMS

Verbs: Future Perfect Tense

Look at this sentence:

"Cum ad Forum crās **redieritis**, Eucleidēs omnia vōbīs explicābit." (24:24)
*"When **you will have returned/you return** to the Forum tomorrow, Eucleides will explain everything to you."*

The verb in the subordinate clause in this sentence is in the *future perfect tense*. A verb in the future perfect tense describes an action that will have been completed *before* some other action in future time begins. Thus, the boys will have returned to the Forum *before* Eucleides will explain everything to them. Note that Latin verbs in the future perfect tense are often best translated by the present tense in English as in the example above, *When you return…* The literal translation is *When you will have returned….*

The endings of the future perfect tense are the same for *all* Latin verbs. They look like the future tense of **esse,** except for the 3rd person plural:

Singular			Plural		
	1	*-erō*		1	*-erimus*
	2	*-eris*		2	*-eritis*
	3	*-erit*		3	*-erint*

These endings are added to the perfect stem, which is found by dropping the *-ī* from the end of the third principal part, e.g., **redeō, redīre, rediī,** perfect stem **redi-**.

Singular	1	redi*erō*	Plural	1	redi*erimus*
	2	redi*eris*		2	redi*eritis*
	3	redi*erit*		3	redi*erint*

EXERCISE 24d

Read each sentence aloud. Identify each verb in the future perfect tense and explain how the action it describes will have been completed before the action of the other verb takes place. Then translate:

1. Sī baculum coniēceris, canēs ferōciter lātrābunt.
2. Cum ad Portam Capēnam advēnerimus, ē raedā dēscendēmus.
3. Sī equī raedam ē fossā extrāxerint, Cornēliī ad urbem iter facere poterunt.
4. Nisi caupō alium lectum in cubiculum mōverit, Aurēlia ibi dormīre nōlet.
5. Crās puerī, cum surrēxerint, strepitum plaustrōrum audient.
6. Eucleidēs et puerī, ubi Circum relīquērunt et Palātīnum circumiērunt, Forum intrāvērunt.
7. Cum ad arcum Tiberiī advēnerint, Cornēliō occurrent.
8. Crās puerī dēfessī erunt, sī omnia aedificia in forō vīsitāverint.
9. Aurēlia et Cornēlia, cum domum advēnerint, sē quiētī dabunt.
10. Aurēlia et Cornēlia, cum ē lectīs surrēxerint, lānam trahent.

   moveō, movēre, mōvī, mōtus, *to move*

EXERCISE 24e

Using the sentences in Exercise 24d and the charts of pluperfect and future perfect forms as guides, give the Latin for:

1. The boys had already thrown the stick.
2. We had already arrived at the Porta Capena.
3. The horses had not yet dragged the carriage out of the ditch.
4. Unless you will have moved/you move another bed into the bedroom, we will not be willing to sleep here.
5. Tomorrow when you will have gotten up/you get up, Sextus, you will hear the noise of wagons.
6. Eucleides and the boys had already left the Circus and had gone around the Palatine.
7. When we will have arrived/we arrive at the Arch of Tiberius, we will meet Cornelius.
8. Yesterday the boys had visited all the buildings in the forum. At night they were tired from their exertion/labor and the heat.
9. Aurelia and Cornelia had already rested.
10. What will you do when you will have gotten up/you get up, Aurelia and Cornelia?

Go Online
PHSchool.com
Web Code: jfd-0024

CULTURAL ASSIMILATION

In "Rome and Northern Europe" on pages 193–195, you were introduced to the Ubian girl Helge and her Roman legionary husband Lucius. Their story continues here.

One day, shortly before Helge's child was born, an officer of the **Legiō XX Valeria** came to Helge's hut and saw that she was weaving a colorful tartan for her husband. The men of the legion needed new tunics and cloaks, and the officer decided that the legionaries' women (**focāriae**) could weave and make tunics and cloaks for the legion. When Helge finished the tartan, she then wove cloth for legionary tunics and cloaks. Afterward, whenever she and the other Ubian legionary wives saw their men wearing the tunics and cloaks they had made, she and her friends felt pride in their work.

Helge bore a son, and when he was nine days old Lucius, the proud father, gave the baby his name and placed a **bulla** containing good luck charms around the child's neck in accordance with the Roman custom. Because Helge was not the daughter of a Roman citizen, little Lucius did not inherit Roman citizenship from his father. Lucius the legionary, however, knew that if his son served in a Roman auxiliary unit, he would be given citizenship upon discharge after twenty-five years of service. Helge knew that Roman citizenship brought certain privileges: exemption from taxation, the right to run for public office, and rights of appeal in cases of litigation in the Roman court.

As little Lucius grew from child to young man, the Romanization process continued. Lucius grew up speaking both Latin and the language of his mother's people. When the boy was seven years old, his father enrolled him in a school run by a Greek freedman. Helge learned that while the customs of her people allowed only the priests to know how to read and write, the Romans permitted literacy to everyone.

The population of the Roman settlement increased, and to meet its needs the men of the **Legiō XX Valeria** and the **Legiō I Germānica** built an underground aqueduct to bring water to the city from springs in the nearby hills. The legionaries also built a head-quarters (**praetōrium**) for the Roman governor of Lower Germany and a wall to enclose and protect the inhabitants. In addition, a road and a dock alongside the Rhine were built.

The years passed and Helge and Lucius were now the parents of four children. In addition to the first son, a daughter and two other sons had been born to them. Their first son joined the auxiliaries and looked forward to receiving the coveted Roman citizenship. Although years earlier Helge had been reluctant to accept Roman ways, she now had grown to appreciate the advantages of Roman civilization, especially after she

Roman parents enjoyed providing their children with toys such as this toddler's pull-toy in the form of a Roman cavalry soldier.
Wheeled toy, Romano-German, Cologne, first to third centuries A.D.

and a merchant were involved in a dispute over a price and the matter was settled in the court before a Roman magistrate (**praetor**) with both sides satisfied, instead of by a fight in which someone might have been killed. When she went shopping, she used Roman coin, which was acceptable to all the tradesmen instead of the complicated system of barter used by her own people and the clans on the other side of the Rhine.

Finally, Lucius received his honorable discharge (**missiō honesta**) from the legion, and, using his mustering-out pay of 3000 sesterces, he opened up a small tavern where he and his old comrades and other legionaries met to drink, spin tales of past campaigns, and play at **latruncul ī** (a game like chess). His two younger sons also joined the auxiliaries and along with their older brother participated in the invasion of Britain in A.D. 43.

And so we see how a common foot soldier peaceably helped spread Roman civilization and its benefits. Not all of Rome's conquests were military! The most enduring aspects of its civilization—its laws, its customs, and its architectural and engineering accomplishments—are still embodied in our present-day civilization.

1. List some distinct advantages of Romanization.
2. What disadvantages might the advance of Roman culture bring to the frontier?
3. If you had been Lucius, would you have stayed on the frontier after your discharge from the army or would you have returned to your native Italy? Explain your decision.

Go Online
PHSchool.com
Web Code: jfd-0024

MEMORIAL
INSCRIPTION

The following inscription on a tombstone found in Colchester, England, commemorates a centurion of the **Legiō XX Valeria**, named Marcus Favonius Facilis:

M·FAVON·M·F·POL·FACI
LIS>LEG XX VERECVND
VS·ET·NOVICIUS·LIB·POSV
ERUNT·H·S·E

M(ārcus) Favōn(ius), M(ārcī) f(īlius) Pol(liā)(tribū), Facilis (centuriō) leg(iōnis) XX. Verēcund-
us et Novīcius līb(ertī) posu-
ērunt. H(īc) s(itus) e(st).

Marcus Favonius Facilis, son of Marcus, of the Pollia tribe, centurion of the Twentieth legion. Verecundus and Novicius his freedmen set up this tomb. Here he lies buried.

Write a possible epitaph in English or Latin for Lucius or Helge based on the readings in Frontier Life I and II.

The emperor Domitian built the Arch of Titus in A.D. 81–82 to celebrate Titus's triumphs and his deification.
Rome

Exercise Va: Dative Case 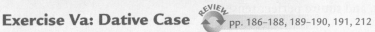 pp. 186–188, 189–190, 191, 212

Supply Latin words to match the English cues. Be sure to use the right endings. Explain the reason for each use of the dative case. Then read each sentence aloud and translate it:

1. Sextus fābulam dē caupōne scelestō _____ nārrābat. (to Cornelia)
2. Eucleidēs mandāta _____ et _____ dabat. (to the slaves) (to the slave-women)
3. Dum Cornēlius fābulam _____ nārrābat, _____ appropinquābant. (to his wife) (the city)
4. Interdiū raedās intrā urbem agere _____ nōn licēbat. (to *or* for the Romans)
5. "_____ necesse est ad Cūriam īre." (For me)
6. Titus respondet, "_____ lectīcāriōs condūxī." (For you, *pl.*)
7. "Ego multa et mīra _____ et _____ explicābō," inquit Titus. (to you, *sing.*) (to Sextus)
8. "_____ in caupōnā pernoctāre necesse erat," inquit Sextus. (for us)
9. Crās Forum vīsitāre _____ licēbit. (to *or* for the boys)
10. Hodiē māne _____ dormīre licet. (to *or* for Cornelia)
11. Cornēlius ē Cūriā mox exībit. _____ Mārcus et Sextus occurrent. (Him)
12. Titus mīra aedificia _____ mōnstrāvit. (to the boys)
13. Crās multa alia aedificia _____ mōnstrābit. (to them)

Exercise Vb: Future, Pluperfect, and 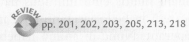 pp. 201, 202, 203, 205, 213, 218
Future Perfect Tenses

Read aloud, identify the tenses of the verbs, and translate:

1. "Sī ego ad Cūriam sērō advēnerō, senātōrēs īrātī erunt," cōgitābat Cornēlius.
2. Sextus numquam aedificia tam magnifica vīderat.
3. Crās Eucleidēs puerōs ad Forum dūcet.
4. Ībisne cum puerīs, Cornēlia?
5. Crās puerī in Forō aderunt et aedificia vidēbunt.
6. Cornēlius fābulam dē caupōne scelestō nārrātam nōn audīverat.
7. "Sī fābulam mīlitis audīverimus, pater, statim cubitum ībimus," inquit Mārcus.
8. Crās Cornēlius fābulam Aurēliae nārrāre poterit.
9. Nēmō caupōnam Apollodōrī anteā reprehenderat.
10. Cum pater manūs lāverit et aliam togam induerit, ad Cūriam statim ībit.

   tam, adv., *so, such*

Exercise Vc: Verb Forms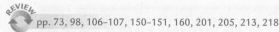

pp. 73, 98, 106–107, 150–151, 160, 201, 205, 213, 218

Give the requested forms of the following verbs in the present, imperfect, future, perfect, pluperfect, and future perfect tenses:

	Present	Imperfect	Future	Perfect	Pluperfect	Future Perfect
1. circumīre (3rd pl.)	———	———	———	———	———	———
2. dēscendere (2nd sing.)	———	———	———	———	———	———
3. ferre (2nd pl.)	———	———	———	———	———	———
4. dare (1st pl.)	———	———	———	———	———	———
5. esse (3rd sing.)	———	———	———	———	———	———
6. respondēre (1st sing.)	———	———	———	———	———	———
7. surgere (3rd pl.)	———	———	———	———	———	———
8. cōgitāre (2nd sing.)	———	———	———	———	———	———
9. conicere (1st sing.)	———	———	———	———	———	———
10. venīre (1st pl.)	———	———	———	———	———	———

Exercise Vd: Reading Comprehension

Read the following passage and answer the questions below with full sentences in Latin:

ROME'S FIERCEST ENEMY

Ubi Hannibal puer novem annōrum erat, pater eius, nōmine Hamilcar, ad Hispāniam multīs cum mīlitibus nāvigāre parābat. Multīs ante annīs Rōmānī Hamilcarem in bellō vīcerant; ab Carthāginiēnsibus īnsulās Siciliam Sardiniam-que cēperant. Nunc in animō habēbat Hamilcar ad Hispāniam trānsīre et ibi imperium novum condere. In Āfricā manēre nōlēbat puer Hannibal, itaque patrī 5 appropinquāvit.

"Pater, pater!" clāmāvit Hannibal. "Dūc mē tēcum ad Hispāniam! Nōlī mē in Āfricā cum puerīs relinquere!"

"Sed tū puer es," respondit pater, quī eō ipsō tempore ōmina ad āram cōnsulere parābat. "Virī Carthāginiēnsēs, nōn puerī, hostēs Rōmānīs sunt." 10

"Puer nōn sum," inquit Hannibal. "Sī tū hostis Rōmānīs es, ego quoque Rōmānīs hostis sum."

"Sī ita cōgitās," inquit Hamilcar, "necesse tibi erit id iūre iūrandō affirmāre." Manum fīliī in capite victimae posuit.

Hannibal, "Ego semper hostis Rōmānīs erō," inquit. "Semper contrā 15 Rōmānōs pugnābō. Nōn quiēscam nisi urbem Rōmam cēperō."

Itaque Hamilcar sēcum ad Hispāniam fīlium Hannibalem dūxit. Multīs post annīs Hannibal, ubi dux Carthāginiēnsium erat, ingentem exercitum contrā Rōmānōs dūxit; multa et mīra perfēcit. Contrā Rōmānōs diū pugnābat et eōs multīs in proeliīs vīcit. Numquam habuērunt Rōmānī hostem ferōciōrem. 20

1 annus, -ī, m., *year*
2 Hispānia, -ae, f., *Spain*
  nāvigō, -āre, -āvī, -ātūrus, *to sail*
  multīs ante annīs, *many years before*
3 bellum, -ī, n., *war*
  Carthāginiēnsēs, Carthāginiēnsium,
    m. pl., *the Carthaginians*
  īnsula, -ae, f., *island*
4 -que, enclitic conj., *and*
5 imperium, -ī, n., *empire*
9 ōmen, ōminis, n., *omen*
  āra, -ae, f., *altar*
10 hostis, hostis, gen. pl., hostium, m.,
   enemy

13 id, *it*
  iūre iūrandō affirmāre, *to affirm by*
   swearing an oath
14 caput, capitis, n., *head*
  victima, -ae, f., *sacrificial victim*
15 contrā, prep. + acc., *against*
16 pugnō, -āre, -āvī, -ātūrus, *to fight*
17 multīs post annīs, *many years later*
18 exercitus, *army*
20 proelium, -ī, n., *battle*
  ferōciōrem, *fiercer*

   3 vincō, vincere, vīcī, victus, *to conquer*
   4 trānseō, trānsīre, trānsiī or trānsīvī, trānsitus, irreg., *to go across*
   5 condō, condere, condidī, conditus, *to found*
 19 perficiō, perficere, perfēcī, perfectus, *to accomplish*

1. How old was Hannibal when his father prepared to sail to Spain?
2. What had the Romans done many years before?
3. What did Hamilcar intend to do?
4. What did Hannibal not want to do?
5. Why did Hamilcar want to leave Hannibal in Africa?
6. What did Hannibal want to be?
7. Where did Hamilcar place Hannibal's hand?
8. Hannibal will never rest unless he does what?
9. How did Hannibal go about trying to fulfill his oath?
10. Did the Romans ever have a fiercer enemy?

Roman battle ship

EXERCISE Ve

1. In lines 1–6 of the passage on page 224, identify two verbs in the pluperfect tense and explain why this tense is used in each instance.
2. In lines 13–16 of the passage on page 224, identify five verbs in the future or future perfect tense, and explain why the tense is used in each instance.

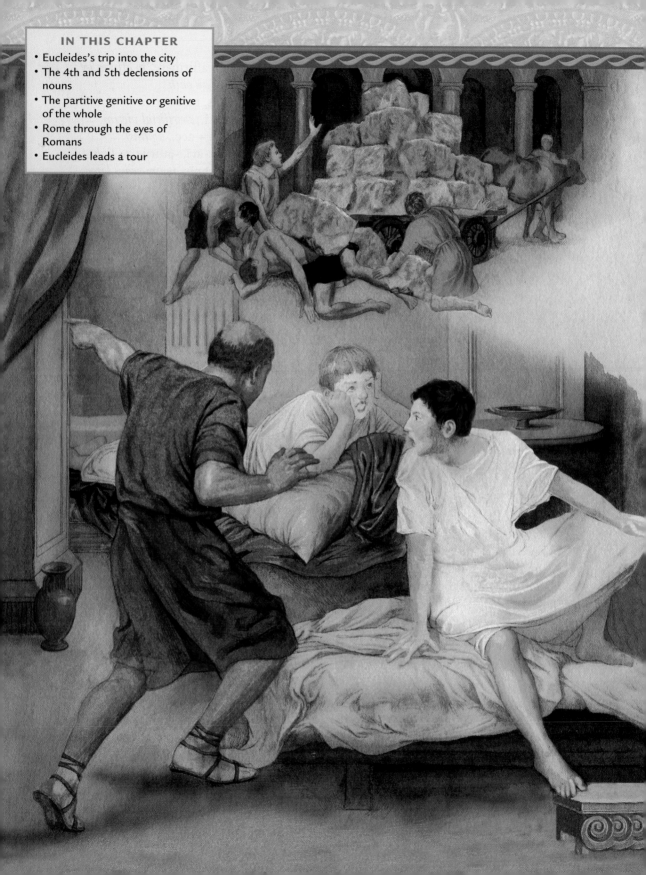

First Morning in Rome

Iam diēs erat. Magnus erat clāmor in urbe. Servī ad Forum magnō tumultū onera ferēbant. Undique clāmor et strepitus! Sed nihil clāmōris, nihil strepitūs ad Mārcum pervēnit. In lectō stertēbat, nam dēfessus erat. Sextus quoque in lectō manēbat sed dormīre nōn poterat. Clāmōribus et strepitū excitātus, iam cōgitābat dē omnibus rēbus quās Titus heri nārrāverat. "Quid hodiē vidēbimus? Cornēliusne nōs in Forum dūcet? 5
Ego certē Forum et Cūriam et senātōrēs vidēre volō."

Intereā Eucleidēs, quī prīmā lūce exierat, iam domum redierat. Statim cubiculum puerōrum petīvit et, "Eho, puerī!" inquit. "Cūr nōndum surrēxistis? Abhinc duās hōrās ego surrēxī. Quod novum librum emere volēbam, in Argīlētum māne dēscendī ad tabernam quandam ubi in postibus nōmina multōrum poētārum vidēre potes. 10
Catullus, Flaccus—"

At puerī celeriter interpellāvērunt quod Eucleidēs, ut bene sciēbant, semper aliquid novī docēre volēbat. "Quid in viīs vīdistī?"

Eucleidēs, "Nihil," inquit, "nisi miserum hominem lapidibus oppressum. Bovēs lapidēs quadrātōs in plaustrō trahēbant ad novum aedificium quod Caesar prope 15
Domum Auream cōnficit. Illud aedificium est ingēns amphitheātrum et mox prīnceps lūdōs ibi faciet. Sī bonī puerī fueritis, fortasse ad lūdōs ībitis."

1 **tumultus**, *uproar, commotion*
4 **excitātus, -a, -um,** *wakened, aroused*
   dē omnibus rēbus, *about everything*
8 Eho! interj., *Hey!*
   abhinc duās hōrās, *two hours ago*
   abhinc, adv., *ago, previously*
10 ad tabernam quandam, *to a certain shop*
   taberna, -ae, f., *shop*

postis, postis, gen. pl., postium, m.,
   doorpost
poēta, -ae, m., *poet*
12 aliquid, *something*
14 **lapis, lapidis,** m., *stone*
   oppressus, -a, -um, *crushed*
15 quadrātus, -a, -um, *squared*
   quod, *which, that*
16 Domus Aurea, *(Nero's) Golden House*

3 **perveniō, pervenīre, pervēnī, perventūrus,** *to arrive (at), reach*
   stertō, stertere, stertuī, *to snore*
15 **trahō, trahere, trāxī, tractus,** *to drag, pull*
16 **cōnficiō, cōnficere, cōnfēcī, cōnfectus,** *to finish*

EXERCISE 25a

Respondē Latīnē:

1. Cūr Sextus dormīre nōn poterat?
2. Quid Sextus facere et vidēre vult?
3. Cūr Eucleidēs in Argīlētum dēscendit?
4. Quid in postibus tabernae vīdit?
5. Quid Eucleidēs in viīs vīdit?
6. Quid prīnceps mox faciet?

Nouns: 4th and 5th Declensions

Most Latin nouns belong to the 1st, 2nd, or 3rd declensions. There are two other declensions, to which a few nouns belong. Most 4th declension nouns are masculine, and most 5th declension nouns are feminine. Note, however, that **diēs** is usually masculine. Be sure to learn these forms thoroughly.

Note endings that could be more than one case and those that could be more than one case and number.

Number Case	4th Declension	5th Declension	
Singular			
Nominative	árcus	díēs	rēs
Genitive	árcūs	diḗī	rḗī
Dative	árcuī	diḗī	rḗī
Accusative	árcum	díem	rem
Ablative	árcū	diē	rē
Vocative	árcus	díēs	rēs
Plural			
Nominative	árcūs	díēs	rēs
Genitive	árcuum	diḗrum	rḗrum
Dative	árcibus	diḗbus	rḗbus
Accusative	árcūs	díēs	rēs
Ablative	árcibus	diḗbus	rḗbus
Vocative	árcūs	díēs	rēs

Nouns of the 4th and 5th declensions will appear in vocabularies as follows:

4th Declension
aestus, -ūs, m., *heat*
aquaeductus, -ūs, m., *aqueduct*
arcus, -ūs, m., *arch*
complexus, -ūs, m., *embrace*
domus, -ūs, f., *house, home*
manus, -ūs, f., *hand*

rīsus, -ūs, m., *smile, laugh*
senātus, -ūs, m., *Senate*
sonitus, -ūs, m., *sound*
strepitus, -ūs, m., *noise, clattering*
tumultus, -ūs, m., *uproar, commotion*

5th Declension
diēs, diēī, m., *day*

rēs, reī, f., *thing, matter, situation*

EXERCISE 25b

Identify the case and number of each of the following nouns (give all possibilities):

1. sonitūs
2. diēbus
3. arcum
4. arcuum
5. diēs
6. senātuī
7. reī
8. diērum
9. rem
10. sonituum
11. rīsū
12. aestus
13. tumultibus
14. rēs
15. domus

ante meridiem, *before noon*
post meridiem, *after noon*
per diem, *a daily allowance for expenses*
in medias res, *into the middle of things*
in situ, *in its original place*

Read aloud, mentally noting the case and number of each 4th and 5th declension noun, paying special attention to each ending that could be more than one case. Then translate:

1. Mediā nocte tumultum magnum audīvī. Quae erat causa huius tumultūs? Magnō cum strepitū bovēs plaustra per viās trahēbant. Prīmum strepitus procul aberat; deinde in viā nostrā erat tumultus.

   causa, -ae, f., *reason*   huius, *of this*

   absum, abesse, āfuī, āfutūrus, irreg., *to be away, be absent, be distant*

2. Multās rēs manibus nostrīs facimus. Eucleidēs manū stilum tenēbat, nam puerōs scrībere docēbat. Puerī arborēs manibus et pedibus anteā ascenderant. Manūs igitur eōrum sordidae erant. Eucleidēs eōs iussit manūs statim lavāre.

   stilus, -ī, m., *pen*   **eōrum,** *of them, their*

3. Multōs diēs in vīllā manēbāmus. Vēnit tamen diēs reditūs. Necesse erat iter trium diērum facere quod ad urbem celerrimē redīre volēbāmus. Eō diē discessimus. Duōs diēs per Viam Appiam iter faciēbāmus. Tertiō diē Rōmam pervēnimus.

   reditus, -ūs, m., *return*   eō diē, *on that day*   tertius, -a, -um, *third*

4. Titus rem mīram nōbīs nārrāvit. Servus, quī nocte per viās urbis ambulābat, subitō fūgit perterritus. Quae erat causa huius reī? In viā occurrerat canī quī, ut ipse dīxit, tria capita habēbat. Dē tālibus rēbus in librīs saepe legimus sed numquam tālem rem ipsī vīdimus. Dē hāc rē omnēs cīvēs multās fābulās nārrant.

   fugiō, fugere, fūgī, fugitūrus, *to flee*   **caput, capitis,** n., *head*

BUILDING THE MEANING

Go Online
PHSchool.com
Web Code: jfd-0025

The Partitive Genitive or Genitive of the Whole

Look at the following sentence:

> Eucleidēs semper **aliquid novī** docēre volēbat. (25:12–13)
> *Eucleides always wanted to teach **something new**.*

The Latin words in boldface literally mean *something of the new*. The word **novī** is an adjective in the neuter genitive singular used as a substantive (see page 200). A better English translation is simply *something new*.

The word in the genitive case refers to a larger whole (*the new*) of which only a part (**aliquid,** *something*) is under consideration. This is called the *partitive genitive* or *genitive of the whole*.

Here are other examples that you have seen in the stories:

> Nihil **malī.** (21:7)   satis **temporis** (24:6)
> *Nothing **of a bad thing**. = There is nothing wrong.*   *enough **of time** = enough time*

Find two examples in line 2 of the story on page 227. For more on the partitive genitive, see page 281.

Go Online
PHSchool.com
Web Code: jfd-0025

ROME

Impressions of Rome

What nation is so far distant, Caesar, or so barbarous that it does not have a representative at the games here in your city? Here come farmers from the Balkans, natives of South Russia nurtured on horse's blood, people from the banks of the Nile, as well as those from the Atlantic's farthest shores. Here too are Arabs, men from Southern Turkey, German tribesmen, and Ethiopians—all so different in dress and in appearance. Their speech too sounds all different; yet it is all one when you are hailed, Caesar, as the true father of our country.

Martial, *De spectaculis* III

Caecilius, in your own eyes you are a polished gentleman, but take my word for it, you are not. What are you then? A clown! You are like the hawker from across the Tiber who trades pale brimstone matches for broken glass or the man

Tunisia

Rome imported grains, wines, and other kinds of food from all over the empire, including North Africa.
Mosaic, Tunisia, second-third centuries A.D.

This terra cotta plaque from the bustling port and commercial center of Ostia shows a shopfront with (far left) the shopkeeper and a customer haggling over the price of a hare; fresh-killed poultry hanging from a rack; an aged customer buying fruit from the shopkeeper's wife; hutches containing hares beneath the counter; and two monkeys on the counter to attract the attention of passers-by.
Funerary stele from Ostia, third century A.D.

who sells to the idle bystanders soggy pease-pudding; like the keeper and trainer of snakes or the cheap slaves of the salt-sellers; like the hoarse-voiced seller of smoking sausages with his hot trays or a third-class street poet.

Martial, *Epigrams* I.41

If duty calls, the crowd gives way and the rich man is borne along rapidly over their heads by stout Liburnian bearers. On the way he will read, write, or sleep, for with the windows shut the litter induces sleep. Even so, he will get there before us. Though we hurry, the sea of humanity in front hinders us, and the great throng following jostles our backs. One man strikes us with his elbow, another with a hard pole; one knocks a beam against our heads, another a barrel. Our legs are plastered with mud, we are trampled on all sides by great feet, a soldier's hob-nailed boot crushes my toe. Newly patched togas are torn. A tall fir tree sways as the wagon rumbles on. Other carts carry pine trees, a nodding menace over the heads of the crowd. If the cart carrying Ligurian stone tilts forward and pours its overturned pile on the crowds, what remains of their bodies?

Juvenal, *Satires* III.239

The Streets of Rome

Roman houses were neither named nor numbered. Hence the very complicated instructions given to those wishing to reach a certain "address":

> Every time you meet me, Lupercus, you ask, "May I send a slave to fetch your book of poems? I'll return it as soon as I've read it." Lupercus, it's not worth troubling your slave. It's a long journey to the Pear Tree, and I live up three flights of steep stairs. You can find what you want closer to home. No doubt you often go down to the Argiletum. There's a shop opposite Caesar's Forum with both door-posts covered with advertisements so that you can in a moment read the names of all the poets. Look for me there.
>
> Martial, *Epigrams* I.117

Domitian, who followed Titus as Emperor of Rome, issued an edict forbidding shopkeepers to display their wares on the streets. This, according to Martial, was a vast improvement:

> The aggressive shopkeepers had taken the whole city away from us and never kept to the limits of their thresholds. But you, Domitian, ordered our narrowed streets to expand and what had been but a path has now become a street. No longer do they chain wine bottles to the pillars in front of their shops, and no longer are officials forced to walk in the middle of the mud. No longer does the barber blindly draw his razor in a dense crowd, and no longer do the greasy fast-food shops take up the whole street. The barbers, bartenders, cooks, and butchers now keep to their own thresholds. Now Rome is a city again, whereas before it was just one big shop.
>
> Martial, *Epigrams* VII.61

Streets had raised stepping stones that allowed pedestrians to cross when the street was flooded with rainwater.
Pompeiian street

Shopping malls are as old as Rome. Here, art lovers admire wares on display in an elaborate portico setting.
Roman Art Lover, *oil on canvas, 1870, Sir Lawrence Alma-Tadema*

Columns and Porticos

The column was one of the main features of Roman architecture. Sometimes a single column was used to support a statue; more often, columns were used to support the roofs or to form the entrance porches of temples and other buildings.

From the idea of the porch, there developed the portico or long covered walk, which afforded the citizens protection from sun and dust, while allowing them to enjoy the fresh air. In the shelter of the portico various activities took place. The Portico of Minucius was used as a corn exchange; in another a vegetable market was held. In the porticos, philosophers lectured, poets recited, schoolmasters held their classes, lawyers met their clients, entertainers performed, snacks were sold, and business deals were concluded. In fact, porticos became so common that it was eventually possible to walk from one end of the city to the other without coming out into the open at all!

According to one writer, porticos covered more than a quarter of the total area of the Campus Martius, the number of columns supporting them being about 2,000. Halls built in the shelter of these housed wall-maps of Rome and the Roman world, exhibitions of wonders from the Far East, natural marvels such as a snake 23 yards or 21 meters long, and, in the Portico of Philippus, a display of wigs and the latest in ladies' hairstyles.

---

1. Summarize Martial's and Juvenal's views of life in the metropolis of Rome.
2. If you had been Cornelius or Aurelia, would you have allowed your children to go out into the city without an escort? Why or why not?

ADDITIONAL READING:
The Romans Speak for Themselves: Book I: "Finding One's Way in Ancient Rome," pages 75–81.

EXERCISE 25d

Take parts, read aloud, and translate:

SEXTUS: Quam dēfessus sum, Mārce! Nam hodiē māne dormīre nōn poteram. Tantus clāmor in viīs erat.

MĀRCUS: Quālem clāmōrem audīvistī? Ego certē nihil clāmōris audīvī.

SEXTUS: Quid? Nōnne audīvistī illōs canēs in viīs lātrantēs? Multās hōrās lātrābant. Numquam audīvī tantum strepitum. Audīvī etiam clāmōrem multōrum   5
hominum quī per viās currēbant.

MĀRCUS: Quid clāmābant?

SEXTUS: Id audīre nōn poteram, nam omnēs simul clāmābant. Certē tamen īrātī erant. Erat quoque strepitus plaustrōrum. Nōs in urbe heri plaustra nōn vīdimus. Unde vēnērunt plaustra?   10

MĀRCUS: Interdiū nōn licet plaustra intrā urbem agere. Nocte igitur necesse est labōrāre. Servī in urbem ferēbant cibum, vīnum, lapidēs—

SEXTUS: Cūr lapidēs in urbem tulērunt?

MĀRCUS: Caesar ingēns amphitheātrum in urbe cōnficit.

SEXTUS: Nōs illud aedificium vīdimus?   15

MĀRCUS: Heri illud cōnspexistī, ubi ad Forum cum patre meō dēscendēbāmus. Heri nōn satis temporis erat id īnspicere quod pater domum festīnābat. Sed mox amphitheātrum iterum vīsitābimus atque id īnspiciēmus. Fortasse Eucleidēs nōs dūcet.

SEXTUS: Dum hoc mihi dīcis, multī hominēs in domum nostram vēnērunt. Quī sunt?   20

MĀRCUS: Nōnne heri in urbe vīdistī multōs cīvēs post senātōrem sequentēs? Hic erat patrōnus, illī erant clientēs. Pater meus est patrōnus multōrum cīvium. Tū audīvistī clientēs domum intrantēs.

SEXTUS: Ēheu! Eucleidēs quoque intrāvit!

12 **vīnum, -ī,** n., *wine*   22 illī, *those men, the former*
21 sequentēs, *following*
hic, *this man, the latter*

Patrōnī were wealthy men who gave food or money to their dependents (**clientēs**). The **clientēs** came to the patron's home early in the morning to receive this dole and then escorted him to the Forum and performed other services for him. Here is Juvenal's satirical comment:

> Now the meager dole sits on the outer edge of the threshold of the patron's house to be snatched up by the clients in their togas. But first the patron inspects each face, fearing that someone might come and claim his due under a false name. Once he recognizes you, you'll get your share.
>
> Juvenal, *Satires* I.95–99

Go Online
PHSchool.com
Web Code: jfd-0025

EUCLEIDES THE TOUR GUIDE

Marcus had always visualized himself showing Sextus around the city of Rome, but he should have realized that Cornelius would never allow Sextus and himself to wander around Rome unsupervised. If neither Cornelius nor Titus were free to act as guide, Eucleides was bound to be their companion. He certainly knew a lot; the trouble was, there was no stopping him.

"Rome," Eucleides was now saying in that pedagogical tone of his, "is built on seven hills, the most famous being the Capitoline and the Palatine. By now, of course, it has far outstripped these petty limits. Augustus divided it into fourteen regions, which are in turn subdivided into 265 **vīcī** or wards. At the last census the population numbered 1,284,602, living in 1,797 **domūs** and 46,602 **īnsulae**."

"I can't see any islands!" complained Sextus, in all seriousness.

"**Īnsulae**," explained Eucleides, "are those apartment buildings, some of them five stories high."

"And the **Īnsula Feliculae** is the biggest in the world," said Marcus.

"There are," said Eucleides, "64 miles of streets, using your Roman measurements."

"Not very wide, are they?" commented Sextus.

"The maximum width according to *The Twelve Tables* can be only 17 feet."

"And some of them are not even paved!" cried Sextus, peering along the dark tunnel they were now traversing between the **īnsulae**.

Reconstruction of an *īnsula* (*center*) in Ostia with shops on the ground floor and apartments on the floors above
Ostia, second century A.D.

"Watch out!" yelled Marcus, pulling Sextus and Eucleides close to the wall to dodge a deluge of slops from a third-floor window.

"We'll have the law on you for that!" shouted Marcus up at the unseen lawbreaker. But Eucleides, not anxious to linger bandying threats, hustled the boys off through the labyrinth of shadowy alleys.

Suddenly they emerged into the blinding sun of the open Forum.

"This," said Eucleides impressively, pointing to a massive column, "is the center of the universe, the *Golden Milestone*. Erected by Augustus, it bears upon it in letters of gilt bronze the distances to all the cities of the Empire."

But it was not the *Golden Milestone* the boys were looking at, nor was it the splendor of the temple of Jupiter Optimus Maximus on the Capitoline Hill behind them. They were gazing into the **Forum Rōmānum,** which glittered with marble and bronze and gold. Senators and businessmen with their slaves were hurrying in and out of the **basilicae** that flanked the Forum. The noise was deafening. Cries of sausage-sellers and pastry-vendors mingled with the uproar of every language under heaven. White toga and tunic jostled with colorful foreign garb of all kinds.

Eucleides, sensing their preoccupation, was just pursing his lips to launch into a lecture on the Forum; but Marcus and Sextus were off, scampering along the **Via Sacra.**

"Come and tell us what's going on here!" they shouted, running to the far end of the Forum where their attention had been caught by the feverish activity of an army of masons engaged, amidst mountains of rubble and building stone, in some mammoth task of demolition or construction—it was hard to tell which.

"The Emperor Nero—" began Eucleides breathlessly as he caught up with them.

"I know," said Marcus. "He's the one that set Rome on fire for fun."

"The Emperor Nero," Eucleides repeated, "on the space cleared of unsightly hovels by a quite accidental fire, built the wonderful **Domus Aurea.**"

"And they're still working at it by the look of it!" said Sextus, grinning.

"No, you idiot!" said Marcus. "Vespasian and Titus pulled down parts of Nero's folly and are putting up things for the citizens of Rome to enjoy, baths, for instance, and—"

"And that terrific statue over there?" pointed Sextus.

"That was a statue of Nero himself," Marcus went on, "but Vespasian put rays around its head and made it into a statue of the sun-god."

"It is 118 feet high," began Eucleides, but his hearers were gone again, toward an immense building nearing completion.

"What's this?" they asked, as an exhausted Eucleides caught up with them.

"This is the **Amphitheātrum Flāvium,**" he gasped. "The Emperor Titus is to dedicate it soon."

ADDITIONAL READING:
The Romans Speak for Themselves: Book I: "Domus Aurea Neronis," pages 82–88.

Forum Rōmānum Aetāte Augustī

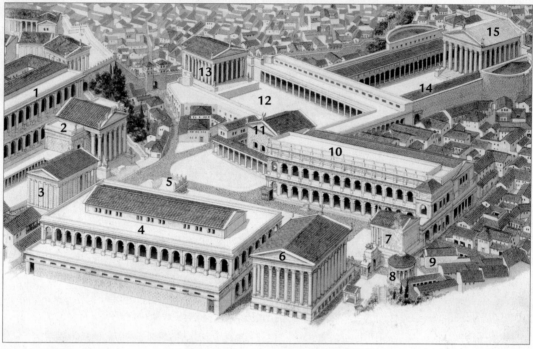

Watercolor, Peter Connolly

1 Tabularium
2 Temple of Concord
3 Temple of Saturn
4 Basilica Julia
5 Rostra
6 Temple of Castor and
   Pollux
7 Temple of the Deified
   Julius Caesar
8 Temple of Vesta
9 Regia
10 Basilica Aemilia
11 Curia Julia
12 Forum of Julius Caesar
13 Temple of Venus
   Genetrix
14 Forum of Augustus
15 Temple of Mars Ultor

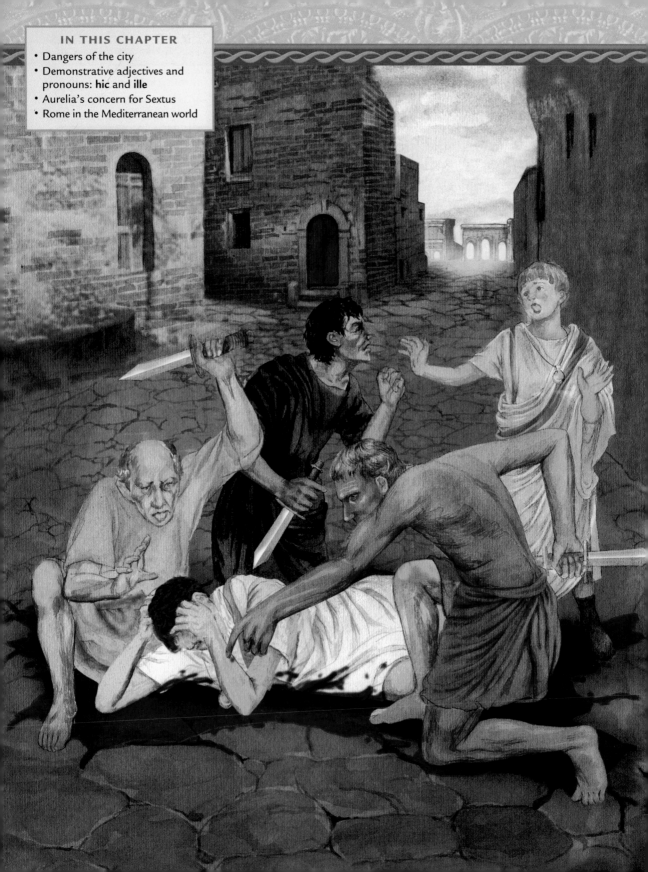

A GRIM LESSON

Eucleidēs et puerī iam domum redierant. Post cēnam Cornēlius et Mārcus et Sextus in ātriō sedēbant.

"Quid hodiē vīdistis, puerī?" inquit Cornēlius.

"Nihil nisi aedificia antīqua," respondit Mārcus. "Nōs in urbem exīre volumus sōlī. Cūr nōn licet?" 5

Cui Cornēlius, "Est perīculōsum sine custōde exīre in viās huius urbis. Sunt multī hominēs scelestī quī bona cīvium arripiunt. Nōnnumquam hī hominēs cīvēs ipsōs necant. Vōbīs igitur nōn licet sine custōde exīre. Iam sērō est. Nunc necesse est vōbīs cubitum īre. Nōlīte cessāre sed īte statim!"

Puerī, labōre diēī dēfessī, simulac cubitum iērunt, obdormīvērunt. 10

Postrīdiē māne Mārcus in lectō suō iacēbat et dē Circō Maximō ita cōgitābat: "Quandō Circum Maximum vīsitābimus? Cūr pater meus nōs exīre vetat? Heri nūllōs hominēs scelestōs in urbe vīdī. Interdiū certē praedōnēs nōbīs nōn nocēbunt. Meum patrem, quod est senātor Rōmānus, praedōnēs timent. Nihil perīculī est."

Brevī tempore, ut Mārcō vidēbātur, puerī ad Circum ībant. Mox mōlem ingentem 15 Circī Maximī Mārcus cōnspexit.

"Ecce!" clāmāvit Mārcus. "Est Circus. Cum intrāverimus, tandem aurīgās ipsōs spectābimus."

Subitō tamen in viam sē praecipitāvērunt trēs hominēs.

"Cavē illōs hominēs!" clāmāvit Sextus. "Illī certē nōs in domūs vīcīnās trahent et ibi 20 nōs necābunt."

Sed frūstrā, nam Mārcus, metū commōtus, postquam Sextum audīvit clāmantem, ad terram cecidit et iacēbat in lutō immōbilis. *(continued)*

2 **ātrium, -ī**, n., *atrium, main room*
4 **nisi**, conj., *unless, except*
6 **sine**, prep. + abl., *without*
   custōs, custōdis, m., *guard*
7 **bona, bonōrum**, n. pl., *goods, possessions*
   nōnnumquam, adv., *sometimes*
11 **postrīdiē**, adv., *on the following day*
   iaceō, -ēre, -uī, -itūrus, *to lie, be lying down*
7 **arripiō, arripere, arripuī, arreptus**, *to grab hold of, snatch, seize*
12 **vetō, vetāre, vetuī, vetitus**, *to forbid*

13 **praedō, praedōnis**, m., *robber*
   noceō, -ēre, -uī, -itūrus + dat., *to do harm (to), harm*
15 ut Mārcō vidēbātur, *as it seemed to Marcus, as Marcus thought*
22 **metus, -ūs**, m., *fear*
23 **terra, -ae**, f., *earth, ground*
   lutum, -ī, n., *mud*

Go Online
PHSchool.com
Web Code: jfd-0026

EXERCISE 26a Respondē Latīnē:

1. Cūr nōn licet puerīs exīre in urbem sōlīs?
2. Quōcum puerīs licet exīre in urbem?
3. Quō ībant puerī?
4. Quī sē in viam praecipitāvērunt?

"Eho!" clāmāvit ūnus ē praedōnibus. "Quō abīs, parvule? Quid est nōmen tuum? Nōnne tū fīlius es senātōris? Nōnne nōmen tuum est Mārcus Cornēlius?" 25

Cui Mārcus, "Quid vultis, scelestī? Nihil pecūniae habeō. Nōlīte mē verberāre! Sī mihi nocueritis, pater meus certē vōs pūniet."

Sed interpellāvit praedō, "Tacē, puer! Tū es captīvus noster neque ad patrem redībis. Nēmō nunc poterit tē servāre. Ipse enim tē necābō."

Tum praedō gladium strīnxit. Sextus stabat perterritus et, "Fer auxilium!" clāmāvit. 30 "Fer auxilium!" Sed nēmō clāmōrem audīvit. Nēmō auxilium tulit. Mārcus oculōs clausit et mortem exspectābat.

Nihil accidit. Oculōs aperuit. In lectō erat suō. Somnium modo fuerat. Hodiē tamen domī manēre cōnstituit Mārcus. Exīre nōluit.

24 parvulus, -a, -um, *small, little*   31 oculus, -ī, m., *eye*
29 **servō, -āre, -āvī, -ātus**, *to save*   34 **domī**, *at home*
30 **gladius, -ī**, m., *sword*

    30 **stringō, stringere, strīnxī, strictus**, *to draw*
    31 **claudō, claudere, clausī, clausus**, *to shut*
    33 **accidit, accidere, accidit**, *(it) happens*
       aperiō, aperīre, aperuī, apertus, *to open*

Respondē Latīnē:

5. Quid fēcit Mārcus postquam Sextum clāmantem audīvit?
6. Cūr praedō gladium strīnxit?
7. Quis vēnit ubi Sextus clāmāvit?

Go Online
PHSchool.com
Web Code: jfd-0026

Demonstrative Adjectives and Pronouns: *hic* and *ille*

Look at the following sentences:

Ille tabellārius equōs vehementer incitāvit.	*That courier fiercely whipped the horses on.*
Quis in **illō** aedificiō habitat?	*Who lives in **that** building?*
Hī canēs lātrant modo.	*These dogs are only barking.*
Est perīculōsum in viās **huius** urbis exīre.	*It is dangerous to go out into the streets of **this** city.*
Sextus, **hīs** clāmōribus et **hōc** strepitū excitātus, dormīre nōn poterat.	*Roused by **these** shouts and **this** noise, Sextus could not sleep.*

You will see from the above examples that both **hic** and **ille** are used adjectivally with nouns to point out someone or something. **Hic** points to someone or something near at hand or near in time, while **ille** points to someone or something further away or distant in time or space. These are called *demonstrative adjectives*, from the Latin verb **dēmōn-strō, dēmōnstrāre,** *to point out, show.*

Here is a chart showing all the cases of **hic** (*this, these*) and **ille** (*that, those*) in masculine, feminine, and neuter genders:

Number Case	Masc.	Fem.	Neut.	Masc.	Fem.	Neut.
Singular						
Nominative	hic	haec	hoc	ílle	ílla	íllud
Genitive	húius	húius	húius	illī́us	illī́us	illī́us
Dative	húic	húic	húic	íllī	íllī	íllī
Accusative	hunc	hanc	hoc	íllum	íllam	íllud
Ablative	hōc	hāc	hōc	íllō	íllā	íllō
Plural						
Nominative	hī	hae	haec	íllī	íllae	ílla
Genitive	hórum	hárum	hórum	illṓrum	illā́rum	illṓrum
Dative	hīs	hīs	hīs	íllīs	íllīs	íllīs
Accusative	hōs	hās	haec	íllōs	íllās	ílla
Ablative	hīs	hīs	hīs	íllīs	íllīs	íllīs

The Latin sentences on page 240 show these demonstrative words being used as *adjectives* modifying nouns; they may also be used without nouns as *pronouns* meaning *he, she, it, this, that,* etc.:

> **Ille**, postquam **haec** audīvit, ē caupōnā sē praecipitāvit.
> *He, after he heard **this** (lit., **these things**), rushed out of the inn.*

> Postquam **hoc** fecit,...   *After he did **this**,...*

> Mārcus patrem, "Quid est **illud**?" rogāvit. *Marcus asked his father, "What is **that**?"*

> "Cavē illōs hominēs!" clāmāvit Sextus. "**Illī** certē nōs in domūs vīcīnās
> trahent et ibi nōs necābunt." (26:20–21)
> *"Watch out for those men!" shouted Sextus. "**They** will certainly drag us into the neighboring houses and kill us there."*

Sometimes **hic** refers to a nearer noun and means *the latter*, while **ille** refers to a farther noun and means *the former*:

> Nōnne herī in urbe vīdistī multōs cīvēs post senātōrem sequentēs? **Hic** erat
> patrōnus, **illī** erant clientēs.   (25d:21–22)
> *Didn't you see yesterday in the city many citizens following behind a senator?*
> ***The latter** (literally, **this one**, i.e., the one last mentioned) was a patron, **the former** (literally, **those men**, i.e., the ones first mentioned) were clients.*

Be careful to distinguish **hic**, the adjective or pronoun, from the adverb **hīc**, *here*:

> Quid tū **hīc**? (9:8)   *What (are) you (doing) **here**?*

EXERCISE 26b

Read aloud and translate:

1. Hic puer in hāc viā, ille in illā habitat.
2. Illa puella in hāc vīllā habitat; hī puerī in illā habitant.
3. Sī in hāc caupōnā pernoctābimus, hic caupō nōbīs certē nocēbit.
4. Illī praedōnēs illōs viātōrēs sub illīs arboribus petunt.
5. Quandō illī haec onera in vīllam portābunt?
6. Nōlī illud plaustrum in hanc urbem interdiū agere!
7. Huic puerō multa dabimus, illī nihil.
8. Hīs rūsticīs licēbit agrōs huius vīllae rūsticae colere.
9. Huic senātōrī ad Cūriam in lectīcā redīre necesse erat.
10. Illī aedificiō appropinquāre perīculōsum est, nam scelestī hominēs ibi habitant.
11. Ūnus ex hīs praedōnibus aliquid illī servō dīcēbat.

EXERCISE 26c

Choose the proper form of **hic** or **ille** to modify the noun in italics, and then read the sentence aloud and translate:

1. Cornēliī in _____ *vīllā* habitant.
2. "Spectāte _____ *arcum*, puerī!" clāmāvit Eucleidēs.
3. Ōlim _____ *puellae* in agrīs ambulābant.
4. Vīlicus cibum _____ *servō* nōn dabit.
5. "Vīdistīne _____ *aedificium*, Mārce?" inquit Sextus.
6. Raeda _____ *mercātōris* prope tabernam manet.
7. Māne _____ *canēs* ferōciter lātrābant.
8. Bona _____ *rūsticōrum* in raedā erant.
9. Ūnus ex _____ *praedōnibus* gladium strīnxit.
10. Nōbīs _____ *arborēs* ascendere nōn licet.
11. _____ *rem* explicāre nōn possum.
12. _____ *strepitus* Mārcum nōn excitāvit.

EXERCISE 26d

Using story 26 and the charts of demonstrative adjectives as guides, give the Latin for:

1. It is not dangerous to go out into the streets of that city.
2. Those wicked men seized the goods of these citizens.
3. Yesterday I saw this wicked man in that city.
4. Sextus had never seen this huge mass of the Circus Maximus.
5. Marcus will never give money to that robber.

Take parts, read aloud, and translate:

AURELIA'S CONCERN FOR SEXTUS

Quīnta hōra est. Domī in tablīnō Gāius Cornēlius strēnuē labōrat sōlus. Iam ā Cūriā rediit et nunc ōrātiōnem scrībit, quam crās apud senātum habēbit. Aurēlia iānuae tablīnī appropinquat et tacitē intrat, nam coniugem vexāre nōn vult.

AURĒLIA:	Salvē, Gāī! Esne occupātus?
CORNĒLIUS:	Ita vērō! Paulisper tamen colloquium tēcum habēre possum. 5
	Quid agis, uxor?
AURĒLIA:	Sollicita dē Sextō sum, coniūnx.
CORNĒLIUS:	Dē Sextō? Cūr? Quid ille puer molestus iam fēcit?
AURĒLIA:	Nihil malī fēcit Sextus. Sollicita sum quod hic puer numquam
	anteā in urbe tantā adfuit. Puerī in urbe sine custōde exīre 10
	nōn dēbent. Necesse est igitur et Mārcō et Sextō custōdem habēre.
CORNĒLIUS:	Titus frāter meus custōs cum illīs ībit. Eucleidēs quoque Sextum
	custōdiet. Ille enim puerōs ad lūdum dūcet.
AURĒLIA:	Frātrī Titō nōn cōnfīdō, et Sextus Eucleidem numquam audiet.
	Nam Eucleidēs numquam tacet. 15
CORNĒLIUS:	(īrātus) Sī Sextus custōdem nōn audīverit, ego ipse eum pūniam!
AURĒLIA:	Minimē, Gāī. Sextus nōn est puer scelestus. Est, ut bene scīs, puer
	strēnuus. Mātrem tamen propter ēruptiōnem Montis Vesuviī nōn
	iam habet Sextus. Certē eam valdē dēsīderat. Dēbēmus Sextum
	dīligenter cūrāre. 20
CORNĒLIUS:	Ita vērō! Estō! Ubi nōn in Cūriā sum, ego ipse puerōs custōdiam.
	Aliter aut patruus Titus aut Eucleidēs verbōsus eōs cūrābit.
AURĒLIA:	Grātiās tibi agō, coniūnx!
CORNĒLIUS:	Nunc, sī vīs, abī! Sōlus esse volō. Mihi necesse est hanc ōrātiōnem
	cōnficere. 25

1 quīntus, -a, -um, *fifth*
  tablīnum, -ī, n., *study*
2 **ōrātiō, ōrātiōnis,** f., *oration, speech*
  quam...habēbit, *which he will deliver*
  apud, prep. + acc., *in front of, before*
3 **coniūnx, coniugis,** m./f., *husband, wife*
5 colloquium, -ī, n., *conversation*
11 **dēbeō, -ēre, -uī, -itūrus** + infin., *ought*
13 **lūdus, -ī,** m., *school*

18 **propter,** prep. + acc., *on account of, because of*
  Mōns Vesuvius, Montis Vesuviī, m., *Mount Vesuvius*
19 **dēsīderō, -āre, -āvī, -ātus,** *to long for, miss*
22 aliter, adv., *otherwise*
  aut...aut..., conj., *either...or...*
23 **Grātiās tibi agō!** *I thank you! Thank you!*
24 sī vīs, *if you wish, please*

10 **adsum, adesse, adfuī, adfutūrus,** irreg., *to be present*
14 **cōnfīdō, cōnfidere** + dat., *to give trust (to), trust*

201–146 B.C.

Go Online
PHSchool.com
Web Code: jfd-0026

ROME IN THE MEDITERRANEAN WORLD

Rome, the victor over Carthage, became an international power, the ruler of the western Mediterranean. Winning the war with Hannibal gave Rome secure control over Sicily, Spain, and Sardinia. Then, after subduing the Gauls in northern Italy, the Romans looked toward the East. Starting with Macedonia, the former ally of Carthage, Rome gradually took control of Greece and the Greek states in Asia Minor. In order to maintain a balance of power, the Romans established a permanent military presence all around the Mediterranean Sea.

The act that symbolized this age of control came in 146 B.C., when the consul Lucius Memmius demolished the city of Corinth and sold her inhabitants into slavery. In the same year, the Senate acceded to Marcus Cato's relentless pronouncement at the close of every speech he made to the Senate, **Carthāgō dēlenda est**, "Carthage must be destroyed." By razing that city, too, the Roman army ended the Third Punic War (149–146 B.C.). The Roman commander, Publius Cornelius Scipio Aemilianus Africanus, adoptive grandson of Hannibal's conqueror, had his troops sow the land with salt to assure its infertility and had them curse the site. The area around Carthage and to the south became the Roman province of Africa.

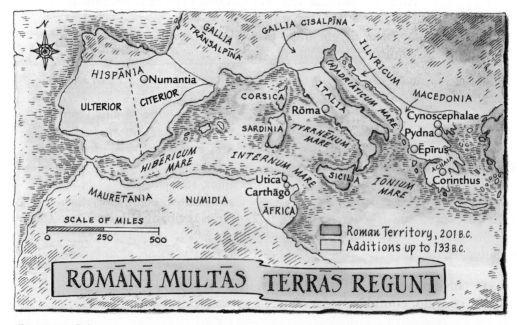

RŌMĀNĪ MULTĀS TERRĀS REGUNT

The Roman Senate emerged as the dominant power in the state during the years of conflict with Carthage and expansion into the eastern Mediterranean. Whereas new consuls, praetors, and other magistrates were elected every year, senators were appointed for life. This stable, more permanent voice of authority directed both foreign and domestic policies and administered finances. The **nōbilēs**, descended from the old families of patrician and plebeian stock, formed a ruling aristocracy, whose ranks supplied most of the consuls and exerted most of the influence on the way the Roman government operated. The Roman Senate organized the newly acquired foreign territories into provinces (**prōvinciae**), whose governors, taken from the pool of former magistrates, were responsible to that same body.

The Italian economy changed when Roman senators spent their share of war-booty and profits from the provinces on the purchase of large estates (**lātifundia**), and under

Carthage maintained her empire with ships from a large circular military harbor that could repair or build 220 ships at a time.

A reconstruction of Carthage's harbors, fourth–second century B.C.

this system there developed a more organized, more profitable type of agriculture that utilized slave labor. The model Roman of earlier times, a citizen-soldier who farmed his own fields, was pushed off his land and into the city. Deriving sufficient wealth from their **lātifundia**, senators chose not to venture into the new realm of international trade; this lucrative opportunity was seized instead by a growing middle class, the equestrian order, members of which emerged as leaders of Roman commerce.

Graecia capta ferum victōrem cēpit, said the poet Horace: "Captive Greece captivated her uncivilized conqueror." Roman life had already been changing during the century before Rome destroyed Corinth and Carthage, as the Romans had gotten to know the Greeks, their language, and their literature, partly through contact with the Greek cities of southern Italy and Sicily.

Both the family-based Roman worship of rustic spirits, who watched over farms, flocks, and storeroom, and the formal state religion began to incorporate Greek rituals, and the Roman gods became associated with the Greek Olympians, who were more human in appearance and personality. At the same time, the Stoic philosophy preached by many Greeks at this time, which offered an intellectual basis for a strong moral code, was welcomed by leading Romans.

Greece also taught Rome the value of literature. Livius Andronicus adapted a Greek play for the Roman stage in 240 B.C., the year after the First Punic War. Gnaeus Naevius composed the *Bellum Punicum*, an epic poem in which he combined the history of the

The nine Muses were among the goddesses of Greek origin that were embraced by the Romans.
Sarcophagus, Rome, second century A.D.

First Punic War with the myth of Queen Dido of Carthage and Aeneas, the Trojan hero and forefather of Rome. In another epic, the *Annales*, Quintus Ennius recounted the glorious history of Rome from its beginnings to his own day. More firmly based on Greek content and form were the comic plays of Plautus and Terence, in which Latin-speaking Italian characters with Greek names romped through Greek plots.

Marcus Cato, fiercely advocating that Romans retain the old standards of Italian independence, wrote the *Origines*, a Roman history book for his son, and the *De agricultura*, advice for Roman landholders. He lamented the appearance of Greek statues in Roman homes and condemned the new interest in barbers and Greek cooks.

Many more Romans, such as Scipio Aemilianus, rather enjoyed the new luxuries, became patrons of the arts, and welcomed the civilizing influence of Greek teachers, writers, and philosophers. Once Rome learned Greek literature and ideas, she evolved into a Hellenized civilization best labeled Greco-Roman. Roman culture and rule of earlier days had both outgrown Italy.

---

1. In what ways was the period discussed in this essay a turning point in Roman history?
2. How would a Cincinnatus have reacted to these changes in the Roman state and agriculture described in this essay?
3. Summarize the fusion of Greek and Roman culture that took place at this time.
4. Which side would you have taken in the "debate" between Marcus Cato and Scipio Aemilianus? Why?

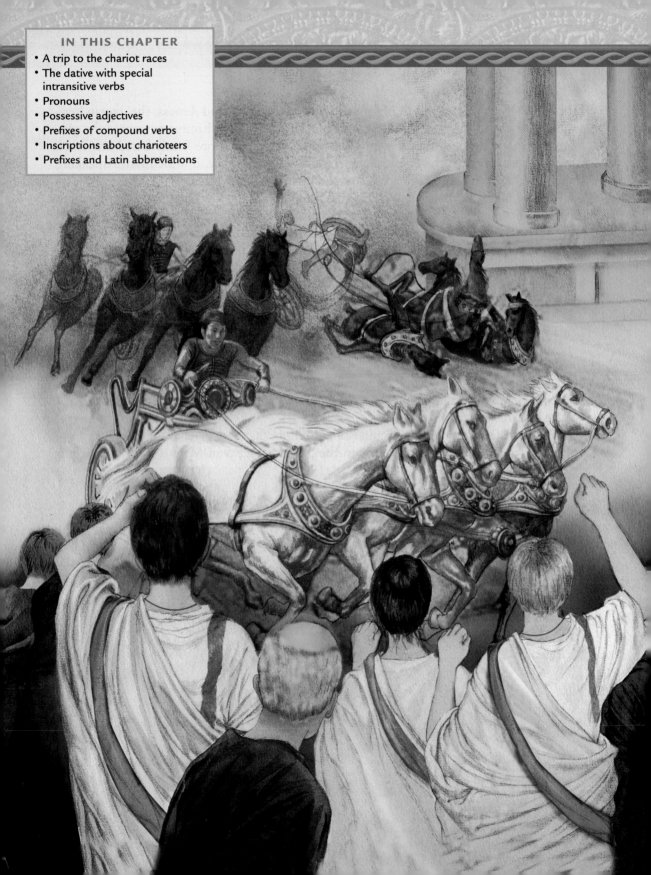

A VISIT TO THE RACES

Chariot races (**lūdī circēnsēs,** literally, *games in the Circus*) were perhaps the most popular spectacle in ancient Rome. It was held in the **Circus Maximus**, a huge open-air stadium in the valley between the Palatine and the Aventine hills. It could hold about 200,000 spectators, seated in tiers around the race track (**curriculum**).

It has been estimated that at one time some 90 holidays (**fēriae**) were given over to games at public expense. On these days the citizens were "celebrating a holiday" (**fēriātī**).

A barrier (**spīna**) ran down the center of the course, and the chariots (**quadrīgae**), each pulled by four horses, had to complete seven laps, about five miles or eight kilometers in all. Fouling was permitted, and collisions were frequent, especially at the turning posts (**mētae**). A race began when the Emperor (**Caesar**) or presiding official gave the signal (**signum**) by dropping a white cloth (**mappa**).

The charioteers, some of whom won great popularity and very high salaries, were employed by four companies (**factiōnēs**), each with its own color—the "Reds" (**russātī**), the "Whites" (**albātī**), the "Greens" (**prasinī**), and the "Blues" (**venetī**). Rival groups of spectators were accustomed to show their support (**favēre**) for each color vociferously.

One charioteer we hear about, Gaius Apuleius Diocles, drove chariots for the Red Stable for twenty-four years, ran 4,257 starts, and won 1,462 victories.

No wonder Marcus, Cornelia, and Sextus are eager to go to the races! As we return to our story, three days after the Cornelii arrived in Rome, Sextus is sitting alone when suddenly Marcus rushes in.

MĀRCUS: Sexte! Sexte! Hodiē nōbīs licet ad lūdōs circēnsēs īre. Eucleidēs mē et tē et Cornēliam ad Circum dūcet.

SEXTUS: Lūdōs circēnsēs amō. Sed nōnne Circus clausus erit?

MĀRCUS: Minimē! Circus nōn erit clausus, nam hodiē cīvēs omnēs fēriātī sunt. Viae erunt plēnae hominum. Virī, mulierēs, līberī Circum celerrimē petent.   5

SEXTUS: Sed cūr nōn nunc discēdimus? Ego sum iam parātus.

MĀRCUS: Simulac Cornēlia ē somnō surrēxerit, statim ībimus.

(*Much to the boys' disgust, Cornelia was rather late in waking up from her siesta, but soon they were all ready to leave.*)

EUCLEIDĒS: Agite! Iam tandem ad Circum īre tempus est. Estisne parātī, puerī? Esne   10 parāta, Cornēlia?

(*Eucleides takes Cornelia and the boys quickly through the streets; they can now hear the noise of the Circus crowds.*)

EUCLEIDĒS: Iam ā Circō nōn procul absumus. Nōnne strepitum audītis? Ecce! Omnēs ad Circum festīnant. Brevī tempore nōs ipsī intrābimus.   (*continued*)   15

5 **mulier, mulieris,** f., *woman*

(They enter the Circus.)

CORNĒLIA: Quam ingēns est turba hominum! Tōtus Circus est plēnus spectātōrum.

EUCLEIDĒS: Ita vērō! Semper multī spectātōrēs in Circō sunt. Hīc cōnsīdēmus?

MĀRCUS: Minimē! Prope curriculum sedēre necesse est quod ibi omnia vidēre poterimus. 20

EUCLEIDĒS: At prope curriculum sedēre perīculōsum est. Pater vester multa dē perīculō dīxit.

MĀRCUS: Nihil perīculī est, nam Titus, patruus meus, cum amīcīs prope curriculum sedēre solet.

SEXTUS: Ecce! Caesar ipse iam surrēxit; signum dare parat. Ego russātīs favēbō. 25

MĀRCUS: Ego albātīs.

CORNĒLIA: Ego venetīs.

MĀRCUS: Ecce! Mappa! Signum est!

CORNĒLIA: Quam ferōciter equōs verberant illī aurīgae! Quam celeriter equōs agunt! Quam temerāriī sunt! Nōnne mortem timent? 30

SEXTUS: Ecce! Russātus meus certē victor erit, nam equōs magnā arte agit.

25 **faveō, favēre, fāvī, fautūrus** + dat., *to give favor (to), support*

This charioteer is approaching the dangerous turning posts where many collisions and accidents occurred.

Roman relief sculpture, Rome, first century A.D.

MĀRCUS:	Ō mē miserum! Aurīga meus equōs dēvertit. Cavē mētam! Cavē mētam! Esne sēmisomnus, fatue? Cūr mētam nōn vītāvistī?
CORNĒLIA:	Ēheu! Ille aurīga cecidit. Humī iacet. Estne mortuus?
SEXTUS:	Minimē! Minimē! Ecce! Animum recuperāvit. Iam surgit.
CORNĒLIA:	Audīvistisne clāmōrēs hōrum spectātōrum? Magnā vōce nōmina aurīgārum et equōrum semper clāmant! Undique ingēns est strepitus! Tantum strepitum ego numquam audīvī.
MĀRCUS:	Russātī vīcērunt, sed mox etiam albātī vincent.
EUCLEIDĒS:	Hoc fortasse accidet, sed Caligula ipse, ut dīcunt, prasinōs amābat.

35

40

(continued)

32 **dēvertō, dēvertere, dēvertī, dēversus,** *to turn aside*
34 **humī,** *on the ground*

39 **vincō, vincere, vīcī, victus,** *to conquer, win*

Charioteers bound their tunics to protect their chests and wore a stiff leather helmet to protect their heads.
Mosaic from villa in Baccano, Tuscany, third century A.D.

(They watch a few more races, but it is not Marcus's lucky day. Eucleides becomes a little anxious as it grows later. He had been caught once before in a crush at the gates.)

EUCLEIDĒS: Iam sērō est. Nunc domum redībimus.

SEXTUS: Nōndum tempus est domum redīre. Ecce! Aurīgae habēnās sūmpsērunt et signum exspectant.

EUCLEIDĒS: Nisi mox discēdēmus, turbam ingentem vītāre nōn poterimus. Agite! Domum!

45

ADDITIONAL READING:

The Romans Speak for Themselves: Book I: "Finding a Date in Ancient Rome or Why Some Men Went to the Chariot Races," pages 89–98; "Pliny's Views on the Chariot Races," pages 93–98.

BUILDING THE MEANING

Go Online
PHSchool.com
Web Code: jfd-0027

Dative with Special Intransitive Verbs

Look at the following sentences:

Sī **mihi** nocueritis, pater meus certē vōs pūniet. (26:26–27)
*If you do harm **to me**, my father will certainly punish you.*
*If you harm **me**, my father will certainly punish you.*

Frātrī Titō nōn cōnfīdō. (26e:14) Ego **russātīs** favēbō. (27:25)
*I do not give trust **to (my) brother Titus.** I will give favor **to the reds.***
*I do not trust **(my) brother Titus.** I will favor/support **the reds.***

The verbs **nocēre,** *to do harm (to),* **cōnfīdere,** *to give trust (to),* and **favēre,** *to give favor (to),* are intransitive and so do not take direct objects in the accusative case. Their meaning is completed by a word or phrase in the dative case. The meaning of the dative case in this type of sentence can be clearly seen in the literal translations of the sentences above: *If you do harm **to me,** I do not give trust **to (my) brother Titus,** and I will give favor **to the reds**.* In translating into idiomatic English, we usually use a direct object, as in the alternative translations above.

These sentences are similar in pattern to those discussed on page 212, Building the Meaning: "Dative with Intransitive Compound Verbs," and may be grouped with those as a basic pattern of Latin sentences.

FORMS

Pronouns: 1st and 2nd Persons

From the early chapters of our story, you have seen many examples of 1st and 2nd person pronouns. They include the words for *I, me, you, we,* and *us*:

1st Person Singular:

Sed **ego** volō cōnsulere Mārcum! (8:16)	*nominative*
Mihi necesse est hīc manēre. (9:18–19)	*dative*
Nihil **mē** terret. (4:7) Multās epistulās ad **mē** mitte! (9:19)	*accusative*

1st Person Plural:

Nōs ad urbem redīre parāmus. (8:7)	*nominative*
Nōbīs necesse est statim discēdere. (8:13–14)	*dative*
Dāvus **nōs** verberāre potest. (11:8)	*accusative*
Vīsne **nōbīscum** lūdere, Cornēlia? (16:19)	*ablative*

2nd Person Singular:

Mārce, cūr **tū** arborem nōn ascendis? (4:5)	*nominative*
Servī meī alium lectum **tibi** parāvērunt. (19:17–18)	*dative*
Quid **tē** terret? (4:5–6)	*accusative*

2nd Person Plural:

Cūr **vōs** ibi sedētis? (8:3)	*nominative*
Servī meī bonam cēnam **vōbīs** statim parāre possunt. (19:2)	*dative*

The following chart includes every case of each of these pronouns:

These words are called *personal pronouns* because they show what person is involved in the action.

For **nōs** and **vōs**, two genitive forms are found, as shown. Their use is limited, as is the use of the genitives of **ego** and **tū**, and you will not meet any of these genitives until later in your study of Latin. They are *not* used to indicate possession (see page 255, "Adjectives: Possessive").

Notice how the preposition **cum** is attached to the end of **nōbīs** in the sentence above from Chapter 16. So also you will find **mēcum**, **tēcum**, and **vōbīscum**.

Number Case	1st	2nd
Singular		
Nominative	égo	tū
Genitive	méī	túī
Dative	míhi	tíbi
Accusative	mē	tē
Ablative	mē	tē
Plural		
Nominative	nōs	vōs
Genitive	nóstrī	véstrī
	nóstrum	véstrum
Dative	nṓbīs	vṓbīs
Accusative	nōs	vōs
Ablative	nṓbīs	vṓbīs

Pronouns: 3rd Person

Now look at these sentences, also from earlier chapters:

Sextus, quod lupus **eum** terret, arborem petit. (5:11)   *accusative, masc., sing.*
Nēmō **eam** cōnspicit. (9:2)   *accusative, fem., sing.*
Lupus **eōs** iam cōnspicit. (5:10)   *accusative, masc., pl.*

Latin 3rd person pronouns include the words for *he, him, she, her, it, they,* and *them*. The adjacent chart shows all cases, singular and plural.

The genitive can be used to indicate possession, e.g., **eius** can mean *his, her,* or *its*, and **eōrum, eārum, eōrum** can mean *their*.

The forms of **is** and **ea** can refer to things: **Flāvia epistulam scrībit; Cornēlia eam legit**, *Flavia writes a letter; Cornelia reads it*.

Number Case	Masc.	Fem.	Neut.
Singular			
Nominative	is	éa	id
Genitive	éius	éius	éius
Dative	éī	éī	éī
Accusative	éum	éam	id
Ablative	éō	éā	éō
Plural			
Nominative	éī	éae	éa
Genitive	eórum	eárum	eórum
Dative	éīs	éīs	éīs
Accusative	éōs	éās	éa
Ablative	éīs	éīs	éīs

EXERCISE 27a

Select, read aloud, and translate:

1. Necesse erat _____ prope curriculum sedēre.   eius/nōbīs
2. Eucleidēs _____ dēmonstrābat circum et aurīgās.   ego/mē/mihi
3. Nōn vult, Sexte, Cornēlia prope _____ sedēre.   tū/tibi/tē
4. Sextus saepe _____ vexat.   eī/eam/eius
5. Cornēlius clāmābat et servī vōcem _____ audīvērunt.   eius/eum/eōrum
6. Sepulcrum vīdimus, sed _____ nōn appropinquāvimus.   id/eum/eī
7. Canēs Getam invēnērunt quod tunicam _____ olfēcerant.   eō/eius/ea
8. Caupō, "Novum lectum," inquit, "_____ parābō."   is/vōs/tibi
9. Equī mētam petunt. Ecce, nunc _____ praetereunt!   id/eōs/eam
10. Aurīgae hodiē bene fēcērunt. _____ laudāre dēbētis.   Eās/Eōs/Vōbīs

Pronouns: Reflexive

Look at these sentences:

Mē in piscīnā vīdī.   Ubi cecidistis, **vōbīs** nocuistis.
*I saw **myself** in the fishpond.*   *When you fell, you hurt **yourselves**.*

The words in boldface are being used as reflexive pronouns. A pronoun is reflexive when it refers to the subject of the sentence, as **mē** in the first sentence refers to the understood 1st person subject of the verb **vīdī**, just as in the translation *myself* refers to *I*.

While the genitive, dative, accusative, and ablative forms of the regular 1st and 2nd person pronouns may be used reflexively, as in the examples, there are special forms for the 3rd person reflexive pronoun, as in the following sentences:

Puellae, ubi cecidērunt, **sibi** nocuērunt.
*The girls hurt **themselves** when they fell.*

Mārcus **sē** in piscīnā cōnspexit.
*Marcus caught sight of **himself** in the fishpond.*

In the first example, **sibi** refers to **puellae**, just as in the translation *themselves* refers to *the girls*.

Here is the complete set of forms of the 3rd person reflexive pronoun:

There is no nominative form. The same forms are used for singular and plural and for masculine, feminine, and neuter. The dative, **sibi**, therefore can mean *to/for himself, to/for herself, to/for oneself, to/for itself,* or *to/for themselves.*

Case	m/f/n s/pl
Genitive	súī
Dative	síbi
Accusative	sē
Ablative	sē

EXERCISE 27b

Read each incomplete sentence to yourself. Select the correct pronoun, remembering that reflexives always refer to the subject. Then read aloud and translate:

1. Aurēlia _____ in aquā cōnspexit.   sibi/sē/suī
2. "Ego _____ in aquā cōnspexī," inquit Aurēlia.   sē/mē/sibi
3. Canēs ē iānuā caupōnae _____ praecipitant.   mē/sibi/sē
4. Nocuistīne _____, ubi cecidistī?   tē/tibi/sibi
5. Ego _____ nōn nocuī.   mihi/sibi/mē

Adjectives: Possessive

In your reading you will not find the genitive of the 1st and 2nd person pronouns or of the reflexive pronouns used to indicate possession. Rather, you will find a *possessive adjective*:

Librum **tuum** legō.
*I am reading **your** book.*

Librum **meum** legō.
*I am reading **my (own)** book.*

The possessive adjectives, corresponding to the personal and reflexive pronouns, are 1st and 2nd declension adjectives, as follows:

meus, -a, -um   *my, my own, mine*
tuus, -a, -um   *your, your own, yours* (singular)
suus, -a, -um   *his own, her own, its own*

noster, nostra, nostrum   *our, our own, ours*
vester, vestra, vestrum   *your, your own, yours* (plural)
suus, -a, -um   *their own*

Notice that just as the pronoun **sē** is used for both singular and plural, so also the adjective **suus, -a, -um** can be singular or plural and mean *his own, her own, its own,* or *their own.*

EXERCISE 27c

Select, read aloud, and translate:

1. Ad lūdōs circēnsēs cum amīcīs _____ ībitis.   vestrī/vestrīs/vestrōs
2. Omnēs spectātōrēs factiōnibus _____ favent.   suae/suīs/suum
3. In somniō _____ appāruērunt praedōnēs scelestī.   meīs/meī/meō
4. In vīllā _____ sunt multī servī.   nostrī/nostra/nostrā
5. Puellae domī cum amīcīs _____ manēbant.   suae/suīs/suō

     factiō, factiōnis, f., *company (of charioteers)*

Note carefully the distinction in use between the adjective **suus, -a, -um** (which is always reflexive) *his own, her own, their own,* and the genitives of the 3rd person pronoun, namely, **eius,** *of him = his,* or *of her = her;* and **eōrum, eārum,** *of them = their:*

Mārcus librum **suum** habet.   Puellae librōs **suōs** habent.
*Marcus has **his own** book.*   *The girls have **their own** books.*

Mārcus librum **eius** habet.   Puellae librōs **eōrum** habent.
*Marcus has **his** (e.g., Sextus's) book.*   *The girls have **their** (e.g., the boys') books.*

EXERCISE 27d

Using the dialogue at the beginning of this chapter and the information on special intransitive verbs, pronouns, and adjectives as guides, give the Latin for the following. Be sure to use pronouns for the emphatic words in italics:

1. As soon as *she* has gotten up, we will go.
2. *We* want to sit near the race track.
3. *I* favor the whites. Do *you* favor them?
4. Look at the blue! *I* favor him.
5. Is your blue winning?
6. My white fell down. Did he hurt himself?
7. *He* is safe, but he harmed his own horses.
8. The horses of your blue are safe.
9. My charioteer did not harm his own horses.
10. It is time for us to return home.

Prefixes: Compound Verbs I

Compare the following sentences:

1. Equī raedam **trahunt**.
   *The horses **pull** the carriage.*
2. Servī lectum **ferēbant**.
   *The slaves **were carrying** the bed.*

1. Equī raedam **extrahunt**.
   *The horses **pull out** the carriage.*
2. Servī lectum **referēbant**.
   *The slaves **were carrying back** the bed.*

In the right-hand column a prefix has been added to the beginning of the verb to give it a more specific meaning. Verbs with prefixes attached to them are called *compound verbs*. Common prefixes are:

ab-, abs-, ā-, *away, from*
ad-, *toward, to*
circum-, *around*
con-, *along with, together*
   (or simply to emphasize)
dē-, *down, down from*
dis-, dī-, *apart, in different directions*
ex-, ē-, *out, out of*
in-, *into, in, on*

inter-, *between*
per-, *through* (or simply to emphasize)
prae-, *in front, ahead*
praeter-, *past, beyond*
prō-, prōd-, *forward*
re-, red-, *back, again*
sub-, *under, below*
trāns-, trā-, *across*

Note that many of these are common prepositions.
Be sure to learn these prefixes thoroughly.

EXERCISE 27e

Read each sentence aloud. Identify each compound verb and give the meaning of its prefix. You are to deduce the meanings of compound verbs that you have not met in the stories. Then translate:

1. Pater līberōs ē vīllā ēdūxit et trāns viam trādūxit.
2. Cornēlius Eucleidem iussit līberōs abdūcere.
3. Eucleidēs līberōs ad hortum redūxit.
4. Servī togās et tunicās in cistās repōnunt.
5. Ubi ad Portam Capēnam veniunt, servī onera dēpōnunt.
6. Ubi plaustrum invēnit, stercus remōvit et corpus extrāxit.
7. Cornēliī Rōmam heri advēnērunt.
8. Homō per viam it. Mox viam trānsībit et ad vīllam redībit.
9. Ubi urbem intrāmus, necesse est Aquam Mārciam subīre.
10. Puerī Circum relīquērunt et Palātīnum circumiērunt.
11. Nihil clāmōris, nihil strepitūs ad Mārcum pervēnerat.
12. Puerōs, quod praecurrēbant, identidem revocābat Cornēlius.

Go Online
PHSchool.com
Web Code: jfd-0027

INSCRIPTIONS ABOUT CHARIOTEERS

Honorary Inscription

P. Aelius, Marī Rogātī fīl(ius), Gutta Calpurniānus equīs hīs vīcī in factiōne venetā: Germinātōre n(igrō) Āf(rō) LXXXXII, Silvānō r(ūfō) Āf(rō) CV, Nitid(ō) gil(vō) Āf(rō) LII, Saxōne n(igrō) Āf(rō) LX, et vīcī praemia m(aiōra) $\overline{L}$ I, $\overline{XL}$ IX, $\overline{XXX}$ XVII.

I, Publius Aelius Gutta Calpurnianus, son of Marius Rogatus, won for the Blue stable with the following horses: Germinator, African black, 92 (times); Silvanus, African chestnut, 105 (times); Glossy, African sorrel, 52 (times); Saxon, African black, 60 (times); and I won major purses of 50,000 sesterces (1), of 40,000 sesterces (9), and of 30,000 sesterces (17).

Sepulchral Inscription

D. M. Epaphrodītus, agitātor f(actiōnis) r(ussātae), vīc(it) CLXXVIII, et ad purpureum līber(ātus) vīc(it) VIII. Beia Felicula f(ēcit) coniugī suō merentī.

To the deified spirits. Epaphroditus, driver for the Red stable, won 178 (times), and after being manumitted to the Purples he won 8 (times). Beia Felicula made (this monument) for her deserving husband.

Curses against Charioteers and Their Horses

Adiūrō tē, daemōn, quīcumque es et dēmandō tibi ex hāc hōrā ex hāc diē ex hōc mōmentō, ut equōs Prasinī et Albī cruciēs occīdās, et agitātōrēs Clārum et Fēlīcem et Prīmulum et Rōmānum occīdās collīdās, neque spīritum illīs relinquās.

I adjure you, demon, whoever you are, and I ask of you from this hour, from this day, from this moment, that you torture and kill the horses of the Green and the White, and that you kill and smash their drivers Clarus and Felix and Primulus and Romanus, and leave no breath in them.

Word Study VII

Prefixes

Knowledge of Latin prefixes will help not only with the meanings of Latin compound verbs but also with the meanings of many English words derived from them. For example, when the Latin simple verb **portāre** is combined with various prefixes, the resulting compound verbs provide English with several words, e.g.:

deport (from **dēportāre**)   report (from **reportāre**)
export (from **exportāre**)   transport (from **trānsportāre**)

Relying on your knowledge of prefixes, can you tell the meaning of each of the English words above?

Some English words are derived from the infinitive base of the Latin compound verb, e.g., *transport* (from **trānsportāre**). Others are derived from the stem of the fourth principal part, e.g., *transportation* (from **trānsportātus**). (For the suffix *-tion*, see Word Study VI.)

EXERCISE 1

After each Latin simple verb below is a group of English verbs that are derived from Latin compounds of that simple verb. (The Latin compound verbs are in parentheses.) Give the meaning of each English verb:

dūcō, dūcere, dūxī, ductus, *to lead, bring*

1. to conduct (**condūcere**)
2. to induct (**indūcere**)
3. to deduct (**dēdūcere**)
4. to reduce (**redūcere**)
5. to produce (**prōdūcere**)
6. to adduce (**addūcere**)

pōnō, pōnere, posuī, positus, *to put, place*

1. to propose (**prōpōnere**)
2. to dispose (**dispōnere**)
3. to expose (**expōnere**)
4. to depose (**dēpōnere**)
5. to transpose (**trānspōnere**)
6. to deposit (**dēpōnere**)

cēdō, cēdere, cessī, cessūrus, *to go*

1. to precede (**praecēdere**)
2. to recede (**recēdere**)
3. to intercede (**intercēdere**)

variant spelling:

4. to proceed (**prōcēdere**)
5. to exceed (**excēdere**)

Note that **cēdere** can also mean *to yield*. From this meaning come the following English derivatives:

6. to cede (**cēdere**)   7. concede (**concēdere**)

ferō, ferre, tulī, lātus, *irreg.*, *to bring, carry, bear*

1. to refer (**referre**)
2. to infer (**īnferre**)
3. to defer (**dēferre**)

4. to transfer (**trānsferre**)
5. to confer (**cōnferre**)
6. to relate (**referre**)

EXERCISE 2

Give the infinitive of the Latin compound verb from which each of the following English nouns is derived. Use each English noun in a sentence that illustrates its meaning:

1. disposition
2. proponent
3. recess
4. inference
5. product

6. exposition
7. relation
8. procession
9. conference
10. precedent

11. translator
12. concession
13. deduction
14. referee
15. reference

EXERCISE 3

Each adjective in the pool below is derived from a Latin compound verb. Choose an adjective to fill each blank and give the Latin compound verb from which it is derived:

1. Eucleides provided an atmosphere for the boys that would lead them to learn. The atmosphere was _____ to learning.
2. Although the horses tried to pull the carriage out, their efforts brought forth no results. Their efforts were not _____.
3. Some masters treat their slaves with violence that goes beyond reasonable limits. Their use of violence is _____.
4. Davus was not unhappy, but he was not as happy as he might have been if he were not a slave. Davus enjoyed _____ happiness.
5. When Cornelius entered a shop, the merchant left the other customers and helped him immediately. Cornelius received _____ treatment.
6. After he considered all of the evidence, the overseer was certain which slave stole the money. The overseer used _____ reasoning to come to his conclusion.
7. When the emperor went by, all the citizens bowed respectfully. The emperor was greeted in a _____ manner.

relative	deferential	conducive
productive	excessive	preferential
deductive		

Latin Abbreviations in English

Many abbreviations used in English are actually abbreviations of Latin words. For example, the common abbreviations for morning and afternoon, A.M. and P.M., stand for the Latin phrases **ante merīdiem** (*before noon*) and **post merīdiem** (*after noon*).

EXERCISE 4

With the aid of an English dictionary, give the full Latin words for the following abbreviations and explain how each is used in English:

1. etc.	5. e.g.	9. cf.
2. A.D.	6. N.B.	10. et al.
3. P.S.	7. ad-lib	11. q.v.
4. i.e.	8. vs.	12. Rx

EXERCISE 5

Replace the words in italics with abbreviations chosen from the list in Exercise 4 above:

1. The senators discussed the most critical problems first, *for example*, the revolt in Judea.
2. Titus was known for his ability to *speak off the cuff* on almost any subject.
3. The eruption of Vesuvius occurred in *the year of our Lord* 79.
4. Titus pointed out the Curia, the Arch of Tiberius, *and the rest*, as they passed them.
5. The announcement of the chariot race read, "Reds *against* Blues."
6. Eucleides said that they would return early, *that is*, before the eleventh hour.
7. At the bottom of the letter Cornelius added an *additional message*.
8. Cornelius had invited Titus, Messala, *and others*, to a dinner party.
9. The abbreviation "B.C." is used to give dates before the birth of Christ. (*Compare* the abbreviation "A.D.")
10. A sign near the Porta Capena read, "*Note well*: It is forbidden to drive wagons or carriages within the city during the day."
11. "*Take this*" was written at the bottom of the doctor's prescription.
12. "*Which see*" is written after a word or topic that needs further explanation, and it directs the reader to find such explanation elsewhere in the book.

Find examples of Latin abbreviations in textbooks, newspapers, or magazines and bring them to class.

Exercise VIa: Demonstrative Adjectives  pp. 187, 228, 240, 241

Select the correct form first of **hic, haec, hoc** and then of **ille, illa, illud** to modify each of the following nouns:

1. diem	(hōrum/hunc/hoc)	(illum/illōrum/illud)
2. arbore	(hōc/hae/hāc)	(illō/illā/illae)
3. lutum	(hoc/hunc/hōc)	(illum/illud/illō)
4. diēbus	(hās/hōs/hīs)	(illās/illīs/illōs)
5. fēminam	(hunc/hanc/hoc)	(illam/illum/illud)
6. terrās	(hōs/hāc/hās)	(illā/illōs/illās)
7. mandātō	(hōc/hoc/hāc)	(illā/illō/illud)
8. terra	(hae/hāc/haec)	(illā/illae/illa)
9. oculō	(hoc/huic/hic)	(illud/ille/illī)
10. arcuum	(hōrum/hārum/hunc)	(illārum/illōrum/illum)
11. somnia	(haec/hae/hanc)	(illā/illa/illam)
12. rīsū	(hāc/hī/hōc)	(illō/illā/illī)
13. vōcum	(hārum/hōrum/hunc)	(illārum/illum/illōrum)
14. diē	(hōc/hoc/haec)	(illud/illō/illa)
15. manūs	(huius/hōs/hī)	(illōs/illīus/illī)

Exercise VIb: Agreement of Adjectives and Nouns pp. 187, 188, 228

From the pool of words below, choose an adjective to go with each noun in Exercise VIa above. Give the noun with the adjective in its proper form to modify the noun.

bonus, -a, -um	īrātus, -a, -um	parvulus, -a, -um
brevis, -is, -e	longus, -a, -um	pūrus, -a, -um
dēfessus, -a, -um	magnus, -a, -um	scelestus, -a, -um
prīmus, -a, -um	multī, -ae, -a	sēmisomnus, -a, -um
īnfirmus, -a, -um	novus, -a, -um	sordidus, -a, -um
ingēns, ingentis	omnis, -is, -e	vester, vestra, vestrum

Exercise VIc: Personal Pronouns pp. 253–254

Give the correct form of the appropriate Latin pronoun to translate the English word or phrase in italics:

1. *I* heard nothing. What did *you* hear, Marcus?
2. *We* heard nothing because we were asleep, but the girls were awake. *They* heard the rumbling of wagons in the street.

3. He didn't see *me*, but I saw *him*.
4. He gave the book *to me*, not *to you*, Cornelia.
5. No, he gave it *to us*.
6. It is really *his* book.
7. But he gave it *to them*.
8. The girls are in the house. I saw *them* there.
9. Did you see *her*?
10. No, Marcus and Sextus, but I saw *you*.
11. The dog is yours, Marcus and Cornelia. Father gave it *to you*.

Exercise VId: Personal Pronouns, Reflexive Pronouns, and Possessive Adjectives

 pp. 254–256

Select the correct form to translate the English word or phrase in italics:

1. I have *my* book. (mihi / meum / meī)
2. Did he give you *your* book, Marcus? (vestrum / tuum / tibi)
3. She hurt *herself* when she fell. (eī / sibi / eae)
4. She saw *herself* in the mirror. (sē / eam / eum)
5. Did you leave *your* books at school, girls? (vōs / vestrum / vestrōs)
6. Yes, we left *our* books there. (nostrōs / nōs / vestrōs)
7. He has *his own* book. (eius / suum / sē)
8. No, he doesn't. He has *her* book. (eius / suum / suam)
9. Do the boys all have *their own* books? (eōrum / suōs / sibi)
10. No, the boys took the girls' books by mistake. So now they have *their* books. (eārum / suōs / eōrum)

Exercise VIe: Verb Forms

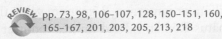 pp. 73, 98, 106–107, 128, 150–151, 160, 165–167, 201, 203, 205, 213, 218

Give the requested forms of the following verbs in the present, imperfect, future, perfect, pluperfect, and future perfect tenses:

	Present	Imperfect	Future	Perfect	Pluperfect	Future Perfect
1. vetāre (*1st pl.*)	___	___	___	___	___	___
2. aperīre (*3rd pl.*)	___	___	___	___	___	___
3. stertere (*2nd pl.*)	___	___	___	___	___	___
4. esse (*3rd sing.*)	___	___	___	___	___	___
5. emere (*3rd sing.*)	___	___	___	___	___	___
6. ferre (*2nd sing.*)	___	___	___	___	___	___
7. arripere (*1st sing.*)	___	___	___	___	___	___
8. docēre (*1st sing.*)	___	___	___	___	___	___
9. posse (*2nd sing.*)	___	___	___	___	___	___
10. velle (*1st pl.*)	___	___	___	___	___	___

Exercise VIf: Reading Comprehension

Read the following passage and answer the questions below with full sentences in Latin:

ROMAN INFLUENCE IN THE EAST: 168 B.C.

Ōlim, ubi Lūcius Aemilius Paulus et Pūblius Licinius cōnsulēs Rōmānī erant, cīvēs Alexandrīnī auxilium ā Rōmānīs petīvērunt. Obsidēbat enim urbem Alexandrīam magnō exercitū Antiochus, rēx Syriae. Hic rēx superbus erat et, quod rēgnum suum augēre in animō habēbat, Aegyptiōs vincere volēbat. Rōmānī Aegyptiīs favēbant, sed exercitum ad Aegyptum mittere nōn poterant. Erat tamen   5
senātor quīdam cōnsulāris, Gāius Popilius Laenās nōmine, quī eō ipsō tempore iter in illīs partibus faciēbat. Hunc senātōrem ad Aegyptum mīsit senātus Rōmānus quod auxilium Aegyptiīs offerre voluit.

Antiochus, ubi Popilius advēnit, ad eum nūntiōs mīsit, nam hunc senātōrem cōnsulere volēbat. Vēnit rēx Syriae ad congressum vestibus magnificīs indūtus   10
cum magnā multitūdine mīlitum. Vēnit Popilius sōlus, togā praetextā indūtus, cum duodecim modo līctōribus. Rēgī appropinquāvit et statim, "Necesse est mihi," inquit, "ad senātum respōnsum tuum, Antioche, referre. Quid ā Rōmānīs petis, bellum aut pācem?"

Stupuit Antiochus et sēcum cogitābat: "Cūr ille Rōmānus mē nōn timet?   15
Nūllum exercitum habet, sed neque commōtus neque sollicitus est." Antiochus ipse vērō commōtus sollicitusque erat et Popiliō igitur respondit, "Necesse est dē hāc rē cum amīcīs meīs cōnsulere."

Habēbat in manū Popilius baculum quod omnēs lēgātī Rōmānī sēcum ferre solēbant. Hōc baculō Popilius circulum in arēnā circum rēgem Syriae scrīpsit.   20
Rēgī, "Antequam ē circulō exieris," inquit, "mihi respōnsum dabis." Attonitus erat Antiochus. Popilium et imperium Rōmānum valdē timēbat. "Faciam," inquit, "id quod cēnset senātus Rōmānus." Ad mīlitēs rediit et exercitum ad Syriam statim redūxit. Tanta erat dignitās et auctōritās huius lēgātī et senātūs Rōmānī.

1 cōnsul, cōnsulis, m., *consul (one of the two chief annual magistrates of the Roman state)*	10 congressus, -ūs, m., *meeting* vestis, vestis, gen. pl., vestium, f., *garment, clothes* indūtus, -a, -um + abl., *dressed (in)*
2 Alexandrīnus, -a, -um, *of Alexandria (a city in Egypt)*	12 duodecim, *twelve* līctor, līctōris, m., *lictor (official attendant)*
3 exercitus, -ūs, m., *army* rēx, rēgis, m., *king* superbus, -a, -um, *arrogant, haughty*	13 respōnsum, -ī, n., *answer*
4 rēgnum, -ī, n., *kingdom* Aegyptiī, -ōrum, m. pl., *the Egyptians*	14 bellum, -ī, n., *war* pāx, pācis, f., *peace*
5 Aegyptus, -ī, f., *Egypt*	17 vērō, adv., *truly* -que, enclitic conj., *and*
6 cōnsulāris, -is, -e, *having the status of an ex-consul*	

20 circulus, -ī, m., *small circle*
  arēna, -ae, f., *sand*
21 antequam, conj., *before*
22 imperium, -ī, n., *empire, power*

24 dignitās, dignitātis, f., *honor, status, dignity*
  auctōritās, auctōritātis, f., *influence, prestige, authority*

2 obsideō, obsidēre, obsēdī, obsessus, *to besiege*
4 augeō, augēre, auxī, auctus, *to increase*
8 offerō, offerre, obtulī, oblātus, irreg., *to provide*
13 referō, referre, rettulī, relātus, irreg., *to bring back*
23 cēnseō, cēnsēre, cēnsuī, cēnsus, *to decree*

1. When did the citizens of Alexandria seek help from the Romans?
2. Who was besieging Alexandria?
3. Why was he wanting to conquer the Egyptians?
4. Whom did the Senate send to Egypt?
5. How did Antiochus come to his meeting with Popilius?
6. How did Popilius come?
7. Was Popilius afraid of Antiochus?
8. Was Antiochus afraid of Popilius?
9. What did Popilius do? What did he say?
10. How did Antiochus respond?
11. What did Popilius do and say in reply?
12. What did Antiochus do?

Exercise VIg: 4th and 5th Declension Nouns

1. In the first, second, and fourth paragraphs of the story above, locate four different 4th declension nouns.
2. In the third paragraph of the story, locate one 5th declension noun.

FORMS

The following charts show the forms of typical Latin nouns, adjectives, pronouns, and verbs in the cases and tenses presented in this book. As an aid in pronunciation, markings of long vowels and of accents are included.

I. Nouns

Number Case	1st Declension	2nd Declension			
	Fem.	Masc.	Masc.	Masc.	Neut.
Singular					
Nominative	puéll**a**	sérv**us**	púer	áger	bácul**um**
Genitive	puéll**ae**	sérv**ī**	púer**ī**	ágr**ī**	bácul**ī**
Dative	puéll**ae**	sérv**ō**	púer**ō**	ágr**ō**	bácul**ō**
Accusative	puéll**am**	sérv**um**	púer**um**	ágr**um**	bácul**um**
Ablative	puéll**ā**	sérv**ō**	púer**ō**	ágr**ō**	bácul**ō**
Vocative	puéll**a**	sérv**e**	púer	áger	bácul**um**
Plural					
Nominative	puéll**ae**	sérv**ī**	púer**ī**	ágr**ī**	bácul**a**
Genitive	puell**árum**	serv**órum**	puer**órum**	agr**órum**	bacul**órum**
Dative	puéll**īs**	sérv**īs**	púer**īs**	ágr**īs**	bácul**īs**
Accusative	puéll**ās**	sérv**ōs**	púer**ōs**	ágr**ōs**	bácul**a**
Ablative	puéll**īs**	sérv**īs**	púer**īs**	ágr**īs**	bácul**īs**
Vocative	puéll**ae**	sérv**ī**	púer**ī**	ágr**ī**	bácul**a**

Number Case	3rd Declension			4th Declension		5th Declension	
	Masc.	Fem.	Neut.	Masc.	Neut.	Masc.	Fem.
Singular							
Nominative	páter	vōx	nómen	árc**us**	gén**ū**	di**ḗs**	r**ḗs**
Genitive	pátr**is**	vóc**is**	nómin**is**	árc**ūs**	gén**ūs**	di**ḗī**	r**éī**
Dative	pátr**ī**	vóc**ī**	nómin**ī**	árc**uī**	gén**ū**	di**ḗī**	r**éī**
Accusative	pátr**em**	vóc**em**	nómen	árc**um**	gén**ū**	díe**m**	re**m**
Ablative	pátr**e**	vóc**e**	nómin**e**	árc**ū**	gén**ū**	dí**ē**	r**ē**
Vocative	páter	vōx	nómen	árc**us**	gén**ū**	di**ḗs**	r**ḗs**
Plural							
Nominative	pátr**ēs**	vóc**ēs**	nómin**a**	árc**ūs**	gén**ua**	dí**ēs**	r**ḗs**
Genitive	pátr**um**	vóc**um**	nómin**um**	árc**uum**	gén**uum**	di**ḗrum**	r**ḗrum**
Dative	pátr**ibus**	vóc**ibus**	nómín**ibus**	árc**ibus**	gén**ibus**	di**ḗbus**	r**ḗbus**
Accusative	pátr**ēs**	vóc**ēs**	nómin**a**	árc**ūs**	gén**ua**	dí**ēs**	r**ḗs**
Ablative	pátr**ibus**	vóc**ibus**	nómín**ibus**	árc**ibus**	gén**ibus**	di**ḗbus**	r**ḗbus**
Vocative	pátr**ēs**	vóc**ēs**	nómin**a**	árc**ūs**	gén**ua**	dí**ēs**	r**ḗs**

II. Adjectives

Number Case	1st and 2nd Declensions			3rd Declension		
	Masc.	Fem.	Neut.	Masc.	Fem.	Neut.
Singular						
Nominative	mágn*us*	mágn*a*	mágn*um*	ómn*is*	ómn*is*	ómn*e*
Genitive	mágn*ī*	mágn*ae*	mágn*ī*	ómn*is*	ómn*is*	ómn*is*
Dative	mágn*ō*	mágn*ae*	mágn*ō*	ómn*ī*	ómn*ī*	ómn*ī*
Accusative	mágn*um*	mágn*am*	mágn*um*	ómn*em*	ómn*em*	ómn*e*
Ablative	mágn*ō*	mágn*ā*	mágn*ō*	ómn*ī*	ómn*ī*	ómn*ī*
Vocative	mágn*e*	mágn*a*	mágn*um*	ómn*is*	ómn*is*	ómn*e*
Plural						
Nominative	mágn*ī*	mágn*ae*	mágn*a*	ómn*ēs*	ómn*ēs*	ómn*ia*
Genitive	magn*órum*	magn*árum*	magn*órum*	ómn*ium*	ómn*ium*	ómn*ium*
Dative	mágn*īs*	mágn*īs*	mágn*īs*	ómn*ibus*	ómn*ibus*	ómn*ibus*
Accusative	mágn*ōs*	mágn*ās*	mágn*a*	ómn*ēs*	ómn*ēs*	ómn*ia*
Ablative	mágn*īs*	mágn*īs*	mágn*īs*	ómn*ibus*	ómn*ibus*	ómn*ibus*
Vocative	mágn*ī*	mágn*ae*	mágn*a*	ómn*ēs*	ómn*ēs*	ómn*ia*

III. Numbers

Case	Masc.	Fem.	Neut.
Nominative	ű́n*us*	ű́n*a*	ű́n*um*
Genitive	ūn*íus*	ūn*íus*	ūn*íus*
Dative	ű́n*ī*	ű́n*ī*	ű́n*ī*
Accusative	ű́n*um*	ű́n*am*	ű́n*um*
Ablative	ű́n*ō*	ű́n*ā*	ű́n*ō*

Case	Masc.	Fem.	Neut.	Masc.	Fem.	Neut.
Nominative	dú*o*	dú*ae*	dú*o*	trēs	trēs	trí*a*
Genitive	du*órum*	du*árum*	du*órum*	trí*um*	trí*um*	trí*um*
Dative	du*óbus*	du*ábus*	du*óbus*	trí*bus*	trí*bus*	trí*bus*
Accusative	dú*ōs*	dú*ās*	dú*o*	trēs	trēs	trí*a*
Ablative	du*óbus*	du*ábus*	du*óbus*	trí*bus*	trí*bus*	trí*bus*

In addition to **ūnus, -a, -um**, the following other adjectives have **-īus** in the genitive singular and **-ī** in the dative singular: **alius, -a, -ud**, *another, other*; **alter, altera, alterum**, *second, one (of two), the other (of two), another*; **nūllus, -a, -um**, *no, not any*; **sōlus, -a, -um**, *alone*; and **tōtus, -a, -um**, *all, the whole.*

IV. Personal Pronouns

Number Case	1st	2nd	3rd		
			Masc.	Fem.	Neut.
Singular					
Nominative	égo	tū	is	éa	id
Genitive	méī	túī	éius	éius	éius
Dative	míhi	tíbi	éī	éī	éī
Accusative	mē	tē	éum	éam	id
Ablative	mē	tē	éō	éā	éō
Plural					
Nominative	nōs	vōs	éī	éae	éa
Genitive	nóstrī	véstrī	eṓrum	eā́rum	eṓrum
	nóstrum	véstrum			
Dative	nṓbīs	vṓbīs	éīs	éīs	éīs
Accusative	nōs	vōs	éōs	éās	éa
Ablative	nṓbīs	vṓbīs	éīs	éīs	éīs

V. Reflexive Pronouns

	Singular	Plural
Nominative	—	—
Genitive	súī	súī
Dative	síbi	síbi
Accusative	sē	sē
Ablative	sē	sē

VI. Relative Pronoun

Number Case	Masc.	Fem.	Neut.
Singular			
Nominative	quī	quae	quod
Genitive	cúius	cúius	cúius
Dative	cui	cui	cui
Accusative	quem	quam	quod
Ablative	quō	quā	quō
Plural			
Nominative	quī	quae	quae
Genitive	quṓrum	quā́rum	quṓrum
Dative	quíbus	quíbus	quíbus
Accusative	quōs	quās	quae
Ablative	quíbus	quíbus	quíbus

VII. Interrogative Pronoun

Number Case	Singular			Plural		
	Masc.	**Fem.**	**Neut.**	**Masc.**	**Fem.**	**Neut.**
Nominative	quis	quis	quid	quī	quae	quae
Genitive	cúius	cúius	cúius	quṓrum	quā́rum	quṓrum
Dative	cui	cui	cui	quíbus	quíbus	quíbus
Accusative	quem	quem	quid	quōs	quās	quae
Ablative	quō	quō	quō	quíbus	quíbus	quíbus

VIII. Indefinite Adjective

Number Case	Masc.	Fem.	Neut.
Singular			
Nominative	quídam	quaédam	quóddam
Genitive	cuiúsdam	cuiúsdam	cuiúsdam
Dative	cúidam	cúidam	cúidam
Accusative	quéndam	quándam	quóddam
Ablative	quṓdam	quā́dam	quṓdam
Plural			
Nominative	quídam	quaédam	quaédam
Genitive	quōrúndam	quārúndam	quōrúndam
Dative	quibúsdam	quibúsdam	quibúsdam
Accusative	quṓsdam	quā́sdam	quaédam
Ablative	quibúsdam	quibúsdam	quibúsdam

IX. Demonstrative Adjectives and Pronouns

Number Case	Masc.	Fem.	Neut.	Masc.	Fem.	Neut.
Singular						
Nominative	hic	haec	hoc	ílle	ílla	íllud
Genitive	húius	húius	húius	illī́us	illī́us	illī́us
Dative	húic	húic	húic	íllī	íllī	íllī
Accusative	hunc	hanc	hoc	íllum	íllam	íllud
Ablative	hōc	hāc	hōc	íllō	íllā	íllō
Plural						
Nominative	hī	hae	haec	íllī	íllae	ílla
Genitive	hṓrum	hā́rum	hṓrum	illṓrum	illā́rum	illṓrum
Dative	hīs	hīs	hīs	íllīs	íllīs	íllīs
Accusative	hōs	hās	haec	íllōs	íllās	ílla
Ablative	hīs	hīs	hīs	íllīs	íllīs	íllīs

X. Regular Verbs

		1st Conjugation	2nd Conjugation	3rd Conjugation		4th Conjugation
	Infinitive	par*ā́re*	hab*ḗre*	mítt*ere*	iác*ere* (-iō)	aud*ī́re*
	Imperative	pár*ā*	háb*ē*	mítt*e*	iác*e*	aúd*ī*
		par*ā́te*	hab*ḗte*	mítt*ite*	iác*ite*	aud*ī́te*
Present	Sing. 1	pár*ō*	háb*eō*	mítt*ō*	iáci*ō*	aúdi*ō*
	2	pár*ās*	háb*ēs*	mítt*is*	iác*is*	aúd*īs*
	3	pár*at*	háb*et*	mítt*it*	iác*it*	aúd*it*
	Pl. 1	par*ā́mus*	hab*ḗmus*	mítt*imus*	iác*imus*	aud*ī́mus*
	2	par*ā́tis*	hab*ḗtis*	mítt*itis*	iác*itis*	aud*ī́tis*
	3	pár*ant*	háb*ent*	mítt*unt*	iáci*unt*	aúdi*unt*
Imperfect	Sing. 1	par*ā́bam*	hab*ḗbam*	mitt*ḗbam*	iaci*ḗbam*	audi*ḗbam*
	2	par*ā́bās*	hab*ḗbās*	mitt*ḗbās*	iaci*ḗbās*	audi*ḗbās*
	3	par*ā́bat*	hab*ḗbat*	mitt*ḗbat*	iaci*ḗbat*	audi*ḗbat*
	Pl. 1	par*ābā́mus*	hab*ēbā́mus*	mitt*ēbā́mus*	iaci*ēbā́mus*	audi*ēbā́mus*
	2	par*ābā́tis*	hab*ēbā́tis*	mitt*ēbā́tis*	iaci*ēbā́tis*	audi*ēbā́tis*
	3	par*ā́bant*	hab*ḗbant*	mitt*ḗbant*	iaci*ḗbant*	audi*ḗbant*
Future	Sing. 1	par*ā́bō*	hab*ḗbō*	mítt*am*	iáci*am*	aúdi*am*
	2	par*ā́bis*	hab*ḗbis*	mítt*ēs*	iáci*ēs*	aúdi*ēs*
	3	par*ā́bit*	hab*ḗbit*	mítt*et*	iáci*et*	aúdi*et*
	Pl. 1	par*ā́bimus*	hab*ḗbimus*	mitt*ḗmus*	iaci*ḗmus*	audi*ḗmus*
	2	par*ā́bitis*	hab*ḗbitis*	mitt*ḗtis*	iaci*ḗtis*	audi*ḗtis*
	3	par*ā́bunt*	hab*ḗbunt*	mítt*ent*	iáci*ent*	aúdi*ent*
Perfect	Sing. 1	par*ā́vī*	háb*uī*	mī́s*ī*	iḗc*ī*	aud*ī́vī*
	2	par*āvístī*	hab*uístī*	mīs*ístī*	iēc*ístī*	aud*īvístī*
	3	par*ā́vit*	háb*uit*	mī́s*it*	iḗc*it*	aud*ī́vit*
	Pl. 1	par*ā́vimus*	hab*úimus*	mī́s*imus*	iḗc*imus*	aud*ī́vimus*
	2	par*āvístis*	hab*uístis*	mīs*ístis*	iēc*ístis*	aud*īvístis*
	3	par*āvḗrunt*	hab*uḗrunt*	mīs*ḗrunt*	iēc*ḗrunt*	aud*īvḗrunt*
Pluperfect	Sing. 1	par*ā́veram*	hab*úeram*	mī́s*eram*	iḗc*eram*	aud*ī́veram*
	2	par*ā́verās*	hab*úerās*	mī́s*erās*	iḗc*erās*	aud*ī́verās*
	3	par*ā́verat*	hab*úerat*	mī́s*erat*	iḗc*erat*	aud*ī́verat*
	Pl. 1	par*āverā́mus*	hab*uerā́mus*	mīs*erā́mus*	iēc*erā́mus*	aud*īverā́mus*
	2	par*āverā́tis*	hab*uerā́tis*	mīs*erā́tis*	iēc*erā́tis*	aud*īverā́tis*
	3	par*ā́verant*	hab*úerant*	mī́s*erant*	iḗc*erant*	aud*ī́verant*
Future Perfect	Sing. 1	par*ā́verō*	hab*úerō*	mī́s*erō*	iḗc*erō*	aud*ī́verō*
	2	par*ā́veris*	hab*úeris*	mī́s*eris*	iḗc*eris*	aud*ī́veris*
	3	par*ā́verit*	hab*úerit*	mī́s*erit*	iḗc*erit*	aud*ī́verit*
	Pl. 1	par*āvḗrimus*	hab*uḗrimus*	mīs*ḗrimus*	iēc*ḗrimus*	aud*īvḗrimus*
	2	par*āvḗritis*	hab*uḗritis*	mīs*ḗritis*	iēc*ḗritis*	aud*īvḗritis*
	3	par*ā́verint*	hab*úerint*	mī́s*erint*	iḗc*erint*	aud*ī́verint*

XI. Irregular Verbs

	Infinitive	ésse	pósse	vélle	nõlle
	Imperative	es éste	— —	— —	nõlī nõlīte
Present	Sing. 1 2 3	sum es est	póssum pótes pótest	vólō vīs vult	nõlō nōn vīs nōn vult
	Pl. 1 2 3	súmus éstis sunt	póssumus potéstis póssunt	vólumus vúltis vólunt	nõlumus nōn vúltis nõlunt
Imperfect	Sing. 1 2 3	éram érās érat	póteram póterās póterat	volébam volébās volébat	nōlébam nōlébās nōlébat
	Pl. 1 2 3	erámus erátis érant	poterámus poterátis póterant	volēbámus volēbátis volébant	nōlēbámus nōlēbátis nōlébant
Future	Sing. 1 2 3	érō éris érit	póterō póteris póterit	vólam vólēs vólet	nõlam nõlēs nõlet
	Pl. 1 2 3	érimus éritis érunt	potérimus potéritis póterunt	volémus volétis vólent	nōlémus nōlétis nõlent
Perfect	Sing. 1 2 3	fúī fuístī fúit	pótuī potuístī pótuit	vóluī voluístī vóluit	nõluī nōluístī nõluit
	Pl. 1 2 3	fúimus fuístis fuérunt	potúimus potuístis potuérunt	volúimus voluístis voluérunt	nōlúimus nōluístis nōluérunt
Pluperfect	Sing. 1 2 3	fúeram fúerās fúerat	potúeram potúerās potúerat	volúeram volúerās volúerat	nōlúeram nōlúerās nōlúerat
	Pl. 1 2 3	fuerámus fuerátis fúerant	potuerámus potuerátis potúerant	voluerámus voluerátis volúerant	nōluerámus nōluerátis nōlúerant
Future Perfect	Sing. 1 2 3	fúerō fúeris fúerit	potúerō potúeris potúerit	volúerō volúeris volúerit	nōlúerō nōlúeris nōlúerit
	Pl. 1 2 3	fuérimus fuéritis fúerint	potuérimus potuéritis potúerint	voluérimus voluéritis volúerint	nōluérimus nōluéritis nōlúerint

		férre	íre	
Infinitive		férre	íre	
Imperative		fer fér**te**	ī́ í**te**	
Present	Sing. 1 2 3	fér**ō** fer**s** fer**t**	é**ō** ī**s** i**t**	
	Pl. 1 2 3	féri**mus** fér**tis** féru**nt**	í**mus** í**tis** éu**nt**	
Imperfect	Sing. 1 2 3	ferḗ**bam** ferē**bā́s** ferē**bat**	ī́**bam** ī**bā́s** ī**bat**	
	Pl. 1 2 3	ferē**bā́mus** ferē**bā́tis** ferē**bant**	ī**bā́mus** ī**bā́tis** ī**bant**	
Future	Sing. 1 2 3	fér**am** fér**ēs** fér**et**	í**bō** í**bis** í**bit**	
	Pl. 1 2 3	fer**ḗmus** fer**ḗtis** fér**ent**	í**bimus** í**bitis** í**bunt**	
Perfect	Sing. 1 2 3	túl**ī** tul**ístī** túl**it**	ī́**vī** ī**vístī** ī́**vit**	or, more usually íī iístī > ī́stī íit
	Pl. 1 2 3	túl**imus** tul**ístis** tul**ḗrunt**	ī́**vimus** ī**vístis** ī**vḗrunt**	í**imus** iístis > ī́stis i**ḗrunt**
Pluperfect	Sing. 1 2 3	túl**eram** túl**erās** túl**erat**	ī́**veram** ī́**verās** ī́**verat**	í**eram** í**erās** í**erat**
	Pl. 1 2 3	tul**erā́mus** tul**erā́tis** túl**erant**	ī**verā́mus** ī**verā́tis** ī́**verant**	i**erā́mus** i**erā́tis** í**erant**
Future Perfect	Sing. 1 2 3	túl**erō** túl**eris** túl**erit**	ī́**verō** ī́**veris** ī́**verit**	í**erō** í**eris** í**erit**
	Pl. 1 2 3	tul**érimus** tul**éritis** túl**erint**	ī**vérimus** ī**véritis** ī́**verint**	i**érimus** i**éritis** í**erint**

BUILDING THE MEANING

I. Parts of Speech

The following are eight basic parts of speech:

Nouns: names of persons, places, things, qualities, or acts (see page 4)

Pronouns: words that stand in place of nouns, e.g., *she* in place of *Cornelia* (see pages 252–255)

Adjectives: words that describe persons, places, things, qualities, or acts (see page 4)

Verbs: words that denote actions (e.g., *sits*) or existence (e.g., *is*) (see page 4)

Adverbs: words that modify verbs, adjectives, or other adverbs (see pages 100–101)

Prepositions: words such as *from*, *in*, and *at*, which introduce prepositional phrases (see page 64)

Conjunctions: words that link other words, phrases, or clauses (see pages 284–286)

Interjections: words that can stand alone and that call attention to a statement or express an emotion, e.g., *Look! Alas!*

II. Core Elements of Latin Sentences

You have met Latin sentences with the following combinations of core elements:

A. Subject and Intransitive Verb (see page 20)

> Cornēlia **sedet.** (1:3)   **Sedet** Cornēlia.   *Cornelia **sits.***

This sentence has only a subject (S) and an intransitive verb (IV). **Cornēlia** is in the nominative case and is therefore the subject of the sentence.

The verb in the above sentence expresses an action that simply tells what the subject is doing. The action of the verb does not affect anyone or anything else. Verbs when so used are called intransitive verbs (IV).

B. Subject, Linking Verb, and Complement (see page 8)

> Cornēlia **est** puella.   *Cornelia **is** a girl.*
> Cornēlia puella **est.**

This sentence has a subject, **Cornēlia**, and a verb, **est**, as well as another word in the nominative case, **puella**. This word is linked to the subject by the verb **est**. The word **puella** is called a complement (C), because it completes the meaning of the sentence. **Est** is called a linking verb (LV) because it links the subject with the complement. The complement may appear before the linking verb, as in the second example above.

The linking verb in the following sentence links the subject with an adjective, which serves as a complement:

Cornēlia **est** laeta. (1:2–3)   *Cornelia **is** happy.*
Cornēlia laeta **est**.
Laeta **est** Cornēlia.
Laeta Cornēlia **est**.

C. Est/Sunt, Subject, No Complement (see page 8)

In pictūrā **est** puella. (1:1)   In pictūrā **sunt** puellae.
There is *a girl in the picture.*   ***There are*** *girls in the picture.*

Note that **est** and **sunt** come before their subjects here.

D. Subject, Direct Object, and Transitive Verb (see page 20)

Sextus Cornēliam **vexat**. (4:1)   *Sextus **annoys** Cornelia.*

In this sentence there is a subject, a direct object (DO: see pages 20 and 40), and a verb. The direct object is in the accusative case, and it names the person or thing that receives the action of the verb. The verbs in such sentences are said to be transitive verbs (TV). The words in the Latin sentence could be arranged in any order and would express essentially the same meaning.

E. Subject, Dative, and Intransitive Verb (see pages 212–213, 252, and 282)

1. Dative with Intransitive Compound Verbs (see pages 212 and 282)

Ibi fortasse patrī tuō **occurēmus**. (24:17)
*Perhaps **we will meet** your father there.*

2. Dative with Special Intransitive Verbs (see pages 252 and 282)

Sī mihi **nocueritis**, pater meus certē vōs pūniet. (26:26–27)
*If **you do harm** to me, my father will certainly punish you.*
*If **you harm** me, my father will certainly punish you.*

III. Sentence Types

Every Latin sentence expresses a statement, a command, an exclamation, or a question.

A. The following are statements:

In pictūrā est puella. (1:1)
There is a girl in the picture.

Flāvia scrībit. (1:5)
Flavia writes.

Sextus Cornēliam vexat. (4:1)
Sextus annoys Cornelia.

B. Sentences may express commands and have their verbs in the imperative (see page 74):

Dēscende, Sexte! (4:6)
Come down, Sextus!

Abīte, molestī! (3:8)
Go away, pests!

Negative commands are expressed with **nōlī** (singular) or **nōlīte** (plural) plus an infinitive (see page 74):

Nōlī servōs **excitāre!** (9:9)
Don't wake up the slaves!

C. A sentence may express an exclamation:

Quam celeriter appropinquat! (15:12)
How quickly it is approaching!

D. Statements can be turned into questions by placing an important word (often the verb) first and attaching the letters **-ne** to it (see page 13):

Puer ignāvus est.
The boy is cowardly.
(statement)

Estne puer ignāvus? (5:4)
Is the boy cowardly?
(question)

Questions are introduced by the word **Nōnne…?** when the speaker clearly expects the answer "yes":

Nōnne cēnāre vultis? (19:2)
*Surely you want to eat, **don't you?***

Questions are often introduced by interrogative words such as the following:

Cui…? *To whom…?* (sing.)
Cuius…? *Whose…?* (sing.)
Cūr…? *Why…?*
Quālis…? *What sort of …?*
Quandō…? *When…?*
Quem…? *Whom…?* (sing.)
Quī…? *Who…?* (pl.)
Quibus…? *To whom…?* (pl.)
Quid…? *What…?*
Quis…? *Who…?* (sing.)

Quō…? *Where… to?*
Quō īnstrūmentō…? *With what instrument…? By what means…? How…?*
Quōcum…? *With whom…?* (sing.)
Quōmodo…? *In what manner…? How…?*
Quōs…? *Whom…?* (pl.)
Quot…? *How many…?*
Ubi…? *Where…?*
Unde…? *From where…?*

IV. More About Verbs

A. Tenses of Verbs

1. Verbs can be in the present tense, describing actions or situations in present time (see page 73):

   a. in a simple statement of fact:

   Cornēliī Rōmam redīre **parant.**
   *The Cornelii **prepare** to return to Rome.*

   b. in a description of an ongoing action:

   Hodiē Cornēliī Rōmam redīre **parant.**
   *Today the Cornelii **are preparing** to return to Rome.*

   c. in a question:

   Auditne Dāvus clāmōrem?
   ***Does** Davus **hear** the shouting?*

   d. in an emphatic statement:

   Clāmōrem **audit.**
   *He **does hear** the shouting.*

   e. in a denial:

   Clāmōrem nōn **audit.**
   *He **does** not **hear** the shouting.*

2. The imperfect tense (see pages 98 and 106–107) shows action in the past that was:

   a. going on for a time:

   Ego et Mārcus **spectābāmus** cisium. (14:10)
   *Marcus and I **were watching** the carriage.*

   Cornēlia dormīre **volēbat.** (13:8)
   *Cornelia **wanted** to sleep.*

   b. repeated:

   Mārcus **vexābat** Cornēliam. (13:7–8)
   *Marcus **kept annoying** Cornelia.*

   c. habitual or customary:

   Dāvus in Britanniā **habitābat.**
   *Davus **used to live** in Britain.*

d. beginning to happen:

> Equōs ad raedam nostrum **dēvertēbat**. (14:11)
> *He **began to turn** the horses **aside** in the direction of our carriage.*

3. The future tense indicates an action that will take place at some time subsequent to the present (see page 201):

> Brevī tempore ad Portam Capēnam **adveniēmus**. (22:26)
> *In a short time **we will arrive** at the Porta Capena.*

4. The perfect, pluperfect, and future perfect tenses are formed from the perfect stem, which is found by dropping the *-ī* from the third principal part of the verb, e.g., **parāvī**, perfect stem **parāv-**. These tenses describe completed actions.

5. The perfect tense refers to an action that happened or to something that someone did in past time (see page 150):

> Eō ipsō tempore ad iānuam caupōnae **appāruit** homō obēsus. (18:12)
> *At that very moment a fat man **appeared** at the door of the inn.*

The perfect tense may also refer to an action that someone has completed as of present time (see page 151):

> Servī meī alium lectum tibi **parāvērunt**. (19:17–18)
> *My slaves **have prepared** another bed for you.*

6. The pluperfect tense describes an action that was completed before some other action in the past took place (see page 213):

> Titus in itinere mōnstrāvit puerīs mīra aedificia quae prīncipēs in Palātīnō **aedificāverant**. (24:19–20)
> *Along the way Titus showed the boys the wonderful buildings that the emperors **had built** on the Palatine.*
> (The emperors had built the buildings *before* Titus showed them to the boys.)

7. The future perfect tense describes an action that will have been completed before some other action in future time begins (see page 218):

> Cum **intrāverimus**, tandem aurīgās ipsōs spectābimus. (26:17–18)
> *When we **enter/will have entered**, we will finally watch the charioteers themselves.*
> (The speakers will have entered the Circus Maximus *before* they will watch the charioteers.)

B. Infinitives

The infinitive is the form of the verb marked by "to…" in English (e.g., "to walk") and by the letters *-re* in Latin (e.g., **errāre, rīdēre,**

ascend*ere*, and **dorm*īre*)** (see page 26). You have seen four uses of the infinitive in Latin sentences:

1. The complementary infinitive (see pages 26 and 162):

    Sextus arborēs **ascendere** *vult*.   *Sextus wants **to climb** trees.*

    Here the infinitive completes the meaning of the main verb. Other verbs and verbal phrases that are often completed with infinitives are: **nōlle, posse, parāre, solēre, timēre,** and **in animō habēre.**

2. The infinitive with impersonal verbal phrase and impersonal verbs:

    Nōbīs <u>necesse est</u> statim **discēdere.** (9.13)   <u>Licet</u>ne nōbīs hīc **cēnāre?** (20:7)
    ***To leave** immediately <u>is necessary</u> for us.*   *Is **to dine** here <u>allowed</u> for us?*
    *<u>It is necessary</u> for us **to leave** immediately.*   *<u>Is it allowed</u> for us **to dine** here?*
          May we dine here?

    The verbal phrase **necesse est** and the verb **licet** are said to be impersonal, because we may translate them with the impersonal phrases *it is necessary* and *it is allowed.* In the Latin sentences, however, the infinitives are the grammatical subjects of the verbs.

3. The infinitive as subject of the verb **est** (see page 162):

    Etiam in caupōnā **pernoctāre** saepe <u>est</u> perīculōsum. (20:19)
    ***To spend the night** in an inn <u>is</u> also often dangerous.*
    *<u>It is</u> also often dangerous **to spend the night** in an inn.*

    Here **pernoctāre,** *to spend the night*, is the subject of the sentence, and **perīculōsum** is a complement after the linking verb. It is neuter in gender because the infinitive used as subject functions as a neuter verbal noun.

4. Accusative and infinitive with **docet** and **iubet** (see pages 72 and 162):

    Aurēlia **Cornēliam** <u>docet</u> vīllam **cūrāre.** (6:11)
    *Aurelia <u>teaches</u> **Cornelia** (how) **to take care of** the country house.*

    Ancillam <u>iubet</u> aliās tunicās et stolās et pallās in cistam **pōnere.** (10:2)
    *<u>She orders</u> **the slave-woman to put** other tunics and stolas and pallas into a chest.*

    Cūr pater meus **nōs exīre** <u>vetat</u>? (26:12)
    *Why <u>does</u> my father <u>forbid</u> us **to go out?***

V. Modifiers

There are many ways in which the thought expressed by a sentence can be elaborated and made fuller and clearer. For example, various kinds of modifiers can be used. Any noun or verb in a sentence can have modifiers.

A. Modifiers of Nouns

1. Adjectives may be used to modify nouns. They must agree with the nouns they modify in gender, case, and number (see pages 34–35, 120–121, and 139–140):

   Flāvia in vīllā **vīcīnā** habitat. (1:4)
   *Flavia lives in a **neighboring** country house.*

   Cum senātōre **Rōmānō** iter facit. (page 121)
   *He travels with a **Roman** senator.*

   Omnēs vīllās, **omnēs** agrōs, **omnēs** arborēs vident. (page 139)
   *They see **all** the country houses, **all** the fields, **all** the trees.*

2. Adjectives that modify the subject of the verb may sometimes best be translated as adverbs:

   Brevī tempore, ubi Mārcus advenit, eum **laetae** excipiunt. (5:12–13)
   *In a short time, when Marcus arrives, they welcome him **happily**.*

3. The Genitive Case

   a. You have also seen a word or phrase in the genitive case used as a modifier (see page 80), usually with another noun. The genitive case relates or attaches one noun or phrase to another:

      Dāvus ad portam **vīllae** stat. (11.17)
      *Davus stands near the door **of the country house**.*

      The genitive case sometimes indicates possession:

      Vīlicus ipse vīllam **dominī** cūrat. (11:3)
      *The overseer himself looks after **the master's** country house.*

   b. Genitive with Adjectives

      You have also seen words or phrases in the genitive case used with adjectives, such as **plēnus** (see page 80):

      Brevī tempore ārea est plēna **servōrum** et **ancillārum.** (11:4)
      *In a short time the space is full **of slaves** and **slave-women**.*

      A word or phrase in the genitive is usually used with adjectives of remembering and forgetting:

immemor **terrōris nocturnī** (22:3)
forgetful **of his fear during the night**

c. Partitive Genitive or Genitive of the Whole

The genitive case may be used to indicate the whole of which something is a part (partitive genitive or genitive of the whole) (see page 229):

"Nihil **malī**," inquit. (21:7)
"_Nothing_ **of a bad thing**," _he said._
"_Nothing bad_" or "_There is nothing wrong._"

Crās satis **temporis** habēbimus. (23f:14)
Tomorrow we will have enough _(_**of**_)_ **time**.

Nihil **pecūniae** habeō. (26:26)
I have nothing **of money**.
I have no money.

With numbers and the words **paucī**, _a few_, **quīdam**, _a certain_, and **nūllus**, _no, no one_, the preposition **ex** or **dē** + ablative is used instead of the partitive genitive:

ūnus **ē praedōnibus** (26:24), _one_ **of the pirates**

4. For subordinate clauses that modify nouns, see section VIII: Main and Subordinate Clauses.

B. Modifiers of Verbs

1. Adverbs may be used to modify verbs (see page 100):

Laeta est Flāvia quod Cornēlia **iam** in vīllā habitat. (1:5)
Flavia is happy because Cornelia _is_ **now** _living in the country house._

Adverbs may express time (e.g., **adhūc**, _still_), place (e.g., **hīc**, _here_), or manner (e.g., **celeriter**, _quickly_) (see pages 100–101).

2. Dative Case
   a. Indirect Object
      You have met sentences like the following:

Sextus Cornēliam vexat. (4:1)   _Sextus_ annoys _Cornelia._

These sentences consist of a subject (S) in the nominative case, a direct object (DO) in the accusative case, and a transitive verb (TV).
This pattern may be expanded with a word or phrase in the dative case (as indirect object, IO; see page 189):

Servī cistās Cornēliōrum **raedāriō** trādidērunt. (22:2)
The slaves handed _the chests of the Cornelii_ over **to the coachman**.

(The indirect object, **raedāriō,** tells to whom the slaves handed over the chests.)

b. Dative with Intransitive Verbs

Intransitive verbs (IV) and verbs that may be transitive but are used without a direct object may be accompanied by words or phrases in the dative case (see page 189):

(Aulus) **Septimō** <u>clāmāvit</u>. (21:8–9)   *(Aulus) <u>shouted</u>* **to Septimus.**

Aulus in somnō **eī** <u>appāruit</u>. (21:4)   *Aulus <u>appeared</u>* **to him** *in (his) sleep.*

c. Dative with Intransitive Compound Verbs

Many intransitive compound verbs are accompanied by words or phrases in the dative case (see page 212):

Iam **urbī** <u>appropinquābant</u>. (22:12)
Already <u>they were coming near</u> **to the city/**<u>approaching</u> **the city.**

Ibi fortasse **patrī tuō** <u>occurrēmus</u>. (24:17)
Perhaps <u>we will meet</u> **your father** *there.*

d. Dative with Special Intransitive Verbs (see page 252)

The dative case is also used with special intransitive verbs, such as **nocēre,** *to do harm (to), harm,* **cōnfīdere,** *to give trust (to), trust,* and **favēre,** *to (give) favor (to), favor, support:*

"Sī **mihi** <u>nocueritis</u>, pater meus certē vōs pūniet." (26:26–27)
"If <u>you do harm</u> **to me,** *my father will certainly punish you."*
"If <u>you harm</u> **me,** *my father will certainly punish you."*

Frātrī Titō nōn <u>cōnfīdō</u>. (26e:14)
I <u>do not give trust</u> **to (my) brother Titus.**
I <u>do not trust</u> **(my) brother Titus.**

Ego **russātīs** <u>favēbō</u>. (27:25)
I <u>will give favor</u> **to the reds.**   *I <u>will favor/support</u>* **the reds.**

e. You have seen the following use of the dative case with the impersonal verbal phrase **necesse est:**

Cūr **mihi** quoque <u>necesse est</u> ad urbem redīre? (8:13–14)
Why <u>is it necessary</u> **for me** *too to return to the city?*

You have met a similar use of the dative with impersonal verbs such as **licet** (see page 190):

"<u>Licetne</u> **nōbīs**," inquit Mārcus, "hīc cēnāre?" (20:7)
"<u>Is it allowed</u> **for us,**" *said Marcus,* "*to eat here?"*
"May we eat here?"

3. Nouns or phrases in the ablative case without a preposition may be used to modify verbs (see pages 90–91). Such nouns or phrases may indicate any of the following:

Cause (see page 213):

Tuā culpā raeda <u>est</u> in fossā. (14:7)
Because of your fault *the carriage* <u>*is*</u> *in the ditch.*
It's your fault that the carriage is in the ditch.

Instrument or Means:

Dāvus Getam **baculō** <u>verberat</u>. (12:17–18)
Davus <u>*beats*</u> *Geta **with his stick**.*

Dāvus Getam **tunicā** <u>arripit</u>. (12:17)
Davus <u>*grabs hold of*</u> *Geta **by the tunic**.*

Manner: a phrase consisting of a noun and adjective in the ablative case may be used to indicate *how* something happens. This is called the ablative of manner:

Tum venit Dāvus ipse et, "Tacēte, omnēs!" **magnā vōce** <u>clāmat</u>. (11:6)
Then Davus himself comes, and <u>*he shouts*</u> ***in a loud voice**, "Be quiet, everyone!"*

The preposition **cum** may be found in this construction when the noun is modified by an adjective, e.g., **magnā cum vōce.**

Respect:

In pictūrā est puella, **nōmine** Cornēlia. (1:1)
*There is a girl in the picture, Cornelia **with respect to her name/by name**.*
*There is a girl in the picture, **named** Cornelia.*

Time When:

Etiam in pictūrā est vīlla rūstica ubi Cornēlia **aestāte** <u>habitat</u>. (1:2)
Also in the picture there is a country house and farm where Cornelia <u>*lives*</u> ***in the summer**.*

Time within Which:

Brevī tempore Flāvia quoque <u>est</u> dēfessa. (2:4–5)
***In a short time** Flavia* <u>*is*</u> *also tired.*

4. Prepositional phrases usually modify verbs. Some prepositions are used with the accusative case (see page 64):

<u>ad</u> **vīllam** (2:7)	<u>*to/toward*</u> **the country house**
Iānitor <u>ad</u> **iānuam** vīllae dormit. (9:3)	*The doorkeeper sleeps* <u>*near/at*</u> **the door** *of the country house.*
<u>in</u> **piscīnam** (3:8)	<u>*into*</u> **the fishpond**
<u>per</u> **agrōs** (9:1)	<u>*through*</u> **the fields**
<u>prope</u> **rīvum** (5:3)	<u>*near*</u> **the stream**

With names of cities and the word **domus**, *home*, the accusative case is used without the preposition **ad** to express the idea "to":

"Eugepae!" clāmat Sextus, quī **Rōmam** īre vult. (7:14)
*"Hurray!" shouts Sextus, who wants to go **to Rome**.*

Prīmum Aurēliam et Cornēliam **domum** dūcam. (23:10)
*First I will take Aurelia and Cornelia **home**.*

Some prepositions are used with the ablative case (see pages 64 and 90):

<u>ab</u> **urbe** (13:12)   <u>*from*</u> **the city**

<u>cum</u> **canibus** (12:9)   <u>*with*</u> **dogs**

<u>ē</u> **silvā**   <u>*out of*</u> **the woods**

<u>ex</u> **agrīs** (2:7)   <u>*out of*</u> **the fields**

<u>in</u> **pictūrā** (1:1)   <u>*in*</u> **the picture**

<u>sub</u> **arbore** (1:3)   <u>*under*</u> **the tree**

5. For subordinate clauses that modify verbs, see section VIII: Main and Subordinate Clauses.

VI. Other Uses of Cases

A. The accusative case is used in exclamations:

Ō **mē miseram**! (9:18)   ***Poor me***!

B. The vocative case is used when addressing a person or persons directly (see page 56):

Dēscende, **Sexte!** (4:7)   *Come down, **Sextus!***

VII. Conjunctions

Conjunctions (Latin **con-**, *together* + **iungere**, *to join*) are words that join things together. A conjunction may show a relationship between sentences. For example, **igitur**, *therefore*, indicates that a sentence describes the result or consequence of what was said in the previous sentence:

Sextus est puer molestus quī semper Cornēliam vexat. Cornēlia **igitur** Sextum nōn amat. (4:1–2)
*Sextus is an annoying boy who always annoys Cornelia. Cornelia, **therefore**, does not like Sextus.*

Other conjunctions may join elements within sentences that are added to one another and are of equal grammatical importance:

Cīvēs, mercātōrēs, servī per portam <u>ībant</u> **atque** hūc illūc <u>currēbant</u>. (23:2)
*Citizens, merchants, slaves <u>were going</u> through the gate **and** <u>were running</u> this way and that.*

Cornēlia <u>sedet</u> **et** <u>legit</u>. (1:3)
*Cornelia <u>sits</u> **and** <u>reads</u>.*

Etiam Sextus <u>dormit</u> **neque** Cornēliam <u>vexat</u>. (6:2)
*Even Sextus <u>is sleeping</u> **and** <u>is</u> **not** <u>annoying</u> Cornelia.*

Mārcus **neque** <u>ignāvus</u> **neque** <u>temerārius</u> est. (5:5–6)
*Marcus is **neither** <u>cowardly</u> **nor** <u>rash</u>.*

Hodiē puellae nōn <u>sedent</u> **sed** in agrīs <u>ambulant</u>. (2:2–3)
*Today the girls <u>are</u> not <u>sitting</u> **but** <u>are walking</u> in the fields.*

VIII. Main and Subordinate Clauses

A clause is a group of words containing a verb. The following sentence contains two clauses, each of which is said to be a *main clause* because each could stand by itself as a complete sentence:

Rīdent Mārcus et Cornēlia, sed nōn rīdet Sextus. (4:10–11)
Marcus and Cornelia laugh, but Sextus does not laugh.

The clauses in this sentence are said to be *coordinate* (Latin **co-**, *together, same* + **ōrdō**, *order, rank*), and the conjunction that joins them, **sed**, is said to be a *coordinating conjunction*. For other coordinating conjunctions, see the examples in section VII: Conjunctions.

Subordinate (Latin **sub-**, *below* + **ōrdō**, *order, rank*) clauses are clauses that are of less grammatical importance than the main clause in a sentence. They are sometimes called dependent (Latin **dē-**, *down from* + **pendēre**, *to hang*) clauses because they hang down from the main clause and cannot stand by themselves. They are joined to the main clause by pronouns, adverbs, or conjunctions.

Subordinate clauses are modifiers. They may be descriptive, like adjectives, and modify nouns:

Cornēlia est puella Rōmāna **quae** <u>in Italiā habitat</u>. (1:1–2)
*Cornelia is a Roman girl **who** <u>lives in Italy</u>.*

Etiam in pictūrā est vīlla rūstica **ubi** <u>Cornēlia aestāte habitat</u>. (1:2)
*Also in the picture there is a country house and farm **where** <u>Cornelia lives in the summer</u>.*

But most subordinate clauses are adverbial, that is, they modify the verb of the main clause or the action of the main clause as a whole and are introduced by subordinating conjunctions that express ideas such as the following:

Cause:

Cornēlia est laeta **quod** <u>iam in vīllā habitat</u>. (1:2–3)
*Cornelia is happy **because** <u>she now lives in the country house</u>.*

Concession:

Quamquam dominus abest, necesse est nōbīs strēnuē labōrāre. (11:7)
Although the master is away, it is necessary for us to work hard.

Condition:

Sī tū puer strēnuus es, ascende arborem!
If you are an energetic boy, climb a tree!

Time:

Dum Cornēlia legit, Flāvia scrībit. (1:4–5)
While Cornelia reads, Flavia writes.

Dum per viam ībant, Aurēlia et Cornēlia spectābant rūsticōs quī in agrīs labōrābant. (13:3–4)
While/As long as they were going along the road, Aurelia and Cornelia were looking at the peasants who were working in the fields.

Dum puerī cibum dēvorant, subitō intrāvit mīles quīdam. (20:13)
While the boys were devouring their food, a certain soldier suddenly entered.
(Here the present tense verb in the **dum** clause is to be translated with the English past tense that describes ongoing action.) (See page 161.)

Puerī, **ubi** clāmōrem audiunt, statim ad puellās currunt. (5:10)
*The boys, **when** they hear the shout, immediately run to the girls.*

Crās, **ubi** surgētis, puerī, clāmōrem et strepitum audiētis.
*Tomorrow, **when** you get up/will get up, boys, you will hear shouting and noise.*

Cum intrāverimus, tandem aurīgās ipsōs spectābimus. (26:17–18)
***When** we enter/will have entered, we will finally watch the charioteers themselves.*
(While the verbs of the subordinate clauses in the two Latin sentences just above are in the future, **surgētis**, and future perfect, **intrāverimus**, we translate them into English as presents; see page 218. The use of the tenses is more exact in Latin.)

Words you have met that may introduce subordinate clauses are:

cum, *when* (22:12)
dum, *as long as* (15:1)
dum, *while* (20:13)
nisi, *if not, unless* (18:16)
postquam, *after* (20b:6)
quamquam, *although* (11:7)
quī, masc., **quae,** fem., **quod,** neut., *who, which, that* (1:1)

quod, *because* (1:3)
sī, *if* (5:1)
simulac, *as soon as* (24:1)
ubi, *when* (5:10)
ubi, *where* (1:2)
ut, *as* (16:17)

PRONUNCIATION OF LATIN

Consonants

The Latin alphabet does not have the letters *j* or *w*; the letter *i* before a vowel is a consonant and is pronounced as *y*, and *v* is pronounced as *w*. The letters *k*, *y*, and *z* occur in few Latin words, the latter two letters only in words taken over by the Romans from their neighbors the Greeks.

In pronouncing Latin you will find the following rules of use.

Most consonants are pronounced as in English, but the following should be noted:
b before **s** or **t** is pronounced as English *p*: **urbs, observat.**
c is always hard and pronounced as English *k*: **cadit.**
g is hard, as in English "get": **gemit.**
gn in the middle of a word may be pronounced as the *ngn* in English "hangnail": **magnus.**
i before a vowel is a consonant and is pronounced as English *y*: **iam.**
r should be rolled: **rāmus.**
s is pronounced as in English "sing," never as in "roses": **servus.**
v is pronounced as English *w*: **vīlla.**

Vowels

The following approximations are offered for the pronunciation of short and long vowels. In addition, long vowels should be held approximately twice as long as short vowels.

Short	Long
a = English "a̲ha" (**ad**)	**ā** = English "father" (**clāmat**)
e = English "pet" (**ex**)	**ē** = English "date" (**dēscendit**)
i = English "sip" (**Italia**)	**ī** = English "sleep" (**īrātus**)
o = English "for" (**arborem**)	**ō** = English "holy" (**in hortō**)
u = English "foot" (**ubi**)	**ū** = English "boot" (**fūrtim**)

The diphthong **ae** is pronounced as the *y* in English "sky" (**amīcae**). The diphthong **au** is pronounced as the *ow* in English "how" (**audit**). The diphthong **ei** is pronounced as the "ay" in English "say" (**deinde**).

Syllables

In dividing Latin words into syllables, note the following rules:

1. A single consonant between two vowels usually goes with the second vowel:

    nō-mi-ne   Rō-mā-na   vī-cī-na

2. Two consonants between vowels are usually divided between the syllables:

    pu-el-la   pic-tū-ra   rūs-ti-ca

Accents

Latin words are accented according to simple rules:

1. If the next to the last syllable (the *penult*) has a long vowel or a diphthong, it will receive the accent:

    discédō

2. If the penult has a short vowel followed by two consonants, it will usually receive the accent:

    exténdō

3. Otherwise, the accent falls on the third syllable from the end (the *antepenult*):

    Británnicus

4. Almost all words of two syllables are accented on the first syllable:

    For example: **légit**   Exception: **adhúc**

Careful observation of the long marks (macrons) over vowels will thus help with both pronunciation and accenting of Latin words.

Latin to English Vocabulary

Latin words in boldface are for mastery; those not in boldface are for recognition (see Introduction, pages xiv–xv). Numbers in parentheses at the end of entries refer to the chapters in which the words appear in vocabulary entries or in Building the Meaning or Forms sections. Roman numerals refer to Review chapters.

A

ā or **ab**, prep. + abl., *from* (13)

ábeō, abíre, ábiī or **abívī, abitúrus**, irreg., *to go away* (3, 9)

   Ábī!/Abíte! *Go away!* (3)

abhínc, adv., *ago, previously* (25)

ábsum, abésse, áfuī, āfutúrus, irreg., *to be away, be absent, be distant* (11, 25)

áccidit, accídere, áccidit, *(it) happens* (14, 26)

accúsō, -áre, -ávī, -átus, *to accuse* (21)

ad, prep. + acc., *to, toward, at, near* (2, 9)

adhúc, adv., *still* (5, 13)

ádiuvō, adiuváre, adiúvī, adiútus, *to help* (6, 21)

admóveō, admovére, admóvī, admótus, *to move toward* (22)

ádsum, adésse, ádfuī, adfutúrus, irreg., *to be present* (26)

advéniō, adveníre, advénī, adventúrus, *to reach, arrive (at)* (5, 23)

advesperáscit, advesperáscere, advesperávit, *it gets dark* (17)

aedifícium, -ī, n., *building* (17)

aedíficō, -áre, -ávī, -átus, *to build* (24)

aestás, aestátis, f., *summer* (1)

  aestáte, *in the summer* (1, 12)

aéstus, -ūs, m., *heat* (24, 25)

áger, ágrī, m., *field* (2)

agnóscō, agnóscere, agnóvī, ágnitus, *to recognize* (18)

ágō, ágere, égī, áctus, *to do, drive* (8, 14, 23)

  Áge!/Ágite! *Come on!* (8)

  Grátiās tíbi ágō! *I thank you! Thank you!* (26)

  Quid ágis? *How are you?* (18)

albátus, -a, -um, *white* (27)

áliquid, *something* (25)

áliter, adv., *otherwise* (26)

álius, ália, áliud, *another, other* (10)

  áliī…áliī…, *some…others…* (9)

  álius…álius, *one…another*

álter, áltera, álterum, *second, one (of two), the other (of two), another* (1)

  álter…álter, *the one…the other* (16)

ámbulō, -áre, -ávī, -ātúrus, *to walk* (2)

amíca, -ae, f., *friend* (2)

amícus, -ī, m., *friend* (3)

ámō, -áre, -ávī, -átus, *to like, love* (4)

amphitheátrum, -ī, n., *amphitheater* (25)

ancílla, -ae, f., *slave-woman* (6)

ánimus, -ī, m., *mind* (16)

  ánimum recuperáre, *to regain one's senses, wake up* (21)

  in ánimō habére, *to intend* (16)

ánteā, adv., *previously, before* (20)

antíquus, -a, -um, *ancient* (26)

apériō, aperíre, apéruī, apértus, *to open* (16, 26)

appáreō, -ére, -uī, -itúrus, *to appear* (15, 18)

appéllō, -áre, -ávī, -átus, *to call, name* (21)

appropínquō, -áre, -ávī, -ātúrus + dat. or **ad** + acc., *to approach, come near (to)* (4, 22)

ápud, prep. + acc., *at the house of, with, in front of, before* (16, 26)

áqua, -ae, f., *water* (6)

aquaedúctus, -ūs, m., *aqueduct* (23, 25)

árbor, árboris, f., *tree* (1)

árcus, -ūs, m., *arch* (24, 25)

área, -ae, f., *open space, threshing floor* (11)

arrípiō, arrípere, arrípuī, arréptus, *to grab hold of, snatch, seize* (5, 19, 26)

ars, ártis, gen. pl., **ártium,** f., *skill* (14)

ascéndō, ascéndere, ascéndī, ascénsus, *to climb, climb into (a carriage)* (4, 22)

Ásia, -ae, f., *Asia (Roman province in western Asia Minor)* (21)

at, conj., *but* (23)

átque, conj., *and, and also* (22)

átrium, -ī, n., *atrium, main room* (26)

atténtē, adv., *attentively, closely* (20)

attónitus, -a, -um, *astonished, astounded* (24)

aúdiō, -íre, -ívī, -ítus, *to hear, listen to* (4, 20)

aúreus, -a, -um, *golden* (25)

auríga, -ae, m., *charioteer* (13)

aúrum, -ī, n., *gold* (21)

aut... aut..., conj., *either...or...* (26)

auxílium, -ī, n., *help* (5, 15)

Fer/Férte auxílium! *Bring help! Help!* (5)

B

báculum, -ī, n., *stick, staff* (10, 15)

Báiae, -árum, f. pl., *Baiae*

béne, adv., *well* (22)

bónus, -a, -um, *good* (12)

bóna, -órum, n. pl., *goods, possessions* (26)

bōs, bóvis, m./f., *ox, cow* (15)

brévis, -is, -e, *short* (2)

brévī témpore, *in a short time, soon* (2, 12)

Británnia, -ae, f., *Britain* (8)

Británnicus, -a, -um, *British* (3)

C

cádō, cádere, cécidī, cāsúrus, *to fall* (3, 22)

caélum, -ī, n., *sky* (17)

Caésar, Caésaris, m., *Caesar, emperor* (27)

cálidus, -a, -um, *warm* (5)

Calígula, -ae, m., *Caligula (emperor, A.D. 37–41)* (27)

cánis, cánis, m./f., *dog* (12)

cántō, -áre, -ávī, -átus, *to sing* (21)

cápiō, cápere, cépī, cáptus, *to take, catch, capture* (21)

captívus, -ī, m., *prisoner* (26)

cáput, cápitis, n., *head* (25)

cāríssimus, -a, -um, *dearest* (16)

caúda, -ae, f., *tail* (18)

caúpō, caupónis, m., *innkeeper* (17)

caupóna, -ae, f., *inn* (17, 20)

caúsa, -ae, f., *reason* (25)

cáveō, cavére, cávī, caútus, *to be careful, watch out (for), beware (of)* (4, 13, 23)

Cávē!/Cavéte! *Be careful! Watch out (for)! Beware (of)!* (4, 13, 23)

celériter, adv., *quickly* (8, 13)

celérrimē, adv., *very fast, very quickly* (14)

célō, -áre, -ávī, -átus, *to hide* (11)

céna, -ae, f., *dinner* (19)

cénō, -áre, -ávī, -átus, *to dine, eat dinner* (19)

céntum, *a hundred* (15)

cértē, adv., *certainly* (19)

céssō, -áre, -ávī, -ātúrus, *to be idle, do nothing, delay* (14)

cíbus, -ī, m., *food* (6)

circénsis, -is, -e, *in/of the circus* (27)

lúdī circénsēs, *games in the circus, chariot races* (27)

circúmeō, circumíre, circúmiī or **circumívī, circúmitus,** irreg., *to go around* (24)

Círcus Máximus, -ī, m., *Circus Maximus (a stadium in Rome)* (23)

císium, -ī, n., *light two-wheeled carriage* (14, 15)

císta, -ae, f., *trunk, chest* (10)

cívis, cívis, gen. pl., **cívium,** m./f., *citizen* (13)

clámō, -áre, -ávī, -ātúrus, *to shout* (3)

clámor, clāmóris, m., *shout, shouting* (5)

claúdō, claúdere, claúsī, claúsus, *to shut* (26)

claúsus, -a, -um, *shut, closed* (24)

clíēns, cliéntis, gen. pl., **cliéntium,** m., *client, dependent* (25)

cógitō, -áre, -ávī, -átus, *to think* (21)

collóquium, -ī, n., *conversation* (26)

cólō, cólere, cóluī, cúltus, *to cultivate* (23)

commótus, -a, -um, *moved* (14)

compléxus, -ūs, m., *embrace* (9, 25)

compléxū, *in an embrace* (9)

cóncidō, concídere, cóncidī, *to fall down* (14)

condúcō, condúcere, condúxī, condúctus, *to hire* (23)

cōnfíciō, cōnfícere, cōnfécī, cōnféctus, *to finish* (25)

cōnfídō, cōnfídere + dat., *to give trust (to), trust* (26)

conícíō, conícere, coniécī, coniéctus, *to throw* (21)

cóniūnx, cóniugis, m./f., *husband, wife* (26)

cōnsídō, cōnsídere, cōnsédī, *to sit down* (23)

cōnspíciō, cōnspícere, cōnspéxī, cōnspéctus, *to catch sight of* (4, 21)

cōnstítuō, cōnstitúere, cōnstítuī, cōnstitútus, *to decide* (23)

cónsulō, cōnsúlere, cōnsúluī, cōnsúltus, *to consult* (7)

cónvocō, -áre, -ávī, -átus, *to call together* (12)

cóquō, cóquere, cóxī, cóctus, *to cook* (6)

Cornēliánus, -a, -um, *belonging to Cornelius, Cornelian* (10)

Cornéliī, -órum, m. pl., *the Cornelii* (10)

córpus, córporis, n., *body* (21)

crās, adv., *tomorrow* (10, 13)

crótalum, -ī, n., *castanet* (21)

cubículum, -ī, n., *room, bedroom* (8, 15)

cúbitum íre, *to go to bed* (19)

cui, *to whom, to him, to her* (19)

Cúius…? *Whose…?* (22)

culína, -ae, f., *kitchen* (21)

cúlpa, -ae, f., *fault, blame* (14)

cum, conj., *when* (22)

cum, prep. + abl., *with* (12)

cúnctī, -ae, -a, *all* (14)

Cūr…? adv., *Why…?* (1)

Cúria, -ae, f., *Senate House* (23)

cúrō, -áre, -ávī, -átus, *to look after, take care of* (6)

currículum, -ī, n., *racetrack* (27)

cúrrō, cúrrere, cucúrrī, cursúrus, *to run* (2, 23)

custódiō, -íre, -ívī, -ítus, *to guard* (17)

cústōs, custódis, m., *guard* (26)

D

dē, prep. + abl., *down from, concerning, about* (16)

débeō, -ére, -uī, -itúrus + infin., *ought* (26)

décem, *ten* (15)

dēféndō, dēféndere, dēféndī, dēfénsus, *to defend* (1)

dēféssus, -a, -um, *tired* (2)

deínde, adv., *then, next* (8, 13)

dēmónstrō, -áre, -ávī, -átus, *to show* (24)

dēscéndō, dēscéndere, dēscéndī, dēscēnsúrus, *to come/go down, climb down* (4, 23)

dēsíderō, -áre, -ávī, -átus, *to long for, miss* (26)

dēvértō, dēvértere, dēvértī, dēvérsus, *to turn aside* (14, 27)

dévorō, -áre, -ávī, -átus, *to devour* (20)

dícō, dícere, díxī, díctus, *to say, tell* (20, 21)

díēs, diéī, m., *day* (5, 13, 25)

éō díē, *on that day* (25)

dīligénter, adv., *carefully* (19)

discédō, discédere, discéssī, discessúrus, *to go away, depart* (9, 22)

díū, adv., *for a long time* (15)

dō, dáre, dédī, dátus, *to give* (21)

sē quiétī dáre, *to rest* (23)

dóceō, docére, dócuī, dóctus, *to teach* (6, 21)

dóleō, -ére, -uī, -itúrus, *to be sad* (18)

dómina, -ae, f., *mistress, lady of the house* (17)

dóminus, -ī, m., *master, owner* (11)

dómus, -ūs, f., *house, home* (23, 25)

dómī, *at home* (26)

dómum, *homeward, home* (23)

dórmiō, -íre, -ívī, -itúrus, *to sleep* (4)

dúcō, dúcere, dúxī, dúctus, *to lead, take, bring* (7, 19, 20)

dum, conj., *while, as long as* (1)

dúo, dúae, dúo, *two* (15)

E

ē or **ex,** prep. + abl., *from, out of* (2, 5, 9)

éam, *her, it* (9, 16)

eárum, *their* (27)

Écce! interj., *Look! Look at!* (1)

effúgiō, effúgere, effúgī, *to flee, run away, escape* (11, 21)

égo, *I* (5, 27)

Éheu! interj., *Alas! Oh no!* (7)

Ého! interj., *Hey!* (25)

éī, *to him/her/it* (21)

éī, éae, éa, *they* (22, 27)

éīs, *to them* (22)

éius, *his, her(s), its* (2, 27)

émō, émere, émī, émptus, *to buy* (21)

énim, conj., *for* (20)

éō, íre, íī or ívī, itúrus, irreg., *to go* (7, 17, 19, 20, 21)

   cúbitum íre, *to go to bed* (19)

éō, adv., *there, to that place* (23)

éō díē, *on that day* (25)

éō ípsō témpore, *at that very moment* (10)

eórum, *their* (25, 27)

éōs, *them* (5)

epístula, -ae, f., *letter* (7)

équus, -ī, m., *horse* (10)

érat, *(he/she/it) was* (13)

érrō, -áre, -ávī, -atúrus, *to wander, be mistaken* (5, 18)

ērúptiō, ēruptiónis, f., *eruption* (26)

ésse (see **sum**)

est, *(he/she/it) is* (1)

Éstō! *All right!* (20)

ēsúriō, -íre, _____, -ītúrus, *to be hungry* (19)

et, conj., *and* (1)

étiam, adv., *also, even* (1, 6, 13)

Eúgepae! interj., *Hurray!* (7)

éum, *him, it* (5)

ex or ē, prep. + abl., *from, out of* (2, 5, 9)

excípiō, excípere, excépī, excéptus, *to welcome, receive, catch* (5, 16, 22)

excítō, -áre, -ávī, -átus, *to rouse, wake (someone) up* (8)

   excitátus, -a, -um, *wakened, aroused* (25)

exclámō, -áre, -ávī, -átus, *to exclaim, shout out* (10)

éxeō, exíre, éxiī or exívī, exitúrus, irreg., *to go out* (5, 23)

éxplicō, -áre, -ávī, -átus, *to explain* (19)

   rem explicáre, *to explain the situation* (19)

exspéctō, -áre, -ávī, -átus, *to look out for, wait for* (15)

éxstāns, exstántis, *standing out, towering* (23)

exténdō, exténdere, exténdī, exténtus, *to hold out* (18)

éxtrā, prep. + acc., *outside* (23)

éxtrahō, extráhere, extráxī, extráctus, *to drag out, take out* (14, 21)

F

fábula, -ae, f., *story* (20)

fáciō, fácere, fécī, fáctus, *to make, do* (1, 23)

   íter fácere, *to travel* (13)

   Quid fácit…? *What does…do? What is…doing?* (1)

   Quid fécit…? *What did…do?* (19)

fáctiō, factiónis, f., *company (of charioteers)* (27)

fátuus, -a, -um, *stupid* (13)

fáveō, favére, fávī, fautúrus + dat., *to give favor (to), favor, support* (27)

félēs, félis, gen. pl., félium, f., *cat* (21)

fémina, -ae, f., *woman* (3)

fériae, -árum, f. pl., *holiday, festival day* (27)

fēriátus, -a, -um, *celebrating a holiday* (27)

fériō, -íre, *to hit, strike* (16)

férō, férre, túlī, látus, irreg., *to bring, carry, bear* (5, 12, 17, 21)

   Fer/Férte auxílium! *Bring help! Help!* (5)

feróciter, adv., *fiercely* (13)

festínō, -áre, -ávī, -atúrus, *to hurry* (9)

fília, -ae, f., *daughter* (11)

fílius, -ī, m., *son* (11)

fíniō, -íre, -ívī, -ítus, *to finish* (21)

fortásse, adv., *perhaps* (15)

fórtis, -is, -e, *brave, strong* (18)

Fórum, -ī, n., *the Forum (city center of Rome)* (25)

fóssa, -ae, f., *ditch* (12)

frágor, fragóris, m., *crash, noise, din* (4)

fráter, frátris, m., *brother* (11)

frígidus, -a, -um, *cool, cold* (5)

frōns, fróntis, gen. pl., fróntium, f., *forehead* (12)

frústrā, adv., *in vain* (14)

fúgiō, fúgere, fúgī, fugitúrus, *to flee* (18, 25)

fúī (see **sum**)

fúrtim, adv., *stealthily* (4, 13)

G

Gádēs, Gádium, f. pl., *Gades (Cadiz, a town in Spain)* (21)

gaúdeō, gaudére, *to be glad, rejoice* (14)

gaúdium, -ī, n., *joy* (23)

gémō, gémere, gémuī, gémitus, *to groan* (3)

gérō, gérere, géssī, géstus, *to wear* (10)

gládius, -ī, m., *sword* (26)

   gládium stríngere, *to draw a sword* (26)

Graécia, -ae, f., *Greece* (21)

Graécus, -a, -um, *Greek* (17)

   Graécī, -órum, m. pl., *the Greeks* (I)

grátia, -ae, f., *gratitude, thanks* (26)

   Grátiās tíbi ágō! *I thank you! Thank you!* (26)

H

habénae, -árum, f. pl., *reins* (22)

hábeō, -ére, -uī, -itus, *to have, hold* (10, 20, 26)

   in ánimō habére, *to intend* (16)

   ōrātiónem habére, *to deliver a speech* (26)

hábitō, -áre, -ávī, -átus, *to live, dwell* (1)

hāc, *this* (25)

haéreō, haerére, haésī, haesúrus, *to stick* (14)

héri, adv., *yesterday* (20)

hī, *these* (18)

hīc, adv., *here* (9, 13)

hic, haec, hoc, *this, the latter* (18, 19, 20, 25, 26)

hódiē, adv., *today* (2, 13)

hómō, hóminis, m., *man* (18)

   hóminēs, hóminum, m. pl., *people* (15)

hóra, -ae, f., *hour* (9)

hórtus, -ī, m., *garden* (3)

hóspes, hóspitis, m./f., *host, guest, friend* (16)

hūc illúc, adv., *here and there, this way and that* (23)

húius (genitive of **hic**) (25)

húmī, *on the ground* (27)

I

iáceō, -ére, -uī, -itúrus, *to lie, be lying down* (26)

iáciō, iácere, iécī, iáctus, *to throw* (10, 20)

iam, adv., *now, already* (1, 8, 13)

   nōn iam, adv., *no longer* (2, 13)

iánitor, iānitóris, m., *doorkeeper* (9)

iánua, -ae, f., *door* (9)

íbi, adv., *there* (5, 13)

id (see **is**)

   id quod, *that which, what* (11)

ídem, éadem, ídem, *the same* (3)

idéntidem, adv., *again and again, repeatedly* (13)

ígitur, conj., *therefore* (4)

ignávus, -a, -um, *cowardly, lazy* (5)

ílle, ílla, íllud, *that, he, she, it, the former* (11, 15, 16, 20, 22, 25, 26)

illúc, adv., *there, to that place* (23)

   hūc illúc, adv., *here and there, this way and that* (23)

ímber, ímbris, gen. pl., ímbrium m., *rain* (23)

ímmemor, immémoris + gen., *forgetful* (22)

immóbilis, -is, -e, *motionless* (12)

impédiō, -íre, -ívī, -ítus, *to hinder, prevent* (11)

in, prep. + abl., *in, on* (1, 9)

   in ánimō habére, *to intend* (16)

   in itínere, *on a journey* (10)

in, prep. + acc., *into, against* (3, 9)

íncitō, -áre, -ávī, -átus, *to spur on, urge on, drive* (10)

incólumis, -is, -e, *unhurt, safe and sound* (14)

índuō, indúere, índuī, indútus, *to put on* (8, 23)

īnfírmus, -a, -um, *weak, shaky* (4)

íngēns, ingéntis, *huge* (22)

innocéntia, -ae, f., *innocence* (21)

ínquit, *(he/she) says, said* (7)

īnspíciō, īnspícere, īnspéxī, īnspéctus, *to examine* (21)

intérdiū, adv., *during the day, by day* (23)

intéreā, adv., *meanwhile* (10, 13)

interpéllō, -áre, -ávī, -átus, *to interrupt* (14)

íntrā, prep. + acc., *inside* (22)

íntrō, -áre, -ávī, -átus, *to enter, go into* (8, 19)

inúrō, inúrere, inússī, inústus, *to brand* (12)

invéniō, inveníre, invénī, invéntus, *to come upon, find* (12, 21)

invītus, -a, -um, *unwilling* (21)

iócus, -ī, m., *joke, prank* (16)
   per iócum, *as a prank* (16)

ípse, ípsa, ípsum, *himself, herself, itself, themselves, very* (6, 10)

íra, -ae, f., *anger* (11)

īrátus, -a, -um, *angry* (3)

íre (see éō) (7, 17)

is, ea, id, *he, she, it; this, that* (27)

íta, adv., *thus, so, in this way* (3, 13, 21)
   Íta vérō! adv., *Yes! Indeed!* (3, 13)

Itália, -ae, f., *Italy* (1)

ítaque, adv., *and so, therefore* (16)

íter, itíneris, n., *journey* (10, 13, 15)
   íter fácere, *to travel* (13)

íterum, adv., *again, a second time* (8, 13)

iúbeō, iubére, iússī, iússus, *to order, bid* (10, 19, 21)

L

lábor, labóris, m., *work, toil* (24)

labórō, -áre, -ávī, -átus, *to work* (3)
   labōrántēs, *working* (7)

lácrimō, -áre, -ávī, -átus, *to weep, cry* (9)
   lácrimāns, *weeping* (9)

laétus, -a, -um, *happy, glad* (1)

lána, -ae, f., *wool* (6)
   lánam tráhere, *to spin wool* (6)

lápis, lápidis, m., *stone* (25)

látrō, -áre, -ávī, -ātúrus, *to bark* (12)
   lātrántēs, *barking* (18)

laúdō, -áre, -ávī, -átus, *to praise* (18)

lávō, laváre, lávī, laútus, *to wash* (20)

lectíca, -ae, f., *litter* (23)

lectīcárius, -ī, m., *litter-bearer* (23)

léctus, -ī, m., *bed, couch* (19)

lēgátus, -ī, m., *envoy* (18)

légō, légere, légī, léctus, *to read* (1, 24)

léntē, adv., *slowly* (2, 13)

líber, líbrī, m., *book* (24)

líberī, -órum, m. pl., *children* (10, 11)

lībértās, lībertátis, f., *freedom* (21)

lícet, licére, lícuit + dat., *it is allowed* (20, 24)
   lícet nóbīs, *we are allowed, we may* (20)

líttera, -ae, f., *letter (of the alphabet)* (12)

lóngus, -a, -um, *long* (15)

lúcet, lūcére, lúxit, *it is light, it is day* (6)

lúdī, -órum, m. pl., *games* (24)
   lúdī circénsēs, *games in the circus, chariot races* (27)

lúdō, lúdere, lúsī, lūsúrus, *to play* (16)
   pílā lúdere, *to play ball* (16)

lúdus, -ī, m., *school* (26)

lúpa, -ae, f., *she-wolf* (II)

lúpus, -ī, m., *wolf* (5)

lútum, -ī, n., *mud* (26)

lūx, lúcis, f., *light* (21)
   prīmā lúce, *at dawn* (21)

M

magníficus, -a, -um, *magnificent* (24)

mágnus, -a, -um, *big, great, large, loud (voice, laugh)* (4)
   mágnā vóce, *in a loud voice* (4)
   mágnō rísū, *with a loud laugh* (13)

málus, -a, -um, *bad* (21)
   níhil málī, *nothing of a bad thing, there is nothing wrong* (21)

mandátum, -ī, n., *order, instruction* (22)

máne, adv., *early in the day, in the morning* (21)

máneō, manére, mánsī, mánsus, *to remain, stay, wait (for)* (9, 20, 23)

mánus, -ūs, f., *hand* (18, 25)

máppa, -ae, f., *napkin, white cloth* (27)

máter, mátris, f., *mother* (6, 11)

máximus, -a, -um, *greatest, very great, very large* (23)

mē, *me* (4)
   mécum, *with me* (9)

médius, -a, -um, *mid-, middle of* (20)
   média nox, médiae nóctis, f., *midnight* (20)

Mégara, -ae, f., *Megara (a city in Greece)* (21)

Mehércule! interj., *By Hercules! Goodness me!* (18)

mélior, mélius, gen., melióris, *better* (19)

mercátor, mercātóris, m., *merchant* (22)

méta, -ae, f., *mark, goal, turning post* (27)

métus, -ūs, m., *fear* (26)

méus, -a, -um, *my, mine* (7)

míhi, *for me, to me* (8)

míles, mílitis, m., *soldier* (20)

mílle, *a thousand* (15)

Mínimē! *No! Not at all!* (3, 13)

mírus, -a, -um, *wonderful, marvelous, strange* (23)

míser, mísera, míserum, *unhappy, miserable, wretched* (9)

míttō, míttere, mísī, míssus, *to send* (9, 20)

módo, adv., *only* (18)

mólēs, mólis, gen. pl., **mólium,** f., *mass, huge bulk* (24)

moléstus, -a, -um, *troublesome, annoying* (4)

moléstus, -ī, m., *pest* (3)

mōns, móntis, gen. pl., **móntium,** m., *mountain, hill* (24)

Mōns Vesúvius, Montis Vesúviī, m., *Mount Vesuvius (a volcano in southern Italy)* (26)

mónstrō, -áre, -ávī, -átus, *to show* (22)

mors, mórtis, gen. pl., **mórtium,** f., *death* (21)

mórtuus, -a, -um, *dead* (16)

móveō, movére, móvī, mótus, *to move* (14, 24)

mox, adv., *soon, presently* (6, 13)

múlier, mulíeris, f., *woman* (27)

múltī, -ae, -a, *many* (3)

multitúdō, multitúdinis, f., *crowd* (23)

múrmur, múrmuris, n., *murmur, rumble* (15)

múrus, -ī, m., *wall* (23)

mūs, múris, m., *mouse* (21)

mússō, -áre, -ávī, -atúrus, *to mutter* (11)

N

nam, conj., *for* (8)

nārrátor, nārrātóris, m., *narrator* (8)

nárrō, -áre, -ávī, -átus, *to tell (a story)* (20)

nārrátus, -a, -um, *told* (20)

-ne (indicates a yes or no question) (3)

Neápolis, Neápolis, f., *Naples* (15)

necésse, adv. or indeclinable adj., _ *necessary* (6)

nécō, -áre, -ávī, -átus, *to kill* (20)

némō, néminis, m./f., *no one* (9)

néque, conj., *and...not* (6)

néque...néque, conj., *neither...nor* (5)

nésciō, -íre, -ívī, -ítus, *to be ignorant, not to know* (9)

níhil, *nothing* (4)

níhil málī, *nothing of a bad thing, there is nothing wrong* (21)

nísi, conj., *unless, if...not, except* (18, 26)

nóbīs, *for us, to us* (9)

nōbíscum, *with us* (16)

nóceō, -ére, -uī, -itúrus + dat., *to do harm (to), harm* (26)

nócte, *at night* (12)

noctúrnus, -a, -um, *happening during the night* (22)

nólō, nólle, nóluī, irreg., *not to wish, not to want, to be unwilling* (5, 17, 21)

Nólī/Nólíte + infin., *Don't...!* (9)

nómen, nóminis, n., *name* (1, 15)

nómine, *by name, named* (1)

nōn, adv., *not* (2, 13)

nōn iam, adv., *no longer* (2, 13)

nóndum, adv., *not yet* (6, 13)

Nónne...? *Surely...?* (introduces a question that expects the answer "yes") (19)

nōnnúmquam, adv., *sometimes* (26)

nónus, -a, -um, *ninth* (16)

nōs, *we, us* (8, 27)

nóster, nóstra, nóstrum, *our* (14, 27)

nóvem, *nine* (15)

nóvus, -a, -um, *new* (16)

nox, nóctis, gen. pl., **nóctium,** f., *night* (11)

íllā nócte, *that night* (11)

média nox, *midnight* (20)

nócte, *at night* (12)

núbēs, núbis, gen. pl., **núbium,** f., *cloud* (15)

núllus, -a, -um, *no, not any* (9)

númerus, -ī, m., *number* (11)

númquam, adv., *never* (20)

nunc, adv., *now* (6, 13)

núntius, -ī, m., *messenger* (7)

O

ō, interj., used with vocative and in exclamations (9)

Ō mē míseram! *Poor me! Oh dear me!* (9)

obdórmiō, -íre, -ívī, -ītúrus, *to go to sleep* (21)

obésus, -a, -um, *fat* (18)

obsérvō, -áre, -ávī, -átus, *to watch* (6)

occupátus, -a, -um, *busy* (7)

occúrrō, occúrrere, occúrrī, occursúrus + dat., *to meet, encounter* (24)

óctō, *eight* (15)

óculus, -ī, m., *eye* (26)

olfáciō, olfácere, olfécī, olfáctus, *to catch the scent of, smell, sniff* (12)

ólim, adv., *once (upon a time)* (18)

olīvétum, -ī, n., *olive grove* (14, 15)

ómnis, -is, -e, *all, the whole, every, each* (6, 18)

  ómnēs, *all, everyone* (6)

  ómnia quae, *everything that* (6)

ónus, óneris, n., *load, burden* (15)

oppréssus, -a, -um, *crushed* (25)

óptimus, -a, -um, *best, very good* (20)

  vir óptime, *sir* (20)

ōrátiō, ōrātiónis, f., *oration, speech* (26)

  ōrātiónem habére, *to deliver a speech* (26)

ōrátor, ōrātóris, m., *orator, speaker* (22)

os, óssis, n., *bone* (18)

P

Palātīnus, -a, -um, *Palatine, belonging to the Palatine Hill* (24)

pálla, -ae, f., *palla* (10)

parátus, -a, -um, *ready, prepared* (10)

párēns, paréntis, m./f., *parent* (11)

párō, -áre, -ávī, -átus, *to prepare, get ready* (5, 20)

  sē paráre, *to prepare oneself, get ready* (22)

pars, pártis, gen. pl., **pártium,** f., *part, direction, region* (13)

párvulus, -a, -um, *small, little* (26)

páter, pátris, m., *father* (6, 11)

patrónus, -ī, m., *patron* (25)

pátruus, -ī, m., *uncle* (22)

paulísper, adv., *for a short time* (20)

pecúnia, -ae, f., *money* (21)

per, prep. + acc., *through, along* (6, 9)

  per iócum, *as a prank* (16)

perīculósus, -a, -um, *dangerous* (17)

perículum, -ī, n., *danger* (14, 15)

pernóctō, -áre, -ávī, -ātúrus, *to spend the night* (17, 18)

pertérritus, -a, -um, *frightened, terrified* (5)

pervéniō, pervenīre, pervénī, perventúrus, *to arrive (at), reach* (25)

pēs, pédis, m., *foot* (13)

pétō, pétere, petívī, petítus, *to look for, seek, head for, aim at, attack* (5, 21)

pictúra, -ae, f., *picture* (1)

píla, -ae, f., *ball* (16)

  pílā lúdere, *to play ball* (16)

pīráta, -ae, m., *pirate* (21)

piscína, -ae, f., *fishpond* (3)

plácidē, adv., *gently, peacefully* (14)

plaústrum, -ī, n., *wagon, cart* (15)

plénus, -a, -um, *full* (11)

plúit, plúere, plúit, *it rains, is raining* (23)

poéta, -ae, m., *poet* (25)

Pompéiī, -órum, m. pl., *Pompeii*

pónō, pónere, pósuī, pósitus, *to put, place* (10, 21)

pōns, póntis, gen. pl., **póntium,** m., *bridge* (23)

pórta, -ae, f., *gate* (11)

pórtō, -áre, -ávī, -átus, *to carry* (6)

póssum, pósse, pótuī, irreg., *to be able; I can* (5, 14, 21)

  póterat, *(he/she/it) was able, could* (13)

  pótest, *(he/she/it) is able, can* (5)

post, prep. + acc., *after* (20)

póstis, póstis, gen. pl., póstium, m., *doorpost* (25)

póstquam, conj., *after* (20)

postrídiē, adv., *on the following day* (26)

praecípitō, -áre, -ávī, -átus, *to hurl* (18)

  sē praecipitáre, *to hurl oneself, rush* (18)

praeclárus, -a, -um, *distinguished, famous* (13)

praecúrrō, praecúrrere, praecúrrī, praecursúrus, *to run ahead* (18)

praédō, praedónis, m., *robber* (26)

praéter, prep. + acc., *except* (21)

praetéreā, adv., *besides, too, moreover* (15)

praetéreō, praeteríre, praetériī or **praeterívī, praetéritus,** irreg., *to go past* (15)

praetéxta, tóga, -ae, f., *toga with purple border* (10)

prásinus, -a, -um, *green* (27)

prīmus, -a, -um, *first* (21)

  prīmā lūce, *at dawn* (21)

  prīmum, adv., *first* (23)

prīnceps, prīncipis, m., *emperor* (7)

prócul, adv., *in the distance, far off, far* (15)

prōmíttō, prōmíttere, prōmísī, prōmíssus, *to promise* (9)

própe, prep. + acc., *near* (5, 9)

própter, prep. + acc., *on account of, because of* (26)

puélla, -ae, f., *girl* (1)

púer, púerī, m., *boy* (3)

púlvis, púlveris, m., *dust* (15)

pū́niō, -íre, -ívī, -ítus, *to punish* (21)

pū́rgō, -áre, -ávī, -átus, *to clean* (6)

Q

quadrắtus, -a, -um, *squared* (25)

quadrígae, -árum, f. pl., *team of four horses, chariot* (27)

quae, *who* (1, 11)

Quắlis…? Quắlis…? Quắle…? *What sort of…?* (4, 18)

Quam…! adv., *How…!* (13)

Quam…? adv., *How…?*

quámquam, conj., *although* (11)

Quándō…? adv., *When…?* (12, 21)

quáttuor, *four* (15)

Quem…? *Whom…?* (5)

quem, *whom, which, that* (24)

quī, quae, quod, *who, which, that* (1, 3, 14)

Quī…? *Who…?* (pl.) (6)

Quibúscum…? *With whom…?* (12)

Quid…? *What…?* (1, 4)

  Quid ágis? *How are you?* (18)

  Quid fácit…? *What does…do? What is…doing?* (1)

  Quid fécit…? *What did…do?* (19)

quídam, quaédam, quóddam, *(a) certain* (10)

quiḗs, quiḗtis, f., *rest* (23)

  sē quiḗtī dáre, *to rest* (23)

quiéscō, quiéscere, quiḗvī, quiētū́rus, *to rest, keep quiet* (13, 23)

quīngéntī, -ae, -a, *five hundred* (15)

quīnquāgíntā, *fifty* (15)

quínque, *five* (15)

quíntus, -a, -um, *fifth* (26)

Quis…? Quid…? *Who…? What…?* (1, 4)

  Quid ágis? *How are you?* (18)

  Quid fácit…? *What does…do? What is…doing?* (1)

  Quid fécit…? *What did…do?* (19)

Quō…? adv., *Where…to?* (4)

Quócum…? *With whom…?* (12)

quod (see **quī, quae, quod**)

quod, conj., *because* (1)

Quō īnstrūméntō…? *With what instrument…? By what means…? How?* (12)

Quốmodo…? adv., *In what manner…? In what way…? How…?* (12)

quóque, adv., *also* (2, 13)

Quōs…? *Whom…?* (7)

Quot…? *How many…?* (15)

R

raéda, -ae, f., *carriage* (10)

raedárius, -ī, m., *coachman, driver* (10)

rámus, -ī, m., *branch* (4)

recúperō, -áre, -ávī, -átus, *to recover* (21)

  ánimum recuperáre, *to regain one's senses, wake up* (21)

rédeō, redíre, rédiī or **redívī, réditūrus,** irreg., *to return, go back* (7, 23)

réditus, -ūs, m., *return* (25)

relínquō, relínquere, relíquī, relíctus, *to leave behind* (16, 21)

remóveō, removḗre, remóvī, remótus, *to remove, move aside* (21)

repéllō, repéllere, réppulī, repúlsus, *to drive off, drive back* (5)

reprehéndō, reprehéndere, reprehéndī, reprehénsus, *to blame, scold, reprove* (6)

rēs, réī, f., *thing, matter, situation* (19, 25)

  rem explicáre, *to explain the situation* (19)

respóndeō, respondḗre, respóndī, respōnsū́rus, *to reply* (5, 21)

révocō, -áre, -ávī, -átus, *to recall, call back* (7)

rídeō, rīdḗre, rísī, rísus, *to laugh (at), smile* (3, 21) rīmṓsus, -a, -um, *full of cracks, leaky* (23)

rī́sus, -ūs, m., *smile, laugh* (13, 25)

   mágnō rī́sū, *with a loud laugh* (13)

rī́vus, -ī, m., *stream* (5)

rógō, -áre, -ā́vī, -ā́tus, *to ask* (12)

Rṓma, -ae, f., *Rome* (7)

   Rṓmam, *to Rome* (7)

Rōmā́nus, -a, -um, *Roman* (1)

   Rōmā́nī, -ṓrum, m. pl., *the Romans* (III)

róta, -ae, f., *wheel* (15)

russā́tus, -a, -um, *red* (27)

rū́stica, vī́lla, -ae, f., *country house and farm* (1)

rū́sticus, -ī, m., *peasant* (13)

S

saépe, adv., *often* (2, 13)

saltā́trīx, saltātrī́cis, f., *dancer* (21)

sáltō, -áre, -ā́vī, -ātū́rus, *to dance* (21)

salū́tō, -áre, -ā́vī, -ā́tus, *to greet, welcome* (7)

Sálvē!/Salvḗte! *Greetings! Hello!* (7)

sálvus, -a, -um, *safe* (5)

sátis, adv., indeclinable substantive, *enough* (23)

   sátis témporis, *enough time* (23)

scelḗstus, -a, -um, *wicked* (10)

scíō, -íre, -ī́vī, -ī́tus, *to know* (16)

scrī́bō, scrī́bere, scrī́psī, scrī́ptus, *to write* (1, 24)

sē, *himself, herself, oneself, itself, themselves* (11, 27)

secúndus, -a, -um, *second* (9)

sed, conj., *but* (2)

sédeō, sedḗre, sḗdī, sessū́rus, *to sit* (1, 21)

sēmisómnus, -a, -um, *half-asleep* (9)

sémper, adv., *always* (4, 13)

senā́tor, senātṓris, m., *senator* (7)

sēnā́tus, -ūs, m., *Senate* (25)

sénex, sénis, m., *old man* (I)

séptem, *seven* (15)

séptimus, -a, -um, *seventh* (13)

sepúlcrum, -ī, n., *tomb* (22)

séquēns, sequéntis, *following* (25)

sḗrō, adv., *late* (21)

sérvō, -áre, -ā́vī, -ā́tus, *to save* (26)

sérvus, -ī, m., *slave* (3)

sex, *six* (15)

sī, conj., *if* (5)

   sī vīs, *if you wish, please* (26)

sígnum, -ī, n., *signal* (27)

siléntium, -ī, n., *silence* (15)

sílva, -ae, f., *woods, forest* (5)

símul, adv., *together, at the same time* (9, 13)

símulac, conj., *as soon as* (24)

símulō, -áre, -ā́vī, -ā́tus, *to pretend* (21)

síne, prep. + abl., *without* (26)

sóleō, solḗre + infin., *to be accustomed (to), be in the habit (of)* (10)

sollícitus, -a, -um, *anxious, worried* (4)

sṓlus, -a, -um, *alone* (3)

sómnium, -ī, n., *dream* (21)

sómnus, -ī, m., *sleep* (21)

sónitus, -ūs, m., *sound* (21, 25)

sórdidus, -a, -um, *dirty* (19)

sóror, sorṓris, f., *sister* (11)

spectā́tor, spectātṓris, m., *spectator* (27)

spéctō, -áre, -ā́vī, -ā́tus, *to watch, look at* (7)

spī́na, -ae, f., *barrier (of a racetrack)* (27)

státim, adv., *immediately* (5, 13)

státua, -ae, f., *statue* (3)

stércus, stércoris, n., *dung, manure* (21)

stértō, stértere, stértuī, *to snore* (25)

stílus, -ī, m., *pen* (25)

stō, stā́re, stétī, statū́rus, *to stand* (10, 22)

stóla, -ae, f., *stola (a woman's outer garment)* (10)

strḗnuus, -a, -um, *active, energetic* (2)

   strḗnuē, adv., *strenuously, hard* (6, 13)

strépitus, -ūs, m., *noise, clattering* (23, 25)

strī́ngō, strī́ngere, strī́nxī, strī́ctus, *to draw* (26)

   gládium strī́ngere, *to draw a sword* (26)

stúltus, -a, -um, *stupid, foolish* (23)

stúpeō, -ḗre, -uī, *to be amazed, gape* (23)

sub, prep. + abl., *under, beneath* (1, 9)

súbitō, adv., *suddenly* (3, 13)

súī, síbi, sē, sē, *himself, herself, oneself, itself, themselves* (27)

sum, ésse, fúī, futū́rus, irreg., *to be* (1, 14, 20, 21)

sū́mō, sū́mere, sū́mpsī, sū́mptus, *to take, take up, pick out* (22)

sunt, *(they) are* (2)

súprā, adv., *above, on top* (21)

súprā, prep. + acc., *above* (23)

súrgō, súrgere, surrḗxī, surrēctū́rus,
   to get up, rise (6, 21)

súus, -a, -um, *his, her, one's, its, their (own)*
   (9, 27)

T

tabellā́rius, -ī, m., *courier* (13)

tabérna, -ae, f., *shop* (25)

tablī́num, -ī, n., *study* (26)

táceō, -ére, -uī, -itus, *to be quiet* (9)
   Tácē!/Tacḗte! *Be quiet!* (9)

tácitē, adv., *silently* (9, 13)

taédet, taedḗre, *it bores* (16)

tā́lis, -is, -e, *such, like this, of this kind* (23)

támen, adv., *however, nevertheless* (6, 13)

tándem, adv., *at last, at length* (2, 13)

tántus, -a, -um, *so great, such a big* (24)
   tántum, adv., *only* (15)

tárdus, -a, -um, *slow* (15)

tē (see **tū**), *you* (4)

temerā́rius, -a, -um, *rash, reckless, bold* (5)

témptō, -áre, -ávī, -átus, *to try* (9)

témpus, témporis, n., *time* (2, 8, 12, 15)
   brévī témpore, *in a short time, soon* (2, 12)
   éō ípsō témpore, *at that very moment* (10)
   sátis témporis, *enough time* (23)

téneō, tenḗre, ténuī, téntus, *to hold* (9, 25)

térra, -ae, f., *earth, ground* (26)

térreō, -ére, -uī, -itus, *to frighten, terrify* (4)

térror, terrṓris, m., *terror, fear* (22)

tértius, -a, -um, *third* (25)

tíbi, *to you, for you* (19)

tímeō, -ére, -uī, *to fear, be afraid (to/of)* (5)

tímidus, -a, -um, *afraid, fearful, timid* (21)

tóga, -ae, f., *toga* (8)
   tóga praetéxta, -ae, f., *toga with purple border*
      (10)

tótus, -a, -um, *all, the whole* (21)

trā́dō, trā́dere, trā́didī, trā́ditus,
   to hand over (7, 22)

tráhō, tráhere, trā́xī, tráctus, *to drag,
   pull* (6, 12, 25)

lā́nam tráhere, *to spin wool* (6)

trémō, trémere, trémuī, *to tremble* (21)

trēs, trēs, tría, *three* (13, 15)
   tríbus diḗbus, *in three days* (12, 13)

Trṓia, -ae, f., *Troy* (I)

Troiā́nus, -a, -um, *Trojan* (I)
   Troiā́nī, -órum, m. pl., *the Trojans* (I)

tū (acc. **tē**), *you* (sing.) (4, 27)

tū́lī (see **férō**)

tum, adv., *at that moment, then* (4, 13)

tumū́ltus, -ūs, m., *uproar, commotion* (25)

túnica, -ae, f., *tunic* (8)

túrba, -ae, f., *crowd, mob* (23)

túus, -a, -um, *your* (sing.) (9, 27)

U

úbi, conj., *where* (1), *when* (5)

Úbi…? adv., *Where…?* (10, 12)

Únde…? adv., *From where…?* (12)

ūndécimus, -a, -um, *eleventh* (17)

úndique, adv., *on all sides, from all sides* (23)

únus, -a, -um, *one* (15)

urbs, úrbis, gen. pl., **úrbium,** f., *city* (7)

ut, conj., *as* (16)

úxor, uxṓris, f., *wife* (11)

V

váldē, adv., *very, very much, exceedingly* (19)

Válē!/Valḗte! *Goodbye!* (9)

veheménter, adv., *very much, violently, hard*
   (19)

vehículum, -ī, n., *vehicle* (13, 15)

vélle (see **vólō**)

vénetus, -a, -um, *blue* (27)

véniō, venī́re, vḗnī, ventū́rus, *to come*
   (7, 20)

vérberō, -áre, -ávī, -átus, *to beat, whip*
   (11)

verbṓsus, -a, -um, *talkative* (26)

vértō, vértere, vértī, vérsus, *to turn* (16)

vésperī, *in the evening* (18)

véster, véstra, véstrum, *your* (pl.)
   (22, 27)

vēstī́gium, -ī, n., *track, footprint, trace*
   (12, 15)

vétō, vetáre, vétuī, vétitus, *to forbid* (26)
véxō, -áre, -ávī, -átus, *to annoy* (4)
vía, -ae, f., *road, street* (10)
   Vía Áppia, -ae, f., *the Appian Way* (11)
viátor, viātóris, m., *traveler* (18)
vīcínus, -a, -um, *neighboring, adjacent* (1)
víctor, victóris, m., *conqueror, victor* (27)
vídeō, vidére, vídī, vísus, *to see* (4, 21)
   vidétur, *he/she/it seems* (21)
vígilō, -áre, -ávī, -ātúrus, *to stay awake* (19)
vílicus, -ī, m., *overseer, farm manager* (11)
vílla, -ae, f., *country house* (1)
   vílla rústica, -ae, f., *country house and farm* (1)
víncō, víncere, vícī, víctus, *to conquer, win* (27)
vínea, -ae, f., *vineyard* (12)

vínum, -ī, n., *wine* (25)
vir, vírī, m., *man, husband* (3, 11)
   vir óptime, *sir* (20)
vírga, -ae, f., *stick, rod, switch* (13)
vīs (from **vólō**), *you want* (16)
vísitō, -áre, -ávī, -átus, *to visit* (23)
vítō, -áre, -ávī, -átus, *to avoid* (13)
vix, adv., *scarcely, with difficulty* (24)
vóbīs, *to you, for you* (pl.) (19)
vócō, -áre, -ávī, -átus, *to call* (16)
vólō, vélle, vóluī, irreg., *to wish, want, be willing* (5, 17, 20, 21)
   sī vīs, *if you wish, please* (26)
vōs, *you* (pl.) (8)
vōx, vócis, f., *voice* (4)
   mágnā vóce, *in a loud voice* (4)
vult (from **vólō**), *(he/she) wishes, wants, is willing* (5, 17)

ENGLISH TO LATIN VOCABULARY

All Latin words in this list are in boldface, regardless of whether they are for mastery or for recognition (see Introduction, pages xiv–xv). Numbers in parentheses at the end of entries refer to the chapters in which the words appear in vocabulary entries or in Building the Meaning or Forms sections. Roman numerals refer to Review sections.

A

able, (he/she/it) was, **póterat** (13)

able, to be, **póssum, pósse, pótuī** (5, 14, 21)

about, **dē,** prep. + abl. (16)

above, **súprā,** adv. (21), **súprā,** prep. + acc. (23)

absent, to be, **ábsum, abésse, áfuī, āfutúrus** (11, 25)

accuse, to, **accúsō, -áre, -ávī, -átus** (21)

accustomed (to), to be, **sóleō, solére** + inf. (10)

active, **strénuus, -a, -um** (2)

adjacent, **vīcínus, -a, -um** (1)

afraid (to/of), to be, **tímeō, -ére, -uī** (5)

after, **post,** prep. + acc. (20), **póstquam,** adv. (20)

again, **íterum,** adv. (8, 13)

again and again, **idéntidem,** adv. (13)

against, **in,** prep. + acc. (3, 9)

ago, **abhínc,** adv. (25)

aim at, to, **pétō, pétere, petívī, petítus** (5, 21)

Alas! **Éheu!** interj. (7)

all, **cúnctī, -ae, -a** (14), **ómnis, -is, -e** (6, 18), **tótus, -a, -um** (21)

All right! **Éstō!** (20)

allowed, it is, **lícet, licére, lícuit** + dat. (20, 24)

allowed, we are, **lícet nóbīs** (20)

alone, **sólus, -a, -um** (3)

along, **per,** prep. + acc. (6, 9)

already, **iam,** adv. (1, 8, 13)

also, **átque,** conj. (22), **étiam,** adv. (1, 6, 13), **quóque,** adv. (2, 13)

although, **quámquam,** conj. (11)

always, **sémper,** adv. (4, 13)

amazed, to be, **stúpeō, -ére, -uī** (23)

amphitheater, **amphitheátrum, -ī,** n. (25)

ancient, **antíquus, -a, -um** (26)

and, **átque,** conj. (22), **et,** conj. (1)

and also, **átque,** conj. (22)

and...not, **néque,** conj. (6)

and so, **ítaque,** adv. (16)

anger, **íra, -ae,** f. (11)

angry, **īrátus, -a, -um** (3)

annoy, to, **véxō, -áre, -ávī, -átus** (4)

annoying, **moléstus, -a, -um** (4)

another, **álius, ália, áliud** (10)

anxious, **sollícitus, -a, -um** (4)

appear, to, **appáreō, -ére, -uī, -itúrus** (15, 18)

Appian Way, the, **Vía Áppia, -ae,** f. (11)

approach, to, **appropínquō, -áre, -ávī, -ātúrus** + dat. or ad + acc. (4, 22)

aqueduct, **aquaedúctus, -ūs,** m. (23, 25)

arch, **árcus, -ūs,** m. (24, 25)

are, they, **sunt** (2)

aroused, **excitátus, -a, -um** (25)

arrive (at), to, **advéniō, adveníre, advénī, adventúrus** (5, 23)

as, **ut,** conj. (16)

as a prank, **per iócum** (16)

as long as, **dum,** conj. (1)

Asia, **Ásia, -ae,** f. (21)

ask, to, **rógō, -áre, -ávī, -átus** (12)

astonished, **attónitus, -a, -um** (24)

astounded, **attónitus, -a, -um** (24)

at, **ad,** prep. + acc. (2, 9)

at last, **tándem,** adv. (2, 13)

at length, **tándem,** adv. (2, 13)

at night, **nócte** (12)

at the house of, **ápud,** prep. + acc. (16)

atrium, **átrium, -ī,** n. (26)

attack, to, **pétō, pétere, petívī, petítus** (5, 21)

attend to, to, **cúrō, -áre, -ávī, -átus** (6)

attentively, **atténtē,** adv. (20)

avoid, to, **vítō, -áre, -ávī, -átus** (13)

awake, to stay, **vígilō, -áre, -ávī, -ātúrus** (19)

away, to be, **ábsum, abésse, áfuī, āfutúrus** (11, 25)

B

bad, **málus, -a, -um** (21)

Baiae, **Báiae, -árum,** f. pl.

ball, **píla, -ae,** f. (16)

ball, to play, **pílā lúdere** (16)

bark, to, **látrō, -áre, -ávī, -ātúrus** (12)

barking, **látrāns** (18)

barrier (of a racetrack), **spína, -ae,** f. (27)

be, to, **sum, ésse, fúī, futúrus** (1, 14, 20, 21)

be away, to, **ábsum, abésse, áfuī, āfutúrus** (11, 25)

Be careful! **Cávē!/Cavéte!** (4, 13, 23)

be careful, to, **cáveō, cavére, cávī, caútus** (4, 13, 23)

Be quiet! **Tácē!/Tacéte!** (9)

bear, to, **férō, férre, túlī, látus** (16)

beat, to, **vérberō, -áre, -ávī, -átus** (11)

because, **quod,** conj. (1, 13)

because of, **própter,** prep. + acc. (26)

bed, **léctus, -ī,** m. (19)

bed, to go to, **cúbitum íre** (19)

bedroom, **cubículum, -ī,** n. (8, 15)

before, **ánteā,** adv. (20), **ápud,** prep. + acc. (26)

beneath, **sub,** prep. + abl. (1, 9)

besides, **praetéreā,** adv. (15)

best, **óptimus, -a, -um** (20)

better, **mélior, mélius,** gen., melióris (19)

Beware (of)! **Cávē!/Cavéte!** (4, 13, 23)

beware (of), to, **cáveō, cavére, cávī, caútus** (4, 13, 23)

bid, to, **iúbeō, iubére, iússī, iússus** (10, 19, 21)

big, **mágnus, -a, -um** (4)

big, such a, **tántus, -a, -um** (24)

blame, **cúlpa, -ae,** f. (14)

blame, to, **reprehéndō, reprehéndere, reprehéndī, reprehénsus** (6)

blue, **vénetus, -a, -um** (27)

body, **córpus, córporis,** n. (21)

bold, **temerárius, -a, -um** (5)

bone, **os, ossis,** n. (18)

book, **líber, líbrī,** m. (24)

bores, it, **taédet, taedére** (16)

boy, **púer, púerī,** m. (3)

branch, **rámus, -ī,** m. (4)

brand, to, **inúrō, inúrere, inússī, inústus** (12)

brave, **fórtis, -is, -e** (18)

bridge, **pōns, póntis,** gen. pl., **póntium,** m. (23)

bring, to, **dúcō, dúcere, dúxī, dúctus** (7, 19, 20)

Bring help! **Fer/Férte auxílium!** (5)

Britain, **Británnia, -ae,** f. (8)

British, **Británnicus, -a, -um** (3)

brother, **fráter, frátris,** m. (11)

build, to, **aedíficō, -áre, -ávī, -átus** (24)

building, **aedifícium, -ī,** n. (17)

bulk, huge, **mólēs, mólis,** gen. pl., **mólium,** f. (24)

burden, **ónus, óneris,** n. (15)

busy, **occupátus, -a, -um** (7)

but, at, conj. (23), **sed,** conj. (2)

buy, to, **émō, émere, émī, émptus** (21)

By Hercules! **Mehércule!** interj. (18)

By what means...? **Quō īnstrūméntō...?** (12)

C

Caesar, **Caésar, Caésaris,** m. (27)

Caligula, **Calígula, -ae,** m. (27)

call, to, **appéllō, -áre, -ávī, -átus** (21), **vócō, -áre, -ávī, -átus** (16)

call back, to, **révocō, -áre, -ávī, -átus** (7)

call together, to, **cónvocō, -áre, -ávī, -átus** (12)

can, I, **póssum, pósse, pótuī** (5, 14, 21)

can, he/she/it, **pótest** (5)

capture, to, **cápiō, cápere, cépī, cáptus** (21)

careful! Be, **Cávē!/Cavéte!** (4, 13, 23)

careful, to be, **cáveō, cavére, cávī, caútus** (4, 13, 23)

carefully, **dīligénter,** adv. (19)

carriage, **raéda, -ae,** f. (10)

carriage, light two-wheeled, **císium, -ī,** n. (14, 15)

carry, to, **férō, férre, túlī, látus** (5, 12, 17, 21), **pórtō, -áre, -ávī, -átus** (6)

cart, **plaústrum, -ī,** n. (15)

castanet, **crótalum, -ī,** n. (21)

cat, **félēs, félis,** gen. pl., **félium,** f. (21)

catch, to, **cápiō, cápere, cépī, captus** (21), **excípiō, excípere, excépī, excéptus** (5, 16, 22)

catch sight of, to, **cōnspíciō, cōnspícere, cōnspéxī, cōnspéctus** (4, 21)

catch the scent of, to, **olfáciō, olfácere, olfécī, olfáctus** (12)

certain, (a), **quídam, quaédam, quóddam** (10)

certainly, **cértē,** adv. (19)

chariot, **quadrígae, -árum,** f. pl. (27)

chariot races, **lúdī circénsēs** (27)

charioteer, **auríga, -ae,** m. (13)

chest, **císta, -ae,** f. (10)

children, **líberī, -órum,** m. pl. (10, 11)

circus, in the, **circénsis, -is, -e** (27)

Circus Maximus, **Círcus Máximus, -ī,** m. (23)

citizen, **cívis, cívis,** gen. pl., **cívium,** m./f. (13)

city, **urbs, úrbis,** gen. pl., **úrbium,** f. (7)

clattering, **strépitus, -ūs,** m. (23, 25)

clean, to, **púrgō, -áre, -ávī, -átus** (6)

client, **clíēns, cliéntis,** gen. pl., **cliéntium,** m. (25)

climb, to, **ascéndō, ascéndere, ascéndī, ascénsus** (4, 21)

climb down, to, **dēscéndō, dēscéndere, dēscéndī, dēscēnsúrus** (4, 23)

climb into (a carriage), to, **ascéndō, ascéndere, ascéndī, ascénsus** (4, 21)

closed, **claúsus, -a, -um** (24)

closely, **atténtē,** adv. (20)

cloud, **núbēs, núbis,** gen. pl., **núbium,** f. (15)

coachman, **raedárius, -ī,** m. (10)

cold, **frígidus, -a, -um** (5)

come, to, **véniō, veníre, vénī, ventúrus** (7, 25)

come down, to, **dēscéndō, dēscéndere, dēscéndī, dēscēnsúrus** (4, 23)

come near (to), to, **appropínquō, -áre, -ávī, -átus** + dat. or **ad** + acc. (4, 22)

Come on! **Áge!/Ágite!** (8)

come upon, to, **invéniō, inveníre, invénī, invéntus** (12, 21)

commotion, **tumúltus, -ūs,** m. (25)

company (of charioteers), **fáctiō, factiónis,** f. (27)

concerning, **dē,** prep. + abl. (16)

conquer, to, **víncō, víncere, vícī, víctus** (27)

conqueror, **víctor, victóris,** m. (27)

consult, to, **cónsulō, cōnsúlere, cōnsúluī, cōnsúltus** (7)

conversation, **collóquium, -ī,** n. (26)

cook, to, **cóquō, cóquere, cóxī, cóctus** (6)

cool, **frígidus, -a, -um** (5)

Cornelian, **Cornēliánus, -a, -um** (10)

Cornelii, the, **Cornéliī, -órum,** m. pl. (10)

Cornelius, belonging to, **Cornēliánus, -a, -um** (10)

couch, **léctus, -ī,** m. (19)

could, (he/she/it), **póterat** (13)

country house, **vílla, -ae,** f. (1)

country house and farm, **vílla rústica, -ae,** f. (1)

courier, **tabellárius, -ī,** m. (13)

cow, **bōs, bóvis,** m./f. (15)

cowardly, **ignávus, -a, -um** (5)

cracks, full of, **rīmósus, -a, -um** (23)

crash, **frágor, fragóris,** m. (4)

crowd, **multitúdō, multitúdinis,** f. (23), **túrba, -ae,** f. (23)

crushed, **oppréssus, -a, -um** (25)

cry, to, **lácrimō, -áre, -ávī, -átus** (9)

cultivate, to, **cólō, cólere, cóluī, cúltus** (23)

D

dance, to, **sáltō, -áre, -ávī, -atúrus** (21)

dancer, **saltátrīx, saltātrícis,** f. (21)

danger, **perículum, -ī,** n. (14, 15)

dangerous, **periculósus, -a, -um** (17)

dark, it gets, **advesperáscit, advesperáscere, advesperávit** (17) daughter, **fília, -ae,** f. (11)

dawn, at, **prímā lúce** (21)

day, **díēs, diéī,** m. (5, 13, 25)

day, by/during the, **intérdiū,** adv. (23)

day, it is, **lúcet, lūcére, lúxit** (6)

day, on that, **éō díē** (25)

day, on the following, **postrídiē,** adv. (26)

dead, **mórtuus, -a, -um** (16)

dearest, **cāríssimus, -a, -um** (16)

death, **mors, mórtis,** gen. pl., **mórtium,** f. (21)

decide, to, **cōnstítuō, cōnstitúere, cōnstítuī, cōnstitútus** (23)

defend, to, **dēféndō, dēféndere, dēféndī, dēfénsus** (I)

delay, to, **céssō, -áre, -ávī, -ātúrus** (14)

deliver a speech, to, **ōrātiónem habére** (26)

depart, to, **discédō, discédere, discéssī, discessúrus** (9, 22)

dependent, **clíēns, cliéntis,** gen. pl., **cliéntium,** m. (25)

devour, to, **dévorō, -áre, -ávī, -átus** (20)

difficulty, with, **vix,** adv. (24)

din, **frágor, fragóris,** m. (4)

dine, to, **cénō, -áre, -ávī, -átus** (19)

dinner, **céna, -ae,** f. (19)

direction, **pars, pártis,** gen. pl., **pártium,** f. (13)

dirty, **sórdidus, -a, -um** (19)

distance, in the, **prócul,** adv. (15)

distant, to be, **ábsum, abésse, áfuī, āfutúrus** (11, 25)

distinguished, **praeclárus, -a, -um** (13)

ditch, **fóssa, -ae,** f. (12)

do, to, **ágō, ágere, égī, áctus** (8, 14, 23), **fáciō, fácere, fécī, fáctus** (1, 23)

do?, What did… **Quid fécit…?** (19)

do?, What does… **Quid fácit…?** (1)

do nothing, to, **céssō, -áre, -ávī, -ātúrus** (14)

dog, **cánis, cánis,** m./f. (12)

doing?, What is… **Quid fácit…?** (1)

Don't…! **Nólī!/Nōlíte!** + infinitive (9)

door, **iánua, -ae,** f. (9)

doorkeeper, **iánitor, iānitóris,** m. (9)

doorpost, **póstis, póstis,** gen. pl., **póstium,** m. (25)

down from, **dē,** prep. + abl. (16)

drag, to, **tráhō, tráhere, tráxī, tráctus** (6, 12, 25)

drag out, to, **éxtrahō, extráhere, extráxī, extráctus** (14, 21)

draw, to, **stríngō, stríngere, strínxī, stríctus** (26)

draw a sword, to, **gládium stríngere** (26)

dream, **sómnium, -ī,** n. (21)

drive, to, **ágō, ágere, égī, áctus** (8, 14, 23), **íncitō, -áre, -ávī, -átus** (10)

drive off/back, to, **repéllō, repéllere, réppulī, repúlsus** (5)

driver, **raedárius, -ī,** m. (10)

dung, **stércus, stércoris,** n. (21)

dust, **púlvis, púlveris,** m. (15)

dwell, to, **hábitō, -áre, -ávī, -átus** (1)

E

each, **ómnis, -is, -e** (6, 18)

early in the day, **máne,** adv. (21)

earth, **térra, -ae,** f. (26)

eat dinner, to, **cénō, -áre, -ávī, -átus** (19)

eight, **óctō** (15)

either…or, **aut…aut,** conj. (26)

eleventh, **ūndécimus, -a, -um** (17)

embrace, **compléxus, -ūs,** m. (9, 25)

embrace, in an, **compléxū** (9)

emperor, **Caésar, Caésaris,** m. (27), **prínceps, príncipis,** m. (7)

encounter, to, **occúrrō, occúrrere, occúrrī, occursúrus** + dat. (24)

energetic, **strénuus, -a, -um** (2)

enough, **sátis,** adv., indeclinable substantive (23)

enter, to, **íntrō, -áre, -ávī, -átus** (8, 19)

envoy, **lēgátus, -ī,** m. (18)

eruption, **ērúptiō, ēruptiónis,** f. (26)

escape, to, **effúgiō, effúgere, effúgī** (11, 21)

even, **étiam,** adv. (1, 6, 13)

evening, in the, **vésperī** (18)

every, **ómnis, -is, -e** (6, 18)

everyone, **ómnēs** (6)

everything, **ómnia** (6)

everything that, **ómnia quae** (6)

examine, to, **īnspíciō, īnspícere, īnspéxī, īnspéctus** (21) exceedingly, **váldē**, adv. (19)

except, **nísi**, conj. (18, 26), **praéter**, prep. + acc. (21)

exclaim, to, **exclámō, -áre, -ávī, -átus** (10)

explain, to, **éxplicō, -áre, -ávī, -átus** (19)

eye, **óculus, -ī,** m. (26)

F

fall, to, **cádō, cádere, cécidī, cāsúrus** (3, 22)

fall down, to, **cóncidō, concídere, cóncidī** (14)

famous, **praeclárus, -a, -um** (13)

far (off), **prócul,** adv. (15)

farm manager, **vílicus, -ī,** m. (11)

fast, very, **celérrimē,** adv. (14)

fat, **obésus, -a, -um** (18)

father, **páter, pátris,** m. (6, 11)

fault, **cúlpa, -ae,** f. (14)

favor, to, **fáveō, favére, fávī, fautúrus** + dat. (27)

fear, **métus, -ūs,** m. (26), **térror, terróris,** m. (22)

fear, to, **tímeō, timére, tímuī** (5)

festival day, **fériae, -árum,** f. pl. (27)

field, **áger, ágrī,** m. (2)

fiercely, **feróciter,** adv. (13)

fifth, **quíntus, -a, -um** (26)

fifty, **quīnquāgíntā** (15)

find, to, **invéniō, inveníre, invénī, invéntus** (12, 21)

finish, to, **cōnfíciō, cōnfícere, cōnfécī, cōnféctus** (25), **fíniō, -íre, -ívī, -ítus** (21)

first, **prímus, -a, -um** (21)
first, **prímum,** adv. (23)

fishpond, **piscína, -ae,** f. (3)

five, **quínque** (15)

flee, to, **fúgiō, fúgere, fúgī, fugitúrus** (18, 25)

following, **séquēns, sequéntis** (25)

following day, on the, **postrídiē,** adv. (26)

food, **cíbus, -ī,** m. (6)

foolish, **stúltus, -a, -um** (23)

foot, **pēs, pédis,** m. (13)

footprint, **vēstígium, -ī,** n. (12, 15)

for, **énim,** conj. (20), **nam,** conj. (8)

forbid, to, **vétō, vetáre, vétuī, vétitus** (26)

forehead, **frōns, fróntis,** f. (12)

forest, **sílva, -ae,** f. (5)

forgetful, **ímmemor, immémoris** + gen. (22)

former, the, **ílle, ílla, íllud** (11, 15, 16, 20, 22, 25, 26)

Forum, **Fórum, -ī,** n. (25)

four, **quáttuor** (15)

freedom, **lībértās, lībertátis,** f. (21)

friend, **amíca, -ae,** f. (2), **amícus, -ī,** m. (3), **hóspes, hóspitis,** m./f. (16)

frighten, to, **térreō, -ére,-uī, -itus** (4)

frightened, **pertérritus, -a, -um** (5)

from, **ā** or **ab,** prep. + abl. (13), **ē** or **ex,** prep. + abl. (2, 5, 9)

From where...? **Únde...?** adv. (12)

full, **plénus, -a, -um** (11)

G

games, **lúdī, -órum,** m. pl. (24)

gape, to, **stúpeo, -ére, -uī** (23)

garden, **hórtus, -ī,** m. (3)

gate, **pórta, -ae,** f. (11)

gently, **plácidē,** adv. (14)

get ready, to, **(sē) paráre** (22)

get up, to, **súrgō, súrgere, surréxī, surrēctúrus** (6, 21)

gets dark, it, **advesperáscit, advesperáscere, advesperávit** (17)

girl, **puélla, -ae,** f. (1)

give, to, **dō, dáre, dédī, dátus** (21)

give favor (to), to, **fáveō, favére, fávī, fautúrus** + dat. (27)

glad, **laétus, -a, -um** (1)

glad, to be, **gaúdeō, gaudére** (14)

go, to, **éō, íre, íī** or **ívī, itúrus** (7, 17, 19, 20, 21)

go around, to, **circúmeō, circumíre, circúmiī** or **circumívī, circúmitus** (24)

Go away! **Ábī!/Abíte!** (3)

go away, to, **ábeō, abíre, ábiī** or **abívī, abitúrus** (3, 9), **discédō, discédere, discéssī, discessúrus** (9, 22) go back, to, **rédeō, redíre, rédiī** or **redívī, reditúrus** (7, 23)

go down, to, **dēscéndō, dēscéndere, dēscéndī, dēscēnsúrus** (4, 23)

go into, to, **íntrō, -áre, -ávī, -átus** (8, 19)

go out, to, **éxeō, exíre, éxiī** or **exívī, exitúrus** (5, 23)

go past, to, **praetéreō, praeteríre, praetériī** or **praetervī, praeteritúrus** (15)

goal, **méta, -ae,** f. (27)

gold, **aúrum, -ī,** n. (21)

golden, **aúreus, -a, -um** (25)

good, **bónus, -a, -um** (12)

good, very, **óptimus, -a, -um** (20)

Goodbye! **Válē!/Valéte!** (9)

Goodness me! **Mehércule!** interj. (18)

goods, **bóna, -órum,** n. pl. (26)

grab hold of, to, **arrípiō, arrípere, arrípuī, arréptus** (5, 9, 26)

great, **mágnus, -a, -um** (4)

great, very, **máximus, -a, -um** (23)

greatest, **máximus, -a, -um** (23)

Greece, **Graécia, -ae,** f. (21)

Greek, **Graécus, -a, -um** (17)

Greeks, the, **Graécī, -órum,** m. pl. (I)

green, **prásinus, -a, -um** (27)

greet, to, **salútō, -áre, -ávī, -átus** (7)

Greetings! **Sálvē!/Salvéte!** (7)

groan, to, **gémō, gémere, gémuī, gémitus** (3)

ground, **térra, -ae,** f. (26)

ground, on the, **húmī** (27)

guard, **cústōs, custódis,** m. (26)

guard, to, **custódiō, -íre, -ívī, -ítus** (17)

guest, **hóspes, hóspitis,** m./f. (16)

H

habit (of), to be in the, **sóleō, solére** + infin. (10)

half-asleep, **sēmisómnus, -a, -um** (9)

hand, **mánus, -ūs,** f. (18, 25)

hand over, to, **trádō, trádere, trádidī, tráditus** (7, 22)

happens, (it), **áccidit, accídere, áccidit** (14, 26)

happy, **laétus, -a, -um** (1)

hard, **strénuē,** adv. (6, 13)

harm, to, **nóceō, -ére, -uī, -itúrus** + dat. (26)

have, to, **hábeō, -ére, -uī, -itus** (10, 20, 26)

he, **ílle** (11, 15, 16, 20, 22, 26), **is** (2, 7)

head, **cáput, cápitis,** n. (25)

head for, to, **pétō, pétere, petívī, petítus** (5, 21)

hear, to, **aúdiō, -íre, -ívī, -ítus** (4, 20)

heat, **aéstus, -ūs,** m. (24, 25)

Hello! **Sálvē!/Salvéte!** (7)

help, **auxílium, -ī,** n. (5, 15)

Help! **Fer/Férte auxílium!** (5)

help, to, **ádiuvō, adiuváre, adiúvī, adiútus** (6, 21)

her, **éam** (9, 16), **éius** (2, 27)

her (own), **súus, -a, -um** (9, 27)

her, to, **cui, éī** (19, 21)

here, **hīc,** adv. (9, 13)

here and there, **hūc illúc,** adv. (23)

herself, **ípsa** (6, 10), **sē** (27)

Hey! **Ého!** interj. (25)

hide, to, **célō, -áre, -ávī, -átus** (11)

hill, **mōns, móntis,** gen. pl., **móntium,** m. (24)

him, **éum** (5)

him, to, **cui, éī** (19, 21)

himself, **ípse** (6, 10), **sē** (11, 27)

hinder, to, **impédiō, -íre, -ívī, -ítus** (11)

hire, to, **condúcō, condúcere, condúxī, condúctus** (23)

his, **éius** (27)

his (own), **súus, -a, -um** (9, 27)

hit, to, **fériō, -íre** (16)

hold, to, **hábeō, -ére, -uī, -itus** (10, 20, 26), **téneō, tenére, ténuī, téntus** (9, 25)

hold out, to, **exténdō, exténdere, exténdī, exténtus** (18)

holiday, **fériae, -árum,** f. pl. (27)

holiday, celebrating a, **fēriátus, -a, -um** (27)

home, **dómus, -ūs,** f. (25)

home, at, **dómī** (26)

home(ward), **dómum** (23)

horse, **équus, -ī,** m. (10)

host, **hóspes, hóspitis,** m./f. (16)

hour, **hóra, -ae,** f. (9)

house, **dómus, -ūs,** f. (23, 25)

house, country, **vílla, -ae,** f. (1)

house of, at the, **ápud,** prep. + acc. (16)

How...! **Quam...!** adv. (13)

How...? **Quam...?** adv., **Quō īnstrūméntō...? Quómodo...?** adv. (12)

How are you? **Quid ágis?** (18)

How many...? **Quot...?** (15)

however, **támen,** adv. (6, 13)

huge, **íngēns, ingéntis** (22)

hundred, five, **quīngéntī, -ae, -a** (15)

hundred, one, **céntum** (15)

hungry, to be, **ēsúriō, -íre,   , -ītúrus** (19)

hurl, to, **praecípitō, -áre, -ávī, -átus** (18)

hurl oneself, to, **sē praecipitáre** (18)

Hurray! **Eúgepae!** interj. (7)

hurry, to, **festínō, -áre, -ávī, -ātúrus** (9)

husband, **cóniūnx, cóniugis,** m. (26), **vir, vírī,** m. (3, 11)

I, **égo** (5, 27)

I thank you! **Grátiās tíbi ágō!** (26)

idle, to be, **céssō, -áre, -ávī, -ātúrus** (14)

if, **sī,** conj. (5)

if... not, **nísi,** conj. (18, 26)

ignorant, to be, **nésciō, -íre, -ívī, -ítus** (9)

immediately, **státim,** adv. (5, 13)

in, **in,** prep. + abl. (1, 9)

in a loud voice, **mágnā vóce** (4)

in front of, **ápud,** prep. + acc. (26)

in this way, **íta,** adv. (3, 13, 21)

in three days, **tríbus diébus** (12, 13)

in vain, **frústrā,** adv. (14)

In what manner/way...? **Quómodo...?** adv. (12)

Indeed! **Íta vérō!** adv. (3, 13)

inn, **caupóna, -ae,** f. (17, 20)

innkeeper, **caúpō, caupónis,** m. (17)

innocence, **innocéntia, -ae,** f. (21)

inside, **íntrā,** prep. + acc. (22)

instruction, **mandátum, -ī,** n. (22)

instrument...? With what, **Quō īnstrūméntō...?** (12)

intend, to, **in ánimō habére** (16)

interrupt, to, **interpéllō, -áre, -ávī, -átus** (8, 19)

into, **in,** prep. + acc. (3, 9)

is, (he/she/it), **est** (1)

is able, (he/she/it), **pótest** (5)

Italy, **Itália, -ae,** f. (1)

its, **éius** (2, 27)

its (own), **súus, -a, -um** (27)

J

joke, **iócus, -ī,** m. (16)

journey, **íter, itíneris,** n. (10, 13, 15)

joy, **gaúdium, -ī,** n. (23)

K

keep quiet, to, **quiéscō, quiéscere, quiévī, quiētúrus** (13, 23)

kill, to, **nécō, -áre, -ávī, -átus** (20)

kind, of this, **tális, -is, -e** (23)

kitchen, **culína, -ae,** f. (21)

know, not to, **nésciō, -íre, -ívī, -ítus** (9)

know, to, **scíō, -íre, -ívī, -ítus** (16)

L

lady of the house, **dómina, -ae,** f. (17)

large, **mágnus, -a, -um** (4)

large, very, **máximus, -a, -um** (23)

late, **sérō,** adv. (21)

latter, the, **hic, haec, hoc** (18, 19, 20, 25, 26)

laugh, **rísus, -ūs,** m. (13, 25)

laugh, with a loud, **mágnō rísū** (13)

laugh (at), to, **rídeō, rīdére, rísī, rísus** (3, 21)

lazy, **ignávus, -a, -um** (5)

lead, to, **dúcō, dúcere, dúxī, dúctus** (7, 19, 20)

leaky, **rīmósus, -a, -um** (23)

leave behind, to, **relínquō, relínquere, relíquī, relíctus** (16, 21)

letter, **epístula, -ae,** f. (7)

letter (of the alphabet), **líttera, -ae,** f. (12)

lie, to, **iáceō, -ére, -uī, -itúrus** (26)

light, **lūx, lúcis,** f. (21)

light, it is, **lúcet, lūcére, lúxit** (6)

light two-wheeled carriage, **císium, -ī,** n. (14, 15)

like, to, **ámō, -áre, -ávī, -átus** (4)

like this, **tális, -is, -e** (23)

listen to, to, **aúdiō, -íre, -ívī, -ítus** (4, 20)

litter, **lectíca, -ae,** f. (23)

litter-bearer, **lectīcā́rius, -ī,** m. (23)

little, **párvulus, -a, -um** (26)

live, to, **hábitō, -áre, -ā́vī, -átus** (1)

load, **ónus, óneris,** n. (15)

long, **lóngus, -a, -um** (15)

long for, to, **dēsī́derō, -áre, -ā́vī, -átus** (26)

long time, for a, **díū,** adv. (15)

look after, to, **cū́rō, -áre, -ā́vī, -átus** (6)

Look (at...)! **Écce!** interj. (1)

look at, to, **spéctō, -áre, -ā́vī, -átus** (7)

look for, to, **pétō, pétere, petī́vī, petī́tus** (5, 21)

look out for, to, **exspéctō, -áre, -ā́vī, -átus** (15)

loud laugh, with a, **mágnō rī́sū** (13)

loud voice, with a, **mágnā vóce** (4)

love, to, **ámō, -áre, -ā́vī, -átus** (4)

M

magnificent, **magnī́ficus, -a, -um** (24)

main room, **átrium, -ī,** n. (26)

make, to, **fáciō, fácere, fécī, fáctus** (1, 23)

man, **vir, vírī,** m. (3, 11), **hómō, hóminis,** m. (18)

man, old, **sénex, sénis,** m. (I)

manager, farm, **vī́licus, -ī,** m. (11)

manner...?, In what, **Quómodo...?** adv. (12)

manure, **stércus, stércoris,** n. (21)

many, **múltī, -ae, -a** (3)

mark, **méta, -ae,** f. (27)

marvelous, **mírus, -a, -um** (23)

mass, **mólēs, mólis,** gen. pl., **mólium,** f. (24)

master, **dóminus, -ī,** m. (11)

matter, **rēs, réī,** f. (19, 25)

may, we, **lícet nóbīs** (20)

me, **mē** (4)

me, to/for, **míhi** (8)

me, with, **mécum** (9)

means...?, By what, **Quō īnstrūméntō...?** (12)

meanwhile, **íntereā,** adv. (10, 13)

meet, to, **occúrrō, occúrrere, occúrrī, occursū́rus** + dat. (24)

Megara, **Mégara, -ae,** f. (21)

merchant, **mercā́tor, mercātóris,** m. (22)

messenger, **nū́ntius, -ī,** m. (7)

mid-, **médius, -a, -um** (20)

middle of, **médius, -a, -um** (20)

midnight, **média nox, médiae nóctis,** f. (20)

mind, **ánimus, -ī,** m. (16)

mine, **méus, -a, -um** (7)

miserable, **míser, mísera, míserum** (9)

miss, to, **dēsī́derō, -áre, -ā́vī, -átus** (26)

mistaken, to be, **érrō, -áre, -ā́vī, -ātū́rus** (5, 18)

mistress, **dómina, -ae,** f. (17)

mob, **túrba, -ae,** f. (23)

moment, at that, **tum,** adv. (4, 13)

moment, at that very, **éō ípsō témpore** (10)

money, **pecū́nia, -ae,** f. (21)

moreover, **praetéreā,** adv. (15)

morning, in the, **máne,** adv. (21)

mother, **máter, mátris,** f. (6, 11)

motionless, **immóbilis, -is, -e** (12)

Mount Vesuvius, **Mōns Vesúvius, Móntis Vesúviī,** m. (26)

mountain, **mōns, móntis,** gen. pl., **móntium,** m. (24)

mouse, **mūs, mū́ris,** m. (21)

move, to, **móveō, movére, mṓvī, mótus** (14, 24)

move aside, to, **remóveō, removére, remṓvī, remótus** (21)

move toward, to, **admóveō, admovére, admṓvī, admótus** (22)

moved, **commótus, -a, -um** (14)

mud, **lútum, -ī,** n. (26)

murmur, **múrmur, múrmuris,** n. (15)

mutter, to, **mússō, -áre, -ā́vī, -ātū́rus** (11)

my, **méus, -a, -um** (7)

N

name, **nṓmen, nṓminis,** n. (1, 15)

name, by, **nṓmine** (1)

name, to, **appéllō, -áre, -ā́vī, -átus** (21)

napkin, **máppa, -ae,** f. (27)

Naples, **Neápolis, Neápolis,** f. (15)

narrator, **nārrátor, nārrātóris,** m. (8)

near, **ad,** prep. + acc. (15), **própe,** prep. + acc. (5, 9)

necessary, **necésse,** adv. or indeclinable adj. (6)

neighboring, **vīcínus, -a, -um** (1)

neither...nor, **néque...néque,** conj. (5)

never, **númquam,** adv. (20)

nevertheless, **támen,** adv. (6, 13)

new, **nóvus, -a, -um** (16)

next, **deínde,** adv. (8, 13)

night, **nox, nóctis,** gen. pl., **nóctium,** f. (11)

night, at, **nócte** (12)

night, happening during the, **noctúrnus, -a, -um** (22)

night, that, **íllā nócte** (11)

nine, **nóvem** (15)

ninth, **nónus, -a, -um** (16)

no, **núllus, -a, -um** (9)

No! **Mínimē!** adv. (3, 13)

no longer, **nōn iam,** adv. (2, 13)

no one, **némō, néminis,** m./f. (9)

noise, **frágor, frāgóris,** m. (4), **strépitus, -ūs,** m. (23, 25)

not, **nōn,** adv. (2, 13)

not any, **núllus, -a, -um** (9)

Not at all! **Mínimē!** adv. (3, 13)

not to wish/want, **nólō, nólle, nóluī** (5, 17, 21)

not yet, **nóndum,** adv. (6, 13)

nothing, **níhil** (4)

nothing, to do, **céssō, -áre, -ávī, -ātúrus** (14)

nothing wrong, there is, **níhil málī** (21)

now, **iam,** adv. (1, 8, 13), **nunc,** adv. (6, 13)

number, **númerus, -ī,** m. (11)

O

often, **saépe,** adv. (2, 13)

Oh dear me! **Ō mē míseram!** (9)

Oh no! **Éheu!** interj. (7)

old man, **sénex, sénis,** m. (I)

olive grove, **olīvétum, -ī,** n. (14, 15)

on, **in,** prep. + abl. (1, 9)

on account of, **própter,** prep. + acc. (26)

on top, **súprā,** adv. (21)

once (upon a time), **ólim,** adv. (18)

one, **únus, -a, -um** (15)

one...another, **álius...álius** (10)

one (of two), **álter, áltera, álterum** (1)

one...the other, the, **álter...álter** (16)

oneself, **sē** (11)

only, **módo,** adv. (18), **tántum,** adv. (15)

open, to, **apériō, aperíre, apéruī, apértus** (16, 26)

open space, **área, -ae,** f. (11)

oration, **ōrátiō, ōrātiónis,** f. (26)

orator, **ōrátor, ōrātóris,** m. (22)

order, **mandátum, -ī,** n. (22)

order, to, **iúbeō, iubére, iússī, iússus** (10, 19, 21)

other, **álius, ália, áliud** (10), **álter, áltera, álterum** (1)

other (of two), the, **álter, áltera, álterum** (1)

otherwise, **áliter,** adv. (26)

ought, **débeō, -ére, -uī, -itúrus** + infin. (26)

our, **nóster, nóstra, nóstrum** (14, 27)

out of, **ē** or **ex,** prep. + abl. (2, 5, 9)

outer garment, woman's, **stóla, -ae,** f. (10)

outside, **éxtrā,** prep. + acc. (23)

overseer, **vílicus, -ī,** m. (11)

owner, **dóminus, -ī,** m. (11)

ox, **bōs, bóvis,** m./f. (15)

P

Palatine, belonging to the Palatine Hill, **Palātínus, -a, -um** (24)

palla, **pálla, -ae,** f. (10)

parent, **párēns, paréntis,** m./f. (11)

part, **pars, pártis,** gen. pl., **pártium,** f. (13)

patron, **patrónus, -ī,** m. (25)

peacefully, **plácidē,** adv. (14)

peasant, **rústicus, -ī,** m. (13)

pen, **stílus, -ī,** m. (25)

people, **hóminēs, hóminum,** m. pl. (15)

perhaps, **fortásse,** adv. (15)

pest, **moléstus, -ī,** m. (3)

pick out, to, **súmō, súmere, súmpsī, súmptus** (22)

picture, **pictúra, -ae,** f. (1)

pirate, **pīráta, -ae,** m. (21)

place, to, **pónō, pónere, pósuī, pósitus** (10, 21)

place, to that, **éō,** adv. (23), **illúc,** adv. (23)

play, to, **lúdō, lúdere, lúsī, lūsúrus** (16)

play ball, to, **pílā lúdere** (16)

please, **sī vīs** (26)

poet, **poéta, -ae,** m. (25)

Pompeii, **Pompéiī, Pompeiórum,** m. pl.

Poor me! **Ō mē míseram!** (9)

possessions, **bóna, -órum,** n. pl. (26)

praise, to, **laúdō, -áre, -ávī, -átus** (18)

prank, **iócus, -ī,** m. (16)

prepare, to, **párō, -áre, -ávī, -átus** (5, 20)

prepare oneself, to, **sē paráre** (22)

prepared, **parátus, -a, -um** (10)

present, to be, **ádsum, adésse, ádfuī, adfutúrus** (26)

presently, **mox,** adv. (6, 13)

pretend, to, **símulō, -áre, -ávī, -átus** (21)

prevent, to, **impédiō, -íre, -ívī, -ítus** (11)

previously, **abhínc,** adv. (25), **ánteā,** adv. (20)

prisoner, **captívus, -ī,** m. (26)

promise, to, **prōmíttō, prōmíttere, prōmísī, prōmíssus** (9)

pull, to, **tráhō, tráhere, tráxī, tráctus** (6, 12, 25)

punish, to, **púniō, -íre, -ívī, -ítus** (21)

purple-bordered toga, **tóga praetéxta, tógae praetéxtae,** f. (10)

put, to, **pónō, pónere, pósuī, pósitus** (10, 21)

put on, to, **índuō, indúere, índuī, indútus** (8, 23)

Q

quickly, **celériter,** adv. (8, 13)

quickly, most/very, **celérrimē,** adv. (14)

quiet, to be, **táceō, -ére, -uī, -itus** (9)

quiet, to keep, **quiéscō, quiéscere, quiévī, quiētúrus** (13, 23)

R

racetrack, **currículum, -ī,** n. (27)

rain, **ímber, ímbris,** gen. pl., **ímbrium,** m. (23)

rains/is raining, it, **plúit, plúere, plúit** (23)

rash, **temerárius, -a, -um** (5)

reach, to, **advéniō, adveníre, advénī, adventúrus** (5, 23), **pervéniō, perveníre, pervénī, perventúrus** + ad + acc. (25)

read, to, **légō, légere, légī, léctus** (1, 24)

ready, **parátus, -a, -um** (10)

ready, to get, **párō, -áre, -ávī, -átus** (5)

ready, to get (oneself), **sē paráre** (22)

reason, **caúsa, -ae,** f. (25)

recall, to, **révocō, -áre, -ávī, -átus** (7)

receive, to, **excípiō, excípere, excépī, excéptus** (5, 16, 22)

reckless, **temerárius, -a, -um** (5)

recognize, to, **agnóscō, agnóscere, agnóvī, ágnitus** (18)

recover, to, **recúperō, -áre, -ávī, -átus** (21)

red, **russátus, -a, -um** (27)

regain one's senses, to, **ánimum recuperáre** (21)

region, **pars, pártis,** gen. pl., **pártium,** f. (13)

reins, **habénae, -árum,** f. pl. (22)

rejoice, to, **gaúdeō, gaudére** (14)

remain, to, **máneō, manére, mánsī, mánsurus** (9, 20, 23)

remove, to, **remóveō, removére, remóvī, remótus** (21)

repeatedly, **idéntidem,** adv. (13)

reply, to, **respóndeō, respondére, respóndī, respōnsúrus** (5, 21)

rest, **quíēs, quiétis,** f. (23)

rest, to, **quiéscō, quiéscere, quiévī, quiētúrus** (13, 23), **sē quiétī dáre** (23)

return, **réditus, -ūs,** m. (25)

return, to, **rédeō, redíre, rédiī** or **redívī, reditúrus** (7, 23)

rise, to, **súrgō, súrgere, surréxī, surrēctúrus** (6, 21)

road, **vía, -ae,** f. (10)

robber, **praédō, praedónis,** m. (26)

rod, **vírga, -ae,** f. (13)

Roman, **Rōmánus, -a, -um** (1)

Romans, the, **Rōmánī, -órum,** m. pl. (III)

Rome, **Róma, -ae,** f. (7)

Rome, to, **Rómam** (7)

room, **cubículum, -ī,** n. (8, 15)

room, main, **átrium, -ī,** n. (26)

rouse, to, **éxcitō, -áre, -ávī, -átus** (8)

rumble, **múmur, múrmuris,** n. (15)

run, to, **cúrrō, cúrrere, cucúrrī, cursúrus** (2, 23)

run ahead, to, **praecúrrō, praecúrrere, praecúrrī, praecursúrus** (18)

run away, to, **effúgiō, effúgere, effúgī** (11, 21)

rush, to, **sē praecipitáre** (18)

S

sad, to be, **dóleo, -ére, -uī, -itúrus** (18)

safe, **sálvus, -a, -um** (5)

safe and sound, **incólumis, -is, -e** (14)

said, (he/she), **ínquit** (7)

same, the, **ídem, éadem, ídem** (3)

same time, at the, **símul,** adv. (9, 13)

save, to, **sérvō, -áre, -ávī, -átus** (26)

say, to, **dícō, dícere, díxī, díctus** (20, 21)

says, (he/she), **ínquit** (7)

scarcely, **vix,** adv. (24)

scent of, to catch the, **olfáciō, olfácere, olfécī, olfáctus** (12)

school, **lúdus, -ī,** m. (26)

scold, to, **reprehéndō, reprehéndere, reprehéndī, reprehénsus** (6)

second, **álter, áltera, álterum** (1), **secúndus, -a, -um** (9)

second time, a, **íterum,** adv. (8, 13)

see, to, **vídeō, vidére, vídī, vísus** (4, 21)

seek, to, **pétō, pétere, petívī, petítus** (5, 21)

seems, he/she/it, **vidétur** (21)

seize, to, **arrípiō, arrípere, arrípuī, arréptus** (5, 19, 26)

-self, -selves, **ípse, ípsa, ípsum** (6, 10), **sē** (11, 27)

Senate, **senátus, -ūs,** m. (25)

Senate House, **Cúria, -ae,** f. (23)

senator, **senátor, senātóris,** m. (7)

send, to, **míttō, míttere, mísī, míssus** (9, 20)

seven, **séptem** (15)

seventh, **séptimus, -a, -um** (13)

shaky, **ínfírmus, -a, -um** (4)

she, **éa** (27), **ílla** (11, 15, 16, 20, 22, 25, 26)

she-wolf, **lúpa, -ae,** f. (II)

shop, **tabérna, -ae,** f. (25)

short, **brévis, -is, -e** (2)

short time, for a, **paulísper,** adv. (20)

short time, in a, **brévī témpore** (2, 12)

shout, to, **clámō, -áre, -ávī, -ātúrus** (3)

shout out, to, **exclámō, -áre, -ávī, -ātúrus** (10)

shout(ing), **clámor, clāmóris,** m. (5)

show, to, **dēmónstrō, -áre, -ávī, -átus** (24), **mónstrō, -áre, -ávī, -átus** (22)

shut, **claúsus, -a, -um** (24)

shut, to, **claúdō, claúdere, claúsī, claúsus** (26)

sides, from/on all, **úndique,** adv. (23)

signal, **sígnum, -ī,** n. (27)

silence, **siléntium, -ī,** n. (15)

silently, **tácitē,** adv. (9, 13)

sing, to, **cántō, -áre, -ávī, -átus** (21)

sir, **vir óptime** (20)

sister, **sóror, soróris,** f. (11)

sit, to, **sédeō, sedére, sédī, sessúrus** (1, 21)

sit down, to, **cōnsídō, cōnsídere, cōnsédī** (23)

situation, **rēs, réī,** f. (19, 25)

six, **sex** (15)

skill, **ars, ártis,** gen. pl., **ártium,** f. (14)

sky, **caélum, -ī,** n. (17)

slave, **sérvus, -ī,** m. (3)

slave-woman, **ancílla, -ae,** f. (6)

sleep, **sómnus, -ī,** m. (21)

sleep, to, **dórmiō, -íre, -ívī, -ītúrus** (4)

sleep, to go to, **obdórmiō, -íre, -ívī, -ītúrus** (21)

slow, **tárdus, -a, -um** (15)

slowly, **léntē,** adv. (2, 13)

small, **párvulus, -a, -um** (26)

smell, to, **olfáciō, olfácere, olfécī, olfáctus** (12, 18)

smile, **rísus, -ūs,** m. (13, 25)

smile, to, **rídeō, rīdére, rísī, rísus** (3, 21)

snatch, to, **arrípiō, arrípere, arrípuī, arréptus** (5, 19, 26)

sniff, to, **olfáciō, olfácere, olfécī, olfáctus** (12, 18)

snore, to, **stértō, stértere, stértuī** (25)

so, **íta,** adv. (3, 13, 21)

so great, **tántus, -a, -um** (24)

soldier, **míles, mílitis,** m. (20)

some...others, **áliī...áliī** (9)

something, **áliquid** (25)

sometimes, **nōnnúmquam,** adv. (26)

son, **fílius, -ī,** m. (11)

soon, **brévī témpore** (2, 12), **mox,** adv. (6, 13)

sound, **sónitus, -ūs,** m. (21, 25)

space, open, **área, -ae,** f. (11)

speaker, **ōrátor, ōrātóris,** m. (22)

spectator, **spectátor, spectātóris,** m. (27)

speech, **ōrátiō, ōrātiónis,** f. (26)

speech, to deliver a, **ōrātiónem habére** (26)

spend the night, to, **pernóctō, -áre, -ávī, -ātúrus** (17, 18)

spin wool, to, **lánam tráhere** (6)

spur on, to, **íncitō, -áre, -ávī, -átus** (10)

squared, **quadrátus, -a, -um** (25)

staff, **báculum, -ī,** n. (10, 15)

stand, to, **stō, stáre, stétī, statúrus** (10, 22)

standing out, **éxstāns, exstántis** (23)

statue, **státua, -ae,** f. (3)

stay, to, **máneō, manére, mánsī, mánsus** (9, 20, 23)

stay awake, to, **vígilō, -áre, -ávī, -ātúrus** (19)

stealthily, **fúrtim,** adv. (4, 13)

stick, **báculum, -ī,** n. (10, 15), **vírga, -ae,** f. (13)

stick, to, **haéreō, haerére, haésī, haesúrus** (14)

still, **adhúc,** adv. (5, 13)

stola, **stóla, -ae,** f. (10)

stone, **lápis, lápidis,** m. (25)

story, **fábula, -ae,** f. (20)

strange, **mírus, -a, -um** (23)

stream, **rívus, -ī,** m. (5)

street, **vía, -ae,** f. (10)

strenuously, **strénuē,** adv. (6, 13)

strike, to, **fériō, -íre** (16)

strong, **fórtis, -is, -e** (18)

study, **tablínum, -ī,** n. (26)

stupid, **fátuus, -a, -um** (13), **stúltus, -a, -um** (23)

such, **tális, -is, -e** (23)

suddenly, **súbitō,** adv. (3, 13)

summer, **aéstās, aestátis,** f. (1)

summer, in the, **aestáte** (1)

support, to, **fáveō, favére, fávī, fautúrus** + dat. (27)

switch, **vírga, -ae,** f. (13)

sword, **gládius, -ī,** m. (26)

sword, to draw a, **gládium stríngere** (26)

T

tail, **caúda, -ae,** f. (18)

take, to, **cápiō, cápere, cépī, cáptus** (21), **dúcō, dúcere, dúxī, dúctus** (7, 19, 20)

take care of, to, **cúrō, -áre, -ávī, -átus** (6)

take out, to, **éxtrahō, extráhere, extráxī, extráctus** (14, 21)

take (up), to, **súmō, súmere, súmpsī, súmptus** (22)

talkative, **verbósus, -a, -um** (26)

teach, to, **dóceō, docére, dócuī, dóctus** (6, 21)

team of four horses, **quadrígae, -árum,** f. pl. (27)

tell, to, **dícō, dícere, díxī, díctus** (20, 21)

tell (a story), to, **nárrō, -áre, -ávī, -átus** (20)

ten, **décem** (15)

terrified, **pertérritus, -a, -um** (5)

terrify, to, **térreō, -ére, -uī, -itus** (4)

terror, **térror, terróris,** m. (22)

Thank you! **Grátiās tíbi ágō!** (26)

that, **ílle, ílla, íllud** (11, 15, 16, 20, 22, 25, 26), **is, éa, id** (27), **quī, quae, quod** (1, 3, 14)

that night, **íllā nócte** (11)

that place, to, **éō,** adv. (23), **illúc,** adv. (23)

their, **eórum, eárum, eórum** (25, 27)

their (own), **súus, -a, -um** (27)

them, **éōs, éās, éa** (27)

them, of, **eórum, eárum, eórum** (27)

them, to/for, **éīs** (22, 27)

then, **deínde,** adv. (8, 13), **tum,** adv. (4, 13)

there, **éō,** adv. (23), **íbi,** adv. (5, 13), **illúc,** adv. (23)

therefore, **ígitur,** conj. (4), **ítaque,** adv. (16)

these, **hī, hae, haec** (18, 19, 20, 25, 26)

they, **éī, éae, éa** (27)

thing, **rēs, réī,** f. (19, 25)

think, to, **cógitō, -áre, -ávī, -átus** (21)

third, **tértius, -a, -um** (25)

this, **hic, haec, hoc** (18, 19, 20, 25, 26), **is, éa, id** (27)

this way and that, **hūc illúc,** adv. (23)

thousand, one, **mílle** (15)

three, **trēs, trēs, tría** (13, 15)

threshing floor, **área, -ae,** f. (11)

through, **per,** prep. + acc. (6, 9)

throw, to, **coníciō, conícere, coniécī, coniéctus** (21), **iáciō, iácere, iécī, iáctus** (10, 20)

time, **témpus, témporis,** n. (2, 8, 12, 15)

time, enough, **sátis témporis** (23)

tired, **dēféssus, -a, -um** (2)

to Rome, **Rómam** (7)

to that place, **éō,** adv. (23)

today, **hódiē,** adv. (2, 13)

toga, **tóga, -ae,** f. (8)

toga with purple border, **tóga praetéxta, tógae praetéxtae,** f. (10)

together, **símul,** adv. (9, 13)

toil, **lábor, labóris,** m. (24)

told, **nārrátus, -a, -um** (20)

tomb, **sepúlcrum, -ī,** n. (22)

tomorrow, **crās,** adv. (10, 13)

too, **praetéreā,** adv. (15)

to(ward), **ad,** prep. + acc. (2, 9)

towering, **éxstāns, exstántis** (23)

trace, **vēstígium, -ī,** n. (12, 15)

track, **vēstígium, -ī,** n. (12, 15)

travel, to, **íter fácere** (13)

traveler, **viátor, viātóris,** m. (18)

tree, **árbor, árboris,** f. (1)

tremble, to, **trémō, trémere, trémuī** (21)

Trojan, **Troiánus, -a, -um** (I)

Trojans, the, **Troiánī, -órum,** m. pl. (I)

troublesome, **moléstus, -a, -um** (4)

Troy, **Tróia, -ae,** f. (I)

trunk, **císta, -ae,** f. (10)

trust, to, **cōnfídō, cōnfídere** + dat. (26)

try, to, **témptō, -áre, -ávī, -átus** (9)

tunic, **túnica, -ae,** f. (8)

turn, to, **vértō, vértere, vértī, vérsus** (16)

turn aside, to, **dēvértō, dēvértere, dēvértī, dēvérsus** (14, 27)

turning-post, **méta, -ae,** f. (27)

two, **dúo, dúae, dúo** (15)

U

uncle, **pátruus, -ī,** m. (22)

under, **sub,** prep. + abl. (1, 9)

unhappy, **míser, mísera, míserum** (9)

unhurt, **incólumis, -is, -e** (14)

unless, **nísi,** conj. (18, 26)

unwilling, **invítus, -a, -um** (21)

unwilling, to be, **nṓlō, nólle, nóluī** (5, 17, 21)

uproar, **tumúltus, -ūs,** m. (25)

urge on, to, **íncitō, -áre, -ávī, -átus** (10)

us, **nōs** (8)

us, to/for, **nṓbīs** (9)

us, with, **nōbíscum** (16)

V

vehicle, **vehículum, -ī,** n. (13, 15)

very, **váldē,** adv. (19)

very much, **váldē,** adv. (19), **veheménter,** adv. (19)

victor, **víctor, victóris,** m. (27)

vineyard, **vínea, -ae,** f. (12)

violently, **veheménter,** adv. (19)

visit, to, **vísitō, -áre, -ávī, -átus** (23)

voice, **vōx, vócis,** f. (4)

voice, in a loud, **mágnā vóce** (4)

W

wagon, **plaústrum, -ī,** n. (15)

wait for, to, **exspéctō, -áre, -ávī, -átus** (15)

wait (for) to, **máneō, manére, mánsī, mānsúrus** (9, 20, 23)

wake up, to, **ánimum recuperáre** (21)

wake (someone) up, to, **éxcitō, -áre, -ávī, -átus** (8)

wakened, **excitátus, -a, -um** (25)

walk, to, **ámbulō, -áre, -ávī, -ātúrus** (2)

wall, **múrus, -ī,** m. (23)

wander, to, **érrō, -áre, -ávī, -ātúrus** (5, 18)

want, to, **vólo, vélle, vóluī** (5, 17, 20, 21)

want, (you), **vīs** (16)

wants, (he/she), **vult** (5, 17)

warm, **cálidus, -a, -um** (5)

was, (he/she/it), **érat** (13)

wash, to, **lávō, laváre, lávī, laútus** (20)

watch, to, **obsérvō, -áre, -ávī, -átus** (6),
  spéctō, -áre, -ávī, -átus (7)

Watch out (for)! **Cávē!/Cavéte!** (4, 13, 23)

watch out (for), to, **cáveō, cavére, cávī, caútus** (4, 13, 23)

water, **áqua, -ae,** f. (6)

way, in this, **íta,** adv. (3, 13, 21)

way...?, In what, **Quómodo...?** adv. (12)

we, **nōs** (8, 27)

weak, **īnfírmus, -a, -um** (4)

wear, to, **gérō, gérere, géssī, géstus** (10)

weep, to, **lácrimō, -áre, -ávī, -átus** (9)

weeping, **lácrimāns** (9)

welcome, to, **excípiō, excípere, excépī,
excéptus** (5, 16, 22), **salū́tō, -áre,
-ávī, -átus** (7)

well, **béne,** adv. (2)

What...? **Quid...?** (1, 4)

What sort of...? **Quális...?, Quális...?
Quále...?** (4, 18)

wheel, **róta, -ae,** f. (15)

when, **cum,** conj. (22), **úbi,** conj. (5)

When...? **Quándō...?** adv. (12, 21)

where, **úbi,** conj. (1)

Where...? **Úbi...?** adv. (10, 12)

where...?, From, **Únde...?** adv. (12)

Where...to? **Quō...?** adv. (4)

which, **quī, quae, quod** (1, 3, 14, 24)

while, **dum,** conj. (1)

whip, to, **vérberō, -áre, -ávī, -átus** (11)

white, **albátus, -a, -um** (27)

white cloth, **máppa, -ae,** f. (27)

who, **quī, quae** (1, 3, 14)

Who...? (sing.) **Quis...?** (1), (pl.) **Quī...?** (6)

whole, the, **ómnis, -is, -e** (6, 18)

whom, to, (sing.) **cui** (19)

Whom...? **Quem...?** (5), **Quōs...?** (7),
Quās...?

whom...?, With, (sing.) **Quócum...?**
(12, 26), (pl.) **Quibúscum...?** (12)

Whose...? **Cúius...?** (22)

Why...? **Cūr...?** adv. (1)

wicked, **sceléstus, -a, -um** (10)

wife, **cóniūnx, cóniugis,** f. (26), **úxor, uxóris,**
  f. (11)

willing, (he/she) is, **vult** (5, 17)

willing, to be, **vólō, vélle, vóluī** (5, 17,
20, 21)

win, to, **víncō, víncere, vī́cī, víctus** (27)

wine, **vī́num, -ī,** n. (25)

wish, if you, **sī vīs** (26)

wish, not to, **nṓlō, nṓlle, nṓluī** (5, 17, 21)

wish, to, **vólō, vélle, vóluī** (5, 17, 20, 21)

wishes, (he/she), **vult** (5, 17)

with, **ápud,** prep. + acc. (16, 26), **cum,** prep.
  + abl. (12)

with a loud laugh, **mágnō rī́sū** (13)

With whom...? (sing.) **Quócum...?** (12, 26),
  (pl.) **Quibúscum...?** (12)

without, **síne,** prep. + abl. (26)

wolf, **lúpus, -ī,** m. (5)

woman, **fḗmina, -ae,** f. (3)

wonderful, **mī́rus, -a, -um** (23)

woods, **sílva, -ae,** f. (5)

wool, **lā́na, -ae,** f. (6)

wool, to spin, **lā́nam trāhere** (6)

work, **lábor, labṓris,** m. (24)

work, to, **labṓrō, -áre, -ávī, -átus** (3)

worried, **sollícitus, -a, -um** (4)

wretched, **míser, mísera, míserum** (9)

write, to, **scrī́bō, scrī́bere, scrī́psī, scrī́ptus**
(1, 24)

Y

Yes! **Íta vḗrō!** adv. (3, 13)

yesterday, **héri,** adv. (20)

you, (sing.) **tū, tē** (4, 27), (pl.) **vōs** (8, 27)

you, to/for, (sing.) **tíbi** (19),
  (pl.) **vṓbīs** (19)

your, (sing.) **túus, -a, -um** (9, 27), (pl.)
  véster, véstra, véstrum (22, 27)

INDEX OF GRAMMAR

gender: adjectives, 120–122; 138, 140; adjectives as substantives, 200; *hic*, 241; *ille*, 241

genitive case: forms, 81; noun modification, 80; partitive or whole, 229; singular or nominative plural, 83

hic: demonstrative adjective and pronoun, 240; genders, 241

-īlis, Latin suffix, 145

ille: demonstrative adjective and pronoun, 240; genders, 241

imperative. *See* verbs, imperative

indirect object, 189

infinitives: complementary, 26, 162; consolidation, 162; identifying conjugations, 72; impersonals, 34, 162; subject of verb *est*, 162; verbal phrase, impersonal, 34; verbs with accusative and infinitives, 162; with verbs, 72

intransitive verbs. *See* verbs, intransitive

-(i)tās, Latin suffix, 144

-(i)tūdō, Latin suffix, 144

masculine nouns. *See* nouns, masculine

modification, adjectives, 34–35

mottoes, 103

negative imperative. *See* verbs, imperative

neuter, nouns, 114

nominative case, 41; complement, 41; confusion with genitive singular, 83; plural ending, 43; subject, 41

nouns: adjective agreement, 120–122, 139–140; bases, 144; cases, 41, 186–187; cases and declension forms, 81; dative case, 186–187; dative or ablative, 191; declensions, 41, 186–187; declensions, 4th and 5th, 228; definition, 4; endings *-ās, -ōs, -ēs*, 40; feminine, 34–35; gender, 34–35, 120–122; Latin base words into English, 57–58; masculine, 34–35; neuter, 114; singular and plural forms, 14; vocative, 56

number: adjectives, 121, 140; adjective substantives, 200

numerals and numbers: English derivatives, 123; forms, 116; Roman system, 123

objects, direct, 20

-ōs, noun and adjective ending, 40

parts of speech. *See* nouns, adjectives, verbs

plural, verb and person, 54

positive imperative. *See* verbs, imperative

post merīdiem, 261

prefixes: compound verbs, 257; meanings, 259

prepositional phrases: ablative case, 64, 90; accusative case, 64

pronouns: declensions of personal, 253; demonstrative, 240; personal, 253–254; personal endings, 54; reflexive, 254–255

root words. *See* base words

silent *-e*, 196

singular, verb and person, 54

spellings, Latin derivatives, 22–23

subjects, sentence element, 8

subordinate clauses, conjunction *dum*, 161

substantives: *-iō, -or*, 196; masculine or feminine, 200; neuter gender, 200; plural number, 200

suffixes: adjectives, 144; combining, 145; Latin sources in English, 102; nouns, 145; 3rd declension nouns, 102

tense: future, 201; future of irregular verbs, 205; future perfect, 218; perfect, 150–151, 160; pluperfect, 213; verbs, 73

transitive verbs. *See* verbs, transitive

verbal phrase: impersonal with dative case, 190; impersonal with infinitive, 34

verbs: accusative, 72; accusative and infinitive, 162; compound, 212; compound prefixes, 257; conjugations, 72, 201, 203; definition, 4; endings, 8–9, 203; future active participle, 165; future perfect tense, 218–219; future tense, 201, 205; imperative, positive and negative, 74; imperfect tense, 98, 106–107; infinitives, 72; intransitive, 21, 165, 189; intransitive compound with dative case, 212; intransitive with dative, 252; intransitive with preposition, 189; irregular, 54, 108, 128; irregular principal parts, 166–167; linking, 8; perfect passive participle, 165; perfect tense, 150–151, 160; persons, 54; pluperfect tense, 213; prepositional phrases as modifiers, 64; present or future tense, 203; present tense, 73; principal parts, 165–167; regular, 128; sentence element, 8; transitive, 21; translation, 3

vocative. *See* adjectives, vocative; nouns, vocative

vowels: ablative case, 65; in personal endings, 54, 73

word order, nouns and adjectives, 140

words, functions in sentences, 42

INDEX OF CULTURAL INFORMATION

CREDITS

The publisher gratefully acknowledges the contributions of the agencies, institutions, and photographers listed below:

(p. 170) *A Roman Triumph*, Peter Paul Rubens. National Gallery, London, UK/The Bridgeman Art Library.

Chapter 21
(p. 179) Silver mask. Louvre, Paris, France/The Bridgeman Art Library.

(p. 180) Roman wall painting. Metropolitan Museum of Art, New York, USA/The Bridgeman Art Library.

Chapter 22
(p. 192) © Rome, Italy/Index/The Bridgeman Art Library.

(p. 193) *Vercingetorix before Caesar 52* B.C., Henri-Paul Motte. Bridgeman-Giraudon/Art Resource, NY.

(p. 194) © Norfolk Archaeological Trust, Artist Sue White.

Chapter 23
(p. 202) Detail of reconstructed general view of the Forum Romanum. From *The Ancient City* by Peter Connolly. akg-images/Peter Connolly.

(p. 207) Pont du Gard. ©Steve Vidler/eStock Photo.

(p. 208) ©age fotostock/SuperStock

Chapter 24
(p. 215) *Left*: © Michael Holford. *Right*: Louvre, Paris, France/The Bridgeman Art Library.

(p. 216) *Hannibal Swearing Eternal Enmity to Rome*, Jacopo Amigoni. ©Agnew's, London, UK, Private Collection/The Bridgeman Art Library.

(p. 221) Wheeled toy, Romano-German. M. Williams/Ancient Art & Architecture Collection, Ltd.

(p. 222) ©Altrendo Travel/Getty Images, Inc.

Chapter 25
(p. 230) Mosaic, Tunisia. C M Dixon/AAA Collection Ltd.

(p. 231) Roman funerary stele. ©Erich Lessing/Art Resource, NY.

(p. 232) Courtesy of Elizabeth Lyding Will.

(p. 233) *Roman Art Lover*, Sir Lawrence Alma-Tadema. ©Milwaukee Art Center, WI, USA/The Bridgeman Art Library.

(p. 235) ©Scala/Art Resource, NY.

(p. 237) akg-images/Peter Connolly.

Chapter 26
(p. 245) Fresco. Zvonimir Atletic/YAY Micro/AGE Fotostock

(p. 246) Roman Sarcophagus Showing Frieze with the Nine Muses. ©Lauros/Giraudon, Louvre, Paris, France/The Bridgeman Art Library.

Chapter 27
(p. 250) Roman relief sculpture. ©British Museum, London, UK/The Bridgeman Art Library.

(p. 251) Courtesy of Elizabeth Lyding Will.

TIMELINE